Financial Politics in the United States in the 1890s

"In this rigorous, deeply researched, and well-written study, Wyatt Wells breathes new life into the 'battle of the standards'—the often neglected or misunderstood controversy in the late nineteenth century over whether gold or silver should constitute the primary backing for the U.S. money supply. Partisans in this battle held sharply different views regarding economic development, and the outcome of the battle would have a profound impact on the political economy of the United States for decades to come. A deft blend of economic, business, and political history, *Financial Politics in the United States in the 1890s: The Golden Web* represents a major contribution to the scholarly literature on late-nineteenth-century America."

—Peter A. Coclanis, *Albert R. Newsome Distinguished Professor of History, UNC-Chapel Hill*

Wyatt Wells

Financial Politics in the United States in the 1890s

The Golden Web

palgrave
macmillan

Wyatt Wells
Auburn University Montgomery
Montgomery, AL, USA

ISBN 978-3-031-86764-4 ISBN 978-3-031-86765-1 (eBook)
https://doi.org/10.1007/978-3-031-86765-1

This Palgrave Macmillan imprint is published by the registered company Springer Nature Switzerland AG.
The registered company address is: Gewerbestrasse 11, 6330 Cham, Switzerland

I would like to dedicate this book to
my wife,
Barbara,
and my sons,
Chase, Wyatt, and Robert

Note on Money

Comparing the value of money from different historical periods presents many difficulties, particularly in the years since the Industrial Revolution. New technologies constantly revolutionize our expectations of what money can do. In 1893, Jay Gould, one of the world's richest men, died of tuberculosis. Sixty years later, even poor Americans had access to effective treatments for this disease. Versailles, the impossibly lavish palace of Louis XIV, lacked indoor plumbing. Today, over 99 percent of French homes have flush toilets.

Some statistics put the value of a dollar in the 1890s into perspective. The total output of the United States totaled about $12.5 billion in 1890, increasing to a little over $17.5 billion by 1900. This translated into roughly $200 a year per capita in 1890, and about $230 a year per capita in 1900. Thus, a transaction of $1 million involved a sum equal to the annual income of about 5000 people.

Acknowledgments

I first conceived of this study in the late 1980s, when I was in graduate school. In the interim, I often put it aside to pursue other projects, but I have always returned to the subject. Over the years I have received important assistance in my research from the Auburn University Montgomery Interlibrary Loan Office, the Auburn University Montgomery Professional Improvement Leave program, the Institute for Humane Studies, and the staffs of the many archives in which I conducted research. Michel Aaij, Barbara Wells, Chase Wells, Harwell Wells, and O. Arne Westad each read this manuscript at different points, making valuable suggestions.

Competing Interests The author has no competing interests to declare that are relevant to the content of this manuscript.

Contents

CHAPTER 1

Introduction

In the summer of 1896, Americans turned their political system inside out. The Democrats renounced President Grover Cleveland, the only member of their party to win the White House in forty years, and he returned the favor by doing his best to guarantee that Republican William McKinley won the election to succeed him. Republicans from the Mountain West rallied behind the Democrats' candidate, William Jennings Bryan, as did the Populists, the strongest third party in American history, despite their many grievances against the Democrats. In many states, Bryan's supporters could choose between a Democrat and a Populist for Vice President. The confusion often extended well down the ticket. In Kansas and Nebraska, the Democrats did not nominate anyone for Congress but supported Populist candidates. In North Carolina, an alliance between Populists and Republicans contested state and local offices with the Democrats, but the Populists joined the Democrats in supporting Bryan for the presidency, while the Republicans worked for McKinley.

A single issue drove this upheaval. Should the United States retain the gold standard or adopt the free coinage of silver? From the perspective of the twenty-first century, the emphasis on this question seems strange—our money rests on neither gold nor silver. Yet the underlying issue is familiar. In the late nineteenth century, Americans did not use the term "globalization," but they understood the process. At the time, the world's leading economies—Britain, France, Germany, and the United States—all based

W. Wells, *Financial Politics in the United States in the 1890s*,
https://doi.org/10.1007/978-3-031-86765-1_1

their currencies on gold, stabilizing their relative value. Merchants selling American cotton to Britain, British textiles to Brazil, and Brazilian coffee to the United States did not have to worry about fluctuations in exchange rates. European investors could put capital into American railroads, Argentine utilities, and Malaysian rubber plantations knowing what the money they earned abroad would be worth at home. By eliminating these uncertainties, the gold standard contributed to a huge expansion of international trade and investment.

Many in the United States profited immensely from the gold standard. In the late nineteenth century, Americans borrowed huge sums abroad on good terms to finance the country's headlong economic development. The largest portion of this money went into railroad securities, but Europeans also invested in ranches, farm mortgages, breweries, and more.[1] The country financed most of its foreign trade, and even some of its domestic commerce, through London's money market. Thanks in part to foreign capital, the U.S. economy had by 1890 become the world's largest.

At the same time, many Americans suffered from the gold standard. Between 1870 and 1895, the world's supply of gold did not grow as fast as the volume of transactions it had to support, creating deflation. Falling prices hit farmers in the American South and on the Great Plains particularly hard. Most of them carried substantial debts, and as prices fell, they had to sell more and more cotton and wheat simply to keep up. Ironically, the United States paid the interest and dividends it owed foreign investors by exporting vast quantities of cotton, wheat, beef, pork and edible fats and oil. The nation's prosperity depended on farmers, but they did not fully share in it.

This contradiction defined public life in the United States in the 1890s. Starting in the late 1880s, protests on behalf of farmers spread, with organizations like the Farmers' Alliance growing rapidly. The financial panic of 1893 and the grinding depression that followed pushed financial concerns to the top of the national agenda. Critics of the gold standard rallied around the free coinage of silver, which in practice would replace gold with silver and devalue the dollar. The result would be higher prices (in

[1] In the 1880s, over 200 mortgage companies backed by Northeastern and British capital existed in Kansas and Nebraska alone. John D. Hicks, *The Populist Revolt* (Minneapolis: University of Minnesota Press, 1931), p. 22. For breweries see Mary O'Sullivan, *Dividends of Development: Securities Markets in the History of U.S. Capitalism, 1866–1922* (Oxford: Oxford University Press, 2016), pp. 78–80.

dollars) for farmers who grew wheat and cotton for sale abroad. Those who benefitted from the gold standard naturally came to its defense, warning that devaluation would drive away the foreign investors on whom they believed prosperity depended. The conflict culminated in the 1896 presidential contest between Republican William McKinley, a defender of the gold standard, and Democrat William Jennings Bryan, the champion of free coinage of silver. Contemporaries called it the "Battle of the Standards," and as Bryan wrote soon after the fact, "We witnessed such activity of mind and body as the nation has not witnessed before for thirty years."[2]

The two sides had different visions for the country as well as different interests. Silverites imagined a rural nation dominated by farmers. Advocates of the gold standard envisaged a country in which cities and industry predominated. In a sense, the currency stood for larger concerns, but at the same time, it profoundly affected these concerns. The gold standard financed railroads and manufacturing while squeezing farmers. Silver coinage would raise the income of farmers while cutting off the railroads and manufacturers from the capital they required.

Historians have too often downplayed the choice between gold and silver. In his classic *Age of Reform*, Richard Hofstadter described the free coinage of silver as a "will-o'-the-wisp," and in his influential *Populist Moment*, Lawrence Goodwyn asserted that the matter was a "triumph of form over substance."[3] More recently, in his sweeping *The Republic for Which It Stands*, Richard White concluded, "In the so-called Battle of the Standards, silver stood for equality and fraternity, gold stood for liberty in the old liberal sense of sanctity of property."[4] Despite their substantial differences, Hofstadter, Goodwyn, and White all saw the choice between gold and silver as symbolic of other concerns.

[2] William Jennings Bryan, "Has the Election Settled the Money Question?" *The North American Review*, 163 (December 1896), 704.

[3] Richard Hofstadter, *The Age of Reform* (New York: Vintage Books, 1960), p. 108; Lawrence Goodwyn, *The Populist Moment*, (New York: Oxford University Press, 1976), p. 312.

[4] Richard White, *The Republic for Which It Stands: The United States During Reconstruction and the Gilded Age, 1865–1896* (New York, Oxford University Press, 2017), p. 831. White is not ignorant of finance and includes a clear description of the link between the gold standard and foreign investment (pp. 760–1), but he fails to put the link between these subjects and the political upheaval of 1896 front-and-center in his discussion of the latter.

The history of finance and politics in the 1890s tells a different story. The choice between gold and silver was the most important economic question facing the country. Would the United States remain linked to the international financial system that had provided the capital for its economic development? Or would it cut these ties, reorienting the financial system to the benefit of farmers in the South and on the Great Plains? The choice was momentous, as most Americans of the day well understood.

CHAPTER 2

Context

In the last quarter of the nineteenth century, economic development transformed the United States. Rapid growth created new industries and communities while threatening established institutions and cherished values. Economic expansion involved investment on a massive scale, which required financing, much of which came from abroad. As Americans digested the changes around them, they naturally focused on currency and credit.

The Emerging Colossus

The economic transformation of the United States in the late nineteenth century built on earlier accomplishments. In 1875, farmers still dominated. They were generally efficient, growing large quantities of cotton and grain for export. The textile industry, the largest manufacturing sector by far, employed several hundred thousand, and the country's workshops made many of the most complex products of the day—steam engines, locomotives, and machine tools. American enterprises were the first to use interchangeable parts to build machinery, and companies like Singer Sewing Machines and McCormick Reaper utilized this technique to make revolutionary products. Perhaps most impressive, the country had thousands of miles of railroad track, including a recently completed line spanning the continent.

W. Wells, *Financial Politics in the United States in the 1890s*, https://doi.org/10.1007/978-3-031-86765-1_2

Britain nevertheless remained "the workshop of the world." Though it had a smaller population than the U.S., Britain manufactured far more goods and dominated international trade and finance. Americans bought many manufactured goods abroad—chiefly from Britain—and they would have purchased more but for the tariffs imposed by the U.S. government on imports. Nor did the situation seem likely to change soon. Less than a quarter of the U.S. population lived in towns with more than 2500 people, and factories counted their employees in the hundreds rather than the thousands. Even the railroads, the corporate giants of the day, usually managed only a few hundred miles of track each. Large parts of the West remained unsettled, and the South had yet to recover from the Civil War. Though the country's prosperity seemed secure, industrial dominance appeared unlikely.

In 1879, the United States shook off the economic depression that had hobbled it since 1873 and commenced an extraordinary boom. Between 1879 and 1893, total output increased about 60 percent. Steel production quadrupled, and the output of bituminous coal, the chief source of energy, more than doubled. The country's railroads laid a staggering 90,000 miles of track. The new lines included four transcontinental connections that opened huge sections of the West to settlers—a disaster for Native Americans, but a boon for the hundreds of thousands who flooded into the region. In 1890, the Census Bureau announced that the frontier, defined as a continuous line of settlement, had disappeared. Impressive as the growth of western settlement was, urban expansion surpassed it. Between 1880 and 1890, the population of towns with at least 2500 increased more than 50 percent, and the number of those living in cities with more than 100,000 almost doubled. Sometime around 1890, the output of the country's factories, by value, surpassed that of its farms.[1] At about the same time, the American economy decisively passed Britain's to become the world's largest.

These aggregates tell what happened, but not how. Americans transformed economic life with new technologies and techniques. In 1881,

[1] These factories often depended on agricultural inputs. Such was obviously the case with meatpacking and flour milling, but it was also true for textiles and more. The difference between various economic sectors is often not as clear as statistics suggest, and in many cases, American industry represented an extension of agriculture. The expansion of manufacturing in the 1880s was nevertheless extraordinary.

Gustavus Swift put the first commercially viable refrigerated rail car into service, using it to deliver fresh meat to distant markets. As sales grew, Swift vastly expanded his meatpacking plant in Chicago, which was soon slaughtering hundreds of hogs and cattle a day. His facility was essentially a huge disassembly line, with specialized workers performing the same tasks at a constant speed, which sharply reduced the costs of butchering livestock. Swift also relentlessly exploited the byproducts of meatpacking, selling leather made from hides, glue from bones, and soap and candles from fat. At the time, meatpackers boasted of using all of the hog "except the squeal." By the end of the decade, Swift and a handful of imitators were supplying most of the beef and pork consumed in American cities and exporting large quantities to Europe.[2] Local butchers, a fixture in most communities since time immemorial, could not compete with the low prices the large meatpackers offered and faced ruin. The savvy ones became retailers for meatpackers like Swift, salvaging their economic position but sacrificing their autonomy. Now the survival of their shops depended on their relationship with Swift or one of his competitors. Farmers and ranchers who raised livestock discovered that they no longer sold in a competitive market but in one that a handful of large meatpackers dominated. Again, the savvy ones adapted. Many midwestern farmers started raising hogs alongside corn, feeding the latter to the former and selling the pigs to meatpackers. This strategy created efficiencies and could be quite lucrative, but it depended on getting a good price from Swift or one of his imitators.

Though the exact process varied, many sectors of the economy experienced roughly comparable transformations. Over the course of the 1870s, John D. Rockefeller's Standard Oil bludgeoned most of its competitors into submission. By 1880, Rockefeller and his associates controlled 80–90 percent of the country's refining capacity. During the next few years, Standard Oil concentrated production in a few huge, highly efficient refineries, reducing the cost of refining kerosene, its chief product, by roughly two-thirds. The company also built an extensive pipeline network to channel crude oil to its refineries, as well as a sophisticated marketing

[2] Alfred Chandler, *The Visible Hand: The Managerial Revolution in American Business* (Cambridge, MA: The Belknap Press, 1977), pp. 299–301; Dominic A. Pacyga, *Slaughterhouse: Chicago's Union Stockyards and the World It Made* (Chicago: University of Chicago Press, 2015), pp. 55–57.

organization to sell kerosene.[3] Andrew Carnegie built his first steel mill, the Edgar Thompson Works, in Pittsburg in 1874. At the time, it was perhaps the most efficient producer of steel rails in the world, and it delivered solid profits from the beginning despite the weak state of the American economy at the time. With economic recovery in the 1880s, profits ballooned, and Carnegie expanded further. He and his associates bought control of the Frick Coal Company, which produced the best coke in the country at the lowest cost, and they took over another large mill near Pittsburg, the Homestead Steel Works. These large plants were very efficient, and by relentless effort, Carnegie and his managers made them progressively more so, cutting both costs and prices. Lower prices, in turn, increased sales, which brought further economies. By 1890, Carnegie Steel employed thousands in and around Pittsburg and in Pennsylvania's coal fields.[4]

In these industries, concentration was integral to growth, not incidental to it. The large companies that prospered all enjoyed economies of scale—their large plants, when operating at high capacity, enjoyed lower costs per unit than smaller ones. Such economies were not universal. Textiles, furniture, housewares, machine tools, and many other industries had limited economies of scale. Economies of scale were large in producing steel and most nonferrous metals, refining both petroleum and natural fats, meatpacking, making standardized consumers goods like tobacco, soap, beer, and chocolate, assembling machines like reapers and sewing machines, synthesizing chemicals such as explosives and alkali, and making paper. Entrepreneurs in these fields who recognized the opportunities and built large plants dominated, squeezing out smaller rivals. Such enterprises usually sought to control supply and distribution as well as production. Interruptions in the supply of raw materials or the flow of goods to market could be disastrous because large plants were efficient only when operating at high capacity. Idle, they represented nothing more than a large expense. After purchasing the Frick Coal Company, Carnegie secured a foothold in the rich iron ore mines of the Mesabi Range. Standard Oil

[3] Chandler, *Visible Hand*, pp. 323–6. For a more detailed account, see Ralph W. Hidy, George Gibb, and Henrietta Larson, *The History of the Standard Oil Company of New Jersey, Volume I, Pioneering in Big Business, 1882–1911* (New York: Harper & Brothers, 1955), pp. 24–121.

[4] Chandler, *Visible Hand*, pp. 258–69. For a more detailed account, see John Frazier Wall, *Andrew Carnegie* (New York: Oxford University Press, 1970), pp. 307–420.

gradually bought control of its chief wholesalers and expanded into drilling. Swift and the other meatpackers owned refrigerated rail cars and set up refrigerated warehouses in major cities.

Behind this process of concentration stood the railroads, which were by far the largest enterprises of the day. They employed hundreds of thousands of workers and billions of dollars of capital in a system that shipped goods quickly and cheaply throughout the country. In most communities, they had a monopoly on transportation. Farmers usually moved their crops to market by rail and received manufactured products the same way. Even cities like New York and St. Louis, which had good connections to the outside world by water, relied heavily on railroads. Railroads both represented centers of economic power and allowed others to create such centers. They brought livestock from around the country to the meatpacking plants of Swift and his competitors and distributed their meat in refrigerated rail cars. Standard Oil not only shipped its products throughout the country via rail but also extracted concessions on rates that helped it subdue competitors. Carnegie Steel transported coal and iron to Pittsburg on railroads, and railroads were the market for its steel rails. Producers of soap, condiments, and cigarettes shipped their goods throughout the country by rail. The expansion and consolidation of the American economy was inextricably bound up with the railroads.

The railroads also accounted for the centralization of finance. Frequently, entrepreneurs in manufacturing industries like Swift and Rockefeller could rely on local investors to launch their ventures and on retained earnings to expand. There were exceptions. Andrew Carnegie borrowed $400,000 in London to construct his first steel mill.[5] On the whole, however, manufacturing was self-financing. Not so the railroads. Their construction was extraordinarily expensive, and they did not deliver profits until complete. From the start, promotors sold stock and bonds to finance railroad construction, and because few communities had the capital to finance such large ventures, railroads turned to outsiders. Investors from Boston and Philadelphia financed many companies, but New York City dominated, not so much because of its own wealth but because of its many foreign connections. It was the home of August Belmont (father and son), the American agents of the famous Rothschild's Banks in London and Paris. Seligman Brothers and Speyer Brothers of London both had counterparts

[5] Wall, *Andrew Carnegie*, p. 320.

in New York—J.F. Seligman & Co. and Speyer & Co, respectively. Likewise, Brown Brothers of New York was closely tied to Brown, Shipley of London, and Morton, Bliss & Co. of London to Morton, Rose of New York. Tom Baring, a senior partner in Barings Brothers, one of London's premier banks, lived in New York, where he was also a partner in Kidder Peabody, one of Boston's leading banks. Jacob Schiff, the dominant partner at Kuhn Loeb, was a New Yorker from Germany who maintained strong connections with the land of his birth.[6]

Among these bankers, the most important figure was undoubtedly John Pierpont Morgan. His father, Junius Morgan, was an American who lived in London, where he was the senior partner in a leading bank. J.P. Morgan was a partner in his father's firm, but he operated out of New York City. His chief American partner, Anthony Drexel, lived in Philadelphia. During the 1880s, Drexel gradually reduced his involvement in the business, allowing Morgan to assert control. Junius Morgan died in 1890, leaving his son the senior partner in the London bank as well. J.P. Morgan accepted without question the unspoken code of London's private bankers, which emphasized discretion, probity, and attention to clients' interests. At the same time, he believed that the United States had an unlimited future if only it adhered to "sound" financial policies. He would provide enterprises with the resources they needed to grow and try to guarantee prudent management. Morgan combined extensive contacts, broad experience, an intuitive understanding of finance, and a very forceful personality—others on Wall Street nicknamed him "Jupiter," after the most powerful god of the Roman pantheon.[7]

Unlike commercial banks that focused on taking deposits and making loans, these institutions, eventually known as investment banks, were partnerships rather than corporations. Though most would accept deposits and provide credit, their chief business was buying and selling securities, particularly those of railroads.

[6] Dorothy Adler, *British Investment in American Railways, 1834–1898* (Charlottesville: University of Virginia Press, 1970), pp. 143–6.

[7] Until 1894, Morgan's principal vehicle was Drexel, Morgan, which had partners in both New York City and Philadelphia. Drexel died in 1893, and Morgan eventually reorganized the firm as J.P. Morgan & Co and focused it on New York. The firm's London house was J.S. Morgan & Co., and it retained that name even after the senior Morgan died in 1890. Morgan also had another investment house in Paris: Morgan, Harjes & Co. For the same of simplicity, this study will refer to J.P. Morgan's various banks under the name J.P. Morgan & Co., since he was the dominant figure in all of them during the 1890s.

These bankers channeled vast sums of capital from Europe to the United States for railroad construction. As one student of the subject described it, "Since railroads had first been built in the United States a steady stream of European money had crossed the Atlantic. The Union Pacific had been financed largely by English and Dutch interests; the Great Northern represented large amounts of Canadian and English capital; the Northern Pacific seemed at times to be an exclusively German company; three-fourths of the Louisville & Nashville stock belonged to Europeans."[8] In just five year, from 1886 to 1890, foreign investors put over $1 billion into the United States, a sum equal to roughly 10 percent of the country's total output, with most of the money going into railroad securities. Historian and social critic Henry Adams wrote, "The generation between 1865 and 1895 was already mortgaged to the railroads, and no one knew it better than the generation itself."[9]

The Standard of the World

In 1890, gold united the financial world. The leading economic powers of the day—Britain, France, Germany, and the United States—all based their currencies on gold, as did many smaller but wealthy countries like Switzerland, Belgium, the Netherlands, and Sweden. In theory, the system was simple. Each country minted gold coins that were legal tender for all debts, public and private. Governments coined gold bullion into money on demand, charging no more than the cost of minting and, often, nothing at all—a practice known as "free coinage." At the same time, individuals could melt down gold coins or export them without restriction. Because transforming metal into money and money into metal was so easy, the mint price defined the value of gold. In the United States, an ounce of gold was worth $20.64 because that was the rate at which the government coined gold. At the same time, gold linked the currencies based on it. In the late nineteenth century, the gold in a British pound was worth $4.86, so that was the exchange rate between the dollar and sterling.

In practice, the system was far more complex. Gold coins accounted for only a fraction of transactions. The total volume of business vastly exceeded

[8] E.G. Campbell, *Reorganization of the American Railroad System, 1893–1900* (New York: Columbia University Press, 1938), p. 13.

[9] Henry Adams, *The Education of Henry Adams: An Autobiography* (Boston: Houghton Mifflin, 1918), p. 240.

the supply of gold, most of which did not circulate at all but resided in the vaults of banks and governments. Day-to-day business relied largely on banknotes and, in many cases, silver coins, and large transactions depended chiefly on bank drafts (checks). Legally, holders could convert these assets into gold, but they rarely did so because gold was heavy and bulky. Moreover, bank balances earned interest whereas gold coins did not. Individuals and institutions took most of their revenue in bank notes or drafts and paid their obligations with the same, and the banking system "reconciled" or "cleared" these transactions. The gold standard meant not that all money was gold, but that all money had the same value in gold. A $10 Gold Eagle coin was worth as much as ten silver dollars, a $10 note, or $10 on deposit at a bank.

The same general principle applied to international transactions. Those doing business across borders constantly traded currencies, and some bankers and merchants specialized in these transactions. Usually, no gold changed hands, only currency and credits. Traders, however, always had the option of converting the money of one country into gold, sending the metal to another country, and having the authorities there coin it into money. Such operations entailed costs—shipping and insurance as well as the interest which might otherwise accrue while the gold was in transit—but these usually consumed less than 1 percent of the sum involved. If a country ran a deficit on its balance of payments—that is, spent more abroad than it brought in—the price of its currency would fall because there were more sellers than buyers. Soon the price would hit the "gold point," the level at which shipping gold became profitable. The gold point for the dollar against sterling, for instance, was $4.89. If sales of dollars for pounds drove the price of sterling above $4.89, currency dealers could turn a profit by shipping gold from the United States to Britain. This movement would both settle the imbalance and push currency values back under the gold point.[10]

The gold standard offered stability. First, it guaranteed that the various types of money in circulation—banknotes, silver coins, gold coins, bank credits—all had the same value. Most of the population, even financiers, took this unity for granted, but it could break down, paralyzing or at least imposing heavy costs on the economy. Such had occurred in the United

[10] These incentives worked both ways. If the price of sterling fell below $4.83, gold would move from Britain to the United States.

States during the Civil War. Second, the gold standard kept prices relatively stable. Industrialist Andrew Carnegie insisted, "A gold dollar would always buy a dollar's worth of anything substantially upon the former average of prices. … It knows neither appreciation nor depreciation beyond a range so narrow as to be of no practical account."[11] Carnegie was wrong. The purchasing power of the gold dollar did often change enough year-to-year to be of "practical account." Between 1879 and 1897, prices fell almost 30 percent in the United States, and between 1897 and 1914, they rose about 20 percent. Other countries on the gold standard had comparable experiences. Prices under the gold standard were nevertheless more stable than under any other system with which people of the 1890s were familiar. Some countries had experimented with paper money unbacked by gold, called "fiat currency" because it rested solely on law, or government fiat. Most, however, considered the results unsatisfactory. During the French and American revolutions, political authorities had issued large volumes of paper money that eventually became worthless. Britain and the United States did better with fiat currency during the Napoleonic wars and the Civil War, respectively, but prices in both countries had still increased sharply over just a few years.[12] Most concluded from these experiences that paper money might be necessary in a national emergency, but that under most conditions currency should rest on gold.[13]

Perhaps most important, the gold standard stabilized exchange rates within a range of 1 percent, a range so narrow as to be of "no practical account." This stability contributed substantially to the rapid growth of international trade and investment in the late nineteenth century. By

[11] Andrew Carnegie, "Mr. Bryan, the Conjurer," *The North American Review* 164 (January 1897), p. 114.

[12] During the 1790s, Britain made Bank of England notes legal tender and suspended the requirement that the bank redeem its notes in coin. The government then borrowed from the bank, which printed up notes for the government if it could not find enough investors to absorb the loans. Though different legally and technically from what happened in the United States during the Civil War, when the government simply issued paper money, from an economic point of view, the outcome was the same. Britain returned to gold in 1821.

[13] China had issued paper money in the eleventh century, during the Sung dynasty, and the notes circulated for centuries without too much depreciation. They had disappeared by 1500, however, because the Ming dynasty issued very large quantities of paper, causing its value to fall dramatically. Very few Europeans and Americans knew of this experience—by the nineteenth century, most Chinese had forgotten about it—and it had no impact on the broader discussion of currency in the nineteenth century.

1890, an intricate network based on gold and centered in London financed most international trade. Merchants often purchased goods not with cash but with "acceptances" (IOUs) that promised payment, usually in sixty or ninety days in sterling at a London bank. Sellers could simply wait to collect their money, but most sold their notes to financiers known as merchant bankers at a slight discount that reflected the rate of interest. If interest rates were 4 percent a year, a merchant banker might purchase a note for £100 due in ninety days for £99. These bankers then guaranteed these notes and resold them. Most of London's financiers considered such paper, backed by goods of some sort and guaranteed by the seller, the buyer, and a reputable merchant bank, entirely safe. It circulated almost like cash. Most of these notes found their way into the portfolios of commercial banks, but merchants also used such paper to pay their obligations. An American importer of English ceramics might pay his supplier with a note issued by a British textile mill to purchase American cotton. Such notes were also the chief commodity of bankers who specialized in foreign exchange. Important markets for acceptances existed elsewhere, most notably in Paris and Berlin, but London was the largest by far, and it set the pace. As early as the 1870s, the total volume of such paper outstanding at any one time in London was £55 million, and the amount would grow rapidly over the next forty years.[14]

This system was both extraordinarily efficient and relatively cheap. Because of the immense volume, dealers could accept narrow profit margins while still enjoying solid earnings, so the cost of issuing such paper was only slightly more than the rate of interest. Because large quantities of paper from all over the world traded in London, the "City"—London's money market—could clear the transactions of entire nations. In the late nineteenth century, the United States usually ran a trade surplus with Europe but a deficit with much of Asia and Latin America. Through the London market, American merchants could use credits earned in the former to pay for purchases from the latter. For their part, Europeans could use the surpluses they earned with Asia and Latin America to pay for goods from the United States. Almost every country had such imbalances—surpluses with some trading partners and deficits with others—that they reconciled through London.

[14] David Kynaston, *The City of London: Volume I, A World of Its Own* (London: Pimlico, 1994), pp. 309–310.

Any country on the gold standard could avail itself of these services. An American exporter of cotton could accept payment in sterling with the knowledge that each pound was worth $4.86. Those operating on another basis faced obstacles. As one British official put it, "London is the lending market, and London thinks in gold. London is ready enough to lend upon contracts for repayment in gold, but resistant to enter upon silver transactions or to engage in industrial enterprises in a silver country."[15] China used silver as money, and Europeans and Americans operating there had to deal in both gold and silver. Merchants exporting to China paid suppliers in gold but received silver from their Chinese customers, and those importing from China the reverse. Starting in the 1870s, this position became dangerous as silver depreciated against gold. European bankers and investors were reluctant to buy paper that paid silver because silver might lose value before the notes matured. As the historian of the Sassoon family, a leader in the China trade, wrote, "The glittering rewards held out by trading with China were always tempered by such risks; profitable trades were only half the battle. Could a trader … manage the currency risk?"[16] The Hongkong and Shanghai Banking Corporation (HSBC) stepped into the gap. British merchants operating in China organized it in 1864, and by the 1880s, HSBC had a network of branches in Asia as well as in European centers that traded extensively with the Far East, including London. These accounts provided HSBC with deposits in both gold (Europe) and silver (Asia). This structure allowed HSBC to pursue what it called an "even keel"—in the parlance of a later age, "hedging." It made sure that assets in each metal (commercial paper) roughly equaled its debts in the same metal (deposits), so that changes in the relative value of gold and silver made no difference, on balance. Such arrangements kept China's trade moving, but they added an extra layer of complexity and expense. Moreover, the size of HSBC's Asian deposits limited the volume of exports to China. The bank could always resell paper paying gold in the London market, but it had to rely on its own resources to cover paper paying silver, and deposits at its Asian branches were not particularly elastic.[17]

[15] "Report of the Indian Currency Committee," May 31, 1893, National Archives, Kew, England (NA), CAB 37/341893.

[16] Joseph Sassoon, *The Sassoons: The Great Global Merchants and the Making of an Empire* (New York: Pantheon, 2022), p. 160.

[17] For HSBC's system, see Frank H.H. King, *The History of the Hongkong and Shanghai Banking Corporation, Volume I, The Hongkong Bank in Late Imperial China, 1864–1902, On An Even Keel* (Cambridge: Cambridge University Press, 1987).

The gold standard also had a powerful impact on long-term foreign investment. All investors operating across international boundaries faced risk from shifts in currency values. If the dollar fell against sterling, then so did the value, in sterling, of securities denominated in dollars. Britons investing at home faced no such danger. Securities sold across international borders, therefore, paid a premium to compensate investors for this risk.[18] In the 1870s, before the United States embraced the gold standard, American railroads had to pay 2.5 percentage points more on their bonds than did comparable British railroads. By stabilizing the relative value of currencies, the gold standard substantially reduced exchange risk. By the 1890s, with the U.S. on gold, the premium on its railroad bonds had dropped by half, to 1.25 percentage points. At this time, British investors held about $1.4 billion in American railroad bonds, so the savings were substantial.[19] Under the gold standard, any enterprise from any country that based its money on gold could raise capital in London at rates only a little higher than comparable British concerns paid. By 1890, the securities of twenty American railroads traded on the London Stock Exchange,[20] and between 1888 and 1890, U.S. breweries floated over £12 million in equities in Britain.[21] British investors took these securities because they offered somewhat higher returns than comparable domestic equities. American companies floated issues in London because its market was much larger than that of the United States and offered better prices. Paris, Berlin, and Amsterdam also absorbed substantial volume of foreign securities, including those of American railways.

Borrowers from countries on another basis could secure such rates only by denominating their obligations in foreign currency. London had a huge market for "sterling bonds" issued by foreign governments and companies but denominated in pounds. Even companies from countries on the gold standard sometimes issued such securities to reduce the interest rate further. By the 1890s, U.S. railroads had issued sterling bonds worth as much

[18] In politically or economically unstable countries, these incentives can work in reverse, with investors preferring to hold assets abroad, in foreign currencies. There are few more devastating indictments of a society's political and financial leadership.

[19] Mira Wilkins, *The History of Foreign Investment in the United States to 1914* (Cambridge MA: Harvard University Press, 1989), 197, 202.

[20] Adler, *British Investment in American Railways*, pp. 153–6.

[21] O'Sullivan, *Dividends of Development*, pp. 78–80.

as £50 million.[22] In these cases, the borrower absorbed foreign exchange risk. In 1890, the Great Northern Railway sold £6 million in bonds ($29.16 million) in London, paying 4 percent, to finance the expansion of its line across the Rocky Mountains to the Pacific. The interest on these bonds totaled £240,000 a year.[23] With the United States on gold at $20.64 an ounce, that represented $1.166 million, but if the United States abandoned gold and devalued its currency, this obligation would increase proportionally.

Some scholars have argued that the gold standard conveyed a "good housekeeping seal of approval," assuring investors of financial stability.[24] Countries on gold had to manage their finances cautiously, avoiding large government deficits and reckless spending. European investors might not know much about conditions in, say, Paraguay, but if Paraguay was on gold, they could assume that the country's finances were in order.

To secure the benefits of the gold standard, nations had to submit to its discipline. Ultimately, the supply of gold determined the volume of currency and credit. The exact ratio depended on the financial system. The more sophisticated the system—the more rapidly money changed hands—the less gold it required. Britain's highly developed banking system and London's position at the center of the financial world allowed the United Kingdom to operate with a smaller gold reserve, relative to total transactions, than most other countries. Nations could also accommodate temporary shifts in the demand for currency and credit. Calls for money usually surged during the harvest as farmers sold their crops, but the increase was temporary. Farmers used the funds to repay debts and purchase supplies. Such was also the case during financial crises, when the demand for currency surged as people scrambled for cash to repay debts and protect themselves from uncertainty. When calm returned, the demand for money fell. In both cases, financial authorities could supply extra currency and credit and then withdraw it from circulation once

[22] In the 1890s, *The Economist* listed quotes for sterling bonds traded the previous week, along with a notice of the size of the entire issue. Issues not traded that week were not mentioned. These reports suggest that U.S. railroads had issued sterling bonds worth at least £50 million.

[23] Ralph Hidy et al., *The Great Northern Railway: A History* (Minneapolis: University of Minnesota Press, 2004), pp. 78–9. The Great Northern had to sell the bonds at a slight discount.

[24] Michael Bordo and Hugh Rockoff, "The Gold Standard as a 'Good Housekeeping Seal of Approval,'" *Journal of Economic History* 56 (June 1996): 389–428.

pressure eased.[25] Year-to-year, however, the supply of gold dictated the money supply. A country that expanded currency and credit too fast would find its gold reserve shrinking, while one that was too stingy would find its reserve growing. The former condition dictated restrictions on credit and currency—at least if the country in question wanted to remain on the gold standard. In the latter case, those with extra gold would convert it into money or use it to finance loans, either of which would increase the supply of currency and credit.

The world's supply of gold changed only slowly. Unlike most commodities, the precious metals are not consumed but remain in circulation indefinitely.[26] New production accounts for a small part of the total. That is part of the appeal of gold—the monetary base is relatively stable. Even large discoveries of gold, such as in California and Australia in the 1840s and in Alaska and South Africa in the 1890s, increase the total supply by only a few percent a year. Over time, the impact was substantial, but the change was gradual.

For most countries on the gold standard, the supply of gold fluctuated with the balance of payments—the total flow of money into and out of a country from trade, services, tourism, remittances, investment, and more. A few countries like the United States produced gold, but even in such cases, shifts in the balance of payments usually accounted for unanticipated changes in the supply of gold. Nations had to pay deficits in gold, and they received gold to settle surpluses. A payments deficit, therefore, reduced the volume of currency and credit by shrinking the supply of gold on which they rested, while a surplus did the reverse. Monetary authorities often reacted to an outflow of gold by raising interest rates to attract money from abroad. London bankers had a saying that an interest rate of 7 percent would draw gold "from the Moon."[27] The results were the

[25] This process could work a variety of ways, but most simply, a country's central bank extended loans to those under pressure during the harvest or a financial crisis, printing up the currency needed, and collected the loans when the pressure had eased, thereby removing the extra money from circulation.

[26] A significant amount of precious metal went to jewelry, silverware, and dental work, disappearing from circulation. Even some of that, however, might make its way back into use for money. Louis XIV famously melted down the gold and silver fixtures of Versailles to pay his soldiers during the War of the Spanish Succession, and Indian peasant women accumulated silver jewelry that they could sell to buy food if the monsoons failed and the harvest was poor.

[27] David Kynaston, *Till Time's Last Stand: A History of the Bank of England, 1694–2013* (London: Bloomsbury, 2017), p. 262.

same, however. Higher rates discouraged borrowing, restricting the volume of credit. Ideally, these forces neutralized each other. A country that lost gold would restrict currency and credit, thereby slowing its economy, pushing prices down, and raising interest rates. All of this would reduce the demand for imports, facilitate exports, and attract foreign capital. Countries with a surplus would experience the opposite. Between them, these forces would push the balance of payments toward equilibrium. Most advocates of the gold standard liked this relatively automatic adjustment because it minimized the government's role. Monetary policy reflected economic forces rather than political calculations.

The "gold standard," then, connoted not simply the rules for coining gold but an entire financial system that linked the world's most sophisticated economies and dictated monetary policy. It underwrote the massive expansion of international trade and investment of the late nineteenth century, creating opportunities and imposing costs. An American company building a railroad across the Rocky Mountains could secure capital on relatively good terms from foreign investors. At the same time, London's money market dictated the terms on which a farmer in Kansas could borrow to buy land.

The Flight from Silver

The gold standard, in its classic form, emerged only after 1870. Before then, only Britain and its economic satellite, Portugal, based their money entirely on gold. The German states and the other countries of Central Europe used silver for money, as they had for centuries. France used both gold and silver, an approach ultimately christened "bimetallism," and in 1865 it persuaded Belgium, Switzerland, and Italy to adopt its system and to form the Latin Monetary Union. Greece joined the group later. In practice, bimetallism entailed using not both metals but the cheaper one. France offered free coinage to both gold and silver, valuing one ounce of gold at fifteen-and-a-half ounces of silver. The fixed ration made coins of the two metals interchangeable, but it created a problem. The precious metals traded in the open market, where their relative value fluctuated. If the market ratio between the two metals deviated just 2 or 3 percent from the official one, the more valuable metal vanished from circulation. An increase in the price of gold to, say, sixteen times that of silver meant that its market price exceeded what the French mint paid for gold, and producers would stop bringing gold to the mint. Because gold coins now had a market value greater than their face value—the gold in a twenty-five franc coin might be worth twenty-six francs—those with gold coins would melt them down and sell the metal at the higher market rate. Soon gold coins disappeared.[28] From the early 1800s to about 1850, the market price of gold was, in fact, more than fifteen-and-a-half that of silver, so France was on a de facto silver standard. In the late 1840s and early 1850s, large discoveries of gold in California and Australia gradually drove the price of gold below fifteen-and-a-half that of silver. As a result, after1850 France found itself on a de facto gold standard.

Though completely unplanned, these multiple standards worked fairly well. Britain, then Europe's largest economy, would always absorb gold, Central Europe offered a ready market for silver, and France and the Latin Union would swing between the two. If the relative prices of the two metals shifted, the Latin Union embraced the cheaper and exported the more expensive, reorienting demand and containing the swing. Between 1820 and 1870, the relative price of silver and gold never fell below fifteen-to-one nor rose above sixteen-to-one.[29] Exchange rates, which mirrored the relative value of the two metals, remained within the same bounds. The results did not match the absolute certainty of the gold standard, but they nevertheless represented an extraordinary record of stability.

The Franco-Prussian War of 1870–1871 destroyed this system. The new German Empire that emerged from the conflict decided to abandon silver and base its money on gold, not only backing its new currency with gold but replacing the many silver coins in circulation with gold ones. This step would sweep away the currencies of the various German states, creating a truly national standard. No doubt, the British example influenced German leaders as well. As the first industrial nation, Britain and its institutions had immense prestige, and its currency rested on gold. Finally, gold seemed the wave of the future. The mines of California and Australia provided a ready supply of it, and by 1860, gold had displaced silver in every country that used both.

[28] Under free coinage, the mint price for a precious metal constitutes a floor. The United States coined gold at $20.64 an ounce, so anyone holding gold could get at least that much for it. As a result, in a bimetallic system, the cheaper metal always stands at the mint price. The more valuable metal stands above it, unless the market ratio corresponds to the official one.

[29] Steven P. Reti, *Silver and Gold: The Political Economy of International Monetary Conferences, 1867–1892* (Westport, CN: Greenwood Press, 1998), pp. 185–86.

Germany could pursue such a radical course because it had just extracted $1 billion in war reparations from France. Most of this sum consisted of credits in London or Paris, not bullion, but foreign exchange could command gold. Soon the Germans were replacing silver coins with gold ones and dumping their silver bullion on the world market, forcing its price down. Much of this silver flowed to French mints, riling the French, who feared that the inflow would drain their country of gold to the benefit of Germany. In 1873, France imposed a cap on the amount of silver that it would coin annually. As the price of silver continued to fall, Paris closed its mints to silver altogether. Silver coins continued to circulate in France, as they did in Germany—the rise of gold's price relative to silver convinced Berlin that recoinage was too expensive. Both counties valued these coins in gold, however, giving them a value greater than the silver they contained and so making them the metallic equivalent of notes.

The German and French action led to a flight from silver. As the price of silver declined relative to gold, so too did currencies based on the former depreciate relative to those based on gold. Small countries like Switzerland, Belgium, the Netherlands, and Sweden, which depended on trade with Britain, Germany, and France, had little choice but to follow these countries in adopting gold. The depreciation of their currencies would disrupt the dense network of international transactions on which their prosperity rested. As these countries closed their mints to silver, its relative price declined further, leading other countries that relied on it to rethink their position. Currency became a game of musical chairs in reverse, with each participant fearing that if it remained loyal to silver it would find itself seated atop a depreciating hoard of the metal.

In retrospect, the timing was terrible. In the late 1860s, miners in the American West struck silver, and by the early 1870s, their output was making its way to world markets. Much of this silver came from relatively low-grade ores, but new technology developed in Europe made these mines profitable. From almost nothing in 1860, production in the United States jumped to over nine million ounces in 1869. Volume tripled over the next ten years and doubled again over the subsequent thirteen. Under the system that had existed before 1870, Germany would have absorbed part of this silver, and as its price fell, French mints would have coined silver, driving gold from circulation there. Buoyed by French and German demand, the price of silver might well have stabilized around one-sixteenth that of gold. Instead, the price of the silver fell below sixteen-to-one in 1875 and continued to fall.

But for another development, this downward spiral might have troubled only silver miners. After 1870, the flow of gold from California and Australia abated. In the 1850s, the world produced about 181 tons of it each year, and in the 1860s, 171 tons annually. In the 1870s, however, output fell to 158 tons a year, and over the 1880s, production of gold declined to only 130 tons annually.[30] This development coincided with a large jump in the demand for gold as Germany adopted gold in 1871, the United States did the same in 1879, and many smaller European countries moved to it as well. The increase in the supply of gold did not keep pace with the growing volume of transactions it had to support, creating a shortage of currency and credit. In a telling metaphor attributed to German Chancellor Otto von Bismarck, gold became "a too scanty blanket on a bed occupied by more than one person, each trying to pull as much of the blanket as possible over himself."[31] As a result of the shortage of currency and credit, nations on the gold standard saw prices fall between 20 and 30 percent between the mid-1870s and the mid-1890s.

Rehabilitating silver could relieve this pressure. To that end, Germany and France retained their silver coins, and the United States actually expanded coinage of the silver. These steps provided some relief, but the decision to value these coins in terms of gold limited the impact. The supply of gold still restricted the total supply of money and credit.[32] If silver was to make a major difference, the world would have to base money on it. In the late 1870s, an "international bimetallist" movement developed. Led by the charismatic French-Italian banker Henri Cernuschi, it amassed a significant following in most European countries and in the United States. International bimetallists sought an international agreement extending the French fifteen-and-a-half-to-one ratio between silver and gold to the world and authorizing the free coinage of gold and silver everywhere. An accord encompassing all the leading economies, bimetallists believed, would both fix the relative value of the two metals and expand currency and credit. Exchange rates would remain stable but deflation would stop.

[30] Barry Eichengreen and Ian W. McLean, "The Supply of Gold under the Pre-1914 Gold Standard," *Economic History Review* 47 (1994): 294.

[31] Quoted in Henry B. Russell, *International Monetary Conferences* (New York, Harper & Brothers. 1898), p. 266.

[32] The substitution of silver coins for gold ones was not entirely in vain because the gold thereby conserved would go into the monetary reserve, expanding volume of currency and credit that a country—and the world as a whole—could maintain.

Such an accord posed a variety of challenges. Supporters of the gold standard had long contended that, sooner or later, market forces would render any legal ratio between gold and silver obsolete, and thus far, experience had borne out this belief. Better to pick a metal and stick with it, they argued. International bimetallists insisted that a universal agreement would work where national legislation had failed, but this conclusion required a leap of faith. On a more prosaic level, getting the leading economic powers to act in concert was difficult. Countries with adequate gold reserves—those that had grabbed a large portion of Bismarck's blanket—felt little pressure to compromise. Nations like Germany that had recently gone to considerable trouble to adopt gold were reluctant to retrace their steps. The great powers did not trust each other and looked after their own interests—the common good did not have priority. As the banker Alfred Rothschild complained, "There are … very pronounced international jealousies to contend with which render the position [international bimetallism] much more difficult."[33] Finally, the continued depreciation of silver made its rehabilitation progressively more challenging. In the late 1870s, when the price of silver stood around eighteen-to-one against gold in the open market, restoring the fifteen-and-a-half-to-one ratio seemed possible. By the early 1890s, however, silver had fallen to thirty-to-one, making its rehabilitation a much more daunting proposition. The cause of international bimetallism was not hopeless, but the odds were against it.

In addition to practical considerations, gold possessed an intangible allure that made governments reluctant to abandon it. Thinkers of the Victorian Era had clear ideas about progress, believing that societies moved through well-defined steps from lower to higher levels. Thinkers as diverse as Karl Marx, the father of Communism, and Herbert Spencer, the high priest of Social Darwinism, shared such assumptions, though they defined progress quite differently. Britain was the first industrial nation, and it was the first to adopt the modern gold standard. To many, the lesson was self-evident—the gold standard constituted progress. To buttress this conclusion, many contended that as the volume of commerce increased, the greater value of gold relative to its weight made it more convenient than silver. The American economist Laurence Laughlin, who would play a significant role in the debate over the currency in the 1890s, wrote, "When a new and lighter plow comes into competition with the

[33] Alfred Rothschild to his brothers, [November 1892], Rothschild's Archives, 000/253.

heavy and cumbrous machines of the last century, the latter will go out of use and decline in value. So it will be with the heavier and more cumbrous metal."[34] Laughlin's proposition was dubious. Most people conducted large transactions with paper money or bank drafts that were lighter than either gold or silver coins. The enthusiasm for gold also contained a strong element of idealism. Senator John Sherman (R-OH), brother of the famous Civil War General William Tecumseh Sherman, was one of the leading figures in the Republican Party from the 1860s to the 1890s as well as the Senate's acknowledged expert on finance. Writing about the gold standard in 1867, he insisted that, by facilitating trade and investment, it promoted the brotherhood of man. "The tendency of the age," he insisted, "is to break down all needless restrictions upon social and commercial intercourse. … Prejudices disappear by contact. People of different nations learn to respect each other as they find that their differences are the effect of social and local customs, not founded upon good reasons."[35] Support for gold also tapped into the era's racial assumptions. Gold was the money of Europe and North America, silver of Asia, Africa, and Latin America. As Senator George Gray (D-DL) stated on the floor of Congress in 1893, "The use of silver money and silver ornaments marks the position in the world's civilization of the simple people of India and the dwellers upon the coasts of the unexplored continent [Africa]."[36]

Historian Lawrence O'Malley has gone so far as to describe racial and monetary hierarchies as different sides of the same coin. He writes, "The triumph of the gold standard represents the same impulse as the triumph of segregation."[37] The two developed in the same intellectual milieu, but reducing monetary policy to a proxy for race is far-fetched. The most fervent racists in the United States, southern Whites, enthusiastically supported silver coinage, while Republicans from the Northeast, who were among the strongest partisans of the gold standard, led a serious push for civil rights legislation in the early 1890s. The choice between gold and

[34] J. Laurence Laughlin, *The History of Bimetallism in the United States*, 4th Edition (New York: D. Appleton & Co., 1900), p. 153.

[35] John Sherman to Samuel Ruggles, May 18, 1867, reproduced in John Sherman, *Recollections of Forty Years and the House, Senate, and Cabinet: An Autobiography* (Chicago: Werner, 1895), p. 409.

[36] Speech of Senator George Gray, Sept. 20, 1893, p. 7. Google Books has collected this address and many others together in *Silver Speeches in the U.S. Senate.*

[37] Michael O'Malley, *Face Value: The Entwined History of Money and Race in America* (Chicago: University of Chicago Press, 2012), p. 161.

silver had far-reaching economic implications that affected the well-being of almost everyone in the United States in one way or another. The debate was not a symbolic exercise—Americans used racial arguments to reinforce their financial preferences, not the other way around.

American Exceptionalism

The United States occupied an odd position in the world of finance. By 1890, it was probably the world's largest economy, but it had a relatively primitive financial system. Banking was hopelessly fragmented, with many regional centers and literally thousands of institutions. A variety of currencies, created at different times for different reasons, circulated. The country had no central bank to manage government finances, oversee the currency, and regulate the supply of money and credit. The U.S. Treasury, Congress, urban clearing houses,[38] and a few particularly powerful banks each exercised some authority, but no one was in charge. The contrast with the leading European economies was striking. Britain, France, and Germany each had a government-chartered, privately owned central bank—the Bank of England, the Bank of France, and the Reichsbank—that worked closely with the finance ministry to manage the currency and oversee financial markets. The capital cities—London, Paris, and Berlin—dominated banking and trading in securities, and the large financial institutions based in these cities had national reach. At the same time, borrowers in the provinces received credit on the same terms as those in the metropolis. Historians have long contrasted the institutional weakness of the American government in the late nineteenth century with European governments, most recently Richard White in his *The Republic for Which It Stands.*[39] In few areas was the dichotomy as stark as finance.

[38] Banks constantly take checks drawn on each other. In the nineteenth century, urban centers with several banks usually had a clearing house, which handled all these drafts, reconciling them so that individual banks only had to deal with the overall balance of withdrawals or deposits. This arrangement saved institutions the trouble of reconciling all balances through a multitude of bilateral arrangements, replacing several sets of accounts and payments with a single one. Though they usually began simply as instruments of convenience, clearing houses often developed into institutions through which banks dealt with common problems, particularly during financial crises. The most important clearing house in the United States, by far, was that in New York City.

[39] Richard White, *The Republic for Which It Stands: The United States During Reconstruction and the Gilded Age, 1865–1896* (New York, Oxford University Press, 2017).

The chaotic state of the currency and banking in the United States reflected its political history. Before the Civil War, no issue except slavery had occupied Americans more than banking. Soon after the Revolution, states began to charter banks to mobilize capital and finance trade, and each of these institutions issued its own notes. These banks often became a focus of political controversy, not the least because they frequently enjoyed unique privileges such as limited liability and a monopoly over the issue of notes within a state. The first Treasury Secretary, Alexander Hamilton, sought to create a unified national financial system to support both the new government and economic development. To that end, he persuaded Congress to charter the First Bank of the United States (BUS). From the start, he encountered strong opposition, most notably from Thomas Jefferson, and this contest continued into the next generation, with Andrew Jackson taking up Jefferson's position and Henry Clay Hamilton's. The BUS set up branches throughout the country, regulated the currency issued by state banks, and coordinated the flow of money between regional centers.[40] It was a powerful, centralized organization in a society that valued local autonomy. Though the business community as a whole benefitted from its activities, some entrepreneurs resented the BUS because it limited the issue of banknotes and the creation of credit. The strongest opposition, however, came from farmers, who then constituted the overwhelming majority of the population. Most of them gave priority to maintaining their independence, which they defined as owning their land and avoiding debt. Tenants and debtors were, by definition, dependent on others. As many of them saw it, the BUS and other banks existed to spin webs of credit to trap farmers in debt.[41]

In the 1830s, President Andrew Jackson destroyed the Second Bank of the United States, and with it, the effort to create a national financial

[40] The BUS had a simple but effective system of bank regulation. It purchased notes of other banks at only slightly less than their face value and then redeemed this paper for coin or its own notes. A state-chartered bank that issued more notes than the volume of transactions could accommodate soon found a BUS official at its door with a satchel full of its paper ready clean out its vault.

[41] The most comprehensive study of banking in the United States before the Civil War remains Bray Hammond, *Banks and Politics in America, From the Revolution to the Civil War* (Princeton: Princeton University Press, 1957). More recently, historian Robert Wright has produced a series of valuable volumes on different aspects of the American financial system during this period, including *The First Wall Street: Chestnut Street, Philadelphia, & the Brith of American Finance* (Chicago: University of Chicago Press, 2005) and *One Nation Under Debt: Hamilton, Jefferson, and the History of What We Owe* (New York: McGraw Hill, 2008).

system.[42] After 1846, the federal government conducted business solely in gold and silver coins. Most people conducted private transactions with banknotes that state-chartered banks issued, but without the BUS to regulate the process, the quality of such paper varied immensely. Notes that banks in New England, New York, Louisiana, and South Carolina issued were generally sound because those states had strict banking laws, but paper from elsewhere was an uncertain proposition. To conduct business with confidence, merchants and bankers needed a broad knowledge of the many notes in circulation. Nor did money and credit did flow smoothly through the country. Clearing houses transferred money efficiently within most cities, but moving cash between cities was often a challenge.

The United States also followed its own line on gold and silver, although before the Civil War this issue was not particularly controversial. When Alexander Hamilton established the dollar in 1790, he based it on both gold and silver, offering the two metals free coinage at the rate of fifteen ounces of silver to one of gold. This ratio reflected the market price of the two metals at the time, but silver's price soon fell, leaving it overvalued. Gold, never plentiful in the new republic, soon vanished from circulation, leaving the U.S. on a de facto silver standard. In 1834, Congress altered the ratio of gold to silver, but instead of adopting the French ratio of fifteen-and-a-half-to-one, it settled on sixteen-to-one.[43] Whereas the old rule had overvalued silver, the new one overvalued gold—silver fetched a higher price in France than in U.S., and the reverse held true for gold.[44] Accordingly, silver flowed out of the country while gold flowed in, effectively putting the United States on a gold standard even before the California and Australian gold rushes reversed the position of the two metals in the world market. It is not clear whether most Representatives and Senators understood the implications of this change, but the measure's chief sponsor, Senator Thomas Hart Benton (D-MO), most certainly did.

[42] The charter of the First BUS had expired in 1811, and followers of Jefferson blocked its re-charter. The War of 1812 created financial chaos, however, and in 1816 Congress created the Second Bank of the United States to sort out the mess. Its charter expired in 1836, and Jackson vetoed the second Bank's re-charter.

[43] To do this, the U.S. government slightly reduced the gold content of the dollar. Because almost no gold coins were in circulation in the country, this change required no re-coining of existing currency.

[44] Anyone could exchange fifteen-and-a-half ounces of silver or one of gold in France, ship that gold to the United States, and trade it for sixteen ounces of silver, earning a clear profit of half an ounce of silver, all with a minimum of risk. This trade would continue until France ran out of gold of the United States ran out of silver.

Benton opposed banking in all its forms. He realized that the high weight of silver relative to its value forced those conducting large transactions to use banknotes or drafts. He reasoned that basing the currency on gold, with its higher value per ounce, would eliminate the need for such devices. Benton did not accomplish his goal. Paper was still more convenient than gold coins, and most large transactions still relied on bank notes or drafts. He did, however, shift the basis of the currency to gold.

The Civil War revolutionized finance. The government needed vast sums to fight the war. When the last Confederate forces surrendered in 1865, the federal debt stood at $2.6 billion, the interest on which exceeded the entire federal budget for 1860. The crisis also convinced many Americans that the United States had to strengthen its national institutions, including financial ones. In addition to raising taxes and issuing bonds, the federal government adopted two major innovations to secure the money it needed. The first, the "greenback," was an emergency measure. In 1861, running short of money and unable to borrow except at prohibitive rates, the federal government issued paper currency unbacked by gold that soon became known as greenbacks because of the green ink used to print the reverse of the notes. These were legal tender for all debts, public and private, with two significant exceptions—the government continued to collect tariffs and pay interest on its debts in gold. By the end of the war, Washington had issued $431 million in greenbacks, which traded at a large and variable discount against gold dollars—it took more than $100 in greenbacks to buy $100 in gold coins, sometimes twice as much. Gold dollars nevertheless remained in circulation for foreign trade and the payment of tariffs and interest on government bonds, giving the country a two-tiered currency.

The second innovation, embodied in the National Banking Acts of 1863 and 1864, sought both to expand the market for federal bonds and to standardize the currency. These measures authorized any group of five or more with at least $50,000 in federal bonds to charter a bank. Such institutions could issue banknotes equal to 90 percent of their bond holdings—a bank with $50,000 in bonds could issue $45,000 in notes.[45] Congress initially capped the total issue of national banknotes at $300 million but removed this limit in 1875. The Treasury Department would print the notes and hold the bonds, remitting interest to their owners, and

[45] National banks in town with fewer than 6000 people needed at least $50,000 in capital, but those in towns with 6000 to 50,000 people required $100,000, and in cities with more than 50,000 people, $200,000 in capital was the minimum.

new bureau, the Office of the Comptroller of the Currency, would audit national banks. Washington also levied a prohibitive 10 percent tax on the notes of state-chartered banks, quickly driving such paper from circulation. State banks either reorganized with a federal charter or reoriented their business toward taking deposits and making loans. National banks were supposed to redeem their notes, on demand, in legal tenders, which in the 1860s meant greenbacks. Most of the population, however, understood that federal bonds backed every national bank note in circulation dollar-for-dollar and was content to hold them.

The system had a grave flaw—inflexibility. Issuing new notes or removing old ones from circulation took several months, so banks could not respond to short-term shifts in the demand for money such as occurred during the harvest, when merchants had to pay farmers for the year's crops. Reserve requirements exacerbated instability. National banks had to keep a minimum reserve of 15 percent against total deposits to provide for withdrawals and other contingencies—that is, for every $100 in deposits they had to hold $15 in reserve. They could keep this money either in cash or on deposit with another national bank in one of nineteen reserve cities. Banks in these cities, in turn, had to maintain a 25 percent reserve, either in cash or on deposit at national banks in New York City. Eventually, Congress allowed national banks in Chicago and St. Louis to hold these reserves as well, but New York was always the chief depository for such money. Because deposits in other banks earned interest but cash did not, bankers preferred to keep as much of their reserve as possible on account with another institution. Money, therefore, tended to flow to the center. Yet whenever pressure developed, such as during the harvest, local banks pulled money out of the reserve centers to meet the demands upon them. Banks in reserve cities, in turn, pulled cash from New York, Chicago, and St. Louis, transmitting local strains through the entire system.[46] In the spring, banks at the center were frequently awash in cash, but in the fall, they often faced a shortage.[47]

[46] Robert Sharkey, *Money, Class, and Party: An Economic Study of Civil War and Reconstruction* (Baltimore: Johns Hopkins Press, 1959), pp. 228–9.

[47] For an excellent description of how the system did, and did not, work, see Richard Sylla, "Federal Policy, Banking Market Structure, and Capital Mobilization in the United States, 1865–1913," *Journal of Economic History* 29 (1969): 657–86. National banks outside reserve centers could hold as much as 60 percent of their required reserves of 15 percent in other national banks in reserve centers, while banks in reserve centers could hold half their reserves of 25 percent on deposit with banks in New York, Chicago, and St. Louis. National banks in the last three cities had to hold all their 25 percent reserve in cash.

The "call market" added another layer of instability. The rules of New York's securities market required brokers to pay within one day for stocks or bonds that they purchased. Their customers, however, usually paid only after a transaction was complete, and the money might not arrive for two weeks. As a result, brokers had to carry large amounts of securities on their own books.[48] Banks in New York City usually loaned extra cash to brokers against these securities—"call loans." Money that flowed into the center financed trading of securities, so that when cash flowed back out, financial exchanges were the first to feel the pinch. Most stock market crashes occurred in the fall, when the demands of the harvest drew money from New York's call market.

The inflexibility of reserve requirements made the situation worse. Banks could not legally draw on funds held in reserve. If rural banks pulled deposits out of institutions in New York, the latter could not use their reserves to cover the demand but had to call in loans. This rule nullified one of the reasons for having a reserve in the first place—to accommodate shifts in the demand for money. Congress had imposed this requirement to prevent the over-expansion of credit and to protect depositors in case a bank suffered heavy losses, and giving bankers discretion over reserves would defeat these purposes. The goals were laudable, but in pursuing them, Congress made the financial system even more rigid.

Many agrarian radicals objected to the national banking system because it allowed private entities to issue currency. Political activist Sarah Emery fulminated in *Seven Financial Conspiracies which have Enslaved the American People*, a seminal text of the Populist movement: "Of all the villainous schemes of robbery ever practiced upon any people our national banking system stands preeminent. … On one hand, he [the banker] draws interest from the government; on the other, from the same investment he draws interest from his individual debtors."[49] The Greenback and Populist parties both called for the abolition of national banks, as did the Democrats after they nominated William Jennings Bryan in 1896. Though important to radicals like the Populists, this proposal never generated broad popular excitement. National banks provided a reliable currency, and radicals wanted to expand the supply of money. Abolishing national

[48] In contrast, brokers in London had as much as two weeks to settle transactions, one of several reasons why London's market for securities was more efficient than New York's.

[49] Sarah Emery, *Seven Financial Conspiracies which have Enslaved the American People, 3rd Edition* (Lansing, MI, 1896), p. 25.

banks would do the opposite. Nevertheless, specific arrangements often benefitted one group at the expense of another. Though bankers liked to pretend otherwise, finance was not simply a technical question. Bankers were not as rapacious as most radicals imagined, but they protected their own interests, and national banks had considerable influence over the currency. At the same time, radicals often misunderstood the issue. They believed that, by allowing banks to issue notes, the government sacrificed its sovereignty. Yet every time a bank took deposits to make loans, it created money—borrowers got credit while depositors still had their money on account. Issuing notes was simply a different means to the same end. The question was not one of principle but of costs, benefits, and their distribution. Radicals also erred in believing that banks systematically restricted the supply of money. Historically, they tended to provide too many notes, not too few. Banks earned interest on each note they issued, so when left to their own devices, they usually erred on the side of liberality.

The hostility of radicals like the Populists toward national banks illustrates an important continuity in American history. Jacksonians had sought to eliminate paper currency, but those who claimed Jackson's mantle after the Civil War wanted to expand the supply of money by issuing greenbacks or coining silver. These programs seem to point in opposite directions, but both reflected a deep-seated distrust of banks and finance in general. Andrew Jackson's desire to return to gold and silver coins and William Jenning Bryan's plan to flood the country with silver money had the same goal, to reduce—ideally eliminate—the power of banks.

With the end of the Civil War, the fate of greenbacks became a political issue second only to the Reconstruction of the South. Many Americans wanted to redeem greenbacks and return to the gold standard as soon as possible, but others feared the impact of suddenly withdrawing $431 million in currency from circulation. The doubters included both those who wanted a currency based entirely on greenbacks that political authorities could adjust to the needs of the economy, and those who hoped for a gradual return to gold. The debate was long, shifting, and often raucous, and the late 1870s saw the emergence of a Greenback Party that sent several representatives to Congress. In early 1875, however, Congress voted to return to gold, setting a deadline of January 1, 1879. It also authorized the Treasury Secretary to sell bonds for gold so that the government could accumulate a reserve of it. Senator John Sherman, the chief architect of this legislation, became Treasury Secretary in 1877, and he successfully steered the country back to the gold standard.

This operation did not eliminate greenbacks. After some reductions, Congress fixed their volume at $320 million and explicitly forbade the Treasury from cancelling them.[50] The return to gold meant that the government would convert greenbacks into gold, on demand, at $20.64 an ounce, making them "as good as gold." National banknotes, which holders would redeem in greenbacks or gold, had the same quality. While at the Treasury, Sherman accumulated a reserve of $100 million in gold, which he estimated was sufficient to back the $320 million in greenbacks, an expedient that subsequently assumed great symbolic importance. The gold reserve became a widely followed index of the country's financial health. If the reserve stood over $100 million, the dollar was safe, but if the reserve fell below that level, trouble loomed. As some pointed out, the difference between a reserve of $101 million and of $99 million was insignificant, but people nevertheless gave this measure considerable weight, not the least because the size of the gold reserve was one of the few reliable economic statistics available to the public.

The late 1870s also saw the first stirrings of the silver movement. Since the 1790s, the United States had offered silver free coinage. Since 1834, however, the mint price had been so far below the market price that no one availed themselves of the opportunity. During the 1870s, the immense flow of silver from the American West, coupled with the decline of European demand for it, altered the situation. In 1875, silver fell below $1.29 an ounce, the price at which Washington would coin it. Normally, that would have drawn silver to U.S. mints, and the coinage of a large volume of silver money would have put the United States on a de facto silver standard by 1876 or 1877. Plans to restore the gold standard would inevitably have fallen by the wayside. A technical change in the coinage laws in 1873, however, prevented this outcome. After several years of discussion, Congress simplified the nation's coinage by discontinuing little-used coins, including the silver dollar. This coin, however, was the only silver money subject to free coinage. Ending its production effectively severed the link between the dollar and silver. The privilege of free coinage now attached only to gold.

Subsequently, the advocates of silver spun an elaborate mythology around this decision, which they christened the "Crime of '73." In 1893, Silverites in the House of Representatives issued a report that insisted,

[50] The Treasury could replace notes that had become worn or defaced, or even change the mix of denominations. The $320 million figure was an aggregate.

"The conspiracy formed in the Old World, planned and so successfully carried through there and here, was aimed to confine the debt-paying medium of the nations concerned to a single metal, gold. … Gold decreed to rise rapidly in value, thus adding fifty percent to the value of credits, enriching creditors, public and private, at the expense of debtors and taxpayers."[51] Sarah Emery made the most detailed accusation in her *Seven Financial Conspiracies.* "In 1872," she wrote, "silver being demonetized in France, England, and Holland, a capital of $500,000 was raised, and Ernest Seyd of London was sent to this country with funds, as agent of the foreign bond holders and capitalists, to effect the same object (demonetization of silver), which was accomplished."[52] According to Populists and Silverites, the decline in prices in the United States between 1873 and 1897 was not a product of bad luck, much less of economic forces, but of a conspiracy among creditors.

Framed this way, accusations of conspiracy were nonsense. In 1872, France and the Netherlands still coined silver. Ernest Seyd, a noted British expert on coinage, did not visit the United States in 1872 or 1873. He did write a long memo on the coinage bill for one of its sponsors in Congress, but this document strongly criticized the decision to drop the silver dollar.[53] Subsequently, Seyd became one of Britain's leading bimetallists. No one made a serious effort to lobby Congress about the fate of the silver dollar, and certainly no one from abroad did so. Although Silverites often implied that the bill passed under irregular circumstances, the record clearly shows that enactment followed the usual procedures and that some Representatives and Senators spoke on it. Silverites and Populists were not, however, inclined to let facts get in the way of their story. As Jeffrey Ostler has demonstrated, accounts of a British-led conspiracy to reduce American farmers to serfdom were a staple of their rhetoric.[54]

Samuel DeCanio has discovered that several lawmakers who represented western states and had close ties to owners of silver mines did pay close attention to the bill. They wanted to create a "trade dollar," a slightly

[51] U.S. Congress 52nd Congress, 1st session, Committee on Coinage, Weights, and Measures, *Free Coinage of Gold and Silver*, 1893, p. 3.

[52] Emery, *Seven Financial Conspiracies*, p. 52. France restricted silver coinage in 1873, not 1872, and the Netherlands switched to the gold standard in 1875.

[53] U.S. Senate, 53rd Congress, 1st session, *Letter from Ernest Seyd to Samuel Hooper on the Subject of Coinage*, 1893.

[54] Jeffrey Ostler, "The Rhetoric of Conspiracy and the Formation of Kansas Populism," *Agricultural History* 69 (1995): 1–27.

heavier silver coin that would not be legal tender but would, they hoped, find a ready market in China, which used imported silver coins. DeCanio also provides strong evidence that at least one government official took a bribe in exchange for his support. These lawmakers showed no interest in the demonetization of silver, however. Presumably, they did not think that the price of silver would ever fall below one-sixteenth that of gold, the rate at which it became profitable to bring the metal to the mint.[55]

Defenders of the gold standard developed their own mythology around this event. The 1873 bill was, they insisted, simply a housecleaning measure that discontinued the silver dollar because the government had never coined many of them—only about $7 million since the founding of the Republic. Economist Lawrence Laughlin wrote, "The act of 1873 was a piece of good fortune, which saved our financial credit and protected the honor of the state" by preserving the gold standard.[56] John Sherman, who shepherded the measure through the Senate, argued, "It was fortunate that the United States then dropped the coinage of the old silver dollar. No one then contemplated the enormous yield of silver from the mines, and the resulting fall in the market value of silver."[57] This tale of serendipity was, at best, only partly true. In 1873, few Representatives or Senators

[55] Samuel DeCanio, "Populism, Paranoia, and the Politics of Free Silver," *Studies in American Political Development* 25 (2011): 1–26. DeCanio suggests that an influential group of westerners led by banker William Ralston, who had large interests in silver mining, actively supported demonetization, and he provides suggestive evidence. Supposedly, they feared that the demonetization of silver in much of Europe would lead to huge imports of silver to the U.S., which would drive down the price of silver in America. Demonetization in the United States would, they imagined, prevent this outcome. This reasoning was dubious. World markets determined silver's price, and a decline in its value in Europe would inevitably make itself felt in the U.S., free coinage of not. It is hard to imagine that a banker with large interests in the industry did not understand the situation. Certainly, farmers in the Dakotas realized that world markets set the price of their grain, and farmers in Mississippi understood that the same was true for their cotton. It seems more likely that Ralston and the lawmakers with whom he worked assumed that the price of silver would never fall below sixteen-to-one and, therefore, that silver would never find use as money in the United States. In that case, the fate of the silver dollar was moot. Of course, it is always possible that Ralston and his associates were remarkably stupid. In either case, they focused on the creation of the trade dollar, which they hoped would open a new market in China for American silver. In this, they were disappointed. The Chinese had been using Mexican silver dollars since the sixteenth century and showed no interest in changing.

[56] J. Laurence Laughlin, *The History of Bimetallism in the United States*, 4th Edition (New York, 1900), p. 93.

[57] Sherman, *Recollections of Forty Years*, p. 469.

paid much heed to the coinage measure. At the time, neither gold nor silver circulated freely. Greenbacks were the issue, and most probably did think of the bill deleting the silver dollar simply as an effort to tidy up the coinage. Those in the Treasury and Congress who drafted and guided this bill to passage, however, were financial sophisticates who knew better, recognizing that the measure severed the link between the dollar and silver. To them, the coinage bill was not merely a housekeeping measure but part of a broader effort to reestablish the gold standard. Historian Walter Nugent has discovered that at least some of those who pushed to end silver coinage had access to reports describing the rapid growth in American silver output, though he also notes that other reports available to them were more skeptical of the potential of American mines. The ore in many of these deposits was of a relatively low grade, and its successful exploitation depended on exploiting new technologies imported from Europe.[58] The decision was more important in retrospect than at the time, however. In 1873, no one alive could remember when the price of gold had stood above sixteen ounces of silver, the point at which it became profitable to bring silver to U.S. mints. The French mint remained open to silver at the more lucrative rate of fifteen-and-a-half-to one. Despite Sarah Emery's assertions to the contrary, France only limited coinage later that year. Perhaps most important, the authors of the 1873 measure apparently had no inkling of the slowdown in gold production that would soon convert the gold standard into a force of deflation. They may have recognized silver's potential for inflation but not gold's for the reverse. As economist Barry Eichengreen writes, "There was no basis for forecasting the magnitude of the price-level decline that began in the 1870s. Only in the 1880s, after a decade of deflation, was this understood."[59] Assigning motives is difficult, but the authors of the 1873 Act probably imagined that they were merely completing a movement toward gold begun when the government overvalued it in 1834.

Irrespective of the motives behind it, the demonetization of silver had profound implications. Had the country's mints remained open to silver, the United States would have found itself on a de facto silver standard by 1876 or 1877. American demand might have stabilized the price of silver

[58] Walter T.K. Nugent, *The Money Question During Reconstruction* (New York: Norton, 1967), pp. 76–85.

[59] Barry Eichengreen, *Globalizing Capital: A History of the International Monetary System, 3rd edition* (Princeton: Princeton University Press, 2019), p. 17.

and even encouraged France to keep its mints open to it, an outcome that could well have mitigated deflation, not only in the United States but also in Europe. As eminent an authority on money as Nobel Laureate economist Milton Friedman considered such an outcome likely.[60] Defenders of the gold standard such as Laughlin and Sherman—less brilliant than Friedman, but closer to events—dismissed such scenarios. They insisted that free coinage would simply have made the United States the dumping ground for the world's silver, saddling the country with a constantly depreciating currency. In any case, the opportunity passed. When Americans turned their attention back to silver, the country was on gold and the price of silver had fallen well below the official price of $1.29. Under these circumstances, the free coinage of silver would have entailed a major devaluation—a very different proposition than the country faced in the mid-1870s, when the issue was how to stabilize the currency. One recurring theme in the history of finance is "path dependency." Decisions have consequences, and much as individuals and even entire societies might wish otherwise, undoing them is difficult, sometimes prohibitively so. Such was the case after the U.S. returned to the gold standard in 1879. Having set the value of the dollar at a certain level, the country could not alter it without thoroughly disrupting existing financial arrangements.

Between 1873 and 1879, the United States suffered a grinding depression characterized by, among other things, falling prices, which explains much of the enthusiasm for greenbacks. Many Americans believed that an expansion of the supply of money would raise price levels. As the price of silver fell, those battered by hard times increasingly viewed its coinage as another means to the same end. Indeed, silver had several advantages over greenbacks. Silver dollars would not challenge the widespread belief that only the precious metals were "honest money," and free coinage of silver would be simpler than greenbacks, whose issue depended on government discretion.[61] Finally, silver had a natural constituency—silver miners—who provided support.

[60] Milton Friedman, "The Crime of 1873," *Journal of Political Economy* 98 (1990): 1159–94.

[61] Some advocates of basing the currency on greenbacks had proposed the "convertible bond," which would pay 3.65 percent. Holders of these bonds could convert them into greenbacks on demand, and holders of greenbacks could convert them into these bonds on demand. The idea was to fix the rate of interest at 3.65 percent because that was supposedly the rate at which productivity increased in the long run. See Sharkey, *Money, Class, and Party*, p. 60. How supporters of greenbacks divined the 3.65 percent rate is not clear—they had no reliable statistics on productivity—nor is it clear why interest rates should equal the

In 1878, supporters of silver in Congress sought to restore the free coinage of silver ("free silver"), the first of many such drives over the next twenty years. Unlike subsequent efforts, however, this one yielded a constructive compromise. The Bland-Allison Act, named after Rep. Richard Bland (D-MO), silver's most consistent champion in Congress, and Senator William Allison (R-IO) , a leading Republican in the Upper House and a defender of "sound finance," directed the Treasury to buy between $2 to $4 million of silver a month at the market price and coin it, with the exact amount left to the discretion of the Treasury Secretary. Purists never liked Bland-Allison. Silverites wanted free silver, not more money under the gold standard. Even Bland considered the measure but a first step toward that goal. Defenders of the gold standard feared that the silver dollars coined under the Bland-Allison Act would drive gold from circulation. President Rutherford B. Hayes vetoed the measure—Congress overrode his veto—and President Grover Cleveland called for its repeal in his December 1885 State of the Union message. More flexible and financially sophisticated defenders of the gold standard, like Senators Sherman and Allison, did not object. They calculated that, because the supply of silver dollars would be limited, the government could keep them at par with gold. Silver coins would become the metallic equivalent of greenbacks. Moreover, during the life of the Bland-Allison Act the Treasury Department coined only the minimum amount authorized, making it that much easier to maintain the silver dollar's value against gold.

At first, Americans resisted using the new silver dollars. Since the early days of the Republic, the population had used paper money for day-to-day transactions, and it was not inclined to change, not the least because bills were lighter than coins. To solve this problem, the government issued silver certificates—paper money backed, dollar-for-dollar, by silver coins in Treasury vaults. In this form, silver money found a warm reception. Subsequently, defenders of the gold standard insisted that the government was sitting on a vast hoard of silver dollars coined under the Bland-Allison Act that no one wanted. In fact, most of these coins backed silver certificates in circulation.

increase in productivity. Such a system would guarantee that, in an economic downturn, as profits (and interest rates) fell, individuals would convert currency into bonds, shrinking the supply of money and aggravating the decline. During a boom, when prices (and interest rates) were rising, individuals would convert bonds into cash, increasing the money supply and intensifying inflation. The convertible bond would, therefore, intensify economic instability rather than restrain it.

Silver money, coins and certificates, played a useful role. The American economy expanded very fast in the 1880s, and the country had to finance the transactions that went with this growth. Bank drafts accounted for most large exchanges—bank deposits increased from $1.36 billion in 1880 to $2.99 billion in 1890—but day-to-day business required currency.[62] Silver money was particularly important because the volume of greenbacks remained static and another type of money, national banknotes, contracted. These notes rested on federal bonds. During the 1880s, the federal government consistently ran a surplus, which it used to reduce its debt, shrinking the supply of bonds. Just as important, banks' financial calculus changed. Between them, the gold standard and the federal surplus drove interest rates down. Federal bonds paid 4–6 percent, and as rates in financial markets fell below 4 percent, these securities traded at a substantial premium—a bond with a face (or "par") value of $100 commanded more than $100 in the market.[63] The amount of notes a bank could issue, however, depended on the face value of the bond, not its market value. As a result, banks had to tie up more capital to issue the same volume of notes, and many concluded that they could better use the resources elsewhere. Over the course of the decade, many banks redeemed their notes, sold their bonds, and used the capital to finance the business of taking deposits and making loans. Between 1880 and 1890, the volume of national banknotes shrank from $337 million to $181 million, while that of silver certificates expanded by almost $300 million.

By the early 1880s, the United States had seven types of currency in circulation—greenbacks, national banknotes, gold coins, silver dollars, fractional silver coins (dimes and quarters),[64] silver certificates, and gold

[62] U.S. Bureau of the Census, *Historical Statistics of the United States, Colonial Times to 1970, Bicentennial Edition, Part II*, Washington, D.C., 1975, pp. 992–3.

[63] Take, for example, a bond with a face value of $1000 that pays $50 a year, or 5 percent, and runs for 20 years. If interest rates drop to 4 percent, investors will pay a premium for it, somewhere around $1100, accepting a loss at maturity in exchange for higher income over the life of the bond.

[64] The U.S. government minted "fractional" silver coins, chiefly dimes and quarters. These coins had less than the official amount of silver in them—$1.29 of these coins contained less than an ounce of silver. More important, Washington controlled their volume according to its estimates of how much small change people needed—there was no "free coinage"—and they were not legal tender for obligations over $5. In practice, these coins did what they were supposed to—provide small change—and they played little if any role in the debate over the currency.

certificates.[65] The Treasury had to keep the value of all equal. Silver coins and certificates posed the greatest challenge because holders could not convert them into gold on demand. In contrast to greenbacks, the Treasury would not exchange them for gold. Silverites had no desire to subordinate silver coins to gold, and defenders of the gold standard did not want to increase demands on the country's limited reserve of gold. If the demand for gold surged for some reason, those holding silver money might find themselves paying a premium for it—$1 in gold might fetch more than a silver dollar. If such a premium persisted very long, it would either drive gold from circulation or create a two-tiered currency, with gold for some transactions, silver for others, and constant trading between the two at a varying price. Such a relationship had existed between gold and greenbacks during and after the Civil War, and few wanted to return to it. The country avoided this outcome. The supply of silver money was limited—silver did not enjoy free coinage. The economy was growing and the supply of national banknotes was falling, so Americans could use the silver money created every month in their routine business. The federal government also enjoyed a surplus throughout the 1880s, and Washington accepted silver money for most taxes. Those holding silver coins and certificates knew that Washington would take them at face value, so idle silver money quickly found its way into federal coffers.

The federal surplus also mitigated the other chief weakness of the American monetary system, its inflexibility. The country could not easily expand the supply of currency and credit to accommodate seasonal shifts in demand, much less a financial crisis. Interest rates almost always jumped during the harvest because merchants and brokers needed cash to pay farmers. In the 1880s, however, the surplus gave the Treasury flexibility. If the demand for money was slack, it would let cash pile up in its vaults—Washington collected most of its revenue in greenbacks and coins. Should demand increase, however, it could inject money into financial markets by repaying federal bonds. The effect was somewhat like the open market operations through which, in the twentieth century, the Federal Reserve conducted monetary policy.

Though hardly ideal, this system worked. Currency and credit grew with the needs of the economy, the country had enough money to move

[65] Gold coins held by the Treasury backed gold certificates dollar-for-dollar, just as silver coins backed silver certificates. Many preferred gold certificates because they were more convenient than coins.

the harvest, and financial crises did not spin out of control. This edifice rested on a delicate foundation, however. The government had to coin just enough silver to provide for the economy's needs but not so much as to push gold to a premium. The Treasury had to run a surplus large enough to give it room to maneuver but not so large as to drain the economy of money. The margin of error was small.

Down on the Farm

The boom of the 1880s exacerbated social divisions. It did not profit everyone equally, or in some cases at all, and it challenged widely held social values. Historically, the American economy was decentralized, with goods moving through a network of small, independent merchants, none of whom controlled their markets. Increasingly, however, large industrial corporations and railroads, with the support of integrated financial markets, dominated economic life. Ranchers discovered that their livelihood now depended on the decisions of Chicago's meatpackers, as did urban butchers. Workers in the country's burgeoning factories and mills depended on wages doled out by managers whom they rarely saw, much less knew. Farmers shipped their crops to market on railroads that, as their managers said, charged "what the market will bear," which in practice meant skimming off as much of cultivators' profits as possible.

Change imposed particularly heavy burdens on farmers, who were still the largest part of the American population by far. Many of them did thrive under the new order. In the Midwest and Northeast, large numbers turned to truck or dairy farming, providing fruit, vegetables, milk, and cheese to rapidly growing cities. Others in the Midwest focused on raising hogs for the expanding meatpackers. Such "mixed farming" offered considerable benefits. Statistics compiled by the state of Minnesota indicated that, in counties where farmers had shifted their focus from growing wheat to more diverse offerings, mortgage foreclosures decline 80 percent over the course of the 1880s.[66] Unfortunately, diversification was not an option for farmers on the Great Plains who grew wheat or in the South who raised cotton. They were distant from the burgeoning urban markets of the Northeast and Industrial Midwest, and few had the capital to reorient their operations. For them, times were hard. The price of wheat and cotton increased some in the early 1880s, recovering from the depressed

[66] *Princeton Union* (Princeton, MN), Oct. 5, 1893, p. 3.

levels of the 1870s, but prices declined again in the second half of the decade. Between 1880 and 1884, the price of wheat and cotton averaged ¢92 a bushel and ¢9.6 a pound, respectively. Between 1885 and 1889, the averages were ¢75 a bushel and ¢8.4 a pound—a decline of 18.5 and 12.5 percent, respectively.

Debt compounded the problem. Between 1879 and 1892, the price of almost everything fell, providing farmers with some relief—though the prices of manufactured goods generally declined less than those of agricultural commodities. Debts, however, did not fluctuate with prices. Farmers in the Northeast and those parts of the Midwest settled before the Civil War had, for the most part, paid off the obligations incurred in buying their land, and many had accumulated some capital. Such was not the case further west, in areas settled after the Civil War. Over 200 mortgage companies operated in Kansas and Nebraska alone, most of them backed by Northeastern or British investors.[67] Lindley Keasbey, an economist, wrote in 1894, "He [the farmer] needed the money at the outset to redeem the barren lands stretching out before him. He has needed extra funds ever since to enlarge his original holdings. With his face turned resolutely toward the setting sun, for years the western farmer has toiled assiduously, striving to save enough to pay off his eastern debt after providing at least a decent living for his family. The harder he labored, and the greater the amount of produce he sent to eastern markets, just so much more difficult—or so it seemed to him—it grew to keep up with the ever-accruing interest on his eastern farm mortgage."[68]

Conditions in the South were worse. The Civil War had severely damaged the region's physical capital—railroads, livestock—and had almost completely wiped out its financial capital. The war had also created an immense class of freedmen who, upon emancipation, had "nothing but freedom." To restart production, farmers had borrowed heavily. Most of the freedmen became sharecroppers, renting land in exchange for a share of their crop. They paid for tools, seeds, and provisions with loans secured by liens on their crops, in effect borrowing against cotton in the ground—the "crop lien." As the *New York Times* described it, "Ninety percent of the cotton crop is sold when it is planted, and the crop is grown on credit. The farmer owes the merchant, the merchant owes the banker, and the

[67] Hicks, *The Populist Revolt*, p. 22.

[68] Lindley Keasbey, "The New Sectionalism: A Western Warning to the East," *The Forum* 16 (1894): 580.

banker in many cases owes his Eastern correspondent [banker]."[69] Such loans were risky—a crop might not come in. Because few southerners had money to lend, borrowers had to pay rates high enough to attract capital from outside the region. Accordingly, money was expensive, often costing as much as 30 percent a year. After the harvest, once they had handed over a portion of their crop to their landlord and paid off the crop lien, most sharecroppers found themselves no better off than when they had first planted. Whites who owned small farms stood in a somewhat better position because they did not have to pay rent, but most of them also relied on the crop lien for seeds, tools, and provisions. Interest payments weighed heavily, and more than a few lost their land after defaulting on debts. As one southerner put it, "Each year the plunge into debt is deeper; each year the burden is heavier. ... Cares are many, smiles are few, and the comforts of life are scantier."[70]

Farmers' debts not only imposed economic hardship but also threatened their social position. The country had changed greatly since the days of Thomas Jefferson, and the self-sufficient yeoman whom he had idealized had given way to the commercial farmer, at least in most places. The latter, however, still cherished independence, albeit in modified form. Farmers wanted to deal with the market on their own terms, which meant owning their land, eschewing debt, and accumulating enough money to ride out bad harvests and fluctuations in farm prices. Historian Allan Nevins described such an independent commercial farmer, William Ford, the father of industrialist Henry Ford: "William Ford believed that a farmer's life in the United States was exceptionally independent, self-respecting, and satisfying. As a boy [in Ireland] he had experienced the hardships and frustrations of tenantry; and his experience in Ireland had made him deeply appreciative of owning his own farm, and being able to save money against hard times. ... What more could a man desire?"[71] Debt robbed farmers of their independence and dignity, and low prices for their crops prevented them from reclaiming it.

Many farmers in the cotton- and wheat-producing regions attributed their plight to a shortage of money. Thomas Shearman, a prominent

[69] *New York Times*, September 21, 1890, p. 16.

[70] Quoted in C. Vann Woodward, *Tom Watson: Agrarian Rebel* (Charlottesville: University of Virginia Press, 1955), p. 161.

[71] Allan Nevins, *Ford: The Times, the Man, the Company* (New York: Charles Scribner's Sons, 1954), p. 71.

New York City attorney sympathetic to their plight, wrote, "The bulk of transactions in rural districts, especially in the South and Southwest, are carried on with even less use of money than is usual in the great cities of the North and East. … Everyone keeps an account at the country store and everything is done upon credit." He continued, "This vast class of producers are fully convinced that they would obtain far better prices for what they sell, and would pay lower prices for what they buy, if they were supplied with money … instead of depending upon store trading."[72] Silverites in the U.S. House of Representatives drafted a report that concluded, "Agriculturalists are compelled, purely for want of sufficient money, to run their farms on credit, and no business can be successfully done in that way. … Agriculture will never prosper again until the farmers can sell for cash, and they can never do so until the money is put into existence."[73] Some went further, arguing that the entire financial system was inherently fraudulent. One writer from Kansas insisted, "The radical and fundamental defect of the present banking system is the theory of 'doing business upon the money of depositors, with nominal capital.' Why indeed should not banks, like individuals, do business upon their own resources?" He continued, "We [farmers] have unbounded confidence in the dollars which jingle in our pockets, but very little in those which exist only in the imagination, and are represented by stocks, bonds, checks, drafts, clearing-house certificates, and other devices, which always fail to perform the function of money in the last extremity, when money is most needed."[74] Sen. William Allen (P-NE) offered a more balanced critique, stating, "Another prolific source of evil contributing … in large measure to produce the distress we are now experiencing, lies in over expanding bank credit, making money panics probable, or at least possible, by sudden and extreme inflation or contracting of the volume of currency. We have too much credit … and not enough actual money."[75] Agrarian radicals hoped that a large expansion of the currency would reduce—perhaps even eliminate—farmers' need for credit.

[72] Thomas Shearman, "Need, Not of 'More Money,' But of Better Exchange," *The Forum* 16 (December 1893): 463.

[73] U.S. House of Representatives, 52nd Congress, 2nd session, *National Money System: Views of the Minority*, 1893, p. 11.

[74] Charles Millard, "An Open Letter to Eastern Capitalists," *The Arena* 18 (August 1897): 215.

[75] Speech of Senator William Allen, August 24, 1893, p. 17, *Silver Speeches*.

To many farmers, the gold standard constituted the chief obstacle to improvement. It limited the supply of currency, forcing prices lower and requiring farmers to rely on credit. As one rural newspaper put it, gold was "a standard, not of valuation, but of spoilation and confiscation."[76] It favored bankers, domestic and foreign, who were not only creditors but also financed the railroads that squeezed farmers. The situation threatened not simply the country's economic well-being but the fabric of democracy. Sarah Emery wrote, "Instead of 'robber king' and 'brigand chief' we have today the money king, the coal king, the cattle king, the railroad magnate, the telegraph monopolist, and the lumber baron. Instead of spoils and plunders, we have interest, dividends, revenue, and rents."[77] The corrupting power of these groups explained why the government had embraced a monetary standard self-evidently at odds with its citizens' interests. As Senator James George (D-FL) stated on the floor of Congress, "Demonetization [of silver] was the result of a conspiracy, and the conspirators, Sir, were monarchical Europe, the money-lenders, the holders of money securities in Europe and this country."[78] *Coin's Financial School*, the most influential Silverite tract of the 1890s, insisted, "The integrity of the government had been violated. A financial trust has control of your money, and with it, is robbing you of your property. Vampires feed upon your commercial blood."[79]

Though no evidence supported accusations of conspiracy, farmers of cotton and wheat had a solid economic case. Prices fell for almost everything during the long boom from 1879 to 1893. Many defenders of the gold standard insisted that advances in productivity accounted for this phenomenon. David A. Wells, a distinguished scientist and former Special Commissioner of Revenue for the federal government, argued, "Man, within the last thirty or fifty years, has attained such a degree of control over the forces of nature, and has so compassed their use, that he has been able to do far more work in a given time and produce far more product, measured by quantity in ratio to a given amount labor, than ever before. … We have, therefore, a natural, sufficient, and non-disputable cause of the

[76] *Farmer's Alliance*, September 6, 1890, p. 1

[77] Emery, *Seven Conspiracies*, p. 10.

[78] Speech of Senator James Z. George, Sept. 20 and 22, 1893, p. 7, *Silver Speeches*.

[79] William Hope Harvey, *Coin's Financial School* (Chicago: Coin Publishing Company, 1894), pp. 143–4.

remarkable decline in prices under consideration."[80] Wells relied on the "labor theory of value," which economists such as Adam Smith, David Riccardo, and Karl Marx also used. They contended that the cost of a good or service reflected the amount of labor needed to produce it. This is wrong—were it true, prices would have been falling even since the Industrial Revolution began in the late eighteenth century. As economist Irving Fisher would point out, the price level is a product of the level of output, the volume of currency and credit, and the pace at which money changes hands. Farmers were right. The price level is largely a monetary phenomenon, and under the gold standard, the supply of gold limited the supply of currency and credit.[81] In the 1880s, the supply of gold did not increase as fast as output, forcing prices ever lower. In many sectors, advances in productivity allowed producers to cut prices even while maintaining wages and profits—such was the case with Carnegie's steel mills and Standard Oil's refineries—but growers of cotton and wheat scored no such gains to offset lower prices. Critics of the gold standard did sometimes exaggerate their case. After 1879, the gold standard did not reduce the supply of currency, as some claimed, but simply limited its growth. Moreover, reform of the financial system could increase prices, at least up to a point, by accelerating the pace at which money changed hands and increasing the volume of credit, which in practice serves as money. On the main issue, however, the critics were right. The gold standard fostered deflation.

Other economic developments at home and abroad exacerbated farmers' problems. In the 1870s and 1880s, Americans settled much of the Great Plains and started growing wheat there. Meanwhile, Argentines worked along similar lines, bringing the Pampas under the plow and constructing railroads linking these farms to ports, even as the Suez Canal

[80] David A. Wells, *Breakers Ahead: Cause of the Present Crisis* (New York, 1896), p. 7, reprinted in *Gold and Silver in the Presidential Campaign of 1896* (New York: Arno Press, 1974).

[81] Economists describe the relationship between the money supply, prices, and output as $m*v = p*q$. The supply of money multiplied by the rate at which it changes hands (velocity) equals the price level multiplied by the quantity of output. This simple formula hides many points of contention. Is the rate at which people spend money (velocity) constant, or does it change frequently? What exactly constitutes "money"? Under what conditions will a larger supply of money raise output, and under what raise prices? Few economists, however, doubt that a large change in the supply of money will have a significant impact on output, prices, or both.

gave growers of wheat and cotton in India better access to European markets. New railroads made it easier for Russian and Ukrainian peasants to ship their crops to the world's consumers. Modern steamships linked all these producers to Europe, the chief market. As an 1896 pamphlet written in support of William McKinley's presidential campaign noted, production of wheat in the United States had doubled between 1870 and 1895, and "nobody pretends there were twice as many people in the country to eat up the flour." At the same time, other nations had roughly tripled their exports of grain. "I don't see," the author continued, "how any amount of silver coined at our mints is going to stop these fellows raising wheat and shipping it to Liverpool."[82] Because American farmers exported most of their cotton and a large portion of their wheat, sharper competition abroad reduced prices at home. From 1873 to 1897, the price level as a whole fell about 30 percent in the United States, but cotton and wheat prices declined almost 50 percent. Even with an expanding currency, farm prices would have declined relative to others. This problem had a monetary dimension too, however. India used silver money, and its depreciation relative to gold made exports from the Subcontinent that much cheaper. The same was true of Russia until it opted for the gold standard in 1897. As a House report that Silverites drafted noted, "Nearly the whole of our exports of agriculture go to European or gold-using countries, to be sold in competition there with countries on the single silver basis." Therefore, "Free coinage [of silver in the United States] would put … the American farmer on equality with the Hindoo [*sic*] and other silver-using peoples."[83] Inevitably, some attributed the situation to conspiracy. One Silverites insisted, "Britain *can* depress the price of silver bullion, and it is in her interest to do so."[84] Another contended, "by cheapening the price of silver[,] the exports of wheat and cotton from India, which compete with your exports from here, must force down the price of these staples."[85] The

[82] *A Farmer's Letter on the Silver Question*, [1896], 8, reprinted in *Gold and Silver in the Presidential Campaign of 1896.*

[83] U.S. House of Representatives, 52nd Congress, 1st session, *Free Coinage of Gold and Silver*, 1893, pp. 5–6.

[84] *Proceedings of the Second National Silver Convention held at Washington, May 26th, 27th, and 28th 1892, Including the Organization of the American Bimetallic League* (Washington, D.C.: Geo. R. Gray, Printers, 1892), p. 136.

[85] Address of Morgan Frewen, *Second National Silver Convention*, p. 175.

result was cheaper bread for British workers and cheaper cotton for British textile mills. In fact, the British government could not control the price of silver. Indeed, its officials feared that silver's decline would create economic problems for their huge Indian empire. Silverites were nevertheless right to link the fall in silver's value with the intensification of foreign competition.

Critics of the gold standard also believed that it fostered high interest rates, but here their case was weaker. Interest rates are, in a sense, the price of money, so the supply of currency and credit strongly affects it. All things being equal, the more money, the lower interest rates. At the same time, lenders factor perceived risks into rates—not only the danger of default, but also the possibility of inflation or devaluation. If lenders consider a nation's money stable, they will accept lower interest rates. The effect on long-term interest rates is particularly strong. Moreover, by tying the dollar to the pound, franc, mark, and other European currencies, the gold standard greatly expanded the pool of capital from which Americans could draw. Defenders of the gold standard insisted that these factors reduced interest rates. Judge George Aldredge of Texas stated, "Interest has declined since 1873 in my part of the country (Texas) from 3 percent a month to 6 and 8 percent per annum. There is no denying the fact that the goldbugs did that. … Interest is always low under an honest standard."[86] Railroads, the country's largest debtors, paid lower rates in the 1880s than in the 1870s, largely because they could get better terms in London's money market. The Grain Belt seems to have benefitted from cheaper money as well, with the interest rate on mortgages declining about two percentage points over the course of the 1880s.[87] Unfortunately, the acute shortage of capital in the South and the risks associated with lending against crops in the ground meant that farmers there reaped little if any benefit from declines in interest rates elsewhere.

Defenders of the gold standard blamed the rickety system of rural credit for the high interest rates charged some farmers. Thomas Shearman wrote, "Is not the only real relief [for farmers' credit woes] to be found in the

[86] George Aldredge in *The White Elephant: Silver as seen by Prominent Statesmen* (Boston, 1896), p. 17, reprinted in *Gold and Silver in the Presidential Campaign of 1896.*

[87] Jeffrey Ostler, *Prairie Populism: the Fate of Agrarian Radicalism in Kansas, Nebraska, and Iowa, 1880–1892* (Lawrence: University of Kansas Press, 1993), p. 16.

extension to every town and village in the land of safe and sound banking agencies, with which farmers can do business on precisely the same terms as New York merchants?"[88] Most farmers, however, wanted freedom from debt, not better terms on their loans. Every proposal for monetary reform that Populists or Silverites floated in the 1890s sought to flood the country with currency, with the object not only of raising prices but of reducing—ideally eliminating—the need for credit. As historian Lawrence Goodwyn argues, the chief aim of the Farmers' Alliance and the People's Party was to "remove furnishing merchants, commercial banks, and chartered mortgage companies from American agriculture."[89]

Behind matters such as prices and interest rates lurked broader questions about the shape of American society. In 1892, a prominent Silverite lamented, "Our late census shows that the large increase in population is confined to the cities and towns. It also shows a large decrease of population in many sections of our country which were once prosperous."[90] Though he exaggerated, the United States was becoming more urban and more industrial. In the Northeast and parts of the Midwest, farmers no long constitution the majority, and everywhere cities were growing. Barring some radical change, this trend would continue. As a leader of the Southern Farmers' Alliance, Leonidas Polk, said, "Retrogression in American agriculture … means national decay, and powerful and promising as is this young giant republic, yet its power and glory touch not the degradation of the American farmer."[91] Many Americans, including many who lived in cities, believed that farmers constituted the backbone of any healthy society and found their eclipse disturbing.

The currency question also fed into concerns about national sovereignty. The gold standard was an international system that gave participants access to trade and capital on good terms but regulated monetary policy. Those in sectors that profited from the system—railroads, manufacturing—considered the benefits worth the costs. The country lost financial autonomy but gained strength in other ways, expanding output. Farmers of cotton and wheat had a different experience. They believed that the international financial system ruined them for the benefit of

[88] Shearman, "Need, Not of 'More Money,' But of Better Exchange," p. 463.
[89] Goodwyn, *The Populist Moment*, p. 92.
[90] *Second Silver Convention*, p. 136.
[91] *New York Times*, December 8, 1890, p. 5.

foreign creditors. Americans had to reassert their sovereignty. As one Silverite insisted, "It is the unwritten law of this nation, that we should not form any alliance with any foreign power. …We believe that we should adopt and maintain a distinct American monetary system, just as we maintain a distinct American tariff system."[92] Another urged Silverites to "spurn the un-American, insulting proposition to refer the question of our coinage law to foreign enemies as England, Germany, or the Latin Union. As well refer to foreign courts our jurisprudence or tax code—our very form of government."[93]

[92] *Second Silver Convention*, p. 26.
[93] *Second Silver Convention*, p. 116.

CHAPTER 3

The Politics of Silver

In the early 1890s, the financial stability that the United States had enjoyed during the 1880s gradually fell apart. It had depended on a delicate balance between the gold standard, limited silver coinage, the federal surplus, and, not the least, foreign investment. Unfortunately, the nation's leaders mistook this fortuitous equilibrium for strength and launched a series of reckless experiments that undermined it. Events abroad compounded the error, creating new pressures just as the government weakened its own ability to respond to them.

An Embarrassment of Riches

In the late 1880s, the United States suffered from an enviable malady—the Federal Treasury had too much money. It contained over $200 million in gold as well as large quantities of greenbacks and silver certificates, and this hoard was constantly growing because the government was running a surplus. Previously, Washington had used surplus funds to retire debt, but that option was becoming less attractive. The government had reduced its total debt to less than $1 billion, and most of the remainder consisted of bonds that would not mature for many years. The government could purchase these in the open market, but because interest rates had fallen since their issue, Washington would have to pay a premium. Retiring $1 in debt would cost more than $1. Politicians resisted this option, not the least

W. Wells, *Financial Politics in the United States in the 1890s*,
https://doi.org/10.1007/978-3-031-86765-1_3

because bankers and foreign investors would reap most of the windfall. Moreover, many federal bonds backed notes that national banks had issued, so repaying them would shrink the supply of currency. Yet the Treasury could not safely continue to pile up cash. The gold and currency it held were out of circulation, contracting a money supply that many already considered inadequate. European governments could simply deposit surplus funds in the central bank, which could then make the money available to borrowers, but the United States had no such institution. Washington could deposit money in national banks, but politicians shied away from this option. The law was murky on whether the Treasury had the authority to make such deposits.[1] The country had several thousand national banks, and those that did not receive deposits might well protest and lobby for funds themselves. If a bank holding federal deposits failed, the government could lose its money, as had happened during the financial crises of the late 1830s. During 1887 and 1888, the Treasury did make some deposits in national banks, but it required that they pledge federal bonds against the money. This condition both reduced the volume of bonds available to support national banknotes and made such deposits far less attractive to banks, and Washington abandoned the experiment after 1888.[2] Reducing the surplus seemed the best solution to the problem.[3]

Responsibility for the problem fell on President Grover Cleveland. Until 1881, he had enjoyed a successful but unremarkable career in the law and politics in Buffalo, New York, where he was a leader among local Democrats. That year, Cleveland won election as mayor, and in office he earned a reputation as a determined foe of corruption. This notoriety

[1] The various statutes governing federal money suggested that it could deposit revenue from excise taxes with national banks, but not the money received from tariffs. Once funds went into the Treasury, however, it was impossible to determine their precise origins. If 40 percent of government revenue came from excise taxes, could it then deposit 40 percent of its cash in banks? Or did it have to put money received from excises directly into banks as soon as it received payment for the deposit to be legal? No one knew, and no one settled the question definitively until the creation of the Federal Reserve rendered it moot.

[2] Esther Rogoff Taus, *Central Banking Functions of the United States Treasury, 1789–1941* (New York: Columbia University Press, 1941), pp. 82–4.

[3] Washington could have utilized repurchase agreements ("repos") to put its cash back into circulation, purchasing federal securities while promising to return them to the original owner after a certain period of time at a specified price that reflected the rate of interest. Such transactions are common in the twenty-first century. There is no evidence, however, that anyone in the United States considered this possibility in the late 1880s.

propelled him into the governor's mansion the next year, where he continued to battle graft, earning the enmity of New York City's powerful Democratic organization, Tammany Hall. Despite Tammany's hostility, he won the Democratic nomination for the presidency in 1884. As the popular governor of the country's largest state, he seemed the party's best chance to capture the White House. Cleveland narrowly defeated the charismatic but controversial Republican nominee, James G. Blaine, becoming the first Democrat elected to the White House since before the Civil War. The new president possessed genuine integrity and courage. At each step in his political ascent, he had stood against corruption that more cautious politicians might have ignored, in the process earning powerful enemies. Cleveland's agenda extended beyond "good government," however. He was what later generations would call a "classical liberal," committed to minimum government, free markets, and individual self-reliance. Cleveland strongly supported the gold standard, which removed monetary policy from the hands of government and left it to an impersonal market. As president he vetoed literally hundreds of bills funding specific projects, most notably pensions for veterans of the Civil War. For him, these questions were as much matters of principle as opposition to corruption, and too often, he conflated hostility to this agenda with self-interest and dishonesty. The pragmatic compromises inherent to democratic politics did not come naturally to him. Cleveland's unimaginative integrity both accounts for his popularity and explains the difficulty he often had governing.

In late 1887, President Cleveland hurled a political thunderbolt. He devoted almost all his December 1887 State of the Union Message to the Treasury surplus, insisting, "It is a condition which confronts us, not a theory." Cleveland warned that the Treasury had become a "hoarding place for money needlessly withdrawn from trade and the people's use, thus crippling our natural energies, suspending our country's development, threatening investment in productive enterprise, [and] threatening financial disturbance." The President then examined various solutions. He did not want to increase spending, which would encourage "schemes of public plunder." The alternative was tax reduction. The federal government raised almost all its revenue from excise taxes and tariffs, and the President insisted that cuts should begin with tariffs that protected domestic producers against foreign competition. Not only did they represent the sort of government favoritism anathema to Cleveland, but these tariffs raised prices out of proportion to the revenue collected. The duty on imported cloth, for instance, both raised the price of imports and allowed domestic producers, freed from foreign competition, to charge more. Tariff reductions that entailed relatively modest reductions in revenue could, therefore, deliver large savings to consumers.[4]

The President's message electrified the political world. Since Reconstruction, loyalties formed during the Civil War had defined the two major political parties. People "voted as they shot," with southern Whites and northerners who had opposed the war supporting the Democrats, and southern Blacks and northern defenders of the Union backing the Republicans. Economic issues cut across party lines. New England manufacturers and farmers on the Great Plains both supported the Grand Old Party (GOP), but they differed on tariffs and the currency. The same was true of the southern Whites and New York merchants who backed the Democrats. Politicians in Washington did their best to avoid such issues, crafting compromises that offended as few as possible, such as the Bland-Allison Act. Grover Cleveland broke with this pattern, offering voters a real choice on an important economic issue, and he carried his party with him. Within a few months, the House of Representatives, in which the Democrats had a majority, passed a measure reducing tariffs, though the Republican-controlled Senate ignored the bill. The platform the Democrats adopted at their national convention in 1888 stated, "The price of nearly everything they [consumers] buy is increased by the favoritism of an unequal system of tax legislation," and it urged substantial reductions.[5]

The Republicans accepted the challenge. Their 1888 platform declared, "We are uncompromisingly in favor of the American system of protection. We protest against its destruction as proposed by the President and his party. They serve the interests of Europe; we will support the interests of America. We accept the issue, and confidently appeal to the people for their judgment."[6] For the Presidency they nominated Benjamin Harrison, a former senator from Indiana as well as a grandson of President William Henry Harrison. James G. Blaine had decided not to seek the nomination, and most of his supporters rallied to Harrison, giving him a majority at the convention. Though not as prominent as James G. Blaine or John Sherman, Harrison was an experienced politician familiar with Washington.

[4] Grover Cleveland, *Third State of the Union Address*, 1887, American Presidency Project (APP), University of California at Santa Barbara (UCSB).

[5] Democratic Party Platform of 1888, APP, UCSB.

[6] Republican Party Platform of 1888, APP, UCSB.

He conducted a "front porch" campaign. Tradition held that aspirants to the White House should not actively campaign—"the office seeks the man." Harrison and his campaign managers evaded this taboo by bringing supporters to his home in Indianapolis, where he greeted them with brief addresses, the texts of which the party subsequently circulated throughout the country. This tactic played to Harrison's capacity for to-the-point speeches that, although lacking rhetorical flourish, effectively deployed logic and example. During the fall of 1888, several hundred thousand visited Indianapolis to hear Harrison warn that lower tariffs would lead to "a vast and sudden increase in importations" that would "diminish work in our American shops."[7]

Though tariffs dominated the campaign, the Republicans laid out a broad agenda. They proposed to expand pensions for veterans of the Union army, declaring, "In the presence of an overflowing treasury it would be a public scandal to do less for those whose valorous service preserved the government."[8] More generous pensions would have the added advantage of absorbing the surplus. The GOP also promised legislation "to secure the integrity and purity of elections, which are the foundation of all political authority." Democrats in the South frequently employed fraud and intimidation to disenfranchise Blacks and win elections, and Republicans did not exaggerate when they insisted, "The present Administration and the Democratic majority in Congress owe their existence to the suppression of the ballot by a criminal nullification" of the votes of African-Americans.[9] Nor did the Republicans ignore the currency. Their platform declared "in favor of the use of both gold and silver as money, and condemns the policy of the Democratic Administration … to demonetize silver."[10] At the time, this statement appeared safe enough. Early in his presidency, Cleveland had called for the repeal of the Bland-Allison Act, which even many supporters of the gold standard considered harmless. The President's suggestion had made no headway in Congress, but the Republicans wanted to remind Silverites of the episode. Unfortunately, the language of the platform was vague. It might constitute no more than an endorsement of the current regime—the gold

[7] Quoted in Charles W. Calhoun, *Minority Victory: Gilded Age Politics and the Front Porch Campaign of 1888* (Lawrence, KA: University of Kansas Press, 2008), p. 156.

[8] Republican Party Platform of 1888.

[9] Republican Party Platform of 1888.

[10] Republican Party Platform of 1888.

standard with limited silver coinage—or it could represent a call for the free coinage of silver. In the West, Republicans campaigned on the latter interpretation, creating expectations that the party would be hard-put to fulfill.

Harrison defeated Cleveland by a narrow margin, winning a majority in the Electoral College but losing the popular vote. Some at the time and since have questioned whether such a victory constituted a mandate for anything. Cleveland's popular majority, however, depended on large margins in the southern states, where the canvass was notoriously corrupt. An honest count would almost certainly have given Harrison a majority of the popular vote and, probably, more electoral votes.[11] The GOP also won a majority in the House of Representatives for the first time in years, and it retained its majority in the Senate. After Harrison's inauguration, the party would be in a position to deliver on its many promises.

The Alliance

The growing influence of the Farmers' Alliance complicated the political landscape, adding to the challenges that the victorious Republicans faced. The Alliance embodied a persistent current of economic, social, and political discontent that historians have dubbed "anti-monopoly" and that, in the past, had coalesced in a variety of organizations—the Grange, the Greenback Party, the Union Labor Party, and the Knights of Labor. Each of these addressed specific grievances such as railroad rates, the state of the currency, and working conditions, but all shared a broader critique of American society. They contended that economic centralization, be it through railroad systems, industrial combinations, or the New York money market, threatened the economic well-being and social autonomy of farmers, workers, and small proprietors. This tendency, they argued, was not the product of impersonal economic forces but of an alliance between corrupt politicians and businessmen eager to increase their wealth and power. Reform was not simply a question of economic reorganization but of political renewal.

[11] African-Americans constituted a majority in Mississippi and South Carolina, and they voted overwhelmingly for the Republican Party, the party of Abraham Lincoln and emancipation. Had Democratic officials counted Blacks' votes in those states, Harrison almost certainly would have carried them.

These movements usually enjoyed only a brief time in the limelight. Organization was often slack, and money was always tight. Members could quickly become disillusioned. These groups had ambitious programs that promised social transformation, and they could generate immense enthusiasm. Maintaining commitment was difficult, however, particularly in the face of a major setback. In 1885, the Knights of Labor won a strike against a railroad that financier Jay Gould controlled, and its numbers rapidly increase from 100,000 to 700,000. The next year, a strike against another of Gould's lines failed completely, and the Knights' membership collapsed, dropping back to 100,000 by 1890.

In the late 1880s, the Farmers' Alliance took the leadership among anti-monopolists. As one Alliance organizer described the situation, "The farmer needed everything. He needed protection against the merchant in selling to him at usurious rates of credit. … The farmer saw cotton corners made by speculators. … He saw syndicates organized to inflate the price of everything that he bought. The railroads organized against him."[12] Local chapters of what would become the Alliance initially appeared in the mid-1870s, and the organization had its first national meeting in Chicago in 1880.[13] Both the leaders and the rank-and-file of the Alliance thought of themselves as champions of the "producing classes" against exploiters such as bankers and railroads. Membership, however, clustered in the Great Plains and the South, which depended on wheat and cotton, respectively. In those regions, it was a power. Historian Jeffrey Ostler estimates that, by 1891, the Kansas Alliance had about 100,000 members, the Nebraska Alliance 70,000, and the Iowa Alliance 47,000.[14] Assuming comparable membership in the other states of the Grain and Cotton Belts, the Alliance must have counted at least one million members by 1890, and perhaps twice as many.

The Farmers' Alliance was not monolithic. The state alliance was its basic unit. These organizations issued charters to local chapters, which by the late 1880s numbered several thousand. State alliances coordinated the activities of local branches but could not issue orders. Chapters set their own course. State alliances, in turn, belonged to one of three umbrella organizations—the Northern Alliance, the Southern Alliance, and the

[12] Quoted in the *Atlanta Constitution*, February 28, 1888, p. 7.
[13] Hicks, *The Populist Revolt*, pp. 96–100.
[14] Ostler, *Prairie Populism*, pp. 181–3.

Colored Farmers' Alliance.[15] The first united the states bordering on the Missouri and upper Mississippi rivers, the second the states from North Carolina to Texas where cotton was king, and the third southern Blacks, whom the all-white Southern Alliance refused to admit. The last two cooperated, but at arm's length. The Northern and Southern Alliances discussed merger several times but never followed through. Apparently, the northern body feared that the larger Southern Alliance would dominate the coalition. Two factors united this diverse group. The first was an extensive network of small Alliance newspapers, most of which belonged to the National Reform Press Association. They circulated stories and editorials extensively among themselves, providing subscribers with a steady stream of news and opinion from the perspective of the Alliance. Second, the Alliance supported a cadre of lecturers who traveled the Cotton and Wheat Belts like evangelists, spreading the gospel of the Alliance. Newspapers editors and lecturers often became leaders in the organization.

Like any large organization in a diverse society, the Alliance encompassed a variety of opinions. Richard Hofstadter dismissed the Alliance and its progeny, the Peoples' Party (Populists), as reactionary, looking back to an era when the United States was almost entirely rural and agricultural.[16] In contrast, Lawrence Goodwyn portrayed them as a radical force that sought to build a cooperative commonwealth.[17] Charles Postel thought of these groups as earnest reforms who systematically studied social problems, forerunners of twentieth-century reformers like the Progressives.[18] Hofstadter, Goodwyn, and Postel each had little trouble finding evidence to support their views. The Alliance included Jeffersonians, social democrats, and progressive reformers. As C. Vann Woodward demonstrated in his biography of Tom Watson, Georgia's leading Populist, all these impulses sometimes existed within the same person.[19] The common theme was a profound suspicion of economic centralization, be it through

[15] The formal name of the Southern Alliance was the National Farmers' Alliance and Industrial Union, of the Northern Alliance the National Farmers' Alliance, and of the Colored Farmers' Alliance the Colored Farmers' National Alliance and Cooperative Union. At the time, most observed used the terms Southern Alliance, Northern Alliance, and Colored Farmers' Alliance, and this study does the same for the sake of clarity and simplicity.

[16] Hofstadter, *The Age of Reform*, pp. 23–130.

[17] Goodwyn, *Populist Moment*.

[18] Charles Postel, *The Populist Vision* (New York: Oxford University Press, 2007).

[19] Woodward, *Tom Watson: Agrarian Rebel*.

the railroads, large industrial enterprises, or financial markets. This process, they believed, was the product of collusion among politicians, bankers, and industrialists. The Alliance would smash this malign cabal, restoring not simply the economic fortunes of farmers but also American democracy.

The currency always occupied a central place in the thinking of Alliance members. As Charles Postel wrote, "Whether in local Farmers' Alliance lodges or Peoples' Party clubs, the study of the money supply had a regular place on the agenda."[20] The quality of this discussion varied greatly. Sarah Emery's *Seven Conspiracies* received considerable attention, as would *Coin's Financial School*, an equally terrible book. As one critic of the movement complained, "The average western American is a man of unbounded energy, unbounded self-conceit, and unbounded ignorance. ... The ignorance of the western American is an artificial and acquired ignorance. He absorbs it from the newspapers which form his only reading. These not only teach him the most absurdly false doctrines in matters of political economy and finance, but they also flatter his vanity."[21] Nevertheless, members of the Alliance and its successor, the People's Party, often produced solid analyses of money. Senators William Peffer (P-KA) and William Allen (P-NB), the leading Populists in the Upper House, discussed the subject as intelligently as anyone in Congress.[22] Most notably, they recognized that currency need not rest on gold or silver. This observation shocked many contemporaries. Senator John Sherman dismissed such views as "a mild form of lunacy" and accepted as "an axiom, that gold and silver, or coined money, have been proven by all human experience to be the best possible standards of value."[23] On this matter Sherman, the Senate's foremost expert on finance, was wrong. A fiat currency, managed carefully, can work well. This important insight led Postel to conclude, "The Populists' soft-money treatises were usually superior to the formulaic arguments about the alleged virtues of gold."[24]

Fiat currencies, however, require careful handling, and history is full of disastrous examples of government mismanagement.[25] Political authorities

[20] Postel, *The Populist Vision*, p. 150.

[21] W.L. Alden, "War to the Knife," *The Nineteenth Century* 40 (1896): 202–203.

[22] See their addresses in *Silver Speeches in the Senate*.

[23] Sherman, *Recollections of Forty Years*, p. 590.

[24] Postel, *Populist Vision*, p. 152.

[25] During the American and French revolutions, political authorities issued large quantities of paper currency that became worthless, as did the Confederacy during the American Civil

must constantly adjust policy, sometimes injecting money into the economy and sometimes withdrawing it. In most cases, they rely on a central bank, and in every instance, they operate through financial markets. Even the Soviet Union, which abolished most forms of private property, used banks to manage the currency and allocate funds for investment.

Thinking among members of the Alliance about credit and finance, unfortunately, was much weaker. For instance, Charles Postel notes that Populists and members of the Alliance "looked to the Bank of France as a model."[26] It had, as Postel writes, "broadly inflated the currency with both paper money and silver coins."[27] Unfortunately, the Bank of France that members of the Alliance and Populists described was quite different from the institution located in Paris. In the 1880s and 1890s, France relied on the gold standard with limited silver coinage, as did the United States. The Bank of France countered seasonal shifts in the demand for money and acted as "lender of last resort" in a crisis, both of which benefitted farmers and workers immensely, but so did the much-reviled Bank of England. The French government had more control over the Bank of France than did Whitehall over the Bank of England, but the two institutions operated in a similar fashion for similar ends. Undoubtedly, an institution like the Bank of France could redress many of the United States' financial problems, but no prominent member of the Alliance or the People's Party ever suggested creating an American central bank, even one owned entirely by the federal government. They considered President Jackson's destruction of the Bank of the United States a triumph of democracy. Such an organization, they feared, would further centralize the financial system and increase the power of bankers—these institutions are called "central banks" for a reason. The Populists also produced reams of information on the amount of currency circulating in the United States, with particular focus on the amount per capita. As Postel writes, "The Populist embedded their arguments in statistical tables, legislative chronologies, and other incontrovertible evidence required by the businesslike, efficient, and

War. After World War I, Germany, Austria, Hungary, and Russia all suffered from hyperinflation, with paper currency becoming worthless not just once but over and over again as prices doubled and redoubled every week. In these cases, war and political crises all played a major role, but so did the incompetence of political authorities. In the 1970s, all the industrial democracies suffered from high inflation that did considerable economic and social damage even though there was no general war or political upheaval.

[26] Postel, *Populist Vision*, p. 281.

[27] Postel, *Populist Vision*, p. 152.

rational demands of the 'science of economical government.'"[28] Unfortunately, these estimates paid little attention to credit. Statistics on bank deposits and loans were much harder to find, but Populists and members of the Alliance did not seem to have tried very hard. The omission was unfortunate. Currency and credit are often different sides of the same coin. France, for instance, had more money in circulation per capita than Britain, but the British had a significantly higher average income because the latter's sophisticated financial system rendered currency less important.

Finance presents a world of "bounded rationality." It is not a blank slate but a complex system involving a wide variety of people and institutions, and any reform must take these into account. Economist Barry Eichengreen described the development of the gold standard as "one of the great monetary accidents of modern times."[29] It emerged because Britain, the pioneer in the Industrial Revolution, based its money on gold. As the economies of other countries gravitated toward this powerhouse, their governments adopted gold to facilitate exchange with it. Over time, bankers and governments built upon gold a powerful, efficient system to finance trade and investment throughout the world. Nations that wanted to avail themselves of the benefits of this system had to embrace gold. Critics who observed that gold's exalted place was arbitrary were correct, but all monetary standards are arbitrary—gold, silver, paper, wampum, or seashells. The standard is utility. The question Americans faced in the 1890s was not, "Is the gold standard rational?" but, "Does the gold standard serve the nation's interest better than any possible alternative?"

In the 1890s, supporters of both gold and silver often ruminated at length on the superiority of the metal they championed, insisting that God or Nature had ordained its use as money. The results were tiresome and not a little silly. In 1893, Senator William Bate (D-TN) stated on the floor of Congress, "Silver is the friend of poverty and the handmaiden of charity. … the promise of a family, the nursery, the virtue, defense, and glory of the state."[30] It is no surprise that historians wading through such drivel find the arguments of members of the Alliance and the Populists about money refreshing. Most of the time, however, the discussion of money and finance among supporters of both gold and silver turned on concerns

[28] Postel, *Populist Vision*, p. 153.
[29] Eichengreen, *Globalizing Capital*, p. 5.
[30] Speech of Sen. William Bate, September 23, 1893, *Silver Speeches.*

like prices, interest rates, and exchange rates. Even the frequent invocations of morality usually turned on how changes and prices and standards affected the relationship between debtors and creditors.

The money question gradually dominated the Alliance's agenda. In the late 1880s, it pursued a variety of initiatives, demanding an expansion of the currency but also lobbying for government regulation of railroads, grain elevators, and cotton trading as well as organizing farmer-owned cooperatives that would allow members to buy and sell on better terms. The Texas Exchange represented the most ambitious of the latter undertakings. It was the creation of Charles Macune, who was both the editor of the *National Economist*, the most widely read Alliance paper, and a leader of the Texas Alliance, the country's largest. He was energetic and charismatic but lacked managerial skill and sometimes displayed poor judgment. Macune imagined the Texas Exchange as a sort of "Farmers' Trust" that would handle both the sale of crops and the purchase of manufactured goods for all the Alliance cooperatives in Texas. The scale of these transactions would allow it to extract better prices for members. Managed in this fashion, the Texas Exchange might have succeeded. At about the same time, British reformers were developing a vigorous cooperative movement that catered to that country's working class. Behind British coops stood two national wholesalers that supplied them, and by 1913, these two organizations were probably the world's largest retailers. Traditional coops did not, however, address cotton farmers' chief need—credit. Such organizations sold only for cash. Customers owned the coops, and people cannot loan money to themselves. Nevertheless, Macune harkened to the desires of his constituents and extended loans to local coops so that members could buy on credit. These loans quickly consumed the Texas Exchange's limited capital, and efforts to borrow from banks yielded little. They were reluctant to prop up a potential rival and dubious about many of the coops' loans. Cotton prices were falling, and many borrowers would indeed default. Macune's management exacerbated the problems. He miscalculated the Exchange's expenses and unknowingly sold many items below cost. The Texas Exchange, launched with enthusiasm in 1887, was in deep trouble by early 1888 and closed its doors in the fall of 1889.[31]

[31] In California, citrus farmers aligned with the Alliance organized a coop among themselves that survives to this day as Sunkist. It did not extend credit to members. This organization stands as an example of what the Alliance might have achieved with better leadership.

Macune, however, was not finished. In the fall of 1889, he unveiled the Subtreasury Plan. Under it, the federal government would construct a network of warehouse facilities for agricultural commodities in which farmers could store their crops. Depositors could then take out loans against crops in storage equal to 80 percent of their market value, receiving fiat currency on which they would pay 1 percent annually. Should a farmer fail to withdraw his crops within twelve months, the government would sell them at auction. This arrangement would supply farmers with credit and the country with an expanding currency. As one Alliance paper argued, "The subtreasury offer[s] an escape for the people from the power of the banks."[32] Macune soon convinced the other leaders of the Southern Alliance to put the Subtreasury Plan at the top of its political agenda.

The Subtreasury Plan had several weaknesses. Critics within the Alliance noted that it offered nothing to those who produced perishable goods like livestock, milk, fruit, or vegetables. Nor did it provide for mortgages on land, the chief debts members of the Northern Alliance carried. It was largely a program for southern cotton farmers enmeshed in the crop lien. More broadly, the Subtreasury would, by issuing large volumes of paper money to farmers, tie the supply of money to the amount of cotton and wheat in storage. Macune and other defenders of the program asserted that this approach was superior to using gold or silver because the currency would adjust to the needs of commerce. In fact, it would tie the currency to the vagaries of the wheat and cotton crops. A drought on the Great Plains would contract the currency, while a bumper cotton crop would expand it. As a Texas paper insisted, "An abundant money supply which is subject to sudden and speedy contraction does not increase prices."[33] Basing currency on the precious metals created rigidities, but at least the supply of metal did not fluctuate randomly. Critics of the Alliance hammered away at these points, and even many within the organization feared that the Subtreasury would create dangerous monetary instability.[34] The Subtreasury's goals were not quixotic. Americans could have created a market for short-term loans against grain in elevators and cotton in warehouses, and a central bank could expand the supply of credit and currency during the harvest by buying or "rediscounting" such paper as needed. Such expedients were, however, anathema to members of the

[32] *The Great West* (St. Paul, Minnesota), December 25, 1891, p. 6.

[33] *Fort Worth Gazette*, July 5, 1891, p. 1.

[34] Hicks, *The Populist Revolt*, pp. 198–204.

Alliance and the People's Party because they would extend the reach of the financial system. Instead, these groups saddled themselves with the risky and probably unworkable Subtreasury.

Over the last fifty years, historians have given the Subtreasury far too much credit. Lawrence Goodwyn gushed, "The sub-treasury plan benefitted all of the nation's 'producing classes,' and the nation's economy itself. For the greenback dollars for the farmers created a workable basis for a new and flexible national currency originating outside the exclusive control of Eastern commercial bankers."[35] Richard White was more restrained, but he still insisted, "The most plausible [solution to the country's financial problems] was the Populist proposal for subtreasuries."[36] Charles Postel described the Subtreasury as "one of the most innovative proposals for federal intervention in the economy ever to enter American politics."[37] The first serious historian of Populism, John D. Hicks, who published his *Populist Revolt* in 1931, had a clearer view. Though generally sympathetic to the Alliance, he noted that the Subtreasury's critics "found it fairly easy to pick flaws in the plan." Hicks reports that in early 1983 Tom Watson of Georgia proposed a modified version of the Subtreasury that provided for loans against crops stored in private grain elevators and cotton warehouses and limiting the total amount of credit to $100 million.[38] Framed this way, the Subtreasury might well have worked, even within the confines of the gold standard. The problem was political. These changes would transform a utopian effort to remake the American economy into a source of financing for farmers of wheat and cotton—useful but hardly revolutionary, and irrelevant to those outside the Wheat and Cotton Belts. Watson's contemporaries and most historians have overlooked his suggestion. Lawrence Goodwyn does not even mention it in *The Populist Moment*, his shorter history of Populism.

Whatever its defects, the Subtreasury Plan committed the Alliance to radical monetary reform. Heretofore, the Northern Alliance had focused most of its political efforts on regulating railroads, but despite some reluctance, it now followed the lead of the Southern Alliance and gave the Subtreasury equal priority. The financial crisis that engulfed that United States in the 1890s would only increase the emphasis on the currency.

[35] Goodwyn, *The Populist Moment*, p. 92.
[36] White, *The Republic for Which It Stands*, p. 833.
[37] Postel, *Populist Vision*, p. 153.
[38] Hicks, *The Populist Revolt*, p. 197, 203.

The Silver Movement

The silver movement represented a less radical response to the concerns that animated the Alliance. For that reason, its appeal was broader, and the established political parties would find it even harder to ignore than the Farmers' Alliance. The First National Silver convention, which met in November 1889 in St. Louis, demonstrated its growing power. The St. Louis Mining Stock Exchange, which traded shares of companies that mined silver, sponsored the event—silver miners would always play a major role in the movement. Enthusiasm for silver extended well beyond the ranks of miners, however. Adoniram J. Warner, a Civil War veteran and a former Democratic representative from Ohio, chaired the Convention. Attendance was broad. The organizers had asked the governor of each state and territory to appoint delegates, though as one of the organizers put it, some states "are so unfortunate as to have a governor who, because of his ties to Wall Street interests, has not accepted his privilege."[39] Representatives from the Northeast were few, but the rest of the country supplied plenty of enthusiastic delegates, including such prominent politicians as Representative Richard Bland and Senator William Stewart (R-NV). Organizers exaggerated when they declared the gathering "as truly national as any Convention ever held in the United States," but not by much.[40]

Delegates at the gathering put forward arguments that, over the next decade, would dominate political discourse. Representative Bland described the end of free coinage for silver in 1873 as "a fraud upon Congress and the American people."[41] Senator Stewart was even blunter, painting the decision as a product of "a conspiracy … among the bondholders of Europe to cut off one-half of the supply of precious metal." "Mark the result!" he continued, "Prices declined … more than 33 ½ percent in fifteen years."[42] Free coinage would undo this damage. It would also improve the position of the United States in world markets. Silverites understood the relationship between the monetary standard and exchange rates. As the price of silver fell relative to gold, currencies based on the former depreciated relative to those based on gold. Stewart pointed out

[39] *Proceedings of the First National Silver Convention at St. Louis November 26, 27, and 28, 1889* (St. Louis: Buxton & Skinner, 1889), p. 15–16.

[40] *First National Silver Convention*, xv.

[41] *First National Silver Convention*, p. 92.

[42] *First National Silver Convention*, pp. 109–111.

that American exporters of cotton and wheat competed with sellers from India and Russia, who used silver money, and that the depreciation of the silver had allowed these vendors to undercut U.S. exporters in world markets.[43] Bland went further, noting, "On this continent to the south of us, and to the west in Asia, there are 800 million of people who use only silver as money. … We ought to have this trade. Proper legislation on the silver question will greatly aid us in securing it."[44]

Most delegates at the Convention insisted that the gold standard threatened not merely prosperity but democratic government. Stewart warned, "I am aware that the money kings have become all-powerful," stating, "The orders to our Treasury Department for the past twenty-five years have come directly from the Bank of England through Wall Street."[45] The implications were grim. "The farmers of our own country today," Stewart lamented, "in consequence of the machinations of the money kings, and the gold monometalists, are losing their independence of character for which they have been noted. Their mortgages are making them cowards."[46] Nevertheless, democracy would be the solution to the problem. Stewart said, "I have faith that the free people of the United States will not always endure these outrages."[47] Another speaker noted, "There is nothing in the way of free coinage but the banker and bondholder. They are but a small portion of the people, and, knowing their methods, we should be able now to cope with them."[48] This mixture of cynicism and naiveté was a hallmark of the silver movement. The benefits of free coinage of silver were so self-evident, Silverites believed, that only conspiracy could explain gold's triumph. At the same time, they were confident that the population would reject gold if only exposed to the truth.

International bimetallists, who believed that only an international agreement could rehabilitate silver, received little hearing. One delegate complained, "What is the use of going over there [Europe] and asking for a thing that they have refused repeatedly to consider."[49] Negotiations were simply an excuse for delay. The likelihood that bankers would have a large role in any talks—if only for their technical expertise—increased skepticism.

[43] *First National Silver Convention*, p. 117
[44] *First National Silver Convention*, p. 101.
[45] *First National Silver Convention*, pp. 113–4.
[46] *First National Silver Convention*, p. 110.
[47] *First National Silver Convention*, pp. 113–4.
[48] *First National Silver Convention*, p. 244
[49] *First National Silver Convention*, p. 72.

Stewart insisted, "I am opposed to all international negotiations until the United States is placed upon the proper footing [the free coinage of silver]."[50]

The Silver Convention did not create the enthusiasm for silver. Over the previous decade, Congress had demonstrated considerable interest in silver coinage. Nor did it mark the emergence of free coinage as the premier issue in American politics. Missouri Governor David R. Francis, in his address opening the gathering, conceded that silver was "second in importance ... to the great question of taxation [tariffs]."[51] Nevertheless, the convention represented the first national gathering of Silverites as Silverites, marking the transformation of what had been a broad sentiment into a self-conscious movement focused on a specific goal—free coinage. Its delegates returned home eager to spread the word and confident of ultimate success.

Over the next few years, A.J. Warner laid the institutional foundations of the silver movement. In 1890 and 1891, he personally raised $22,000 from silver miners in Nevada and Idaho and used it to circulate literature supporting the free coinage of silver.[52] The effort had limited impact, in part because Warner worked in his spare time without a staff, but it was the precursor of a much larger effort to come.

Historians have often treated Silverites as an afterthought. The books on the Alliance and the Populists fill shelves, but sources on Silverites are thin. Silverites almost certainly outnumbered members of the Alliance and the People's Party, however, and they shared with the latter an abiding suspicion of economic centralization. Only by working with them could the Alliance and the Populists hope to permanently change American politics and society.

Silver and Tariffs

The Republicans under President Harrison arrived in Washington in 1889 with narrow majorities and an ambitious agenda. They wanted to raise tariffs, expand veterans' pension, and secure the voting rights of southern Blacks, all of which were controversial. Success would require careful management. American political parties are diverse coalitions whose members

[50] *First National Silver Convention*, p. 68.
[51] *First National Silver Convention*, pp. 87–8.
[52] *Second National Silver Convention*, pp. 278–81.

have their own interests and agendas, and they splinter easily. Intellectually, the new president understood the challenge, but temperamentally, he was ill-suited to meet it. Benjamin Harrison was intelligent, honest, and diligent. He was a gifted lawyer who thoroughly understood the government's workings. He could manage most departments as well as their secretaries and occasionally had to do so, but he lacked the easy familiarity that most politicians cultivate. Harrison could be warm with intimates, but to most of the world he presented a stern face. Many described him as "crusty." He recognized the necessity of compromise but lacked the charm that made others want to work out differences with him. Exacerbating difficulties, Harrison's wife was seriously ill throughout the last year of his presidency, dying in October 1892, and her decline distracted and isolated the President.

Harrison never had a firm grip on his own party either. A rift opened almost immediately with senators Matthew Quay (R-PN) and Thomas Platt (R-NY), who dominated the GOP in their home states, the country's largest. Quay had managed Harrison's 1888 campaign, and Platt's hard work had secured Harrison's victory in New York, which had provided the margin of victory in the electoral college. Both expected a generous reward, but the new president believed that they asked too much. Quay wanted absolute control over federal appointments in Pennsylvania, but Harrison insisted on vetting Quay's recommendations because he realized that, if something went wrong, he would receive the blame. Platt hoped to be Secretary of the Treasury, but Harrison refused because western Republicans did not want a New Yorker in charge of government finances. As far as they were concerned, New Yorkers already had too much control over banking and money.[53] In both cases, Harrison's instincts were probably correct, but Quay and Platt never forgave him, and they were powerful enemies. Harrison also managed to fall out with Representative Thomas Reed (R-ME), the capable, sharp-tongued Speaker of the House, largely because of disagreements over patronage. James G. Blaine presented an even larger problem. He was the most popular figure within the party and, had he sought it, probably could have secured the presidential nomination

[53] Harrison ended up appointing William Windom Secretary of the Treasury. Windom was an experienced Minnesota politician who had served, briefly, as Treasury Secretary under James Garfield, but in the mid-1880s, he had moved to New York City, where he made his living in finance. As such, his roots were in the Midwest, but he did have ties with the country's financial hub.

over Harrison in 1888. In recognition of Blaine's prominence, Harrison appointed him Secretary of State. Unfortunately, Blaine had trouble subordinating himself to Harrison, who before winning the presidency had been a far less important figure in the GOP. Blaine also apparently regretted not seeking the Republican nomination himself in 1888. For the first half of Harrison's administration, the two managed to work together effectively on foreign policy, but starting in 1891, Blaine's health deteriorated, forcing the President to take over the management of his department.[54] Blaine added insult to injury by dallying with Harrison's enemies within the party, allowing them to put him forward for the presidential nomination at the 1892 Republican convention.

The new Congress would not convene in regular session until December 1889, so patronage and planning occupied the first eight months of Harrison's administration. Most federal jobs were still the gift of the executive, who rewarded political supporters with positions. Unfortunately, the number of applicants always vastly exceeded the number of jobs, and inevitably each appointment created disappointment among those passed over. The art lay in knowing whom the executive could safely alienate. In addition to political considerations, the President needed to appoint honest, capable officials—one corrupt or incompetent appointees created a bad impression that ten good selections could not erase. On the whole, Harrison's record was good, but he made one serious mistake. To lead the Pension Bureau he chose James Tanner, a Civil War veteran and a leader of the Grand Army of the Republic, a veterans' organization closely aligned with the GOP. During the 1888 campaign, the Republicans had promised to liberalize the rules for pensions, and they would fulfill this pledge once Congress met. Tanner was impatient, however. Declaring "God help the surplus," he approved many pensions that the law, as of 1889, clearly did not authorize. After a few months, Harrison removed Tanner, but the damage was done. Democrats used the incident to portray the administration as profligate, emptying the Treasury to provide favors to political supporters.[55]

[54] Harrison's papers during this period are full of detailed documents concerning matters like a conflict with Canada and Britain concerning seal hunting in the Bering Sea that normally Blaine, a capable diplomat, would have handled. Blaine died in early 1893.

[55] Charles Calhoun, *Benjamin Harrison* (New York: Times Books, 2005), loc. 1243 (Kindle).

During 1889, the Republicans also moved to strengthen their control over the Senate. Six western territories drafted state constitutions and applied to join the Union—Washington, Idaho, Montana, Wyoming, and North and South Dakota. Congress rapidly granted their requests. All had enough people to qualify for statehood, and all were chafing under the restrictions of territorial government. All were also overwhelmingly Republican, and GOP leaders calculated that they would send a phalanx of Republicans to Congress. In the House, their numbers would be negligible—the six states combined had fewer Congressmen than New Jersey. In the Senate, however, they would provide twelve members out of a total of eighty-eight, converting the narrow GOP majority into a sizeable one.

The arrival of these twelve western senators in Washington changed the dynamics of the silver issue. In several of these states, silver mining was a major industry. All produced commodities—grain, copper, lead—whose prices had declined. Many of their people, as recent settlers, had substantial debts. For the most part, the citizens of these new states believed that the financial system favored eastern interests and that the free coinage of silver would redress the balance, raising commodity prices and facilitating the repayment of debts by expanding the currency. Their senators, together with those from Colorado and Nevada—states whose economies depended heavily on silver mining—constituted a powerful block committed to elevating silver, and the term "Silver Republican" soon entered the political lexicon. From the start, they made it clear that they would support the GOP's broader program only if it included "something for silver."

Silver, a secondary issue in most of the country during the 1888 campaign, suddenly became central. The President and his Treasury Secretary, former Minnesota senator William Windom, opposed the free coinage of silver unless sanctioned by international agreement because they believed that it would almost certainly lead to a major devaluation of the dollar. Nevertheless, Harrison and Windom recognized that they had to mollify Silver Republicans to achieve their other goals. In his first annual report, issued at the end of 1889, Windom recommended that the government "issue Treasury notes, against deposits of silver bullion at the market price of silver bullion deposited, payable on demand in such quantities of silver bullion as will equal in value, at the date of presentation, the number of dollars expressed in the notes at the market price of silver, or in gold, at the option of the government, or in silver dollars at the option of the holder."[56] Washington would accept these Treasury notes for taxes, and national banks could count them as reserves against deposits. At the same time, Washington would repeal the Bland-Allison Act. In effect, this proposal would allow free coinage of silver, but at the market price, not the official price of $1.29. Windom hoped that this approach would increase the demand for silver and expand the currency without threatening the gold standard. The proposal bore some resemblance to the Alliance's Subtreasury Program, allowing holders of silver to convert it, on demand, into government paper. A few of the delegates to the National Silver Convention that had just adjourned had endorsed such an approach.[57] The Treasury notes issued would not be legal tender, which created the possibility that they might trade at a discount to other formers of money. The administration hoped that, because the government would accept the notes at face value for taxes and because holders could exchange them for silver with the same market price, that would not happen. The country had endured a two-tiered currency during and after the Civil War—gold and greenbacks—and few wanted to return to that state.

In early 1890, the House of Representatives passed a measure similar to Windom's recommendation. The formidable Speaker, Thomas "Czar" Reed, dominated that body. He had unilaterally overruled the tactics Representatives had long used to slow or halt business and would keep Republican Congressmen together through the long 1889–1890 session, passing one bill after another despite the party's narrow majority.[58] The Senate exhibited no such discipline. Silver Republicans constituted a third of the party's strength in the upper house, and their leader was Henry Teller (R-CO), an intelligent, honest, hard-working legislator whom all respected. The Silver Republicans, in alliance with southern Democrats, amended the House bill, substituting the free coinage of silver for

[56] *Annual Report of the Secretary of the Treasury, 1890* (Washington: Treasury Department, 1890), XLVII-XLVIII.

[57] *First National Silver Convention*, pp. 31, 35, 36. The convention as a whole endorsed the free coinage of silver.

[58] The most common tactic Representatives used to halt action was to call for and then refuse to answer a quorum call, because without a quorum, the House could not transact business. To halt this maneuver, Reed simply marked Congressmen who were present "present," even if they did not answer the quorum call. Supposedly, when a member complained of this new practice, Reed replied, "I have noted the gentleman's presence. Does he wish to deny it?" Calhoun, *Benjamin Harrison*, loc. 1446–1449.

Windom's complex scheme. This measure, however, had no chance of becoming law. Reed supported the gold standard, and as long as he was Speaker of the House, free silver would not pass. Though President Harrison reserved comment—Senator Stewart had somehow managed to convince himself that the President supported free coinage—Harrison opposed free coinage outside of an international agreement. He undoubtedly would have vetoed a free silver bill.[59] Simply killing the measure, however, would drive Silver Republicans into opposition and end hopes for other major legislation, particularly a new tariff bill. In the conference committee that convened to reconcile the two very different measures from the House and Senate, Senator John Sherman managed to impose a compromise subsequently known as the Sherman Silver Purchase Act. The measure repealed the Bland-Allison Act and, in its place, directed the Treasury to buy 4.5 million ounces of silver a month—roughly the country's entire output—at the market price, paying for it with Treasury bills. These notes would be legal tender, and the government would redeem them, on demand, "in coin." The term was intentionally vague, but most believed that it allowed the government to pay out either gold or silver, at its discretion. At the same time, the measure stated that it was "the established policy of the United States to maintain the two metals on a parity with each other upon the present legal ratio [sixteen-to-one]."[60] Ideally, federal purchases would drive the market price of silver up to $1.29, at which point the United States could embrace free silver without risk of devaluation. Until then, however, the language suggested that Washington would redeem Treasury notes in gold if holders demanded it.[61]

No one liked the compromise. Silverites recognized that it fell far short of free coinage. Senator Teller warned, "I have not much doubt that if this conference report is accepted and this bill becomes a law, we shall find that it is not entirely what we supposed it would be. ... [but] If this bill is not

[59] Homer Socolofsky and Allan Spetter, *The Presidency of Benjamin Harrison* (Lawrence: University of Kansas Press, 1987), p. 56.

[60] Quoted in Robert F. Hoxie, "The Silver Debate of 1890," *Journal of Political Economy* 1 (September 1893): 543.

[61] Historian Scott Nelson wrote, "The Sherman Act committed the federal government to buying—at an inflated price—$50 million of silver a year," then stated, "The Treasury notes [used to pay for silver] ... would have traded at a substantial discount." Scott Nelson, *Nation of Deadbeats: An Uncommon History of America's Financial Disasters (New York: Alfred A. Knopf, 2012)*, p. 186. Both statements are wrong. The government would pay the market price for silver, and the Treasury notes circulated at par because they were legal tender and the government would redeem them in gold.

made a law I see no promise of any relief whatever to the stagnated business of this country."[62] Supporters of the gold standard feared that, by authorizing a rapid expansion of the currency backed by gold, it would undermine the gold standard. John Sherman later stated, "I voted for it, but the day it became a law I was ready to repeal it, if repeal could be had without substituting in its place absolute free coinage."[63] Senator Henry Blair (R-NH) summed up the situation with disarming frankness. "I think that nothing so adds to the happiness of the surroundings," he said on the floor of the Senate, "as for a sick man to take his medicine cheerfully; and … after listening to one Senator from Oregon who finds in it [the Silver Purchase Act] the gold standard, … and the other Senator from Oregon who finds in it unlimited or free coinage in substance, and the Senator from Kansas who is satisfied that it is a free-coinage bill, and the Senator from Colorado who is not satisfied precisely what it is, but it very well satisfied with it, I thought that I would vote for the bill, but that I would give notice to the Senate that under no circumstances whatever … would I ever give a single reason for so doing."[64]

Subsequently, Republican leaders in Congress like Reed and Sherman insisted that they had supported the Silver Purchase Act because it constituted the only alternative to free coinage. Senator Sherman wrote, "A large majority of the Senate favored free silver, and it was feared that the small majority against it in the other House might yield and agree to it. The silence of the President on the matter gave rise to an apprehension that if a free coinage bill should pass both Houses he would not feel at liberty to veto it."[65] Sherman was rationalizing. Free coinage did not have a majority in the House, where the populous states of the Northeast had greater weight. Speaker Reed supported the gold standard, and it is difficult to imagine any important measure passing over his opposition. Had Congress passed a free silver bill, however, President Harrison would have vetoed it. He did not want to alienate western voters if he could avoid it, but forced to choose, he would defend the gold standard. The Silver Purchase Act had a different objective—clearing the way for an increase in tariffs by mollifying Silver Republicans. As two Democrats observed, fail-

[62] Quoted in Fred Wellborn, "The Influence of the Silver-Republican Senators, 1889–1891," *The Mississippi Valley Historical Review* 14 (March 1928): 469.

[63] Sherman, *Recollections of Forty Years*, p. 1170

[64] Quoted in Hoxie, "The Silver Debate of 1890," p. 469

[65] Sherman, *Recollections*, p. 1170.

ure to "do something for silver" would have "let the impression go abroad that the Republican Party was 'unfriendly to silver.' What would have been the effect of this? Merely that … [the bill to increase tariffs] would have failed."[66]

The Republicans' focus on tariffs gave the debate on the Silver Purchase Act a strange quality. As one supporter of the gold standard noted with irritation, "The main issue was avoided, and the endeavor made to confine the discussion to compromise measures which should be forced through Congress with little or no discussion of the main topic as possible."[67] Silverites interpreted this silence as evidence of their strength. The speaker opening the 1889 Silver Convention had crowed, "The gold monometalists have virtually given up the defense of such a policy."[68] Such was not the case. Most Republican leaders opposed free coinage of silver, at least outside an international agreement. They refused to debate the currency in 1890 not because they had no answer to Silverites' arguments but because such a contest would have alienated Silver Republicans, whose support they needed to raise tariffs.

The Silver Purchase Act accomplished its real purpose, clearing the way for a tariff bill. Leadership on that issue fell to Representative William McKinley (R-OH), chairman of the House Ways and Means Committee. McKinley had served with distinction in the Union Army during the Civil War, rising from a private to the rank of major. Supporters often referred to him as "The Major," a title he preferred to all others. After the war he practiced law in Canton, Ohio, playing an active role in local politics before securing election to Congress in 1876. McKinley was the complete politician who, besides his devotion to his invalid wife (who probably suffered from epilepsy), had no other interests. He was handsome, charming, and persuasive. The Major had many acquaintances but few intimates—he almost never let others know his thoughts. Naturally cautious, he paid close attention to public opinion and only rarely miscalculated it. Since first arriving in Congress in 1877, McKinley had made a careful study of tariffs, mastering their numbing complexities. The country had hundreds of different duties on various items, many of which, like the tariff on raw wool and wool cloth, were related. He was a committed protectionist who

[66] A.B. and H. Farquhar, "Congress and the Currency," [1893], Grover Cleveland Papers, Library of Congress, reel 78.

[67] Hoxie, "The Silver Debate of 1890," pp. 549, 574.

[68] *National Silver Convention*, p. 20.

believed that Americans should produce as much as possible themselves. Just as important, he viewed tariffs as a device to reconcile the country's many, varied economic interests, creating social harmony or, at least, reducing discord.

McKinley's committee produced a bill that raised tariffs to the highest level thus far in American history. It contained some deft pieces of industrial policy. The measure imposed a stiff duty on tin-plated steel, almost all of which the country imported, with the provision that protection would cease within a few years unless domestic producers substantially increased output. That they did, developing a variety of new techniques that sharply reduced costs and allowed American companies to compete in world markets with British producers, who had heretofore dominated the industry.[69] Ultimately, however, tariff-making was a political process, and rates reflected political calculations first and foremost. For instance, the McKinley tariff protected domestic wool, which many farmers produced. Unfortunately, their costs were high, so this levy forced domestic producers of woolen textiles to pay more for their chief raw material than did foreign competitors. To compensate, the new tariff also sharply raised the duty on imported wool cloth, allowing American producers to dominate the home market but imposing a double burden on consumers. Congress enacted such a self-defeating provision because the tariff bill had to offer something to farmers, who constituted a majority of the population. Wool was the only agricultural commodity produced in the U.S. besides sugar that faced substantial foreign competition. The case of wool was particularly egregious, but in many instances, levies reflected the political clout of those protected more than any economic calculation.

In retrospect, the most momentous provision of the McKinley Tariff reduced a tariff. Sensitive to charges that the bill would increase consumer prices, the bill's authors abolished the duty on imported sugar, a household staple. (It retained the ¢½ per pound duty on refined sugar.) To compensate the relatively small number of domestic producers of sugar for the loss of protection, the bill provided them with a cash bounty based on the volume of production.[70] The duty on sugar had been a major source

[69] Donald Earl Dunbar, *The Tin-Plate Industry: A Comparative Study in its Growth in the United States and Wales* (Boston & New York Houghton Mifflin, 1915).

[70] Sugar growers clustered in the South, in states dominated by the Democratic Party. As a result, they had far less influence over tariffs than sheep ranchers in states that usually voted Republican.

of revenue, and higher duties on most other items generated little new income because they reduced the total volume of imports. Customs revenue in fiscal 1892 declined $53 million from the previous year—a drop of 24 percent—enough to consume most of the surplus even before taking into account new spending on pensions, which advanced $54 million.[71]

Historian Scott Nelson attributes this outcome to the machinations of the Sugar Trust, which dominated the industry within the United States. It was locked in a rivalry with producers on the West Coast who had access to duty-free raw sugar from Hawaii.[72] Eliminating the tariff improved the relative position of eastern producers. Nelson concludes, "The tussle in 1890 between eastern and western sugar barons … drained the U.S. Treasury and helped create a financial panic [in 1893]."[73] No doubt, the Sugar Trust was delighted to see the cost of its chief raw material fall and would have been so even without the threat of competition from the West Coast. Cutting the duty on raw sugar was an obvious ploy for Republicans who were busy raising duties on almost everything else, including many consumer goods. The Sugar Trust was pushing on an open door.

In the nineteenth century, most Americans were of two minds about tariffs. They wanted to protect American workers, who generally earned higher wages than did laborers in other countries, but they did not want to pay higher prices to fatten manufacturers' profits.[74] The line between these two impulses was unclear, but many Americans concluded that the new tariff bill had crossed it. McKinley and other Republicans had badly miscalculated public opinion—in McKinley's case, a rare error. It did not help that, after the tariff bill's passage, some retailers launched advertising campaigns urging consumers to buy before the new measure drove prices up. In November 1890, less than two months after they had passed the

[71] Fiscal 1892 began on July 1, 1891, so it was the first full fiscal year in which the new tariff was in effect. The figures on pensions come from Socolofsky and Spetter, *The Presidency of Benjamin Harrison*, p. 36.

[72] Hawaii had a trade agreement with the United States that, among other things, allowed raw sugar grown there into the country without paying a duty.

[73] Nelson, *A Nation of Deadbeats*, p. 182.

[74] Though defenders of protection often exaggerated the difference, Americans workers did in most cases earn higher wages that European ones. In his *Tin Plate Industry*, Dunbar estimated that unskilled workers in American mills producing tin plated steel earned $4 to $5 a day in the early 1900s, whereas skilled British workers earned $12 to $15 a week (pp. 59, 68).

McKinley Tariff, the Republicans suffered a crushing defeat in the off-year elections—one of the worst in the party's long history. Half the GOP members in the House of Representatives lost their seats, including McKinley. Iowa, Pennsylvania, and Massachusetts, traditionally Republican strongholds, elected Democratic governors. As the British publication *The Economist* put it, "The Democrats have, in a word, swept the country, and their successes have far exceeded the prognostications of even the most sanguine of party prophets."[75] The party in power usually loses ground in off-year contests, but this setback was special. In parts of the Midwest, Republican-controlled state legislatures had imposed laws restricting the sale of alcohol, discouraging parochial schools, and mandating that schools teach in English, all of which antagonized German immigrants who usually voted Republican. The economy also suffered a mild recession in 1890, which hurt. Most of all, however, voters reacted strongly against the Republican program. No one liked the Silver Purchase Act, the expansion of pensions seemed profligate, and the tariff bill looked like a huge collection of favors for special interests. *The Economist* insisted, "The elections turned directly on the tariff question."[76] Pundits had already christened the fifty-first Congress the "Billion Dollar Congress." It was not a term of endearment.[77]

The Baring's Crisis

The Silver Purchase Act and the McKinley Tariff coincided with the worst financial disaster to hit London's money market in a generation—the Baring's Crisis. Baring Brothers, a venerable firm that many considered second only to Rothschild's among London's merchant (investment) banks, specialized in securities from the Americas. In the 1880s, only Morgan's sold as many U.S. railroad bonds to British investors as Baring's. It aggressively solicited business, and some of the projects it backed were sounder than others. It was the chief backer of the ambitious Atchison, Topeka, & Santa Fe Railroad, which went bankrupt in the 1890s. Baring's

[75] *The Economist*, November 8, 1890, p. 1406.

[76] *The Economist*, November 8, 1890, p. 1407.

[77] In fact, federal spending remained well below $1 billion and would continue to do so until World War I. Critics of the Republican program insisted that it would increase federal spending by $1 billion over several years.

downfall, however, owed not to developments in the United States but in Argentina.

Like the United States, Argentina had boomed in the 1880s. For decades, political and financial instability had thwarted its development. In the late 1870s, however, a new regime had imposed a measure of order, allowing Argentines to exploit their country's considerable potential, particularly in farming and ranching. This effort required capital to build railroads, upgrade ports, and more, and this British investors happily provided. Between 1885 and 1890, they put £100 million into the country, which at the time had fewer than four million people. Baring's dominated this business, underwriting £17.5 million in securities and extending many short-term credits as well. In particular, it was deeply involved in the Buenos Aires water works, a huge project plagued by poor management, cost overruns, and (possibly) corruption.[78]

By 1890, British investors had developed doubts about Argentina. By almost any measure, the country was financially overextended, with immense foreign obligations that required careful management. The Argentine government, however, continued borrowing and spending with little care about how it would service these debts. Investors ceased buying Argentine securities. Baring's, which had continued to lend even as more cautious firms had backed off, found itself saddled with a huge portfolio of unsalable bonds financed, for the most part, by its own borrowing.

Throughout 1890, the situation drifted. Knowledgeable observers realized that Baring's and other firms faced heavy losses on Argentine investments. In self-defense, London's investors and bankers began to accumulate cash by restricting credits and, often, selling securities. The investing public's appetite for issues from the Western Hemisphere soured, affecting the United States as well as Latin America. The United States was in far better shape than Argentina, but it had plenty of heavily indebted railroads. Moreover, the growing silver movement raised the prospect of devaluation, casting a pall over all obligations denominated in dollars. The Bank of England both raised interest rates to attract gold from abroad and extended loans generously to those under pressure, albeit at a high interest rate, acting as the "lender of last resort." Meanwhile, it fortified its own position, borrowing £3 million in gold in Paris—chiefly from the Bank of

[78] Philip Ziegler, *The Sixth Great Power: A History of One of the Greatest of all Banking Families, the House of Barings, 1762–1929* (New York: Alfred Knopf, 1988), pp. 236–7.

France—and purchasing another £1.5 million in gold in Russia.[79] Such was Baring's prestige, however, that few imagined it might not survive, and within the firm, even those with a complete view of the situation only gradually accepted this grim reality.

In November 1890, Baring's chief, Lord Revelstoke (Edward Baring), finally admitted to officials at the Bank of England that his firm was on the verge of collapse. All found the prospect appalling. Baring's had borrowed extensively from other banks, and its failure would saddle these organizations with large, possible fatal losses. At the least, Baring's default would force them to restrict credits further and sell more securities on a falling market. Even worse, Baring's was the largest dealer in the commercial paper (IOUs) that financed international trade. It had endorsed £15 million in such instruments, and if other dealers refused to accept is guarantee, the results could paralyze the entire system.[80] Baring's bankruptcy could well transform the recession already unfolding in Britain into a crushing depression.

The Bank of England rose to the challenge. After the government refused to provide direct financial support, the Bank created a "guarantee fund" whose members promised to make good any debts that Baring Brothers failed to repay. The Bank itself put in £1 million and persuaded (or cajoled) other London banks to do the same, ultimately assembling £17 million in commitments. With this huge fund in place, Baring's creditors were willing to exercise forbearance. This measure prevented the worst. There was no financial panic, and though Britain and much of Europe suffered a severe recession over the next few years, it was not nearly as bad as the depression that would hit the United States in 1893. The guarantee fund allowed the orderly liquidation of Baring's, a task that took several years. This process consumed all of the firm's capital and a large portion of its partners' fortunes, but ultimately the guarantee fund itself suffered no loss. Soon most of Baring Brothers' partners and staff organized a limited liability company of the same name. Members of the Baring clan who were not active in the old firm when it collapsed provided financing, and in time, the new company joined the ranks of London's top merchant banks.

The crisis profoundly affected the United States. During most of the 1880s, the country enjoyed a trade surplus, exporting more than it

[79] Zeigler, *Sixth Great Power*, pp. 248–9. 253–54.
[80] Ziegler, *Sixth Great Power*, p. 247.

imported. At the same time, it suffered a large deficit in services—chiefly shipping and related fields like insurance—as well as in remittances immigrants sent home. Perhaps most important, the country had to pay interest on its substantial foreign debts. As a result, in most years the United States had a deficit on its current account of $150 million to $200 million. The country made up the difference by selling securities abroad, chiefly railroad bonds. The Baring's crisis not only sharply curtailed the appetite of British investors for new American securities but led some of them to reduce their current holdings. They feared that the United States might follow Argentina's path. Even if it did not, many wanted cash to reduce their own debts and to provide a cushion against financial uncertainty. The demand for railroad securities dropped sharply, and that for the securities of American industrial companies dried up almost completely.[81] As an English correspondent of New York banker August Belmont wrote in 1891, "New business in London is almost stagnant, and the British investor will not even look at anything new."[82] Baron Edmund Rothschild, of the Paris branch of the family, wrote Belmont in late 1891, "Investors over here, particularly in France, have lost heavily of late years in transatlantic ventures, and consequently are little inclined, at present, to embark in such investments."[83]

Unable to cover its balance-of-payments deficit by selling securities, the United States had to export gold. Since the currency rested on the gold, this outflow translated into a contraction of money and credit. By the fall of 1890, even before Baring Brothers applied to the Bank of England for help, pressure had become acute. The harvest, with its demand for cash, was approaching, and foreign investors were taking money out of the country. Fortunately, the Treasury still had a surplus. The government had been reluctant to purchase Treasury bonds in the open market because they commanded a premium—extinguishing $1 in debt cost more than $1. The deteriorating financial situation and the lack of alternatives, however, led President Harrison and Treasury Secretary Windom to act despite

[81] O'Sullivan, *Dividends of Development*, p. 78.

[82] Hamilton Smith to August Belmont, Oct. 31, 1891, Belmont Papers, box 12. Series I catalogued correspondence, Columbia University Archives.

[83] Edmund Rothschild to August Belmont, Dec. 19, 1891, Belmont Papers, box 5, collected correspondence. Rothschild was referring, in part, to the Panama debacle. A French company tried to dig a canal through Panama, connecting the Atlantic and Pacific oceans, but had failed miserably, not the least because yellow fever and malaria had decimated the workforce.

the obvious disadvantages. In September, the government spent $16 million to purchase bonds at a 26 percent premium, and it also prepaid the interest on other outstanding securities.[84] This injection of funds stabilized financial markets and allowed the harvest to proceed smoothly, and the sale of crops abroad brought an influx of gold.

The basic problem nevertheless remained. European investors were not buying American securities, and Washington was not in a position to step into the breach again. The McKinley Tariff and heavier spending on pensions had eliminated the federal surplus, which fell from $85 million in fiscal 1890 (which ended June 30, 1890) to $26 million the next year and then vanished altogether.[85] As the Secretary of the Treasury admitted, the bond purchases of 1890 had "exhaust[ed] the available surplus."[86] Good luck delayed the reckoning. The European harvest of wheat in 1891 was poor, while the United States enjoyed a bumper crop. In 1892, the value of grain exports tripled, reflecting both larger volume and higher prices. This windfall allowed the country to cover its payments deficit without further investment from abroad, and, on the whole, 1892 was prosperous. The country had secured no more than a respite, however.

Silver and Segregation

Hopes that the Silver Purchase Act would rehabilitate silver proved vain. As Congress debated the issue in the summer of 1890, silver's price increased to $1.21, the highest level in years. With the passage of the Silver Purchase Act, however, the price began to fall, dropping below $1 by the end of the year. By 1894, silver had fallen to a little over $0.60 an ounce. This decline had a variety of causes. In 1890, speculators bid up silver on the expectation that the American government would take action to raise its price. When the Silver Purchase Act became law, they had to unwind their positions, dumping silver on the market. The impact of this selling was temporary, however, and cannot explain the decline after 1891. The recession that settled on Europe in the wake of the Baring's Crisis drove down the prices of all commodities, including silver. Hard times

[84] George Batchellor to E.W. Halford, Sept. 17, 1890; William Windom to Benjamin Harrison, Sept. 14, 1890, both Harrison Papers, reel 29.

[85] The fiscal year started on July 1 of the previous year—that is, fiscal 1891 started July 1, 1890.

[86] Windom to Harrison, Sept. 14, 1890.

reduced the demand for jewelry and silverware. Meanwhile, American output continued to increase. With prices falling, miners had to wrestle more silver from the earth just to maintain their incomes. Only when prices approached \$0.60 an ounce did production finally fall back, largely because at that price, smaller, less-efficient mines could not pay their expenses.

The Silver Purchase Act may well have contributed to this fall. Commodity traders always find the existence of a large stockpile of any good unsettling because holders can dump this "overhang" on the market whenever prices increase. Under Bland-Allison, the federal government had bought a good deal of silver, but authorities had coined the metal and put it into circulation, directly or through silver certificates. Not so with the Silver Purchase Act. In theory, holders could convert the new Treasury bills into silver coins, but such redemptions were quite rare. At home, the notes were legal tender, so holders had no incentive to convert them into less convenient coins. In foreign trade, silver dollars were useless because the metal in them was worth less than their face value—the silver in a silver dollar had a market value of less than \$1. If holders of Treasury bills converted them into anything, it was gold. Unlike the silver coined under Bland-Allison, that acquired under the Silver Act was idle, and the government's hoard was growing at the rate of 4.5 million ounces a month. As one politician wrote several years later, "The immense pile of silver bullion in the Treasury now is a constant menace to the price of silver."[87]

Whatever its cause, the decline of silver had momentous consequences. Depression settled on mining districts as producers cut wages and scrambled to pay their debts. By 1893, small mines were closing, leaving owners as well as workers unemployed. In 1890, the Denver & Rio Grande Railroad sent dozens of cars every week to and from silver mining districts in Colorado and Arizona, but by 1894, this traffic had almost completely evaporated.[88] As an inhabitant of a mining town in New Mexico wrote in 1893, "Everything here is closed down. Men are shouldering their blankets and leaving the camp and they don't know where they are going. … Now I must get out of here until silver recovers, and I have no money to make a start."[89]

[87] David Francis to Grover Cleveland, March 20, 1894, Cleveland Papers, reel 83.

[88] Campbell, *The Reorganization of the American Railroad System*, p. 289.

[89] W.E. Marable to Manton Marable, June 30, 1893, Manton Marable Papers, Vol. 79, Library of Congress.

In the realm of international finance, the decline of silver hastened the flight from it. As silver depreciated, so did the value of currencies based on it. During the 1880s, the gradual decline of silver relative to gold had offered some advantages to countries that used it. They avoided the deflation that went with the gold standard, and the modest devaluation of their currencies boosted exports. After 1890, however, the gradual decline of silver gave way to headlong collapse. Enterprises and governments doing business in silver found international financial markets closed to them unless they borrowed in gold, in which case the size of these debts, in domestic terms, ballooned. An Indian firm that borrowed sterling, a currency based on gold, needed one third more silver rupees to service this debt in 1893 than it did in 1890. Swapping silver for gold became more and more attractive. Austria-Hungary had used silver as money for centuries, but it had closed its mints in 1879 as the price of silver fell. The Dual Monarchy did not adopt the gold standard, however. Instead its currency "floated" in the market, declining relative to gold, but not so much as silver bullion.[90] The sudden jump in the price of silver in the first half of 1890 drove up the value of the Empire's currency and hurt its exports, while the sharp decline that began in the fall opened the possibility of a major devaluation that would derange commercial relations with countries on the gold standard, including the Dual Monarchy's largest trading partner, Germany. Opinion about the currency, heretofore diverse, coalesced behind the gold standard, and in the summer of 1892, Austria-Hungary launched a new gold currency, though it did not recall silver coins already in circulation but valued these in terms of gold.[91]

The sharp drop in silver prices also alarmed members of the Harrison administration. In December 1890, Treasury Secretary Windom recommended a one-time purchase of 13 million ounces of silver, which he hoped would bolster prices by eliminating what he saw as a temporary glut.[92] Windom died suddenly in early 1891, but his successor Charles

[90] The term "float" is an anachronism, but in the 1890s, bankers and government officials understood the concept of a floating currency, even if they did not use the term. Though silver coins continued to play a central role in the currency of Austria-Hungary, the volume of these ceased to expand. Since these were legal tender in the Dual Monarchy, their volume remained fixed, and Austria-Hungary's economy continued to grow, they took on a value greater than the silver they contained.

[91] Russell, *International Conferences*, pp. 373–4; Frederick Grant to James G. Blaine, May 30, 1892, Harrison Papers, reel 35.

[92] Memo from William Windom, Dec. 12, 1890, Harrison Papers, reel 29.

Foster suggested a new issue of greenbacks and changes that would make it easier for national banks to issue notes.[93] The President, however, decided to stand pat. "The silver bill gives a steady and large increase [to the currency]," he wrote Foster.[94] In his December 1891 State of the Union Message, the President stated, "Upon this subject [the currency], … my recommendation is that the existing laws be given full trial and that our business interests be spared the distressing influence which threats of radical change always imparts."[95] The federal government was already buying fifty-four million ounces of silver a year, roughly a third of the world's output. Tinkering with the program seemed unlikely to raise the price of silver much. Indeed, the President had begun to have doubts about the whole effort. Though not a doctrinaire advocate of the gold standard, he strongly opposed devaluing the dollar. He feared that further unilateral efforts by the United States to bolster silver would put the country on a silver basis. A public letter released in the spring of 1891 reflected Harrison's frustration. In it, he stated that he had hoped that the Silver Purchase Act would raise the price silver to $1.29, "and keep it there. That anticipation has not been realized."[96] Privately, the President stated that his administration might be "forced to advocate the repeal of this silver [purchase] bill."[97]

Silverites drew a different conclusion from the experience. Only the free coinage of silver, they believed, could resurrect silver and, more broadly, resolve the country's financial problems. Silver Republicans were determined to push the matter when Congress reconvened in December. Though the country had elected a new Congress in 1890, the old one still had one more session beginning in December. After their crushing defeat in November, Republicans' morale was not high. As one observer wrote, "I find that Republicans generally in both the House and the Senate are apathetic and almost hopeless as to the next election."[98] Western Republicans, however, had largely avoided defeat. They attributed survival

[93] Benjamin Harrison to Charles Foster, Oct. 19, 1891, Harrison Papers, reel 33.

[94] Harrison to Foster, Oct. 12, 1891, Harrison Papers, reel 33.

[95] Benjamin Harrison, Third State of the Union Address, December 1891, American Presidency Project, University of California Santa Barbara.

[96] Benjamin Harrison to the Western States Commercial Congress, April 7, 1891, American Presidency Project, University of California Santa Barbara.

[97] Harrison to Foster, Oct. 12, 1891.

[98] Francis G. Newlands to Benjamin Harrison, February 21, 1891, Benjamin Harrison Papers, Reel 31.

to their support for silver and, in many cases, believed that free silver could save the Republican Party as a whole.

This effort would collide with another Republican priority, voting rights. During the 1888 campaign, Republicans had promised to secure the voting rights of southern Blacks. This commitment reflected both self-interest and principle. In much of the South, Democrats had deprived African-Americans of the franchise through a mixture of fraud, intimidation, and violence, creating what became known as the "Solid South" under exclusive Democratic control. Republicans had a strong interest in breaking this political monopoly. Because Blacks voted overwhelmingly for the GOP, the party of Lincoln and emancipation, securing them an honest ballot offered a means to this end. At the same time, most Republicans were proud of their party's record on civil rights. Many of its leaders were veterans of the Civil War, including Harrison and McKinley. As a party operative active in the Grand Army of the Republic reported, "Our people are just as anxious for the passage of new elections laws as they were for the pension bill."[99] The need was pressing. In 1890, a petition from Blacks in Oklahoma to President Harrison lamented, "The passage of unfair law affecting elections, labor and the landlord and tenant system, by the legislatures of southern states has caused widespread unrest and discontent" and "produced a feeling of profound discouragement and utter dismay among Africo-American voters in the entire country."[100] Soon after convening in late 1889, the House of Representatives had launched an investigation into elections in the South. Representative Henry Cabot Lodge (R-MA) chaired the effort, which documented pervasive abuses. Based on this evidence, Lodge introduced what soon became known as the "Force Bill." It would allow voters in any Congressional district to petition for federal oversight of elections there. If federal tallies differed from state ones, a federal court would determine the outcome. Though less radical than the voting rights measures enacted during the Reconstruction and Civil Rights eras—among other things, the Force Bill applied only to elections for federal office, not state or local ones—it would have provided a brake on the electoral chicanery pervasive in the South.

Southern Democrats stubbornly resisted the Force Bill. They supported white supremacy—it was, indeed, the only major question on

[99] L.T. Mitchner to H.E. Halford, July 10, 1890, Benjamin Harrison Papers, reel 28.
[100] Petition, April 1890, Benjamin Harrison Papers, reel 27.

which they all agreed. They also recognized that, in many parts of the South, fair elections would eject them from office. Southern Democrats could not prevent the Force Bill from passing the House, but in the Senate they filibustered, taking advantage of rules that allowed unlimited debate to bring business to a halt. Republicans found themselves in a dilemma. They could probably break the filibuster, but the process would take the rest of the session, preventing action on other priorities, particularly raising tariffs. Instead, they decided to postpone consideration of the Force Bill to the second session. The manager of the measure, Senator George Hoar (R-MA), acquiesced to the decision but extracted a major concession. He got every Republican Senator save one—agrarian radical Richard Pettigrew (R-SD)—to sign a pledge promising the bring the Force Bill to a vote in the next session. This agreement guaranteed that, except for routine business, voting rights would consume the next meeting of the Senate.

Silver Republicans desperately wanted a vote on free coinage. The price of silver was falling, creating hardship in mining districts of the West. The Silver Purchase Act had clearly failed in its purpose. Silver Republicans sought to reassure constituents of their devotion to silver and, ideally, to lay the foundation for free coinage—if not in 1891, then later. Unfortunately, a battle over the Force Bill would preclude any vote on silver. Accordingly, the Silver Republicans struck a deal with southern Democrats. The latter were desperate to kill the Force Bill, and many were sympathetic to the free coinage of silver. Like the West, the South depended on the production of commodities—chiefly cotton—and debt weighed even more heavily on southerners than on the people of the West. Together, these two groups united in a procedural vote that pushed the Force Bill well down the agenda, guaranteeing that it would not come to a vote. Senator Hoar and other supporters of the measure were furious at Silver Republicans' breach of faith, but they could not do much. The Silver Republicans then introduced a free coinage bill, which passed with the support of southern Democrats. Their bill languished in the House, however. The formidable Speaker, Thomas Reed, no longer had any reason to conciliate Silver Republicans, and he made short work of the measure.

Historians have long struggled with the relationship between race relations and agrarian radicalism—the Alliance and the Populist Party as well as Silverites. The Populists often sought the support of African-American voters, in several states cooperating with Republicans. Tom Watson, perhaps the most famous southern Populist, stoutly defended Black's voting rights. Yet "Pitchfork" Ben Tillman, who dominated South Carolina's politics with the enthusiastic support of the Alliance, was a particularly vicious racist, even by the low standards of southern Democrats in the 1890s. The 1890 meeting of the Southern Alliance in Ocala, Florida, which drafted what would become the Populist Party's platform, also adopted a resolution condemning the Force Bill.[101] Nevada's Silver Party, which Senator Stewart organized in 1892, offered a platform with but two planks—free silver and opposition to the Force Bill. It declared that the latter was "destructive of free government and designed to secure Negro domination in the South."[102] Race relations have always been a part of the matrix of American politics. In the 1890s, southern Democrats gave white supremacy absolute priority over all other questions. Southern Populists who challenged them naturally reached out to African-American voters, and western Silverites seeking an alliance with southern Democratic naturally embraced white supremacy. Their motives were essentially opportunistic or, as they might have said, "realistic."

This opportunism had profound implications. Had Congress enacted the Force Bill in 1891, it would have imposed a brake, however imperfect, on the electoral chicanery rampant in the South. Perhaps more important, it would have sent a clear message to southern Democrats that Washington remained concerned with the fate of African-Americans. In blocking this measure, Silver Republicans like Senators Teller and Stewart—who heretofore had supported civil rights—opened the way for the consolidation of Jim Crow.

The Brussels Conference

By the summer of 1891, the Harrison administration's financial policy was in shambles. The Silver Purchase Act had neither raised the price of silver nor conciliated Silver Republicans. The budget surplus had evaporated, and the balance of payments had slipped into deficit, necessitating the export of gold. To combat the drain, the Treasury had paid out most of its surplus funds, and the volume of gold in the Treasury was nearing the psychologically important $100 million level. The Democratic victory in the 1890 elections made new legislatives initiatives impossible. The

[101] *New York Times*, December 4, 1890, p. 2.

[102] *Eureka Weekly Sentinel* (NV), Nov. 19, 1892, p.1.

fortuitous combination of a bad harvest in Europe with a good one in the United States granted a respite for 1892, but no more.

To escape these problems, the administration sought to negotiate an international agreement to establish the free coinage of both gold and silver at a universally agreed ratio. Such had always been the program of "international bimetallists," a group of which Harrison counted himself a member. Advocates of unilateral free coinage usually dismissed such views because they considered such an accord hopeless. The prospect of negotiations, they insisted, merely allowed supporters of the gold standard to feign sympathy to silver, confident that talks would yield nothing. With a few exceptions such as Richard White, most historians have accepted this conclusion—to the degree that they have noticed the phenomenon at all. In some cases, this assessment is fair. Despite the occasional kind word for international bimetallism, John Sherman clearly preferred the unalloyed gold standard, and Grover Cleveland was even less interested. His mentions of international bimetallism always had the air of an afterthought. An international agreement, however, promised to square the financial circle, expanding the supply of currency without deranging international finance. International bimetallism had considerable support in Europe, where it was practically synonymous with the silver movement, and many of its American advocates were entirely sincere, including Harrison.

Unfortunately, the Silver Purchase Act—the Harrison Administration's unilateral attempt to prop up the price of silver—complicated any talks. Other governments were inclined to wait and see the results. The measure might stabilize silver prices without requiring anything of them. On the other hand, if it failed—as seemed increasingly probable—then the experience cast further doubt on the possibility of resurrecting silver.

President Harrison nevertheless considered successful talks possible. The collapse of the price of silver relative to gold had created alarm. Most of the countries of Latin America and Asia still based their money on silver, and its fall had deranged commercial relations between them and nations on gold. As banker August Belmont put it, "The silver question is a menace in its present condition to every important commercial country in the world. ... Silver cannot be shelved and therefore had best be treated if possible in a way to cause the least trouble to the world's interests."[103] Even the British, who had the longest experience with gold, worried

[103]August Belmont to Lord Rothschild, March 22, 1892, Belmont Papers, box 22, Letterpress books.

because their huge Indian empire used silver. Officials in the India Office asked the British government to "lend your support to any proposal by the United States of America, or by any other country, for the settlement of the silver issue by international agreement," adding, "We fear that a refusal on the part of Great Britain to adopt the system of double legal tender [international bimetallism] may be fatal to an international agreement."[104] In a discussion with the American ambassador in early 1892, the British Prime Minister, Lord Salisbury, "spoke of himself as a 'silver man' and of Mr. [Arthur] Balfour [his chief lieutenant] and Mr. [Henry] Chaplin [minister in charge of agriculture] as being 'apostles,'" though Salisbury added that other members of his cabinet were more skeptical.[105] Harrison hoped that the flow of gold from Europe to the United States over 1892 to pay for grain would encourage flexibility. As he wrote in 1891, "My own view of the situation is that England and Germany will not adopt the bi-metallic standard until they feel the squeeze more than they have yet." He continued, "If we are able, by the marketing of our large crops, to recover our lost gold and largely increase our reserve of that metal, Europe may be better disposed towards the question."[106] The President also knew that Senator Teller, the leader of the Silver Republicans, thought talks worth pursuing.[107] A serious effort to secure an international agreement might reconcile at least some of the Silverites within Harrison's own party.

By this point, Harrison had little to lose. The Silver Purchase Act had not achieved its objective, and the President refused to consider unilateral free coinage. That left an international agreement, which might conceivably rescue the situation. The administration invited European countries to send delegates to a conference scheduled to convene in Brussels in November 1892, and most agreed. The timing largely reflected logistics—formal invitations only went out in the spring of 1892—but the President may also have hoped that the prospects of negotiations would mollify Silver Republicans during the fall campaign.

Even before the conference opened, problems arose. It was clear that many participants would not agree to the free coinage of silver. German

[104] Government of India Finance and Commerce Department, No. 160 of 1892, June 21, 1892, NA, CAB 37/311892, No. 12.

[105] Robert Lincoln to James Blaine, January 27, 1892, Harrison Papers, reel 34.

[106] Benjamin Harrison to Jefferson Coolidge, August 14, 1891, Harrison Papers, reel 32.

[107] Charles Foster to Benjamin Harrison, January 16, 1892, Harrison Papers, reel 34.

officials told American diplomats that they were "satisfied with its [Germany's] currency."[108] The Austrians, who had just embraced the gold standard, were no more encouraging. Accordingly, Harrison stated officially that the conference was "for the purpose of conferring as to what measures, if any, can be taken to increase the use of silver as money," though he made clear his own support for an agreement on free coinage.[109] This concession was probably inevitable, but it created the possibility that the conference would never address the subject for which it was convened—remonetizing silver. Officials in Britain's India Office, where support for silver was strong, "observe with regret that the Conference has been summoned ... not for the purpose of considering the adoption of an international agreement for the free coinage of gold and silver."[110] Further difficulties arose in July when William Gladstone's Liberals won elections in Britain against Lord Salisbury's Conservatives. The Conservatives were divided over the currency whereas the new Prime Minister and his followers strongly supported the gold standard. The British election had impact across the Channel. France had relied on bimetallism for decades and still had a large reserve of silver. American officials assumed that it would be eager for an agreement, but Paris did not feel strong enough to act on its own. Speaking with the American ambassador in Paris, the French Finance Minister "indicated that the action of France would be in conformity with that of Britain."[111]

Bad management made an unpromising situation worse. The President put Senator William Allison of Iowa in charge of the American delegation. He was "sound" on most financial questions—like Harrison, he supported free coinage of silver only in the context of an international agreement—but as a midwesterner, Allison possessed a credibility with westerners that no eastern politician enjoyed. Unfortunately, Allison did almost no groundwork in advance. One of the British delegates to the Brussels Conference believed that Allison and his associates only realized that Europeans were unlikely to agree to free coinage when they visited London on their way to Brussels.[112] It is not clear why they failed to grasp this fact

[108] William Wharton to Benjamin Harrison, May 28, 1892, Harrison Papers, reel 35.

[109] Quoted in Russell, *International Conferences*, p. 380.

[110] No. 160 of 1892, Department of India, Finance and Commerce Department, June 21, 1892, NA, CAB 37/31, 1892.

[111] Henry Vignaud to James G. Blaine, [June 22, 1892], Harrison Papers, reel 35.

[112] Alfred Rothschild to his brothers, November 23, 1892, Rothschild's Archives, 000/253.

earlier given the signals from London, Paris, Berlin, and Vienna. In his opening address to the conference, Senator Allison announced, "The establishment of some fixity of values between gold and silver and the full use of silver as a coin metal, upon a ratio to gold to be fixed by an agreement between the great commercial nations of the world, would very greatly promote the prosperity of all classes of people."[113] At the same time, he recognized that support for such a course did not exist at the conference, but he had no alternative ready. He asked the assembly for a three-day recess in which to devise one, but upon his return, he provided little more than a general statement endorsing the broader use of silver.

The American delegates had no idea what to do. Gold was again flowing out of the United States. A good harvest in Europe in 1892 had reduced the continent's need to import wheat, and a weak cotton harvest had reduced exports of it. Sentiment for repeal of the Silver Purchase Act was growing at home, and the United States could not ask others to do more for silver if it reduced its efforts. Grover Cleveland had defeated Harrison in the fall election, and the President-elect showed no interest in the negotiations. Alfred Rothschild, a member of London's most prominent banking family and a member of the British delegation, lamented, "It is really quite impossible to get anything out of the Americans."[114]

At this point, Rothschild intervened. He declared to the Conference, "The stock of silver in the world is estimated at some thousands of millions, and if this conference were to break up without arriving at any definite result there would be a depreciation in the value of that commodity which would be frightful to contemplate, and out of which a monetary panic would ensue, the far-spreading effects of which it would be impossible to foretell."[115] To prevent such a disaster, he proposed a European version of the Silver Purchase Act. Between them, the nations of the continent would agree to purchase £5 million worth of silver a year for several years, or about $25 million annually.[116] With no other viable proposal on the table, Rothschild's suggestions quickly became the focus of discussion,

[113] Quoted in Russell, *International Monetary Conferences*, p. 380.

[114] Alfred Rothschild to his brothers, December 2, 1892, Rothschild's Archives, 000/253.

[115] Quoted in Russell, *International Conferences*, p. 384.

[116] Rothschild also suggested increasing the use of silver coins as small change—in the case of Britain, increasing the use of such coins by making them legal tender for transactions as large as £5, up from the current ceiling of £2. Such action was not particularly controversial—many countries already made extensive use of silver coins. Unfortunately, it would not increase the demand for silver enough to alter conditions in the silver market significantly.

and the conference appointed a committee that included an American to translate his idea into a specific agreement.

This committee soon deadlocked. Rothschild had acted on his own initiative. At least one member of his own delegation opposed his plan, and it was not clear that the government in London would agree to participate in his scheme even if the Conference embraced it.[117] France and Germany already had large stocks of silver to which they had no desire to add. Rothschild reported, "The attitude of France remains ... sullen, not to say sulky and reserved beyond words."[118] For their part, the Germans decided that they lacked authority from their government even to discuss the subject. Ironically, the Silver Purchase Act had robbed the United States of most of its leverage. It committed the country to buy silver regardless of what other countries did. Allison and his associates could not use the prospect of American purchases to extract promises of similar action from Europeans. Nor did the record of that measure, which coincided with the destabilization of the silver market, encourage emulation. British delegates, and presumably others as well, knew that sentiment for repeal of this measure was growing in the United States, and none were willing to buy silver if the U.S. stopped doing so. The committee failed to produce a specific recommendation, and the conference as a whole adjourned in December. At the time, some hoped that it might reconvene in May 1893, but by then conditions had changed radically, and the delegates never met again. In November 1893, President Grover Cleveland formally ended the effort.[119]

In retrospect, conditions for an accord were not good. It is hard to imagine Gladstone's government agreeing to remonetize silver under any but the most desperate conditions, and no one else was likely to act unless the British cooperated. Nor was American diplomacy brilliant. In particular, the failure to prepare a fallback proposal in case the conference refused to consider free coinage is shocking. More broadly, hammering out any complex agreement at a large conference is extremely difficult because the process involves so many governments and diplomats. Failure is far more common than success. Usually, such forums produce agreements only if

[117] Niall Ferguson, *The House of Rothschild; The World's Banker, 1849–1999* (New York: Viking, 1999), pp. 349–51.

[118] Alfred Rothschild to his brothers, December 5, 1892, Rothschild's Archives, 000/253.

[119] Note from the Belgian Minister in London relative to the Monetary Conference, November 23, 1892, NA, MINT 12/247.

the chief participants have agreed in advance upon the outline of an accord, and the Harrison administration had done no preliminary work.[120]

The entire project smacked of desperation. The Republicans had lost control of Congress in 1890, and the GOP's chief financial initiative, the Silver Purchase Act, had clearly failed to raise the price of silver. Not only did Harrison have to fight a reelection campaign in 1892, but his wife was desperately ill, and she died in October. The Secretary of State, Blaine, was also ill, and he spent most of his waning energies on plots against Harrison. John W. Foster, an experienced diplomat, replaced Blaine in June, but he had little time in which to make an impression. The President undoubtedly hoped that the conference would yield an agreement, but the operation was a "Hail Mary."

[120] The most successful international monetary conference, that at Bretton Woods in 1944, followed this pattern. The United States and Britain dominated proceedings, and the leaders of their delegations, John Maynard Keynes and Harry Dexter White, had already devised the outline of the agreement.

CHAPTER 4

The End of Compromise

In 1893, the political equilibrium that had characterized the United States since the end of Reconstruction began to fall apart. For a generation, loyalties formed during the Civil War had determined party affiliation. Since 1874, Democrats and Republicans had been evenly balanced, with small shifts constituting the difference between victory and defeat. Both sides focused on mobilizing their own supporters and avoided issues that might divide them. The currency was just such a question, and the Sherman Silver Purchase Act represented the latest effort to neutralize it. The Panic of 1893 and the ensuing depression would render this balancing act impossible.

Alliance to Populism

In 1890, the Farmers' Alliance faced a critical decision. Over the previous decade, it had attracted more than one million committed members among farmers in the Wheat and Cotton Belts with the promise of a better life. Their enthusiasm was its chief asset, and members required a steady diet of success. Victory galvanized them, laying the foundation for new initiatives, while defeat disheartened them, creating the prospect of decay. In the 1870s and 1880s, the Grange and the Knights of Labor had both enjoyed rapid growth and wide influence only to suffer major setbacks and go into steep decline, and the Alliance seemed likely to follow a similar

W. Wells, *Financial Politics in the United States in the 1890s*,
https://doi.org/10.1007/978-3-031-86765-1_4

trajectory. Banker August Belmont opined in 1890, "Like the Knights of Labor, which are no longer of any great political importance, a few years will see its [the Alliance's] great success and subsequent decay."[1]

In 1889, the Southern Alliance experienced both defeat and victory. Its ambitious effort to organize cooperatives finally collapsed, destroying the hopes invested in this project. The Subtreasury Plan offered a new program, but its appeal was untested. At the same time, the Southern Alliance had scored a major victory over the "jute trust." Cotton farmers gathered their crop in cheap bags made of jute, and in 1888 the producers of these sacks had conspired to raise prices sharply. In response, the Alliance organized a boycott that forced producers to rescind the increase, saving members money and demonstrating the potential of collective action.

Increasingly, the Alliance pivoted to politics. The Northern Alliance had always given high priority to controlling railways, which would require government action. With the collapse of its cooperatives, the Southern Alliance embraced the Subtreasury Plan, which required federal legislation. By 1890, members of the Alliance differed not so much on political involvement as on its nature. Some wanted to organize a new party while others sought to work through the existing ones. Members of the Northern Alliance inclined to the first course, while those of the Southern Alliance favored the second.

The Northern Alliance drew on an existing network of activists who had, over the previous twenty years, played leading roles in the Greenback, Union Labor, and other third parties. They had gravitated toward the Alliance in the late 1880s largely because they considered it the country's best chance for radical reform. As historian John D. Hicks put it, "Many people joined the Alliance precisely because they expected independent political action."[2] These activists had little interest in working through the existing parties, and the existing political organizations had little interest in cooperating with them. As the Alliance moved into politics, the experience of these people was invaluable, giving them considerable influence.

Conditions in the South were quite different. As the editor of one Alliance paper wrote, "The Democratic Party at the South is something more than a mere political organization. … It is a white man's party, organized to maintain white supremacy and prevent a repetition of the

[1] August Belmont & Co. to Rothschilds Brothers, August 5, 1890, Belmont Papers, Box 23, Letterpress Books.

[2] Hicks, *The Populist Revolt*, p. 157.

destructive rule of ignorant negroes and unscrupulous Whites [during Reconstruction]. … The safety of the South … as well as the conservation of free institutions on these shores, depend upon the strength, unity, and perpetuity of the Democratic party."[3] People throughout the United States took their political affiliations quite seriously, but in most of the country, social, family, and working relationships spanned party lines. Not so in the South, where any white man who challenged the Democratic Party was a traitor to his race and an enemy of civilization.

Going into the 1890 elections, members of the Alliance agreed to disagree. The Northern Alliance supported "independent" candidates, while the Southern Alliance sought to take control of the region's Democratic Party. Members threw themselves into these campaigns, following the admonition attributed to activist Mary Lease to "raise less corn and more Hell!"[4] As one observer of the Alliance campaign in Kansas in 1890 wrote, "It was a religious revival, a crusade, a Pentecost of politics in which a tongue of flame sat upon every man."[5] Both approaches enjoyed substantial success. In the South, "Pitchfork" Ben Tillman and James Hogg, both of whom had strong support from the Alliance, won election as governors of South Carolina and Texas, respectively. Alliance candidates running as Democrats did well in Georgia and Tennessee too. In Kansas and Nebraska, independent candidates won control of at least one house of the state legislature, and independent candidates secured election to the U.S. House of Representatives in both states as well as in Minnesota. Kansas even sent a member of the Alliance, William Peffer, to the U.S. Senate.

Over the next year, members of the Alliance debated the next step. Efforts by the Southern Alliance to capture the Democratic Party and by the Northern Alliance to create a new party had both yielded gains, and much depended on the Alliance's goals. At a December 1890 meeting in Ocala, Florida, the Southern Alliance devised a program known as the "Ocala Demands," which the Northern Alliance embraced within a year. In time, it formed the basis of the Populist platform. The Ocala Demands called for (1) the abolition of national banks and the issue of fiat currency (greenbacks) through the Subtreasury Plan, (2) a ban on the trading of commodity futures, (3) free coinage of silver, (4) a ban on foreigners

[3] Quoted in Hicks, *The Populist Revolt*, p. 239.

[4] Quoted in Hicks, *The Populist Revolt*, p. 160. This quotation may be apocryphal, but it sums up the mood nicely.

[5] Quoted in Hicks, *The Populist Revolt*, p. 159.

owning land, (5) an income tax, (6) government ownership of the railways and telegraphs, and (7) popular elections of U.S. Senators.[6] This program was quite radical—only the fifth and seventh point would ever become law, though at different times some states have restricted the ability of non-citizens to purchase land. This radicalism narrowed the Alliance's options. The national Democratic and Republican parties would not embrace anything so far-reaching because doing so would alienate established interests and repel many voters. To work through them, the Alliance would have to compromise, but having committed itself to radical goals, the Alliance could not easily abandon them. The promise of thoroughgoing change motivated members, and if their enthusiasm waned, so would the Alliance. Its radical program effectively committed the Alliance to a new party, whatever the reservations among the organization's southern members.

In a series of meetings and conventions that stretched from late 1890 into early 1892, the Alliance launched the People's Party—the Populists. The organization's first formal convention, at St. Louis in February 1892, proclaimed, "A vast conspiracy against mankind has been organized on two continents and is taking possession of the world." "The fruits of the toil of millions are boldly stolen to build up colossal fortunes, unprecedented in the history of the world, while their possessors despise the republic and endanger liberty." "The old political parties have allowed the existing dreadful conditions to develop without serious efforts to restrain or prevent them." As a result, "The newspapers are subsidized or muzzled; public opinion is silenced; business prostrated, our homes covered with mortgages, labor impoverished, and the land concentrated in the hands of capitalists."[7]

The People's Party did not simply represent another face of the Alliance. Many of the latter's members refused to abandon long-held party loyalties, particularly in the South. Charles Macune, the father of both the cooperative movement and the Subtreasury, was among those who did not make the leap—though for a while he did try to play both sides.[8] In compensation for this loss, new groups not previously associated with the Alliance joined the Populists. The Knights of Labor supported the new party, though by 1892 this organization was a mere shadow of its former

[6] Hicks, *The Populist Revolt*, pp. 430–2.
[7] Quoted in Hicks, *The Populist Revolt*, pp. 435–39.
[8] Hicks, *The Populist Revolt*, p. 204.

strength. Western Silverites represented the largest accretion of support. Free coinage of silver was but one part of the Populist program, and not necessarily the most popular among party activists. Delegates at the St. Louis convention cheered the proposal to nationalize the railroads more heartily than free silver.[9] It was silver that attracted the westerners from the mountains, however—silver mining was a major industry in those states. The composition of the western contingents of the People's Party varied. In Nevada, the Silver Party, an organization that Silver Republicans controlled, doubled as the People's Party. Elsewhere Populists challenged established Republican organizations. In either case, the prospect of free silver, and in many cases that alone, motivated Populists in the Mountain West.

The People's Party had clear limits. With the important exception of silver miners, it was a movement by farmers for farmers. As one enthusiastic supporter of the new party wrote, those who tilled the soil had "a certain sturdy intelligence ... which again and again has proven the salt of the world, the reinforcing element of society, and is today the hope of our nation." He continued, "The People of the East will never understand the merit and magnitude of the present political movement, until they give the farmer credit for intelligence of a superior order."[10] The Populist platform complained that "imported, pauperized labor beats down their [workers'] wages." Ignatius Donnelly, the leader of the party in Minnesota, wrote, "The Eastern States are simply a semi-Europeanized fringe, standing between the New and the Old World. The real power of American is in the Valley of the Mississippi."[11] Such rhetoric appealed to few besides farmers, and it positively repelled immigrants and inhabitants of the Northeast. The new party made little impression in the Northeast or the Industrial Midwest (Ohio, Indiana, Michigan, Illinois, and Wisconsin).

Populism represented a political protest as much as an economic one. Historian Jeffrey Ostler, in his comparative study of the Alliance and the Populist Party in Kansas, Nebraska, and Iowa, noted that despite considerable similarities, these three states followed different political trajectories. All had strong Alliance movements, but whereas the Populists had great

[9] Hicks, *The Populist Revolt*, p. 231.

[10] R.B. Hassell, "The Independent Party and Money at Cost," *The* Arena, August 1891, pp. 344, 345, 347.

[11] Quoted in Hicks, *The Populist Revolt*, p. 436; Ignatius Donnelly, *The American People's Money* (Chicago: Laird & Lee, 1896), p. 7.

impact in Kansas and Nebraska, their influence in Iowa was small. Before the advent of the Populists, the Republicans who dominated Kansas and Nebraska had largely ignored farmers' complaints. In Iowa, however, the GOP accommodated the Alliance, most notably passing a strong measure to regulate railroads. Its actions fell well short of the Alliance's most radical demands, but members had no reason to feel disenfranchised. Ostler attributed the difference to structural factors. The Democratic Party was quite weak in Kansas and Nebraska, so Republican leaders there believed that they could ignore public opinion when it suited them. Though Iowa certainly tilted toward the GOP, it had a substantial Democratic organization. Republican leaders there understood that they ignored public opinion at their peril.[12] The same pattern held in Ohio, where "Independent" candidates made a serious effort in 1890 and 1891 but failed to elect anyone at any level. The state legislature, which Republicans controlled, had passed several measures farmers demanded, in particular tax reform that lightened the burden on agriculture. Meanwhile the state's Democrats had embraced the free coinage of silver. Farmers had no reason to think of the existing parties as indifferent to their concerns.[13]

Similar tendencies manifested in the South. The Texas Alliance was probably the country's largest, but Populists made a limited impression in the state. Governor James Hogg championed railroad regulation and other measures that appealed to farmers, and his faction of the Democratic Party fought a constant battle with more conservative elements. Existing political arrangements in the Lone Star State gave farmers a voice. The Populists did successfully contest some elections there, but they never threatened the Democrats' hold on state government. The case of South Carolina was even starker. There "Pitchfork" Ben Tillman dominated the political landscape with the enthusiastic support of the state's Alliance, and Populism in the Palmetto State was largely confined to the Black population until the new state constitution that Tillman engineered in 1895 eliminated them from public life.[14] In contrast, Democrats in Georgia and Alabama showed little interest in reform, and these states developed strong

[12] Jeffrey Ostler, *Prairie Populism*.

[13] Michael Pierce, *Farmers and the Failure of Populism in Ohio, 1890–1891*, *Agricultural History* 74 (2000), pp. 58–85.

[14] Omar H. Ali, "Standing Guard at the Door of Liberty: Black Populism in South Carolina, 1886–1895," *South Carolina Historical Magazine* 107 (2006): 190–203. The situation in the Palmetto State allowed Ben Tillman to combine his two passions: hatred of Blacks and hatred of the old planter elite.

Populist movements. In North Carolina, disgust with the chronic electoral fraud perpetrated by Democrats motivated its formidable Populist organization.[15] Other factors, most notably leadership, played a role as well. Kansas had an extraordinarily large number of capable Populist agitators, and Georgia Populism owed much to the fiery Tom Watson. For the most part, however, Populism thrived where the existing political parties had ignored the grievances of farmers and failed to take root where they had responded.

As the Populists waxed, the Alliance waned. Both depended on the enthusiasm of members, to whom they held out the prospect of radical change through collective action. Both demanded much of adherents, and few individuals could make such a commitment to two separate organizations. After 1892, the Alliance decayed rapidly as its most enthusiastic supporters migrated to the People's Party.

The Silverites' Dilemma

Many Silverites believed that, with the election of a new Congress in 1890, their hour had come. The Democrats had a huge majority in the House of Representatives, and most of them favored free coinage. In the Senate, Silver Republicans and Democrats favorable to silver had a majority. When the new Congress met in early 1892, Representative Richard Bland introduced a bill authorizing free coinage, confident of success.

Instead, the Silverites suffered defeat. Grover Cleveland seemed poised to capture the 1892 Democratic presidential nomination, and his position on the matter was clear. In 1891, he wrote, "The greatest peril would be initiated by the adoption of the scheme embraced in the measure now pending in Congress for the unlimited coinage of silver."[16] He adhered to this line in 1892, even though it put him at odds with powerful elements in his own party. Cleveland groused to a friend, "Congress will do about all the fool things it can, nearly as quite (as far as they can) committing the party to the silver craze."[17] In another letter he wrote, "If the Democratic

[15] James Beeby, "'Equal Rights for All and Special Privileges for None: Grass-Roots Populism in North Carolina," *North Carolina Historical Review* 78 (2001): 156–86.

[16] Cleveland to Ellery Anderson, February 10, 1891, Grover Cleveland, *The Letters of Grover Cleveland,* Allan Nevins, ed. (New York: Houghton Mifflin Company, 1933), p 246. Cleveland intended this letter for publication.

[17] Cleveland to William S. Bissell, March 1, 1891, *Letters of Grover Cleveland*, p. 279.

House of Representatives permits a free silver bill to go to Mr. Harrison for his veto, those responsible for it will in my opinion stand a chance to gain the same splendid notoriety as the man who burned the temple of Diana."[18] For Cleveland, the gold standard was a matter of principle, and he could not imagine that anyone had a legitimate grievance against it.

More calculating politicians had doubts too. Ever since the Civil War, Democrats had assumed that they could not win the presidency without carrying New York, and indeed the elections of 1880, 1884, and 1888 had all turned on the Empire State. Most New Yorkers supported the gold standard. They had a sophisticated banking system, ample currency and credit, and close commercial and financial ties with Europe. Many Democrats—even some sympathetic to free silver—believed that President Harrison's best chance to carry New York and secure reelection was for Democrats in Congress to pass a free silver bill that he could then veto. As the editor of *The Nation* wrote, "Certain members of Congress are under the necessity of stirring around and making a show of activity for silver—all this for home consumption—but … the Democratic party is not going to disembowel itself at the beginning of a presidential campaign."[19]

The matter played out as *The Nation* predicted. As *The Economist* noted, "The result of the first engagement between the silver and anti-free-silver men in the House of Representatives is a surprise to the country at large, including those directly engaged in the encounter."[20] Except for those from the West, Republicans solidly opposed Bland's bill, and Democrats proved less enthusiastic than expected. A motion to table the bill, effectively killing it, failed by a single vote—and that only because the Speaker took the unusual step of voting himself. The closeness of the vote stunned and demoralized Silverites, and soon thereafter a reconsideration of the motion to table the bill carried.[21] As a prominent Silverite complained, "Enough [votes] were found to postpone the question, in the interest of some presidential candidate [Cleveland]; to make it easy for some man to carry New York."[22]

[18] Cleveland to Michael D. Harter, July 7, 1892, *Letters of Grover Cleveland*, p. 291.

[19] *The Nation*, February 11, 1892, p. 103.

[20] *The Economist*, April 9, 1892, p. 484.

[21] *Harper's Weekly*, April 9, 1892, p. 340. There was a dispute over the tally of votes in the first motion to table the silver bill, and a second counting resulted in its defeat.

[22] *Second National Silver Convention*, p. 33.

By this time, President Harrison had clarified his position. He had never supported the free coinage of silver outside an international agreement, but neither had he wanted to antagonize Silver Republicans if he could avoid it. For a long time, he avoided saying anything definitive on the matter. In the spring of 1891, however, he stated in a public letter, "When any issue of paper or coined dollar is, in buying or selling, rated as less than other paper or coined dollars, we have passed the limit of safe experimentation. If we have dollars of different value, only the poorest will circulate. The farmers and laborers who are not in hourly touch with the ticker and the telegraph will require, above all other classes in our community, a dollar of full value. Fluctuations and devaluations are always at the first cost of these classes in our community." Harrison then sifted focus, insisting, "Nothing, in my judgment, would so much retard the restoration of the free use of silver by the commercial nations of the world as legislation adopted by us that would result in placing this country upon a basis of silver monometallism."[23] If the United States embraced free silver, other countries would stand aside to see what happened, or worse, dump their silver in this country. Harrison was not as clear and forthright as Cleveland, in part because his views on the currency were less dogmatic, but no one who read this statement could imagine that he favored unilateral free coinage.

This was the situation that Silverites faced when the Second National Silver Convention met in Washington, D.C., in May 1892. The leaders of the two major parties opposed free coinage, and party loyalty had stymied legislation in Congress. Silverites had also begun to recognize the limits of their movement's appeal. One speaker at the convention noted sourly, "I find New York and New England virtually joining in the schemes of commercial freebooters ... led by British astuteness and avarice."[24] Addresses at and letters to this convention focused almost solely on the impact of the gold standard on farmers of wheat and cotton. As one speaker remarked, "Free coinage is a measure for the prevention of the evils—overwhelming and destructive—of Asiatic competition in the production and sale of our greatest American staple products—our wheat, cotton, oil [cotton] seeds, and other products—a grievance primarily to farmers and planters."[25] This

[23] Message of President Harrison to the Western States Commercial Convention, April 7, 1891, American Presidency Project, UCSB.

[24] *Second Silver Convention*, p. 228.

[25] *Second Silver Convention*, p. 213.

statement reflected a solid understanding of links between the value of silver, exchange rates, and commodity prices, but it ignored those who did not grow cotton or wheat.

Most of those at this convention still hoped to secure action through one or both of the major parties. The Chairman of the Convention, A.J. Warner, stated, "We propose to say to the [Republican] convention that is to meet in Minneapolis and the [Democratic] convention that is to meet in Chicago, 'Gentlemen, you shall not evade this great question.'"[26] Several others voiced comparable sentiments. Senator Stewart, however, warned the gathering, "The gold ring … proposed to run two men [Harrison and Cleveland] of the same principle and belonging to the same gold party, and occupy the attention of the people with discussing non-essentials."[27]

The Populists offered an alternative. As one speaker at the convention said, "We can still go to [the Populist convention in] Omaha, and there find a party that will not ask, 'Please, Madam Europe, what can we do on the currency question?'" The Populists, however, had embraced free coinage as an afterthought, preferring the issue of greenbacks through the Subtreasury or some other device. In an almost condescending address to the convention, Representative Jerry Simpson (P-KA) made it clear that he considered free silver a second-best solution to the country's financial problems. Senator William Peffer (P-KA) was more encouraging, urging Silverites, "Come to us at Omaha with your party manacles off your limbs." Still, he made it clear that Silverites would have to embrace Populism, "Don't ask us to compromise our principles," he said, "we are not built that way."[28]

Ultimately the Silver Convention fell back on a program of education and agitation. A.J. Warner insisted, "The surest road to the re-establishment of bimetallic coinage in the United States … [is] a purely educational work, through public discussion and by the publication and distribution of sound literature on the question, and by enlisting the support of as many of those interests in the cause as possible."[29] Since the 1889 Silver

[26] *Second Silver Convention*, p. 35.

[27] *Second Silver Convention*, p. 61.

[28] *Second Silver Convention*, pp. 269–70. Ironically, both Simpson and Peffer would be among those Populists who, in 1896, urged the party to embrace free coinage of silver and abandon the Subtreasury Plan and other, more radical aspects of the Populist program.

[29] *Second Silver Convention*, p. 279.

Convention, Warner had managed such a campaign almost single-handedly, but by 1892, he realized that more was necessary.[30] Warner proposed, and the Convention accepted, a Bimetallic League "to educate the people and organize a movement throughout the country for the restoration of … free bimetallic currency."[31] Warner would lead the new organization, which would have a full-time staff, and members would pay a subscription fee to defray its expenses. Over the next four years, the Bimetallic League would play a major role promoting free silver, providing a forum through which Silverites of different political stripes could coordinate their activities. Though Silverites agreed with the Populists' critique of American society in many ways, they were not ready to abandon the major parties.

The Election of 1892

As the Populists coalesced and Silverites debated their course, the two major parties settled into a temporary stasis. The crushing Democratic victory in the 1890 elections had robbed the Republicans not only of their majority in the House of Representatives but of any claim to a popular mandate. The GOP still controlled the Senate and White House, however, so the Democrats could not initiate change. Bland's free silver bill, introduced and tabled in 1892, was the proverbial exception that proved the rule. The political world fixed its gaze on the 1892 elections, which most observers assumed would see a rematch between Benjamin Harrison and Grover Cleveland.

Neither man lacked for critics in his own party. Senators Quay and Platt detested the President, Speaker Reed cordially disliked him, and Secretary of State Blaine considered himself Harrison's superior. As a sitting President, however, Harrison allocated patronage, which gave him power over the party organization throughout much of the country. Such was particularly true in the South, where in most states the GOP was quite weak and federal office-holders had considerable clout. Nor did Harrison's enemies have a candidate. Blaine did challenge him at the 1892 convention, but his health was poor, and most knew it—Blaine died in early 1893. Unhappiness with Harrison drove the Silver Republicans to support

[30] *Second Silver Convention*, p. 281.

[31] *Second Silver Convention*, p. 3.

Blaine, but outside the Mountain West, their numbers were not great. The popular William McKinley might have posed a threat. He had rebounded from his failure to win reelection to the House in 1890 by capturing the governor's mansion in his native Ohio in 1891. McKinley had no desire to challenge Harrison, however, and he no doubt recognized that his party's chances in 1892 were not good. He might well have entered the fray had the convention deadlocked, but for the time being, he kept his distance. Nevertheless, he received as many votes at the convention as Blaine, who actively sought the nomination.[32] Yet most Republicans, even those not enamored of Harrison, concluded that they had little choice but to nominate him. The electorate had punished the GOP in 1890 not because voters disliked Harrison per se but because they were skeptical of the Silver Purchase Act, heavy spending on pensions, and particularly, the McKinley Tariff. The entire party had supported this program, and with the important exception of the Silver Purchase Act—about which Harrison and many others in the GOP had developed doubts—Republicans remained committed to it. Abandoning Harrison would smack of desperation. Ironically, Harrison himself was not at first sure that he wanted to stand for reelection, but the machinations of his opponents within the party convinced him that he had to, if only to defend his good name.

Grover Cleveland too had plenty of critics. David Hill, governor of and soon to be senator from New York, hated the former president. Hill had close ties to Tammany Hall, and Cleveland had never bothered to conceal his opinion that Hill was a corrupt hack. Hill may well have been corrupt, but he was a gifted politician and a formidable enemy. Southern Democrats with ties to the Alliance, like Tillman and Hogg, considered Cleveland an ally of the conservative "bourbon" Democrats who were their rivals in state politics. Nevertheless Cleveland, like Harrison, seemed inevitable. The party had won the 1890 elections by attacking the McKinley tariff and heavy government spending, and Cleveland was the Democrats' leading champion of frugal government and tariff reduction. His appeal had always rested on his rocklike integrity in public affairs, and he had brought the tariff issue to the forefront. Cleveland also had the aura of success. He was the only Democrat to win the Presidency since before the Civil War. As one of his supporters put it, "The [Democratic] party ever since the

[32] J.S. Clarkson to Matthew Quay, April 27, 1982, Quay Papers, Box 3, Library of Congress.

war has been on the hunt for a herd of swine to run into and go with into the sea. It was lifted up by Mr. Cleveland, put on ideal ground, infused with sentiment, transfixed by that arrow of truth which is the cannon law of unselfishness."[33] Though overblown, this statement accurately described Cleveland's position within his party. The Democratic Party was an alliance of former Confederates, northern Copperheads (anti-war activists), and Irish immigrants defined more by opposition to the Republicans than by any principles of its own. Even after disenfranchising Blacks in the South, it fell short of a majority. Its history meant that even those disenchanted with the GOP often felt they had no choice but to vote Republican. Cleveland brought with him a respectability that represented the margin between victory and defeat. He was not typical of his party—that was the point. He was a Democrat because he was a "classical liberal" who firmly believed in minimal government—a stance most other Democrats embraced chiefly because it offered a common rationale for their opposition to Republican initiatives ranging from civil rights to prohibition. Cleveland was a bridge to middle- and upper-class supporters of "good government," by which they meant frugal, honest management, who were unhappy with the Republicans but skeptical of the Democrats. In 1884, Cleveland had received J.P. Morgan's vote for president, the only Democrat so honored in the banker's long life. As one delegate from South Carolina to the National Democratic Convention stated, "I believe Cleveland ... would control the greatest number of the independent votes of the North and East and he is the best candidate that can be put forward by the Democratic Party."[34] Though in some ways out of step with his followers, Cleveland was in 1892, "the choice of seven-tenths of the Democrats of the whole country."[35]

Cleveland made sure his party did not embrace free silver. In 1891 and again in 1892, he reaffirmed his commitment to "sound currency," and before the convention he insisted that the platform "must be sound—especially in the money plank."[36] Democratic Silverites had a stark choice—turn against the likely nominee and the party's best chance to carry the White House or remain silent. Cleveland did give a little on the platform,

[33] George Irish to Manton Marable, March 1, 1892, Marable Papers, volume 76.

[34] *New York Times*, May 23, 1892, p. 9.

[35] George Irish to Manton Marable, March 1, 1892.

[36] Cleveland to William Bissell, June 11, 1892, *Letters of Grover Cleveland*, p. 287.

but not too much. The final draft condemned "the Sherman [Silver Purchase] Act of 1890 as a cowardly makeshift," calling for "its speedy repeal." More broadly, the platform called for "the coinage of both gold and silver without discriminating against either metal ... but the dollar unit of coinage for both metals must be of equal intrinsic and exchangeable value, or be adjusted through international agreement or by such safeguards of legislation as shall insure the maintenance of the parity of the two metals and the equal power of every dollar at all times in the markets and in payment of debts; and we demand that all paper currency be kept at par with and redeemable in such coin."[37] This statement was a masterpiece of obfuscation—it called for the free coinage of silver but then insisted on keeping silver at par with gold, which was impossible under free coinage. The platform did, however, allow those on both sides of the silver issue to claim its support. It also called for the repeal of the 10 percent tax on notes issued by state banks, enacted during the Civil War, that had driven such paper from circulation. This proposal opened up the prospect of increasing the supply of currency through banks without abandoning the gold standard. Along with repeal of the Silver Purchase Act, it might have formed the basis of a coherent program, but the question of gold and silver coinage commanded most of the public's attention.

Harrison approached the issue more cautiously than Cleveland, but his position was nevertheless clear. Issues of paper and silver coins were acceptable only as long as the government could maintain their value in gold. Free coinage was acceptable only as part of an international agreement. In these opinions, Harrison was in tune with most Republicans, with the important exception of Silver Republicans from the West. The party's platform called for "the use of both gold and silver standard money, with such restrictions and under such provisions, to be determined by legislation, as will secure ... the parity of value of the two metals so that the purchasing and debt-paying power of the dollar, whether of silver, gold, or paper, shall be at all times equal." It also endorsed "the wise and patriotic steps already taken by our government to secure an international conference, to adopt such measures as will insure a parity of value between gold and silver for use as money throughout the world."[38] Though hardly a model of clarity, this language did suggest a consistent policy, maintaining the gold

[37] 1892 Democratic Platform, American Presidency Project, UCSB.
[38] 1892 Republican Platform, American Presidency Project, UCSB.

standard while continuing limited silver coinage. Meanwhile, the Brussels Conference held out the hope of remonetizing silver through an international agreement.

This position did not satisfy the party's Silverites. In April their leader, Senator Teller, said on the floor of the Senate, "We have local issues which are paramount. We supported the McKinley [tariff] bill, not because it was in our interest to do so—for we are not manufacturing states, and if manufactured goods can be had cheaper, it is better for us—but because we believed the prosperity of the whole nation was bound up in the protective system. ... We make no threats, but we cannot continue to insist upon government by a party hostile to every local interest we have." "If the Republican party stands for the gold standard the four silver producing states of Colorado, Montana, Nevada, and Idaho will not hereafter be able to act in cooperation with the Republicans in this or any other body."[39] Despite such complaints, most Silver Republicans remained loyal in 1892. Cleveland was even less flexible on the currency than Harrison, and the new People's Party was an uncertain experiment. Nevada was the exception. There, Silver Republicans had organized the Silver Party, which dominated the state government and, in 1892, supported the Populists. Elsewhere, the GOP held firm. Free coinage nevertheless remained the chief issue in the Mountain States, and Teller's criticism of the administration and the rest of his party had an impact. Republican operatives warned Harrison that the matter was "being effectively used against you in all the silver-producing states, and in Nebraska and Kansas."[40] Teller did take the stump in Colorado against Cleveland, but it was hard to him to retract his own words. After the fact, one Republican supporter complained, "[T]he Republicans would have carried Colorado but for the eight months of abuse of President Harrison by Senators [Edward] Wolcott [R-CO] and Teller."[41] This statement probably exaggerates Teller's and Wolcott's impact, but they certainly did not help.

The Populists provided the contest's chief drama. Neither Cleveland nor Harrison campaigned actively. Harrison's wife was on her deathbed, and he later wrote, "I was so removed from the campaign that I can scarcely realize that I was a candidate."[42] Cleveland was more active, but

[39] *Rock Island Daily Argus*, April 21, 1892, p. 1.

[40] John Michael to Benjamin Harrison, September 26, 1892, Harrison Papers, reel 37.

[41] S.V. Leech to Benjamin Harrison, November 11, 1982, Harrison Papers, reel 37.

[42] Harrison to W.O. Bradley, Nov. 16, 1892, Harrison Papers, reel 37.

he operated through surrogates, allowing them substantial leeway. The Populist candidate, James Weaver, did pursue an active campaign, speaking extensively, particularly in the Cotton and Wheat Belts. A veteran of the Civil War, he was also a veteran of third-party politics who had served in the U.S. Congress as a member of the Greenback Party and had run as its presidential candidate in 1880. A level-headed man of conservative habits—prohibition was one of his causes—Weaver reassured many put off by the Populists' radicalism. The new party generated considerable enthusiasm but also strong resistance. In the South, Democrats used fraud and intimidation against Populists just as they had against Republicans. Nor did it help among southerners that Weaver was a veteran of the Union Army. Many Alliance men, particularly in the South but also in the West, refused to abandon their traditional loyalties. On the other hand, the new party received an enthusiastic reception in the mountains of the far west, particularly in those states that produced silver, where the Alliance had had little presence. In Nevada, Silver Republicans controlled the People's Party, but elsewhere it challenged the dominant GOP, including established champions of silver like Senator Teller.

Everywhere, Populists faced the question of fusion—alliance with an existing party. In the South, the Republicans were weak, and the same was true of the Democrats in the Wheat Belt and the mountains of the far west. At the same time, in both areas these parties had voters and organizations that could well tip the scales in favor of the People's Party. Each side was wary of fusion, however. They differed on important issues, and each feared that the other would swallow it. The national Democratic Party urged cooperation in the West, even if doing so allowed Weaver to carry states. Democratic leaders apparently calculated that, in a close election, Populist victories in traditional Republicans strongholds could throw the election into the House of Representatives, where the Democrats had a large majority. Each state had its own story, but cooperation between Democrats and Populists helped the latter win a tight contest in Kansas and to win one elector in North Dakota (the Democrats and Republicans each carried one elector there as well).

In the South, fusion entailed even greater complications because it meant working with the African-Americans who constituted the large majority of GOP voters. If victorious, it meant governing with them. Democrats denounced any such arrangement in apocalyptic terms, playing on the racial fears of Whites, and no one doubted that they would use fraud and intimidation to defeat such a coalition. These calculations, as well as their own commitment to white supremacy, led most southern Populists to eschew fusion for the moment. This decision did not insulate the People's Party from Democratic race-baiting and, worse, fraud and intimidation. In his southern tour, Weaver was, as one historian described it, beset by "howling mobs, brass bands, [and] hoodlums with rocks and eggs." According to one Populist, Weaver "was made a regular walking omelet by the southern chivalry of Georgia."[43] Fraud almost certainly cost the People's Party victories in Alabama's gubernatorial election and at least one House contest in Georgia, and it may have been decisive elsewhere.

Overall, Grover Cleveland and the Democrats won an impressive victory. Cleveland carried not only the "Solid South" and traditional "swing states" such as Indiana, New Jersey, Connecticut, and New York, but also Illinois, Wisconsin, and California, which no Democrat had won since the Civil War. He came close in the GOP strongholds of Ohio and Michigan as well. His party lost a little ground in the House of Representatives, but it retained a very large majority there, and the Democrats won a narrow majority in the U.S. Senate for the first time since the Civil War. Cleveland would take office in a stronger position than any president since Ulysses S. Grant twenty years before.

The Populists had reason to be pleased too. Weaver carried Kansas, Colorado, Nevada, and Idaho, and he polled almost 10 percent of the vote nationwide. With a fair count in the South, he probably would have crossed that threshold. The party also elected eleven representatives, increased its number of senators to three, and carried the governor's mansions in Colorado and Kansas. This performance concealed two major weaknesses, however. First, the new party made little impression in any state east of the Mississippi River and north of the Ohio and Potomac rivers, the richest and most densely populated part of the Union. Even among the many farmers of the Industrial Midwest, its following was not large. They carried smaller debts than their brethren in the Wheat and Cotton Belts, had better access to credit, and depended less upon export markets. Second, the Populists were the only party to embrace silver in 1892. This factor accounted for their victories in the Mountain States and certainly contributed to their success in Kansas. Should one of the major parties take up the cause of free coinage, Silverites might well defect.

[43] Quoted in Hicks, *The Populist Revolt*, p. 244.

In defeat, President Harrison seemed almost relieved. As he wrote a friend, "My own family troubles were such that it was not possible for the election results to disturb me much." During the election, "I was a leader in prison." The outgoing President also recognized, "Our successful opponents face great difficulties" that (he implied) he lacked the personal energy and political strength to manage.[44] Harrison was one of the few residents of the White House genuinely happy to leave it.

The Panic of 1893

In 1893, a disastrous financial panic swept across the United States, initiating a severe depression. In part, it reflected the regular ebb and flow of capitalism. The country had enjoyed a long period of prosperity during which many individuals and enterprises had overextended themselves, borrowing to finance risky projects. Since 1890, Europe had suffered from a recession that had reduced demand for American exports. Any significant economic setback could well set off a chain of bankruptcies among overextended businesses or those who relied on foreign markets, like the farmers of cotton and wheat.

Two factors converted a difficult situation into a catastrophic one. First, the American financial position was unstable. The United States faced a large deficit on its balance of payments. Throughout the 1880s, the country had spent more abroad on goods and services and to service debt than it had earned—roughly $150 to $200 million a year. Foreign investment had covered the shortfall. Put simply, British subjects and other Europeans had enough confidence in the long-term prospects of the United States to finance its short-term debts. The Baring's Crisis had largely halted this inflow of money. The combination of a poor grain crop in Europe in 1891 with a bumper one in the United States had allowed the country to balance its current account for a time by exporting more wheat at higher prices. By the end of 1892, however, European agriculture had recovered, while in the U.S., a poor cotton crop reduced exports of the South's staple from $291 million in 1891 to $258 million the next year and $189 million in 1893. By December 1892, the balance of payments had returned to deficit, and to cover the shortfall, Americans had to export gold. Over the course of 1893, the country would export about $88 million of it. Even

[44] Harrison to W.O. Bradley, November 16, 1892.

taking into account the substantial American production of gold, the country's supply of it declined by $60 million between late 1892 and June 1893.[45] Historian Jonathan Levy claims, "The cause of the Panic of 1893 was nothing other than the normal operation of the international gold standard."[46] Other factors were at work too, but the drain of gold was critical.

The problem initially manifested through the banking system. Both law and prudence required that banks keep cash reserves against deposits. Gold played a central part in international trade and finance, so it was a key part of banks' reserves—particularly in New York City, the country's financial capital. As gold flowed out, these institutions had to restrict credit. Because $1 in reserves might support $4 of deposits, the loss of $1 in gold usually contracted credit substantially more than $1. Unlike during the Baring Crisis in 1890, the Treasury could not intervene. Higher spending and lower tax revenue had converted the large surpluses of the late 1880s into deficits. Washington enjoyed a surplus of only $2 million for fiscal 1893 (which ended on June 30 of that year) and suffered a hefty $62 million deficit in the following fiscal year. In and of themselves, these shortfalls were manageable. The sums involved were less than half of one percent of total output, and investors were willing to lend to the U.S. government at the relatively low rate of 3–4 percent. Unfortunately, the Treasury also played a key monetary role, acting as the lender of last resort during the harvest or a financial crisis. It accumulated funds during good times and, when trouble developed, made the money available. As the editor of *The Nation* put it, "The Treasury has become the United States Bank. … What is done in this behalf by the Bank of England and the Bank of France in those countries respectively is done here by the Treasury Department."[47] By the end of 1892, the U.S. Treasury had no surplus funds. Indeed, as the demand for gold to cover foreign obligations grew, merchants and bankers exchanged greenbacks and Treasury bills for gold, further draining government coffers. Instead of being able to release cash as financial pressure increased, Washington had to join the scramble for gold.

[45] *The Economist*, June 3, 1893, p. 656.

[46] Jonathan Levy, *Ages of American Capitalism: A History of the United States* (New York: Random House, 2021), p. 310.

[47] *The Nation*, April 27, 1893, p. 306.

The Sherman Silver Purchase Act exacerbated the problem. It required the government to buy 4.5 million ounces of silver a month with Treasury notes. These were legal tender that holders could convert into gold on demand. Between 1878 and 1890, Washington had issued over $2 million silver dollars and certificates each month under the Bland-Allison Act without ill effect. Holders could not convert their silver directly into gold, but the money was legal tender and, as a practical matter, was interchangeable with gold. The Silver Purchase Act substantially increased the amount of money the government issued (the exact sum varied with the price of silver). These notes were government obligations, though they did not appear in calculations of the deficit. Had the population used these bills in the ordinary course of business, as had been the case with money coined under Bland-Allison, their creation would have entailed no problem. Unfortunately, the larger sum issued under the Silver Purchase Act was more than the country could readily digest. Under a regime of fiat currency, excess money translates into inflation as people use it to bid up the price of goods. Under the gold standard, people exchange extra currency for gold, which will presumably hold its value come what may. Treasury notes piled up in banks, and importers used them to pay tariffs while those with foreign obligations converted them into gold with which to pay these debts. Had the government still been running a large surplus, it probably could have managed the situation. The notes would have accumulated in the Treasury, effectively removing them from circulation. Without a surplus, however, Washington had to spend all the money it received, so the government redeemed Treasury notes in gold, then reissued them to pay its obligations, and the notes subsequently returned to the government, drawing out more gold. As President Cleveland wrote, "We have an endless chain in operation constantly depleting the Treasury's gold."[48]

The Treasury provided the ultimate guarantee of the gold standard. As long as it could convert greenbacks and Treasury notes into gold on demand, the dollar was "as good as gold." If the Treasury ran out of gold, paper money—greenbacks, national banknotes, Treasury notes—would cease to have value in gold. Since the gold standard fixed the value of the dollar against other currencies, its collapse would, in effect, devalue the dollar, imposing substantial losses on foreigners who had invested in the

[48] Grover Cleveland, *State of the Union Address*, December 3, 1894, Presidency Project, UCSB.

United States. Doubts about the future of the gold standard both discouraged new investment by foreigners and encouraged those who already held American securities to sell. The prominent banker James Stillman wrote, "Few people have any idea of the amount of property of every description in this country that is owned by foreigners,"[49] and should these investors all rush to sell at once, the results would be catastrophic. The United States also financed most of its foreign trade and some domestic transactions through London. If bankers there refused to extend credit to Americans, commerce could grind to a halt. Fortunately, no such panic materialized, but uncertainty about the future created a constant drain of capital. Abandoning the gold standard promised trouble at home too. As the American correspondent for *The Economist* noted in 1891, "Contracts have already begun to appear here, in which 'the gold clause' is inserted," requiring repayment in gold or its equivalent.[50] Companies increasingly found it necessary to guarantee payment of their bonds in gold as well. As long as the dollar was "as good as gold," such provisions mattered little, but if the currency depreciated against gold, all such obligations would increase proportionally, threatening otherwise solvent individuals and enterprises with bankruptcy. For these reasons, people watched the country's gold reserve closely.

The financial weakness of many railroads represented a second threat to American prosperity. These were the nation's largest companies by far, and railroad securities held abroad accounted for the largest part of the foreign capital invested in the U.S. These organizations not only dominated transportation but were the country's largest consumers of steel and machinery and sponsored huge construction projects. Unfortunately, changes in the industry during the 1880s had left many railroads in precarious financial condition. Since they had first appeared in the 1840s, these companies had concentrated on a specific region that they dominated or "drained," in the clumsy terminology of the industry. These organizations happily accepted through traffic—freight that neither originated nor terminated with them—but managers assumed that earnings depended on business associated with their own region. Building and organizing a new railroad was a huge challenge in and of itself, and few promoters or managers had the time or energy to devote to the issue of through traffic, which seemed

[49] James Stillman to William Curtis, July 31, 1894, Cleveland Papers, reel 86.
[50] *The Economist*, January 31, 1891, p. 144.

secondary. Even the first transcontinental line consisted of two separate companies, the Central Pacific and the Union Pacific (UP), which exchanged traffic in Utah.

As the American economy became more integrated, through traffic became more important. In the 1870s, railroads carried livestock from farm to city, and the distances were often relatively short. By the late 1880s, railroads were carrying livestock from all over the west to Chicago, and meat from Chicago's packing plants went in refrigerated rail cars to cities throughout the country. Most of this freight qualified as through traffic. The same was true of the consumer goods distributed by large companies, and much more. Rates on through traffic were lower than on local shipments, but so were expenses—through traffic required neither loading nor unloading—and this business increasingly represented the difference between profit and loss. As long as connecting roads passed on through traffic, dividing it equally among competing lines, most railroad managers were content. Taking control of or building new connections to control such traffic was expensive and risky. If, however, a rival bought a connecting road and, with it, the through traffic it carried, a railroad had to respond. Few could afford to lose this business.

Jay Gould did more than anyone else to set change into motion. A speculator notorious for insider dealing, Gould was also a strategic genius who assembled railroad systems to capture through traffic, creating organizations whose value would, he hoped, exceed the sum of their parts. In the late 1860s, his operations had forced the Pennsylvania and New York Central railways to buy control of the lines linking them to Detroit, St. Louis, and most important, Chicago, the nation's emerging rail hub. They purchased the lines to prevent Gould from doing so and channeling these lines' through traffic over the Erie Railroad, which he controlled. During the long depression of the 1870s, Gould focused on rehabilitating the troubled Union Pacific even while lining his own pockets at its expense. In the 1880s, however, he sold his UP holdings and returned to his former tactics, buying and selling railroads to control through traffic, particularly in the West, where such shipments constituted a larger portion of shipments. Gould's schemes failed at least as often as they succeeded, but competitors could not ignore them. A significant amount of railroad construction in the 1880s sought not to accommodate growing shipments but to establish links for through traffic even if that meant duplicating existing tracks. The process became known as "system building." The Burlington, which connected Chicago to the Union Pacific's terminal at

Council Bluffs on the Missouri River, had to respond to the UP's efforts to secure its own connection to Chicago. The Burlington built and bought lines through Nebraska, Kansas, and Colorado to Denver, where it could exchange traffic with another railroad tied to the Central Pacific. It also established a link to Minneapolis, where it connected with the Northern Pacific and the Great Northern, both of which eventually ran to the Pacific. System-building was often a zero-sum game, with the success of one road coming at the expense of another. Indeed, it could become a negative-sum game, with competing roads building two lines where there was only enough traffic to support one, doubling expenses without increasing revenue. The railroads would then make the situation worse by bidding against each other for what traffic there was, driving rates down. During the 1880s, rates on through traffic fell sharply throughout the country.[51]

Successful system-building required strategic vision, disciplined management, and good luck. The process also required capital, which the railroads acquired by borrowing both at home and abroad, and the revenue from new lines had to cover the interest on these debts as well as operating expenses. The leaders of the Great Northern, Burlington, Illinois Central, and Louisville & Nashville all proved equal to the task, as had those of the Pennsylvania and New York Central in the 1870s. Their systems were indeed more valuable than the sum of their parts. Failure was at least as common as success, however. In the West, the Union Pacific, Northern Pacific, and Atchison, Topeka, and Santa Fe were all overextended by 1890, and in the East, the same was true of the Richmond Terminal, Baltimore & Ohio (B&O), Reading, and Erie. Often, corruption exacerbated the problem—the Richmond Terminal was notorious for insider dealing, and the accounts of the Atchison, Topeka, and Santa Fe concealed significant malfeasance. By 1890 these organizations had more debt than they could manage, and an ugly reckoning loomed.

The crisis developed slowly. The drain of gold that began in December 1892 continued month after month, bringing with it a gradual but relentless tightening of credit. As credit became tighter, business activity contracted. Over 2800 merchants with liabilities of $33 million defaulted in the last quarter of 1892—a substantial increase over previous months. In the first quarter of 1893, the number jumped to 3200 with over $47

[51] Chandler, *The Visible Hand*, pp. 159–170. For a more thorough account, see Julius Grodinsky, *Transcontinental Railway Strategy, 1869–1893: A Study of Businessmen* (Philadelphia: University of Pennsylvania Press, 1962).

million in debts.[52] Unstable firms—those with more debt than they could readily manage—went first, but most commercial enterprises are both creditor and debtor. Each bankruptcy affected others, transferring the problems of the weak to the strong.

Credit markets took another blow in late February when the Reading Railroad went into receivership. Its chief business was carrying coal from mines in Pennsylvania to the cities and factories of the Northeast. The company had suffered significant reverses in the early 1880s, but between 1886 and 1888, J.P. Morgan led group of bankers who reorganized it, putting the road on a sound footing. Unfortunately, new management had taken control of the Reading in 1890 and had launched an ill-considered program of system-building. The company owned several unprofitable coal mines, and the new leadership decided to resolve the problem by purchasing more mines, along with connecting roads. They hoped to create a monopoly that would allow them to raise the price of coal. At about the same time, the road expanded into New England with the idea of controlling the distribution of coal there, buying several local railroads. Borrowing financed both investments, and neither yielded a profit. By early 1893, the Reading had about $10 million in short-term debts coming due that it lacked the money to pay. It tried to sell long-term bonds to cover the obligation, but J.P. Morgan & Co. not only refused to handle the issue but began to sell its own holding in the company, which encouraged others to do the same. The Reading's expansion into New England had challenged the New York Central, a client far more important to Morgan than the Reading, and Morgan was undoubtedly miffed that the Reading had abandoned the safe course that he had marked out for it just a few years earlier. In any case, his refusal to involve himself doomed the issue, and the Reading defaulted on its debts and filed for receivership.[53]

In and of itself, the Reading's default was not catastrophic. Its failure dragged few others into bankruptcy. Many British investors held Reading securities, however, and they were furious. Until the very end, the Reading's management had concealed the size of its debts and the scale of its losses, even borrowing to pay dividends. *The Economist* pointed with irritation to, "Philadelphia and Reading income mortgages, the deeds of

[52] W. Jett Lauck, *The Causes of the Panic of 1893* (Boston & New York: Houghton, Mifflin and Company, 1907), p. 105.

[53] Stuart Daggett, *Railroad Reorganization* (New York: August Kelly, 1967), pp. 120–7.

which were supposed to be 'very carefully draw.' Yet the directors in one year found it possible to take the income to which the bonds were entitled and devote it … to the purchase of four new collieries."[54] Its default raised questions about whether even "sound" American securities were safe, encouraging further selling. *The Economist* opined, "Investors in this country [Britain] should entirely leave alone all contingent American railway securities [equities or stock]."[55] Another blow came from Australia, where a severe financial crisis had forced most of the continent's banks to suspend payment. These defaults imposed new strains on the London money market and further soured its investors on foreign commitments. As August Belmont wrote Lord Nathaniel Rothschild, "The collapse of the Australian banks and the consequent nervousness resulting in London added to our difficulties."[56] Calculations at the time suggested that, on balance, foreign investors disposed of $100 million worth of American securities between July 1892 and June 1893.[57]

The Harrison administration sought to delay the reckoning until it was safely out of office. Its motives were cynical—it hoped to cast the blame for any disaster on its successor—but its leaders also realized that they lacked the political strength for decisive action. It did explore the possibility of purchasing gold with bonds to replenish the dwindling Treasury reserve. The 1875 Act that had returned the United States to the gold standard authorized such sales. The administration managed to avoid this contingency. In late February, Treasury Secretary Foster persuaded New York banks to exchange $8 million in gold for greenbacks, allowing him to hand over to the incoming Cleveland administration a gold reserve of slightly more than $100 million.

The inauguration of a new president did nothing to halt the slide. Gold continued to leave both the Treasury and the country, interest rates continued to rise, and bankruptcies continued to grow. Soon after President Cleveland's swearing-in, *The Economist* reported, "Country banks [are] drawing their reserve balances from New York banks." Institutions around the country were losing deposits and so pulled cash from New York. This pushed up interest rates at the center—those borrowing in the call market

[54] *The Economist*, July 7, 1894, p. 827.

[55] *The Economist*, February 25, 1893, p. 229.

[56] August Belmont to Lord Rothschild, May 7, 1893, Belmont Papers, box 23, letter books.

[57] *The Economist*, January 20, 1894, p. 82.

against securities had to pay as much as 50 percent.[58] In mid-April, the amount of gold in the Treasury fell below $100 million. The new Treasury Secretary, John Carlisle, announced that the government would stop issuing gold certificates. These were notes backed, dollar for dollar, by gold held in the Treasury, and they represented a significant convenience for those dealing in gold. By halting their issue, the Treasury would force those who wanted the convenience of paper money to entrust their gold to its general reserve. Most approved of this step, but such was not the case with Carlisle's next major announcement. He was an experienced Kentucky politician who had served as Speaker of the U.S. House and was an expert on tariffs. Carlisle possessed a substantial reserve of common sense but had no special knowledge of finance, and sometimes it showed. On April 22, he announced that the government would redeem its paper on demand, in gold, "so long as he [the Treasury Secretary] had gold lawfully available to that purpose." In the panicked atmosphere of New York, some interpreted this statement to mean that the government would start redeeming the Treasury notes issued under the Silver Purchase Act in silver, which it had the legal right to do. As this rumor spread, so did the demand for gold. As one observer commented, "the declaration only created uncertainty, and in the minds of some people almost consternation."[59] In fact, Carlisle was simply stating that the government could not tap gold earmarked specifically for gold certificates, which had never counted as part of the general Treasury reserve—a legal nicety that almost all financiers understood.[60] The situation, however, demanded a show of resolution, not attention to legal details. Two days later, President Cleveland managed to calm markets by announcing, "The President and his Cabinet are absolutely harmonious in the determination to exercise every power conferred upon them to maintain the public credit, to keep the public faith and to preserve the parity between gold and silver and between all financial obligations of the Government."[61] Nevertheless, the drain of gold to pay foreign creditors continued. As one lawyer wrote President Cleveland in late April, "Gold today has gone to a premium. This is a fact

[58] *The Economist*, March 25, 1893, p. 357.

[59] *The Economist*, May 6, 1893, p. 542.

[60] Diary of Charles Hamlin, November 13, 1894, Charles Hamlin Papers, Library of Congress, reel 1.

[61] Quoted in James A. Barners, *John G. Carlisle: Financial Statesman* (Gloucester, MA: Peter Smith, 1967), pp. 233–9.

(though not generally observed) inasmuch as sterling bills [IOUs paid in British pounds] have been sold for gold at a lower price than for currency."[62]

In May, the bankruptcy of National Cordage transformed the crisis into a full-blown panic. National Cordage, a merger of companies that produced rope, twin, and string, collapsed because it could not secure loans for working capital—funds to purchase raw materials, pay workers, and carry inventory. In retrospect, National Cordage had inherent weaknesses. Its organizers had sought to increase profits by raising prices, but its technology offered few economies of scale and entering the business was easy. As a result, when National Cordage increased prices, it attracted competition. Its response was to buy out these challengers—ten in all by early 1893—which naturally attracted more competitors. Nevertheless, National Cordage was a darling of Wall Street—its board included August Belmont and other financial luminaries. The company went under not because of long-term strategic challenges, but because it could not get short-term credits—a shocking development for such a well-connected enterprise.[63] If the shortage of money could bring down National Cordage, nothing was safe. Many who held stock decided to sell before conditions worsened, and others sold to accumulate cash, which seemed to offer the only safe haven. During the first week of May, a record 2.6 million shares changed hands on the New York Stock Exchange.[64] As prices fell, those who had bought on credit found themselves owing more than their investments were worth, provoking further sales as well as bankruptcies. As news of the disaster spread, regional banks accelerated withdrawals from New York, and credit became progressively tighter. In May, one of President Cleveland's New York correspondents pointed to "an almost total cessation in the sale of commercial paper, the notes of perfectly solvent houses failing to find a market at even 8, 9, and 10 percent."[65]

By June, many citizens had lost all confidence in financial institutions and were lining up at banks to withdraw their cash—a "bank run." No bank ever has enough money on hand to pay all its depositors because these institutions loan out most of the money entrusted to them, so runs threaten even strong institutions with disaster. In June, regional banks

[62] Francis Stetson to Grover Cleveland, April 20, 1893, Cleveland Papers, reel 75.
[63] O'Sullivan, *Dividends of Development*, pp. 133–7.
[64] *The Economist*, May 20, 1893, p. 603.
[65] S.R. Thurber to Grover Cleveland, May 6, 1893, Cleveland Papers, reel 75.

withdrew another $33 million from New York.[66] After June 10, the New York Clearing House stopped publishing information on specific banks lest adverse news lead to a run on the bank in question.[67] To protect themselves, banks restricted withdrawals. This step may well have been illegal, but with bankruptcy as the alternative, many institutions took it. As *The Economist* reported, banks throughout the country were "refusing to pay more than relatively limited sums to depositors on demand."[68] One banker stated, "We are paying small cheques, but on large cheques we pay currency only for payroll."[69] The problem was not confined to New York. In New Orleans, banks refused to pay out more than $50 to any depositor, and in Nashville, institutions simply closed for several days in August.[70] Banks in Denver and Kansas City closed as well, hoping that, when the storm had passed, they could resume business. Such measures were understandable, but they increased the demand for cash. As *The Economist's* American correspondent noted, "So scarce has currency become, that several brokerage firms in Wall Street have been offering a premium of from a fraction of 1 to 2 percent for it, while ... round lots of gold have been secured at a small premium by some traders."[71] The "prime rate," the charge on short-term loans backed by solid collateral, stood at 8–12 percent, while call loans backed by securities were available only at astronomical cost. In July, J.P. Morgan wrote an Episcopal priest who had asked for a financial help, "It is absolutely impossible for us to make a time loan," adding, "it is impossible to sell anything here."[72] This refusal indicates just how dire the situation was. Morgan was not only immensely wealthy but a devout Episcopalian who was usually eager to support the church and its priests. A few months later, he told another supplicant, "I have done little else for the last six months but to personally examine into and relieve just

[66] Lauck, *The Causes of the Panic of 1893*, p.100.

[67] Christopher Cotter and Peter Rousseau, "Correspondent Banking, Systemic Risks, and the Panic of 1893," *Munich Personal RePEc Archive*, Paper No. 113340, June 15, 2022, p. 6.

[68] *The Economist*, September 2, 1893, p. 1062.

[69] Quoted in *The Economist*, August 5, 1893, 945.

[70] *The Economist*, August 26, 1893, p. 1033; Don Doyle, *Nashville in the New South* (Knoxville: University of Tennessee Press, 1985), pp. 51–55.

[71] *The Economist*, August 19, 1893, p. 1004. Banks offered a premium for currency by exchanging cashiers' checks for cash, with the check being slightly larger than the sum of cash.

[72] J.P. Morgan to Endicott Peabody, July 31, 1893, Morgan Papers, letter book microfilm, Morgan Library.

such cases; they will soon reach a number in importance and magnitude which it simply enormous, and it has taxed me to the fullest extent of my powers."[73]

The crisis crippled trade. *The Economist*'s American correspondent reported in June, "Larger jobbers, manufacturers, and other wholesale dealers have practically ceased pushing goods, or even offering goods for sale to other than those whom they believed to be abundantly able to pay."[74] Two weeks later he added, "There is no open market for commercial paper in New York City at present, and banks are taking from one-quarter to one-third only of the paper … offered by many of their customers.[75] James Hill, the leader of the Great Northern Railway, wired President Cleveland in August, "Entire situation between Chicago and Pacific Coast very critical. No grain or farm product can move for want of money."[76] In the end, the Great Northern itself provided loans to farmers against grain stored in its elevators, allowing them to ride out the crisis, but elsewhere cultivators were less fortunate.[77]

The crisis crested in August. The New York Clearing House began to issue "Clearing House Certificates," IOUs backed by the city's entire banking community. The clearing houses in Boston, Philadelphia, Baltimore, Pittsburg, and Chicago followed suit. By the end of August, paper of this sort worth $63 million was in circulation, of which $38 million came from New York City.[78] By law, national banks had to hold reserves equal to 15–25 percent of deposits. Unfortunately, no mechanism existed to allow banks to tap this money in a crisis. Paying out their reserves would put them in violation of the law, creating a classic Catch-22. Banks escaped this trap by replacing cash held in reserve with clearing house certificates, freeing up the former for depositors and borrowers.[79] Legally,

[73] J.P. Morgan to W.S. Rainsford, October 14, 1893, Morgan Papers, letter book microfilm.

[74] *The Economist*, June 17, 1893, p. 731.

[75] *The Economist*, July 1, 1893, p. 790.

[76] James Hill to Grocer Cleveland, August 9, 1893, Cleveland Papers, reel 78.

[77] Campbell, *The Reorganization of the American Railroad System, 1893–1900*, p. 296. This example suggests that a system of short-term credits for farmers at the harvest, such as Tom Watson's revised version of the Alliance's Subtreasury program, might have done some good.

[78] Lauck, *The Causes of the Panic of 1893*, p. 104.

[79] Banks had used Clearing House Certificates in previous panics, the earliest case being in 1857. For a description of the workings of this system, see Gary Gorton, "Clearinghouses and the Origin of Central Banking in the United States," *Journal of Economic History* 45 (1985): 277–83.

the maneuver was dubious because the certificates were not legal tender. They served a desperate need, however, and most bankers stifled their doubts. Many farmers and small businessmen, who did not have the luxury of paying their debts with IOUs, did complain. Senator James George of Mississippi attacked the "ingenious device of issuing what is called clearing-house certificates, which are not allowed to circulate among the people, but are kept for use exclusively by the banks, to enable them to persist in locking up the currency by their refusal to pay depositors."[80] The complaint had merit—bankers were using a dubious legal device to save themselves—but clearing house certificates played a key role in resolving the money famine.

At the same time, high interest rates and the premium on cash drew money from abroad. Financial uncertainty deterred foreign investors, but by August, interest rates in the United States were so high that at least some were willing to take a risk. By August 6, $5 million in bullion had landed in New York, and by August 19, *The Economist* reported that the influx had reached £2.5 million, or over $12 million.[81] National banks also stepped into the breach. During the 1880s, low interest rates had made the business of issuing currency less profitable, and many national banks had abandoned it. Higher rates and the premium on currency during the crisis altered the calculus, and some of these banks moved to issue new currency. The process was clumsy—the Bureau of Engraving had to print the bills, and banks had to transfer federal bonds to the Treasury—but by mid-August, national banks had issued roughly $5 million in new notes. The total would increase to $20 million by the end of the year.[82]

As is usually the case in a panic, once banks had enough money to pay depositors, depositors stopped demanding payment. Over the fall, the stringency of credit and cash slowly gave way to a glut. By the middle of October, commercial paper was fetching 5–6 percent again, and the rate fell below 5 percent by the end of the year.[83] In November, August Belmont reported to Leopold Rothschild, "Our financial situation here is

[80] Speech of Senator James George, September 20 & 22, 1893, p. 15, *Silver Speeches*.

[81] *The Economist*, August 19, 1893, p. 999; William E. Curtis to Elizabeth [Curtis?], August 6, 1893, William Curtis Papers, Library of Congress, box 1.

[82] *The Economist*, August 19, 1893, p. 999. Lauck, *The Causes of the Panic of 1893*, p. 104.

[83] Discount rates in New York for Commercial Paper in 1893, [March 1894], Cleveland Papers, reel 83.

a waiting one. Money is going begging, and there is not desire for new business."[84]

The crisis left devastation in its wake. Over the course of 1893, 15,000 businesses failed, leaving debts of over $343 million unpaid.[85] By early 1894, railroads controlling roughly a quarter of the nation's entire network of track—almost 50,000 miles—were in receivership, including the Richmond Terminal, the Reading, the Erie, the Northern Pacific, the Union Pacific, and the Atchison, Topeka, and Santa Fe. Between 1891 and 1895, American railroads reduced their capital spending from $300 million a year to $100 million, dealing a severe blow to the larger economy.[86] Four hundred ninety-six banks had failed, of which sixty-three were national banks—six times as many failures as in the previous year, and twelve times the number in 1890.[87] Farm income dropped sharply simply because merchants did not have money with which to purchase crops. As a result, many farmers defaulted on their debts, and foreclosure sales multiplied. One rural paper in Minnesota contained between eight and fifteen foreclosure notices in each of its weekly issues during the summer of 1894[88]—a grim tally replicated in many other communities. Many once independent farmers found themselves reduced to tenants, and many more escaped that fate only by the narrowest of margins.

Industrial workers suffered as well. The manager of a Georgia lumber mill reported in September, "165 men and our mills are idle because no money is coming in to meet our payrolls here."[89] Such situations were common. Reliable figures on unemployment did not exist at the time. Estimates ranged from one to three million out of a total urban workforce of 15 million, but all agreed that it was high.[90] During 1893 and 1894, newspapers reported on the organization, or re-organization, of relief committees in cities throughout the country. In Wheeling, West Virginia, a new, city-wide relief committee created in December 1893 received over

[84] August Belmont to Leopold Rothschild, November 22, 1893, Belmont Papers, box 23, letter books.

[85] Lauck, *The Causes of the Panic of 1893*, p. 105.

[86] Rendigs Fels, *American Business Cycles, 1865–1897* (Chapel Hill: University of North Carolina Press, 1959), p. 216.

[87] U.S. Bureau of the Census, *Historical Statistics of the United States, Colonial Times to 1970, Bicentennial Edition, Part 2*, Washington, D.C., 1975, p. 1038.

[88] See *Weekly Transcript* (Little Falls, MN), June–September, 1894.

[89] M.F. Amorous to Grover Cleveland, September 22, 1893, Cleveland Papers. reel 79.

[90] *The Economist*, January 6, 1894, p. 15.

200 requests for help on its first day. "Some of the men," a local paper reported, "said they had as many as ten people depending upon them for support, and families of eight and nine were frequent. Nearly all had been out of work for four to six months. … All were willing and anxious to work. … It has been many a day since so many evident cases of poverty were gathered together in one place in this city."[91] For those who remained at work, *The Economist*'s American correspondent reported, "There are hardly any exceptions to the rule of from ten to fifteen percent reduction in wages."[92] The huge number of foreclosures and bankruptcies precluded a rapid recovery. The arteries of trade were damaged, and repairs would take years. Production stopped shrinking sometime in the late summer or early fall of 1894, but improvement after that was slow.

The Great Debate

Most bankers and businessmen attributed the crisis to uncertainty about the currency created by the Silver Purchase Act. Industrialist Andrew Carnegie wrote President Cleveland in April, "From my own experience I can tell you that foreigners have taken alarm and have begun to withdraw their capital in gold. Unless all doubt [about the currency] is put to rest there is still great danger of the country being drained of gold."[93] A Minneapolis grain broker informed the President, "I am in receipt of a letter today from one foreign institution that loaned three millions of dollars in this city last year to help move the crop, in which they say, 'We do not intend to extend any advance until the silver question is settled.'"[94] Domestic hoarding exacerbated the foreign drain. One stockbroker insisted, "I have not the slightest doubt that at least $50,000,000 [in] gold and gold certificates together are now stowed away in Trust Co. vaults and safe deposit boxes."[95] This calculation was a guess, and probably an exaggerated one, but banks and businesses were holding onto gold as long as they could, and at least a few people were hoarding it. As Senator John Sherman put the case, "If the coinage of silver dollars were stopped …

[91] *Wheeling Daily Register*, December 22, 1893, p. 6.
[92] *The Economist*, January 20, 1894, p. 82.
[93] Andrew Carnegie to Grover Cleveland, April 22, 1893, Cleveland Papers, reel 75.
[94] F.H. Peavy, to Grover Cleveland, September 28, 1893, Cleveland Papers, reel 79.
[95] Henry Clews to Grover Cleveland, May 13, 1893, Cleveland Papers, reel 75.

the world would know that we proposed to pay out debts in the world's money—gold—and confidence would be restored. ... When confidence is restored the gold will come back."[96]

Grover Cleveland accepted this analysis, but he considered the currency a moral as well as a technical issue. As he wrote, "The people of the United States are entitled to a sound and stable currency and to money recognized as such in every market of the world."[97] Abandoning gold would represent a breach of faith. Whereas Benjamin Harrison, William Allison, and even John Sherman were willing to compromise with Silverites as long as they could maintain the link between the dollar and gold, Cleveland considered such equivocations dishonest. Only by tying the dollar to an immutable standard—gold—could Americans enjoy financial stability.

The rank-and-file of the Democratic Party was not so sure. The party's substantial Northeastern arm supported the gold standard, and those from the Industrial Midwest were open to persuasion, but in the South and West, Silverites predominated. The mass of patronage requests that flowed to the President around his inauguration highlighted the situation. In state after state, the party divided not only over personalities—a perennial question—but over principles. In many southern and western states one faction claimed patronage on the basis of its support for Cleveland and his policies, including defense of the gold standard. Another claimed the spoils of office despite its opposition to the gold standard on the basis of popular support. Most of the time, both spoke the truth. Democrats could effectively challenge Republicans in the Farm Belt and Mountain West only by embracing silver. Defending the gold standard meant political irrelevance. The South suffered a chronic shortage of money and credit, and many of its citizens believed that the free coinage of silver would relieve the problem. Even southern Democrats dubious about silver had to contend with the Populists, who would challenge any Democrats who defended the gold standard. The most dexterous politician would have had trouble uniting the Democratic Party around a coherent financial program, and Grover Cleveland owed his popularity to his stubborn integrity, not to his skill at compromise.

[96] *New York Times*, July 4, 1893, p. 5.

[97] U.S. House of Representatives, 53rd Cong., 1st Sess., Message of the President of the United States, August 8, 1893.

Cleveland used patronage to whip his party into line. In the late nineteenth century, the President appointed literally thousands of officials throughout the country, and many party activists involved themselves in politics chiefly to secure such jobs. Cleveland wrote John Carlisle in January 1893, "One thing may as well be distinctly understood by professing Democrats in Congress, who are heedless of the burdens and responsibilities of the incoming administration and the duty our party owes to the people. They must not expect us to 'turn the other cheek' by rewarding their conduct with patronage."[98] One of the President's supporters put it even more bluntly, stating, "I don't think it wise to give out patronage until your wishes about silver are carried out."[99] For the time being, such uncompromising tactics worked. Senator Daniel Voorhees (D-IN), a critic of the president who had flirted with silver, wrote Cleveland in March of his "grateful appreciation for your kindness and courtesy … in the appointment of Mr. Riley. … You have indeed made me very deeply and permanently your debtor, and it will be one of the principle pleasures and purposes of my life, and at every opportunity, to recognize and justify, as far as may be in my power, the generous confidence and friendly regard you have extended me."[100] Subsequently, Voorhees championed Cleveland's financial policies in the Senate. Many Democrats resented the administration's heavy-handed tactics, however. Their constituents often favored free silver and might well fail to return defenders of the gold standard at the next election. These politicians had no desire to risk their careers for the President's principles and found his indifference to their political problems infuriating.

To prop up the gold standard and thereby relieve financial stringency, Grover Cleveland and his advisors first considered issuing bonds, as had the Harrison administration. Ideally, these securities would go to Europe in exchange for gold to replenish the Treasury reserve. J.P. Morgan strongly recommended this course.[101] If European investors did not want to hold American railroad securities, then the country had to offer something that they would take, and Morgan believed that government bonds would do. Before taking office, Cleveland extended feelers about a bond

[98] Grover Cleveland to John Carlisle, January 22, 1893, *Letters of Grover Cleveland*, p. 314–5.

[99] Michael Harton to Grover Cleveland, February 1, 1893, Cleveland Papers, reel 73.

[100] Daniel Voorhees to Grover Cleveland, March 20, 1893, *Letters of Grover Cleveland*, p. 321.

[101] J.P. Morgan to Foster, February 17, 1893, Morgan Papers, microfilm, letter books.

issue to the London Rothschild's through their American agent, August Belmont, who was unusual among New York's bankers in being a Democrat.[102] Once in office, however, the new administration abandoned this course. The deteriorating financial situation discouraged any new issue. Cash was scarce, and investors were reluctant to tie it up in long-term investments. Moreover, the bonds authorized under the 1875 Act were payable "in coin," which legally could mean either gold or silver. Investors were reluctant to pay gold for a security on which they might receive silver.[103] Before any successful loan, the American government had to convince investors of its commitment to gold.

Instead, the President and his advisors decided to halt purchases of silver under the Silver Purchase Act.[104] The subject had become an ideé fixe among defenders of the gold standard. As a petition from bankers in Buffalo stated, "The conditions of the past two years and the distress of the last few months are universally admitted to be largely due to its [the Silver Purchase Act's] operations."[105] The President himself wrote, "I believe these things [financial instability], are principally chargeable to Congressional legislation touching the purchase and coinage of silver by the General Government."[106] As one Silverite summed it up, "The public mind ... in the Eastern part of the country dreads the silver [purchase] legislation as if it was a fatal and disgraceful disease."[107] Repeal would, according to one petition, "restore confidence in the money markets of the country and ... attract foreign capital to American investments" by emphasizing the country's commitment to the gold standard.[108] Some did

[102] Cable to Rothschild's, February 21, 1893, Belmont Papers, box 23, letter books; August Belmont to Lord Rothschild, February 28, 1893, Belmont Papers, box 23, letter books; Grover Cleveland to Daniel Lamont, February 19, 1893, *Letters of Grover Cleveland*, pp. 318–9.

[103] Memo from W.E. Curtis, [August 1893], Curtis Papers, box 1.

[104] The Administration would not seek repeal of the entire act but leave the provisions making the Treasury notes issued under it legal tender and committing the government to maintaining the parity between gold and silver currency. Because the purchase of silver was the object of the act, however, almost all spoke of "repeal" in reference to the administration's initiative.

[105] Newspaper clipping, [July 23, 1893], Cleveland Papers, reel 76.

[106] Message of the President of the United States, August 8, 1893.

[107] George Gibson, "The Financial Excitement and its Causes," *The Forum*, June 1893, p. 490.

[108] Resolution Adopted by the St. Paul Chamber of Commerce, Monday, June 12, 1893, Cleveland Papers, reel 76.

take a more nuanced view. Cleveland's Secretary of State, Walter Gresham, wrote the President, "I realized that all this financial trouble is not due [solely] to the Sherman [Silver Purchase] law."[109] Arthur B. Farquhar, a prominent businessman and friend of the President, wrote a pamphlet on the subject in which he asked, "Is the state of the currency the only cause of the business distress?" and answered, "By no means." Farquhar continued, "The reason why stress is laid upon it is that the evil is more easily remedied than any other."[110] The Silver Purchase Act was part of a set of problems that included the federal deficit, an inflexible financial system, and poor and (sometimes) dishonest railroad management. Repealing the Silver Purchase Act, however, was far simpler than balancing the budget, reforming the banking system, or reorganizing the railroads, and in a crisis, time is of the essence.

The drive to repeal the Silver Purchase Act had been gaining momentum since the summer of 1892. At that time, Senator John Sherman had proposed legislation to halt silver purchases and the issue of Treasury notes. Support spread quickly. In January 1893, Sherman insisted, "A large majority of Senators ... are in favor of the repeal or suspension of the purchase of silver bullion."[111] Meanwhile, business and banking groups circulated petitions seeking repeal. Between January 1 and February 7, 1893, the House of Representatives received sixty-three petitions urging repeal and only three opposing it.[112] Silverites insisted that bankers had coerced most of the signatories, but they never produced evidence to back this claim. Outside silver mining regions, most businessmen supported the gold standard because they considered it the foundation of "sound finance."

Silverites mobilized to resist repeal only slowly. They had doubts about the Silver Purchase Act, which they considered at best a half-baked compromise. They only gradually realized that repeal would, by default, leave gold as the sole basis for money and halt further expansion of the currency. At a hastily convened Silver Convention in August 1893, A.J. Warner argued, "Under the law [the Silver Purchase Act] ... about $150,000,000 has been added to our currency. Does anybody believe that the presence

[109] Walter Gresham to Cleveland, July 3, 1983, *Letters of Grover Cleveland*, p. 326.

[110] A.B. and H. Farquhar, "Congress and the Currency," 1893, Cleveland Papers, reel 78.

[111] *New York Times*, January 16, 1893, p. 2.

[112] U.S. House of Representatives, 52nd Cong, 2nd Sess., *Repeal of the Sherman Act*, February 7, 1893.

now of this $150,000,000 in our currency produces the present money famine or makes money scarce and dear?"[113]

For the President, the question was largely one of timing. He considered repeal necessary, and the Democratic platform of the previous year had endorsed it—one of the few financial issues on which the platform was clear. Congress would not meet until December, however, and the President and his advisors were unsure whether they should wait until then or call a special session of Congress devoted to repeal.

News from abroad added urgency. In June, the British government closed India's mints to silver, ending the free coinage of rupees. This news should not have come as a surprise. At the Brussels Conference the previous fall, British delegates had announced that unless the gathering came up with a program to stabilize the price of silver, the Indian government would have to halt free coinage.[114] The reasons were straightforward. As the price of silver fell against gold, so too had the rupee depreciated against the pound. The debt of the Indian government was largely denominated in sterling, so as the rupee lost value the burden of its debt grew, in rupees. A report by officials in the India Office noted a year earlier, "The recent fall in the rate of exchange has already imposed on our [Indian's] finances a burden which we should have some difficult in meeting."[115] Moreover, as another report by the India Office observed, "The fall in exchange has led to claims on the part of their [the Indian Office's] officers, civil and military, who receive salaries in rupees[,] to some compensation for their losses. ... Many of these officials are under the necessity of remitting a considerable portion of their incomes to this country [Britain] for the support of their families and the education of their children."[116] Ironically, another factor behind the decision was fear that the United States would repeal the Silver Purchase Act, causing another major drop in silver's value. London wanted to act before silver declined any more.[117] In any case, India's retreat from silver would likely lead to a further decline in the value

[113] A.J. Warner, *Opening Address of A.J. Warner Delivered Before the Silver Convention (1893)* (Washington, D.C.: Geo. R. Gray, 1893), p. 4.

[114] Alfred Rothschild to his brothers, December 7, 1892, Rothschild's Archives, 000/253.

[115] Government of India Finance and Commerce Department, No. 160 of 1892, June 21, 1892.

[116] "Report of the Indian Currency Committee, May 31, 1893, NA, CAB 37/34.

[117] Government of India Finance and Commerce Department, No. 160 of 1892, June 21, 1892.

of silver, making its rehabilitation that much more difficult.[118] Up until this time, India had absorbed roughly a quarter of the world's silver production (the United States purchased about a third of total output under the Silver Purchase Act).[119] Manton Marable, one of the leading international bimetallists in the United States, insisted, "American free bimetallic coinage [is] impossible without free silver coinage [in] India."[120] President Cleveland did not comment publicly on the change in India, but he made a point of learning as much about it as he could.[121]

Cleveland could not yet face Congress, however. Doctors had diagnosed a cancerous growth on the roof of the President's mouth, likely due to his habit of smoking cigars. In early July, surgeons removed it, along with part of Cleveland's jaw, and he enjoyed a full recovery. The White House suppressed news of the President's illness and operation, which did not become public knowledge for many years. Cleveland and his lieutenants feared the impact of the news on financial markets. Vice President Adlai Stevenson had flirted with silver in the past and would do so again in the future, and the prospect that he might succeed Cleveland almost certainly would have led to a further drain of gold.

In late June, as he was preparing for his surgery, President Cleveland called a special session of Congress for August to consider repeal of the provisions of the Sherman Silver Purchase Act that authorized buying silver with Treasury notes. The financial panic was cresting, and if the government was going to act at all, it needed to do so soon. At the same time, the President hoped that he would have recovered sufficiently from his surgery by August to deal with Congress. When it convened, Cleveland greeted the new session with a brief message in which he pointed to the country's financial distress and the drain of gold from the Treasury, insisting, "The operation of the silver purchase law now in force, leads in the direction of the entire substitution of silver for gold in the government

[118] The decision of the British government to cease coinage in India created considerable economic hardship there. The action halted the supply of new money to an economy used to a fairly rapid increase in coinage. In retrospect, London would have done better to cap the coinage of rupees at a level consistent with the growth of trade. In any case, the British government eventually devised a system that fixed the value of the rupee in sterling, making it, indirectly, convertible into gold, but without the need for a large gold reserve or replacing silver rupees already in circulation.

[119] Report of the Indian Currency Committee, May 31, 1893.

[120] To David Bennet Hill, August 7, 1893, Marable Papers, reel 79.

[121] Daniel Lamont to John Carlisle, July 13, 1893, Curtis Papers, box 1.

Treasury, and . . . this must be followed by payment of all government obligations in depreciated silver." That would saddle the United States with "a currency greatly depreciated according to the standards of the commercial world, [and] we could no longer claim a place among nations of the first class." The government "had no right to injure them [the American people] by financial experiments opposed to the policy and practices of other civilized states, nor is it justified in permitting an exaggerated and unreasonable reliance on our national strength to jeopardize the soundness of the people's money." Cleveland concluded by stating his determination to "put beyond all doubt or mistake the intention and the ability of the Government to fulfill its pecuniary obligations in money universally recognized by all civilized countries."[122]

The administration demanded a "clean" repeal that contained no financial reforms or concessions to silver. Thomas Shearman, an American banker writing from Europe, had urged the President to make a statement "showing your sympathy with the needs of the farmers and planters and your intention to devise and recommend measures which will give them … relief. … We cannot stand forever upon a platform of mere negation. The people justly become impatient with statesmen who never have anything to say but No."[123] At least some Democrats in the House of Representatives suggested repealing the Silver Purchase Act and returning to Bland-Allison, which had worked well enough for a dozen years. Simply returning to Bland-Allsion was risky, however. The act had authorized buying $2 million in silver every month at the market price and coining it. With the sharp decline in silver's price, that would have translated into far more silver money than in the past. Nevertheless, a measure to replace the Silver Purchase Act with limited silver coinage probably would have secured ready approval. In the middle of a crisis, such a half-measure might not have restored confidence—desperate conditions often demand dramatic action. Such calculations do not explain Cleveland's refusal to consider some sort of compromise, however. To his mind, gold was the only honest basis of money, and the crisis offered an opportunity to extirpate the silver heresy.

Repeal moved rapidly through the House of Representatives. The rules of that body gave the leadership considerable power, and the

[122] Message of the President, August 8, 1893.
[123] Thomas Shearman to Grover Cleveland, July 15, 1893, Cleveland Papers, reel 78.

administration's aggressive use of patronage kept most Democrats in line. Members also recognized that the country faced a crisis and desired to do something about it. Petitions arrived from all over the country, chiefly but not solely from business groups, urging repeal. The thirty-three-year-old William Jennings Bryan (D-NB), a second-term Congressmen from Nebraska, did provide some verbal pyrotechnics. Bryan had grown up in Illinois but, seeking broader opportunities, had moved to Lincoln, Nebraska, where he established a successful legal practice and, like many young lawyers, had become active in local politics. One of the state's few Democrats, he had won election to Congress in the Democratic sweep of 1890. Initially, he concentrated his fire on the protective tariff, but once in Washington, he concluded that the currency was more important than tariffs and became a champion of free silver. As the vote in the House neared, Bryan warned, "You may think you have buried the cause of bimetallism; you many congratulate yourselves that you have laid the free coinage of silver away in a sepulcher, newly made since the election, and before the door rolled the veto stone. But, sirs, if our cause is just, as I believe it is, your labor has been in vain, no tomb was even made so strong that it could imprison a righteous cause. Silver will yet lay aside its grave clothes and shroud. It will yet rise."[124] Nevertheless, on August 28 the House approved repeal by a large majority.

In the Senate, progress came to a screeching halt. There, the western and southern states had greater representation, and the body's rules allowed unlimited debate. Silverites filibustered, inaugurating a debate that lasted through October. The contest stoked tempers already running high. Democrats argued at length about whether the vague language of their platform endorsed gold or silver. Those eager to halt silver purchases denounced the "vicious minority" filibustering to "upset the will of the majority."[125] Senator Teller accused Republicans from the Northeast and Midwest, almost all of whom supported repeal, of betrayal. He and other Silver Republicans had voted for the McKinley Tariff in exchange for the party's support for the Silver Purchase Act, and now eastern Republicans were reneging on the bargain.[126] Businessmen from southern cities

[124] Quoted in Richard Franklin Bensel, *The Political Economic of American Industrialization, 1877–1900* (New York: Cambridge University Press, 2000), p. 413.

[125] *The Economist*, October 7, 1893, p. 1205.

[126] Elmer Ellis, *Henry Teller: Defender of the West*, (Caldwell, ID: Caxton Press. 1941), pp. 196–7.

bombarded their senators with petitions for repeal only to discover that, in many cases, lawmakers were listening to others.[127] As Georgia's governor warned the President, "Every election held in this state for the past three months [since June 1893] has gone against the Democratic Party and in favor of the Populists. Ex-Congressman [Tom] Watson, the leader of the Populists, has taken advantage of the conditions, and in speaking over the state to assemblies never less than 2000 sometimes as many as 5000 people."[128] Populists had long insisted that the country suffered from a dearth of money, and the panic seemed to confirm this diagnosis. President Cleveland had sought a show of unity behind the gold standard, but he got a bitter debate that highlighted social and regional divisions.

The filibuster created a forum for a thorough discussion of the currency—the closest thing the Battle of the Standards had to the Lincoln-Douglas debates. The virtues and defects of the Silver Purchase Act were almost beside the point. Even its supporters considered it no more than an ungainly compromise. Silverites defended it, first, because it expanded the currency during a desperate scramble for cash in which not only gold but greenbacks, national banknotes, Treasury notes, and silver dollars and certificates all commanded a premium. Second, the workings of the Silver Purchase Act promised to drain the Treasury of gold and, by default, put the country on a silver basis. Whatever the issue at hand, the underlying question was the choice between the gold standard and the free coinage of silver.

Speakers on both sides kept returning to a few central themes. Silverites invoked tradition. Senator William Allen argued, "For seven hundred years before the Christian era silver was used as money and has been continuously used from that time until the present time throughout the civilized world."[129] Senator John Daniel (D-VA) insisted, "The great men who framed our institution were bimetallists. Our system was devised by Hamilton and Jefferson and approved by Washington; it existed, flourished, and fulfilled its functions from 1793 to 1873. … We flourished as no one nation has ever flourished since time began."[130]

[127] An example of such a petition is in *The Daily American* (Nashville), October 7, 1893, which lists support from 120 of the city's firms for repeal. Tennessee's senators nevertheless opposed repeal and participated in the filibuster. Cleveland Papers, reel 79.

[128] W.J. Norton to Grover Cleveland, September 15, 1893, Cleveland Papers, reel 79.

[129] Speech of William V. Allen, August 23, 1893, p. 14, *Silver Speeches*.

[130] Speech of John W. Daniel, September 14, 1893, p. 31, *Silver Speeches*.

Silverites distrusted the country's banking system and finance in general, and many described it as inherently corrupt. Senator James George contended, "The smaller the amount of real money in circulation … the more is the need for paper money and those contrivances and devices for economy in the actual use of money which are so much relied on by the monometallists. Bank paper and bank contrivances … are the means by which the power of the money class is made absolute."[131] Senator Allen insisted, "The volume of money in this country is so small that eight or ten thousand men can control it."[132] "The Sherman [Silver Purchase] Act," Allen continued, "is the last feeble barrier that stands between the patriotic and industrious masses of our people and that horde of insolent, aggressive, and ravenous money-changers and gamblers of Lombard Street and Wall Street."[133] This argument had a regional dimension as well. Senator James Berry (D-AR) insisted, "The [impact of financial] legislation of the general government since the war has been to collect and concentrate the capital and wealth of the country into one section only [the Northeast]."[134]

Where Silverites saw conspiracy and the violation of tradition, defenders of the gold standard found evidence of progress. Senator George Gray insisted that with "our wonderful civilization we have arrived at a period where the exchanging function of the previous metals and of the currencies of the people is becoming relatively less important." Transactions "are carried on by the process which have been evolved by that magnificent civilization … which has bought mankind to the point where the exchange of commodities … is brought about in 95 percent of the transactions of the world without the intervention of actual money."[135] According to defenders of the gold standard, the best response to a shortage of money was to expand financial markets and institutions. Advocates of repeal had little patience with appeals to tradition. Senator Donelson Caffrey (D-LA) insisted, "It will not do to tell us what Aristotle thought about money. … This is no relief."[136] Senator Joseph Dolph (R-OR) contended, "The merits or demerits of any measure for the use of silver as money today must be

[131] Speech of James Z. George, September 20 & 22, pp. 15–6, *Silver Speeches*.
[132] Speech of William Allen, October 7, 1893, p. 35, *Silver Speeches*.
[133] Speech of William Allen, August 24, p. 18, *Silver Speeches*.
[134] Speech of James Berry, August 16, 1893, p. 4, *Silver Speeches*.
[135] Speech of George Gray, September 20, 1893, pp. 3–4, *Silver Speeches*.
[136] Speech of Donelson Caffery, August 31, 1893, p. 10, *Silver Speeches*.

determined by existing conditions. The question whether previous financial legislation has been wise or unwise is immaterial."[137]

Defenders of the gold standard insisted that the free coinage of silver would bring economic progress to a halt. Senator Johnson Camden (D-WV) noted that gold was "the currency of all civilized nations of the world." Any country that used silver money relied on "the gold standard of exchange in all transactions outside its own country."[138] A shift to silver would devalue the dollar. Senator William Allison insisted, "I have never changed my mind from 1878 to this moment that we could not in and of ourselves restore the parity in value between silver and gold at the ratio of sixteen to one."[139] Senator Dolph warned that, with devaluation, "The credit of the government would have been impaired. Foreign capital would have been permanently withdrawn from our country, our foreign trade demoralized, our prosperity destroyed, and the development of our great resources stopped."[140]

Silverites saw no need to adjust American practices to those of the rest of the world. Senator Wilkerson Call (D-FL) insisted, "We have no need of such [foreign] capital. How can the oppressed, the poorly rewarded labor of Europe compare with our people upon our virgin soil with its vast production?"[141] Others claimed with Senator Fred Dubois (R-ID), "The United States is strong enough, and its wealth and credit are so great that it can decree what the position of silver in the business world is to be."[142] Some skipped over financial and economic questions altogether and appealed to patriotism. Senator Bate insisted, "If Europe is to dictate our financial policy then the declarations of Mr. Jefferson, that these were free and independent states, is not a true declaration."[143] Imaginative Silverites projected a reorientation of American trade toward Latin American and East Asia, which still used silver as money. Senator Dubois claimed, "Free coinage in the United States would at once bring a flood of orders for goods [from these regions]; such fluctuations in exchange would be done

[137] Speech of J.N. Dolph, August 8, 1893, pp. 12–13, *Silver Speeches.*
[138] Speech of J.N. Camden, September 30, 1893, p. 14, *Silver Speeches.*
[139] Speech of William B. Allison, September 16, 1893, p. 20, *Silver Speeches.*
[140] Dolph Speech, pp. 17–8.
[141] Speech of Senator Wilkinson Call, October 4 &6, 1893, p. 33, *Silver Speeches.*
[142] Speech of Senator Fred Dubois, August 22, 1893, p. 13, *Silver Speeches.*
[143] Speech of William B. Bate, September 23, 1893, p. 14, *Silver Speeches.*

away with. The trade would amount to tens of millions of dollars annually; it would permanently turn the general balance of trade in our favor."[144]

Silverites contended that the gold standard imposed insupportable burdens on farmers by forcing down the price of agricultural commodities. Senator Bate said, "It is a generally admitted fact that gold has *appreciated*, and it is denied that silver has *depreciated*. … The purchasing power of silver here remains unchanged except as to gold."[145] Many Silverites went further. Senator Dubois argued "that silver measures the value of all commodities. … It has yet served as a perfect measure of value of the products of labor."[146]

Defenders of the gold standard responded to this argument, the strongest in the Silverite arsenal, in several ways. Senator Gray said, "The theory that the fall in prices for the last twenty years has been occasioned by the appreciation of gold leaves out of sight the enormous advances which have been in the capacity of production all over the world." Gray continued, "I find measured by labor, measured by the wages of the artisans and the toiling people of this country as well as of Europe, that gold has not appreciated, and I have yet to hear why that test is not the best test that can be applied."[147]

Finally, both sides gave their case a moral dimension. Senator Allison said, "Is it the policy of anybody to pay a debt created upon one standard in another standard, and that depreciated? … I submit to do that is a wrong thing, and to do it by stealth is doubly wrong." Allison conceded that the gold standard had only been in place for fifteen years but insisted, "It is stated by those who examined the matter that debts in the average are only nine months old. I appeal to the experience of Senators around me. How many of them owe a debt that they owed in 1873?"[148] Silverites were not impressed. Senator Joseph Blackburn (D-KY) thundered, "Is he the repudiator who offers to discharge the obligation of a dollar by paying you one that represents 100 cents in the open market, or is he the repudiator who claims that you, his debtor, shall pay him … a dollar that represents $1.30?"[149]

As far as the Senate was concerned, this debate changed little. It probably did not alter a single vote. These speakers did, however, define what

[144] Dubois Speech, p. 13.
[145] Bate Speech, pp. 20–21. Emphasis in original.
[146] Dubois Speech, p. 5.
[147] Gray Speech, pp. 17–8.
[148] Allison Speech, pp. 20, 33–4.
[149] Speech of Joseph S, Blackburn, October 4, 1893, p. 12, *Silver Speeches*.

would be the chief issue in American politics over the next three years. Those alarmed by the centralization of economic life found in the free coinage of silver an issue around which they could rally. Alternatives like the Subtreasury fell by the wayside, even among Populists like Senators Allen and Peffer.

The long debate also defined the terms of discussion. Silver was the stuff of tradition while gold was the engine of progress. Silver would lighten the debts of farmers while gold provided access to foreign capital. The financial system either facilitated commerce and investment or allowed clever grifters to accumulate huge fortunes. Honor required the repayment of debts in gold while justice dictated cheaper silver. Politicians would, in some cases, repackage their arguments in more eloquent or digestible form, but they added little of substance. Speeches given during the filibuster raised all the main points found in William Jennings Bryan's famous "Cross of Gold" speech as well as in the huge volume of literature that Republicans issued in the 1896 campaign.

A filibuster is a battle of attrition—victory goes to the dogged. Though the Silver Republicans joined the filibuster, the rest of the Republicans supported repeal, and they viewed the contest with equanimity. When the vote came, they knew where they stood. In the interim, they were happy to see the Democrats tear each other apart. As Senator John Sherman put it, "I prefer to have President Cleveland and his advisers unembarrassed by my advice. … [T]he present dispute over the silver question is a Democratic Party issue," adding, "Mr. Cleveland … is fighting three-fourths of his party."[150] A Republican member of the House put it more bluntly: "Let the Democrats do the talking and voting. … It is their funeral."[151] Senators Hill and Voorhees, despite a history of poor relations with Cleveland, led the push for repeal. Hill sought to change Senate rules to force a vote, while Voorhees kept the Upper House in continuous session for forty hours to break the filibuster. Neither succeeded.[152] After two months of debate, support among Democrats for repeal began to waver. Sensing the

[150] *New York Times*, July 4, 1893, p. 5.

[151] Quoted in R. Hal Williams, *Realigning America: McKinley, Bryan, and the Remarkable Election of 1896* (Lawrence: University Press of Kansas, 2010), p. 33.

[152] The discussion of the legislative maneuvers surrounding the filibuster comes largely from Jeannette Paddock Nichols, "The Politics and Personalities of Silver Repeal in the United States Senate," *American Historical Review* 41 (October 1935): 26–53, and Allan Nevins, *Grover Cleveland: A Study in Courage* (New York: Dodd, Mead & Co., 1932), p. 541–548.

mood, Senator David Gorman (D-MD) tried to forge a compromise. On October 23, after a series of hasty and rather confused meetings, he produced a letter that thirty-seven of the forty-four Democratic Senators had signed outlining an agreement. The deal would end silver purchases after one year, on October 1, 1894, authorize the coinage of idle silver in the government's vaults, and end the issue of notes of less than $10. Notably, it contained no provision authorizing the issue of bonds that explicitly paid gold to replenish the Treasury reserve—something defenders of the gold standard ardently desired. Secretary Carlisle acted as liaison between Gorman and the President, but he did not participate in the negotiations among the Senators, and it is not clear if he understood the arrangement until Gorman presented it to the public.

This compromise would have *increased* the issue of silver-based currency over the coming year. Purchases of silver and the issue of Treasury notes would continue for another eleven months, and on top of that, Washington would coin roughly $55 million of idle silver in its vaults. Under the Silver Purchase Act, the government bought silver at the market price, which ranged as low as $0.60 an ounce, but it carried this silver on its books at $1.29, the official price. At that level, Washington had far more silver than it needed to back the Treasury notes in circulation—about $55 million more—which it could coin if it so desired. This bit of creative accounting soon became known as "coining the seigniorage," because it would exploit the government's authority to turn metal with a market value of $0.60 to $0.70 into coins worth $1.29. The final aspect of the compromise, halting the issue of notes less than $10 in favor of silver coins and certificates, represented a legitimate effort to boost demand for silver. Alfred Rothschild had suggested something similar at the Brussels Conference the previous winter. The United States, however, had already greatly reduced the issue of small notes in favor of silver coins and certificates, so the impact would not have been large.

Silverites had overplayed their hand. Seven Democrats, including David Hill, refused to consider the arrangement. Republicans who supported repeal—about two-thirds of the party in the upper chamber—had no use for legislation designed solely to unite the Democrats. Democrats on the fence—those who supported repeal but had signed the compromise—began to develop doubts as they realized that the arrangement would, for the time being, increase the amount of silver coined. Had Silverites demanded less—for instance, combining immediate repeal with the gradual coinage of the seigniorage—support among Democrats might have been unanimous and enthusiastic. Silverites, however, believed that their opponents were about to give up and drove a hard bargain.

President Cleveland's intervention proved decisive. Compromise was not his métier, and the prospect of an agreement that increased the volume of silver money infuriated him. After receiving Gorman's letter on October 23, he issued a terse statement: "The President adheres to the position that the purchasing clause of the Sherman Silver law should be unconditionally repealed."[153] Privately, he made it clear that he would not make any more patronage appointments until the Senate voted.[154] Compromise was dead, and the filibuster soon followed. Silverites realized that the President would not back down, and their resolve faltered. On October 30, the Senate voted forty-three to thirty-two in favor of repeal.

President Cleveland had won a great personal victory. Banker Jacob Schiff stated publicly and Senator William Allison said privately that only Cleveland could have secured repeal.[155] Congressional action did little to end the financial crisis, however. The vote in the House for repeal did coincide roughly with the easing of the panic. The *Commercial and Financial Chronicle* insisted, "This [the vote in the House] was the turning-point of the whole financial crisis of 1893; confidence was restored like magic; money began to come back into the banks and kept on accumulating."[156] The inflow of gold, however, predated the House's action—at best, the prospect of repeal was but one of several factors encouraging the importation of gold. The real importance of repeal lay in the future. The government stopped buying 4.5 million ounces of silver a month with Treasury notes that holders could redeem in gold. In other words, Washington's liabilities stopped growing. At the same time, so did the supply of currency. In the future, increases in the supply of money would depend almost entirely on finding more gold. Even many with "sound" financial views considered that prospect inadequate for an economy as dynamic as that of the United States. Thomas Jones, the governor

[153] Quoted in Nevins, *Grover Cleveland*, p. 546.

[154] Richard E. Welch, *The Presidencies of Grover Cleveland* (Lawrence: University Press of Kansas, 1988), p. 123.

[155] Jacob Schiff to Grover Cleveland, August 29, 1893, Cleveland Papers, reel 78; Horace White to Grover Cleveland, April 16, 1894, Cleveland Papers, reel 84.

[156] Quoted in Lauck, *The Causes of the Panic of 1893*, p. 108.

of Alabama and a supporter of both Cleveland and the gold standard, wrote, "the repeal of the Sherman purchase clause … should be followed by some measure which will continue the gradual increase of the currency."[157]

Politically, repeal initiated a tectonic shift. Democrats from the South and West were furious with the President, and Cleveland and Northeastern Democrats were hardly less angry with them. Healing this breach would have been difficult even had the economy bounced back quickly from the panic. With the onset of a grinding depression, the chasm became unbridgeable. Though feeling in the GOP was not as bitter as among Democrats, Silver Republicans were also unhappy with the rest of their party. Consensus on issues like tariffs and pensions for veterans of the Civil War could no longer conceal divisions over the currency. Among Populists, free coinage of silver suddenly took on greater prominence. Senators Allen and Peffer had played a leading role in the filibuster, and they and other Populists realized that in silver they had an issue with far broader appeal than the Subtreasury or anything else in their platform. If their party was to continue to advance, it would do so under the banner of silver. William Jennings Bryan was right. Silver was buried, but not dead.

[157] Thomas Jones to Grover Cleveland, November 14, 1893, Cleveland Papers, reel 80.

CHAPTER 5

The Economics of Gold

The defense of the gold standard consumed Grover Cleveland's second term in office. Other matters came and went, but the currency was a constant. Through a series of expedients, the President preserved the gold standard, but at a heavy price. Most Democrats lacked his commitment to "sound finance," and they gradually turned against him, leaving Cleveland politically isolated. In late 1894, he wrote to a friend, "I never did better public service than now; but it is depressing enough to have no encouragement from any quarter."[1]

Silver and Securities

The Panic of 1893 and the struggle to repeal the Sherman Silver Purchase Act had exhausted both the administration and Congress. The Senate did not even formally adjourn in 1893—after the final vote on repeal, most members simply went home. Nevertheless, Congress would convene in December for its regular session. In his year-end *Annual Report*, Treasury Secretary Carlisle advanced two proposals for legislation that he hoped would stabilize the financial situation. He observed, "The laws have imposed upon the Treasury Department all the duties and responsibilities of a bank of issue" but "have not conferred upon the Secretary any part of

[1] Cleveland to Richard Gilder, December 26, 1894, *Letters of Grover Cleveland*, p. 374.

W. Wells, *Financial Politics in the United States in the 1890s*,
https://doi.org/10.1007/978-3-031-86765-1_5

the discretionary powers usually possessed by the executives heads of [such] institutions."[2] To repair this defect, Carlisle wanted the Treasury, at its discretion, to be able to cancel greenbacks and Treasury notes paid into federal coffers and to authorize the issue of short-term bonds to be sold for and repaid in gold (gold bonds). Almost all observers agreed that, if Washington explicitly guaranteed its securities in gold, it could borrow at 3 percent or less. Current law, however, authorized only bonds paid "in coin," which could mean either gold or silver, and the possibility of repayment in silver led investors to demand a higher rate.

The proposal to authorize a new class of bonds addressed a problem to which Carlisle alluded only implicitly in his annual report. The federal government was running a substantial deficit that was draining the Treasury. The Secretary hoped that tariff reform and the return of prosperity would increase revenue, but in the meantime, he wanted to sell bonds not only to replenish the Treasury's gold reserve but to cover the deficit. As one Treasury official insisted, no one "has ever been able to distinguish between what part of the proceeds of bonds sales was used to replenish the gold reserve and what part was used to supply deficiencies [the deficit]."[3] For precisely this reason, Silverites stubbornly resisted the sale of bonds. They wanted to exhaust the Treasury's gold so that Washington would have no choice but to pay its obligations in silver, and they contended that, so long as the government had idle silver in its coffers, it had no reason to borrow. To induce Silverites to go along with his program, Carlisle offered two things that they had sought in 1893. First, he suggested retiring all greenbacks, Treasury notes, and national banknotes with denominations of less than $10 and replacing them with silver dollars and certificates. Second, he recommended coining the seigniorage—the Treasury's idle silver—putting $55 million in silver money in circulation over the course of the next few years. Proposals to coin the seigniorage were always vague about the timetable, but Carlisle calculated that government mints could coin at most $40 million in silver a year.[4]

Bond sales also impinged on the complex politics of national banks. These institutions were a bête noire of Populists and many Silverites because they issued currency, an authority Populists and Silverites wanted

[2] *Annual Report of the Secretary of the Treasury, 1893* (Washington: Government Printing Office, 1893), LXXIII.

[3] Herbert Satterley to George Cortleyou, November 23, 1897, McKinley Papers, reel 2.

[4] *New York Times*, May 21, 1895, pp. 9, 13.

to reserve for the government.[5] National banks nevertheless provided a large volume of money that the public accepted readily. These institutions had to hold federal bonds with a face value of $100 for every $90 of notes they issued. If these securities traded at a premium, banks found themselves using more capital to issue the same amount of currency. In 1894, a $100 bond paying 5 percent and running ten years would fetch about $117 in the market, so a national bank had to tie up $117 to issue $90 in notes. In the 1880s, many national banks had retreated from issuing currency because they could use the capital more profitably taking deposits and making loans. Bonds such as Carlisle proposed, that traded close to their face value because they carried a lower interest rate, might well encourage national banks to issue more notes.[6] This prospect gave Silverites and Populists another reason to oppose such securities.

The Secretary misjudged sentiment among Democrats in Congress. Many—particularly those from the South—had taken a political risk in voting to halt silver purchases. Populists and, in some cases, rivals within their own party attacked their action, claiming that they had sacrificed the interests of their constituents to Wall Street and foreign investors. Had the economy rebounded strongly in 1894, such attacks might not have mattered, but recovery did not materialize. Congress ignored Carlisle's proposals to retire notes and issue gold bonds.

By the end of 1893, Carlisle realized that the Treasury had to replenish its gold reserve. Between the start of 1893 and the end of January 1894, the Treasury lost, on balance, $55.7 million in gold as holders of greenbacks and Treasury notes exchanged them for gold. Most of this gold went abroad to cover the country's payments deficit. These withdrawals had reduced the Treasury's reserve of gold to $65 million, well below the $100 million considered necessary to guarantee the gold standard. Starting in August 1893, high interest rates had attracted gold back to the country, but most of this influx went into the vaults of New York's banks, not the Treasury. The former's holdings had jumped from $62.6 million at the

[5] Populists and Silverites did not generally recognize that by taking deposits and making loans, banks effectively created money, just as national banks did when they issued notes. A strong case exists for reserving the issue of paper money to the government—it allows the government to command the profits from doing so (the seigniorage), and it gives political authorities more control over the supply of money. Allowing private institutions to make such issues does not, however, represent some basic abdication of political authority, as many Populists and Silverites insisted.

[6] *The Economist*, February 3, 1894, pp. 139–140.

end of July 1893 to $129.6 million six months later.[7] Carlisle wanted to move some of this hoard to the government's coffers.

The Treasury would secure gold by selling bonds. When it became clear that Congress would not authorize gold bonds, the government fell back on the 1875 Act which had provided for the country's return to the gold standard and that authorized the sale of bonds to raise gold. This measure had two shortcomings. First, it authorized payment of interest and principal on bonds "in coin"—that is, either gold or silver. The repeal of the Silver Purchase Act had reinforced confidence in the American commitment to gold, but doubts remained, making coin securities less attractive to investors. Second, the bonds authorized by the 1875 Act paid 4–5 percent a year, whereas the going rate for U.S. government securities was closer to 3 percent. These bonds, therefore, commanded a substantial premium. The prospect of paying above face value for securities deterred many small investors and national banks, which were a substantial part of the market for such bonds.

On January 17, 1894, Secretary Carlisle announced that the Treasury would issue $50 million in bonds paying 5 percent, to run for ten years. Bids were due February 1, and Washington would not consider any of less than $117.23 per $100 in bonds, which would yield the government about $58 million. Subscribers would pay in gold.[8] This issue had two purposes. First, the gold raised would replenish the government's depleted supply of gold. Second, the issue would absorb idle currency, raise interest rates, and prevent further exports of gold. The currency shortage of the previous summer had attracted gold from abroad and encouraged the issue of more national banknotes, while the collapse of business in the wake of the financial panic had reduced the demand for loans. As Secretary Carlisle stated in late 1893, "The amount of money in the country is greater than is required for the transaction of the business of the people."[9] As a result, interest rates had fallen sharply, and foreign investors were considering redeploying their money to other countries to secure better returns. Removing over $58 million from circulation, as one economist suggested, "would have created a perceptible void in circulation, contracted the discount market, raised the money rate and checked the

[7] The Gold Movement and Bond Issues, 1893–1896, Curtis Papers.

[8] Circular Inviting Proposals for Five Per Cent Bonds, January 17, 1894, Cleveland Papers, reel 82.

[9] *Annual Report of the Treasury, 1893*, LXXIV.

demand for export gold."[10] The transaction would be, in some respects, similar to the open market operations that the Federal Reserve would use to manage interest rates and the supply of money in the twentieth century.

From the perspective of the twenty-first century, the desire to contract the currency and raise interest rates during a severe depression seems perverse. In late 1893, low interest rates reflected weak demand for credit, not an excess of currency, and authorities should have welcomed cheap money as a force for recovery. Many Silverites instinctively grasped this argument, though they lacked the language that economists like Irving Fisher and Milton Friedman later developed to make their case in technical terms. The gold standard had its own logic, however, subordinating domestic considerations to international ones. The United States had a deficit on its current account, and it had to cover the gap, either by offering foreign investors attractive terms or by exporting gold. Either approach would restrict the supply of currency and credit—higher rates would discourage borrowing, while the export of gold would remove currency and restrict banks' capacity to lend. The country could avoid such action by abandoning gold standard, but that would almost certainly lead foreign investors to sell American securities and withdraw funds, which would also contract the supply of money and credit. As long as it had a deficit on its balance of payments with the rest of the world, the United States had to pay interest rates high enough to attract foreign capital. Hence the obsession of supporters of the gold standard with "confidence." If foreign investors had confidence in the dollar and the American economy in general, they would invest, the supply of money would expand, and the economy would rebound.

The bond issue did not go smoothly. Bids came in slowly, and ultimately the Treasury Secretary had to travel to New York City himself to persuade its bankers to take the securities. Fortunately, they had more gold than they could readily use.[11] In retrospect, the Treasury had not prepared the ground as carefully as it might have. Carlisle was still finding his way in the world of high finance—he did not, for instance, realize that the major insurance companies based in and around New York City were

[10] Alexander Noyes, "The Treasury Reserve and the Bond Syndicate," *Political Science Quarterly* 10 (1895): 589; see also C.N. Jordan to Curtis, January 15, 1895, Curtis Papers, box 4, for similar sentiments.

[11] *The Economist*, February 17, 1894, pp. 210–11.

heavy buyers of securities.[12] The Secretary learned quickly, but he remained uncomfortable with, and suspicious of, Northeastern financiers. In dealing with the banks, he leaned heavily on his assistant secretary, William Curtis, a debonair New York lawyer whom the financial elite of the metropolis respected. An unlikely pairing, the two men formed an effective team, and ultimately they became good friends despite their considerable differences.

Though the sale of bonds raised the government's gold reserve to $106.5 million by the end of February, its limits soon became apparent. The banks that had purchased the majority of these bonds had trouble reselling them, and most ultimately lost money on the transaction. Few Europeans bought, so the sale did little for the payments deficit. Many purchasers withdrew the gold with which they paid for bonds from the Treasury itself, exchanging greenbacks or Treasury notes for gold. The government calculated that at least a quarter of bond sales consisted of such transactions. Meanwhile, the government's fiscal deficit persisted, so much of the money the bonds brought in went back out again. Whenever possible, Washington paid its obligations with greenbacks, Treasury notes, or silver certificates, but that expanded the volume of paper in circulation with a claim on the gold reserve. In May 1894, the gold reserve again fell below the psychologically important level of $100 million.

Silverites and Populists had their own plan to close the financial gap. The bond issue had infuriated them. Senator Peffer thundered, "In the face of idleness, destitution, hunger, and desperation in every State and in every city of the Union, … the President is compelled to sell the people's credit to appease the clamor of these misers of Wall Street."[13] Led by Representative Richard Bland, a stalwart champion of silver for over fifteen years, Congress passed a bill to coin the seigniorage—the roughly $55 million of idle silver in the Treasury—sending it to the President in March 1894. Its supporters insisted that, by providing the government with money to pay its bills, this measure made the issue of bonds unnecessary. The calculus was as much political as financial, however. *The Nation* noted archly, "The seigniorage bill … enables members who were compelled by public opinion to vote for the repeal of the Sherman [Silver Purchase] act, but who did so reluctantly, to say that they have got something in return. They can tell their Populist allies or enemies, as they may

[12] John McCall to Daniel Lamont, January 20, 1894, Cleveland Papers, reel 82.
[13] Quoted in Nevins, *Cleveland*, p. 599.

be, that they are no longer empty-handed. Behold, we are coining silver!"[14] In fact, many Democrats had taken a considerable political risk in supporting repeal, either lured by patronage or driven by loyalty to the administration. Their constituents were, at best, uncertain about their action, and legislators wanted political cover, which coining the seigniorage offered.

The seigniorage bill put President Cleveland in a difficult situation. *The Economist* complained, "It would revive the very evil which the repeal of the Sherman [Silver Purchase] Act was intended to abolish," and if "many millions more of silver certificates are forced into circulation, a similar displacement of gold is almost inevitable."[15] The financial editor of the New York *Evening Post* warned, "This bill would excite alarm among foreign capitalists, check the inward movement of capital, & start gold exports on an extensive scale."[16] Business groups, including those based in the South, opposed the measure. One petition from Galveston, Texas, insisted, "It will again, and justly, undermine the faith of European and Eastern capitalist in our intentions to maintain 'honest money' as evidenced by the Sherman bill repeal."[17] Others were more cautious, doubting whether issuing $55 million in new money over several years would do much harm. The country could presumably absorb this cash as its economy grew—such had certainly been the case in the 1880s with silver coined under the Bland-Allison Act. Yet even they feared, as one of Cleveland's friends wrote, "its effect upon European capitalists" and that "a large part of the benefits realized from the repeal of … the Sherman [Silver Purchase] Act will be lost.[18] Coupled with initiatives to strengthen the gold standard, as Carlisle had wanted, coining the seigniorage probably would have done no harm. Alone, it suggested a weakening of resolve—and in finance, perceptions matter.

Political considerations weighed against the financial ones. As a St. Louis banker wrote the President, "The Democratic party is sorely divided in Missouri at this time and I fear a similar condition obtains in other

[14] *The Nation*, March 8, 1894, p. 170.

[15] *The Economist*, March 3, 1894, p. 266.

[16] A.D. Noyes to Grover Cleveland, March 14, 1894, Cleveland Papers, reel 83.

[17] Julius Runge et al. to Grover Cleveland, March 26, 1894, Cleveland Papers, reel 84. See also Glenn Walker to Grover Cleveland, March 23, 1894; Charles Witt et al. to Grover Cleveland, March 19, 1894; and Citizens of Waxahachie to Grover Cleveland, March 21, 1894, all Cleveland Papers, reels 83 and 84.

[18] A.B. Farquhar to Grover Cleveland, March 13, 1894, and David Dow to Grover Cleveland, March 13, 1894, both Cleveland Papers, reel 83.

western and southern states. In Missouri the decided majority of our party is opposed to your fiscal [currency] policy." "If you should veto the seigniorage bill the Missouri State Convention in May would no doubt pass a resolution condemning the veto and we would lose the state."[19] Governor Thomas Jones of Alabama was just as blunt, warning, "The vast majority [in Alabama] wish its approval. ... A veto would go far to help [Reuben] Kolb," the Populist candidate for governor.[20] Senator John B. Gordon (D-GA) wrote the President, "Nearly all Democrats are profoundly ... anxious that you approve it [the seigniorage bill]. They recognize its defects, but they do not believe that there is really any trouble."[21] Some suggested that, by signing the bill, the President might actually suspend debate over the currency for several years. One Congressman insisted, "It [the seigniorage bill] is the aftermath of the struggle we had last fall and not the beginning of a new free silver crusade. With few exceptions the members of the Senate and House want repose from further agitation."[22]

President Cleveland's public reputation depended, in large part, on his stubborn integrity. As the Dallas *Morning News* stated, "No more derogatory reflection could have been cast upon the president than to have expected that he would sign the bill and step down from his maturely, clearly and signally defined position in defense of sound money."[23] James Stillman, president of New York's powerful National City Bank, opined, "The President would be throwing away the reputation which it has taken years to acquire by not vetoing the bill."[24] James Roosevelt, a prominent New York Democrat and father of future President Franklin D. Roosevelt, wrote Cleveland, "You despise the politicians and they hate you."[25]

President Cleveland vetoed the seigniorage bill. He considered it unwise and acted accordingly. In so doing, he ended any hope of reconciliation with Democratic Silverites on the currency issue. The prospect may have been illusory in any case. Arthur Farquhar, a friend of the President who usually urged moderation, wrote Cleveland, "What is to be gained by trying to propitiate the knaves and fools who have brought this trouble upon you? They should be made aware at once that they can expect

[19] David Francis to Grover Cleveland, March 20, 1894, Cleveland Papers, reel 83.

[20] Thomas Jones to Grover Cleveland, March 23, 1894, Cleveland Paper, reel 84.

[21] James Gordon to the President, March 15, 1894, Cleveland Paper, reel 83.

[22] Josiah Patterson to Grover Cleveland, March 14, 1894, Cleveland Papers, reel 83.

[23] Dallas *Morning News*, March 30, 1894.

[24] James Stillman to Daniel Lamont, March 17, 1894, Cleveland Papers, reel 83.

[25] James Roosevelt to Grover Cleveland, March 21, 1894, Cleveland Papers, reel 83.

nothing."[26] Had Silverites really sought middle ground, they would have adopted Carlisle's proposal, both authorizing gold bonds and coining the seigniorage. On the other hand, in 1893 Cleveland had insisted on unconditional repeal of silver purchases, and Democratic Silverites no doubt considered themselves entitled to a victory. The middle ground between the gold standard and free coinage of silver—limited coinage of silver—was narrow and treacherous. The country had successfully trod this path in the 1880s, but with the Panic of 1893, it may have become untenable. At the same time, the crisis had convinced both sides on the currency debate that they could secure their full demands—either a currency based solely on gold or the free coinage of silver. In any case, Cleveland was a politician of principle who did not seek the middle ground—Americans had elected him, in part, because of his aversion to compromise.

A Bad Year

During 1894, the Cleveland administration suffered one blow after another. Some, like the rejection of Supreme Court nominees, were relatively minor, commanding headlines for a month but quickly fading from memory. The same was true of Coxey's March, a protest in support of public works to provide jobs for the unemployed. Two, however, had long-term implications—the Pullman Strike and the failure of tariff reform. The former alienated Cleveland from workers and urban reformers, while the latter destroyed what remained of the unity of the Democratic Party.

The administration operated against a backdrop of economic hardship. Though the financial panic had lifted in the fall of 1893, its effects still reverberated through the country. As banker August Belmont wrote in the middle of 1894, "The general situation can be summed up in the word stagnant; … I see no element of disaster, but few, if any, for an early revival."[27] In agricultural districts, particularly among debt-ridden cultivators of cotton and wheat, foreclosure sales were frequent. Each such auction erased not only a farmer's investment but years of hard work. For each farmer who went under, several survived by the narrowest of margins thanks to desperate economies and the forbearance of creditors. Conditions in the cities were different, but just as bad. Workers had no unemployment insurance, and few had much savings. Even a couple of months without a

[26] A.B. Farquhar to Grover Cleveland, March 21, 1894, Cleveland Papers, reel 83.

[27] August Belmont to N.M. Rothschild & Sons, July 3, 1894, Belmont Papers, box 23, letter books.

job could reduce them to destitution. The construction of the 1893 Columbian Exposition (World's Fair) in Chicago had attracted to that city thousands of temporary workers who now roamed its streets in search of work. At night, the city opened municipal buildings to the homeless so that they would not freeze to death, and soup kitchens served thousands every day. Conditions varied from city to city, but all had grim stories. All in all, 1894 was perhaps the worst year for Americans economically in the half-century between 1880 and 1930.

The Pullman Strike began in Chicago, where the Pullman Company built the famous sleeping cars that it operated on railroads throughout the country. Demand for new cars collapsed after the 1893 Panic, and like many other employers, Pullman cut both the wages and hours of its workers. Workers' reaction to such decisions depended, in large part, on how managers presented them. In many cases, companies promised to restore wages when prosperity returned, and sometimes they reduced dividends or the salaries of corporate officers. In such circumstances, workers often recognized that employers were reacting to forces beyond their control and that workers were not alone in their sacrifices and so grudgingly accepted reductions. Pullman's managers handled the situation badly. In particular, they refused to cut the rent on company-owned housing in which they required workers to live, even though landlords in adjoining Chicago neighborhoods had reduced rents significantly in response to the economic downturn. Workers struck, but it soon became clear that their cause was hopeless. Demand for sleeping cars had fallen so far that Pullman found it no more expensive to close its plant than to keep it open. The company would wait out workers, whose strike fund and savings were soon exhausted.

At this point, the American Railway Union (ARU) intervened. This organization, under the leadership of Eugene Debs, had recently won a strike against the Great Northern in 1893. It had a reputation for radicalism, largely because it enrolled all railway workers, not just skilled ones. Its members refused to handle Pullman cars, snarling traffic throughout the country and infuriating managers. As historian Thomas Cochran has written, the outlook of the era's executives "left no place for labor unions or collective bargaining between labor and management. ... Even the most liberal entrepreneurs were willing merely to listen to labor's grievances, and then make a 'fair' decision."[28] The strike also raised a broader

[28] Thomas C. Cochran, *Railroad Leaders, 1845–1890: The Business Mind in Action* (New York: Russell & Russell, 1965), p.183.

question. Every company of any size in the United States did business with or through the railroads, and if unions dragged the railroads into every labor dispute, service would always be in question. Railroad managers kept running Pullman cars, in many cases attaching them to U.S. mail cars in hope of securing support from the federal government against the union. Conditions were particularly tense in Chicago, the nation's most important rail hub and the home of the Pullman Company, where the ARU was particularly strong, but other rail centers saw unrest too.

Federal intervention may well have been inevitable. The railroads were not only central to the economy but supplied many cities with food and fuel, and the Chicago hub was key to the entire system. Allowing a local labor dispute to mushroom into a national rail strike would also set a dangerous precedent. Nevertheless, caution was in order. Pullman's workers had legitimate grievances, and the ARU had violated no laws—with a few exceptions, the strike was peaceful. Unfortunately, President Cleveland put Attorney General Richard Olney in charge of the government's response. Though a gifted lawyer, Olney lacked what attorneys call "the judicial temperament." Once committed to a course of action, he pursued it relentlessly with all his considerable ability and energy, brushing aside opposition. Like many attorneys of the day, Olney had worked extensively for railroads, and he saw the dispute from their perspective. He never seriously considered compromise. Instead, Olney secured a sweeping federal court injunction that, as written, seemed to ban *any* strike by railroad workers under *any* circumstances. When the union failed to comply, Olney bombarded the President and the rest of the Cabinet with reports of violence by workers—a task greatly facilitated by alarmist reporting in the press. By July, Cleveland had, with the backing of his cabinet, decided to dispatch federal troops to Chicago. As he told William Curtis of the Treasury, "He proposes to stand up & stamp this out if it takes the whole army & militia to do it."[29] Cleveland acted against the advice of the governor of Illinois and the mayor of Chicago, both Democrats, who insisted—correctly—that violence was greatly exaggerated and urged caution. Notably, both banker August Belmont and Assistant Treasury Secretary William Curtis, neither of whom had the least sympathy for the ARU, considered reports of violence much exaggerated.[30] The arrival of

[29] William Curtis to Mother, July 7, 1894, Curtis Papers, box 3.

[30] Curtis to Mother, July 7, 1894; Belmont to Leopold Rothschild, July 13, 1894, Belmont Papers, box 23, letterbooks.

the Army in Chicago in July 1894 turned simmering unrest into rioting that, over the next several days, took a dozen lives and inflicted huge property damage. In the aftermath of this unrest, the strike and the ARU itself both collapsed, and the government subsequently sent Debs and other union leaders to jail for violating the federal court order that had declared the strike illegal.

At the time, most lauded Cleveland's action. They had the impression that the violence began *before* the President sent in the Army and so concluded that he had acted decisively to preserve order. The U.S. Senate passed a resolution praised Cleveland's "prompt and vigorous measures" against the strike.[31] Even at the time, however, some were critical, and in the following months, as tempers cooled and more information became available, their numbers grew. Increasingly, observers concluded that the President had not acted to preserve order but rather had pushed a delicate situation to the breaking point. In particular, Cleveland earned the undying enmity of Governor John Peter Altgeld of Illinois, who believed that he could have settled the dispute peacefully, given time. Altgeld may have been wrong, but Cleveland could have afforded to let him try—the economic dislocation from the strike had not yet become critical. Heretofore urban reformers like Altgeld, whose chief support was among the working class, had viewed Cleveland favorably because he was a foe of corruption and government favoritism. The Pullman strike changed their minds. It is easy to blame Olney for this outcome, and he did deserve much of the onus. At different times as the crisis developed, however, other members of the Cabinet—Secretary of the Treasury Carlisle, Secretary of State Gresham, and Secretary of War David Lamont—all advised caution, but Cleveland consistently ignored them and followed Olney's advice. The prosecution of Debs and other leaders of the strike was particularly petty, exhibiting a spirit of retribution rather than conciliation.

William McKinley's management of a massive strike in Ohio's coal fields in the spring of 1894 offered a sharp contrast to Cleveland's actions during the Pullman Strike. McKinley had already garnered goodwill among workers by signing a measure making it illegal for employers to dismiss workers because they had joined a union. The depression hit coal mining hard, and mining companies cut wages. Workers struck in response, but the weak state of the economy worked in the favor of management,

[31] Quoted in Nevins, *Grover Cleveland*, p. 624.

which decided to wait out the strikers. As the latter became desperate, some resorted to violence. McKinley, the governor, dispatched the state militia to the coal fields to preserve order, and the strike soon collapsed. He did so, however, only when asked by local officials and only after credible reports of violence. At the same time, he coordinated a successful effort to provide relief for miners and their families rendered destitute by the strike. McKinley's approach cast him as a defender of social order and private property even while reassuring workers that he was not a heartless agent of capital—an image that would serve him well in the future.

Grover Cleveland's greatest political setback in 1894 involved tariff reform. Tariffs had been the chief issue in the 1892 election. When asked in early 1893 whether he would pursue the matter, Cleveland replied, "What were we elected for?"[32] He also realized that the government needed more revenue. Like most of his contemporaries, Cleveland believed as a matter of principle that the government should balance its budget, and he recognized that a surplus would make managing the currency much easier. The House of Representatives started work on the matter during the special session in 1893, when the filibuster occupied the Senate. In the regular session that followed, members presented a comprehensive package of reforms that the House passed in February 1894. This measure substantially reduced duties on finished goods like textiles, hardware, and ceramics. A significant amount of protection remained—despite the claims of its critics, the bill did not institute free trade—but in most cases tariffs ceased to be prohibitive. The bill placed many raw materials—wool, lumber, iron ore, coal—on the "free list," allowing them into the country without paying duty. Ideally, this change would reduce the cost of producing many goods and so improve the competitive position of American manufacturers in world markets, not to mention the prices consumers paid. The bill would also reimpose the duty on raw sugar, which promised considerable revenue. Finally, the measure imposed a modest income tax, 2 percent on all income over $4000 a year. This innovation would diversify the tax base, provide badly needed revenue, and introduce an element of progressivity into the tax code.

The Senate proved unreceptive to most of these innovations. There the Democrats had a majority of but one vote, and Cleveland's old nemesis, Senator David Hill of New York, unalterably opposed any measure that

[32] Quoted in Nevins, *Grover Cleveland*, p. 563.

contained an income tax. Most of the others recognized their leverage and behaved accordingly, seeking more protection for industries in their home states. The bill's managers handled this delicate situation poorly, in essence asking each doubtful Senator what he wanted and granting it. Coal and iron ore went off the free list, and tariffs on textiles and hardware went up—in all, the Senate made 600 amendments to the House bill. Cleveland and other supporters of reform were not pleased, but they looked to the conference between the House and the Senate to reverse many of the changes. In the committee, however, Senators simply refused to yield. One of them benefitted politically from each of the 600 amendments, and the Democrats' margin in the Senate was so thin that the bill needed every vote.

Frustrated, President Cleveland intervened directly. The previous year, his strong stand against the filibuster blocking the repeal of silver purchases had broken resistance, and he imagined that another show of determination would again secure victory. In a letter intended for publication he wrote, "Every true Democrat and every sincere tariff reformer knows that this bill in its present form and as it will be submitted to the conference falls far short of the consummation for which we have long labored. … How can we face the people after indulging in such outrageous discrimination and violation of principal?" In particular, Cleveland insisted "no tariff measure can accord with Democratic principles … that does not provide for free raw materials."[33] This maneuver backfired. Though the press reacted favorably to this missive, the Senators who were its target did not. They resented Cleveland's attempt to bully them and insisted that he had impugned their integrity. Ultimately, the conference committee reported a bill that differed little from the Senate's version.

Cleveland now found himself in a difficult position. Though the tariff bill that arrived on his desk fell well short of his wishes, it did, from his perspective, represent an improvement on the existing system. The measure reduced duties significantly on a few items like ceramics and admitted wool duty-free, eliminating arguably the single worst provision of the existing system. It imposed an income tax as well as a duty on sugar, both of which would deliver needed revenue. The President could reasonably describe the bill as an improvement. Yet having strongly denounced the measure to the public, such a statement would smack of hypocrisy. In the end, the President allowed the tariff bill to become law without his

[33] Cleveland to William Wilson, July 2, 1894, *Letters of Grover Cleveland*, pp. 354–6.

signature. Compounding the mess, in 1895 the Supreme Court ruled the new income tax unconstitutional, eliminating an important source of revenue and the most innovative feature of the bill.

The failure to deliver comprehensive tariff reform was a disaster for President Cleveland and the Democratic Party. Early in 1894, *The Nation* had warned that, if the party did not deliver significant reform, "The people would say that the Democrats had been preaching tariff reform for twenty years and had succeeded in making it the distinctive if not the sole issue in politics, and had finally carried the country on that issue, but were not able, even with the House, Senate, and Executive in their hands, to carry their ideas into effect. What else could follow but the trampling of such a party under foot?"[34] Tariff reform also represented the last chance for Cleveland to reconcile with the southern and western wings of his party. Most of these Democrats would never agree with him on the currency, but they did want a lower tariff. They (and many Populists) believed that reductions would not only cut the cost of living but, by allowing more foreign goods into the country, give people abroad greater resources with which to purchase American cotton and wheat.[35] Had the President delivered substantial reform, he would have had a claim on them. Without it, he was simply the champion of the gold standard.

In November 1894, the Democrats suffered a crushing electoral defeat. In the House, less than half secured reelection, reducing their numbers to fewer than one hundred. Indiana, Connecticut, and New Jersey—states the two parties had hotly contested for a generation—returned not a single Democrat to Congress. Illinois and Wisconsin—which Cleveland had carried in 1892—did the same. The evisceration of the party in the Northeast and Midwest tilted it strongly toward the West and, particularly, the South—a shift that bode ill for Cleveland because of the enthusiasm for the free silver in those regions. Even the Solid South showed cracks, however. Most of the Deep South remained loyal, but the Populists nevertheless demonstrated strength there. They elected two representatives in Alabama and, but for fraud, almost certainly would have taken the governor's mansion in that state. Fraud also kept Populist Tom Watson from winning a House seat in Georgia. The Republicans elected representatives in Tennessee and Virginia, but it was North Carolina that gave Democrats the greatest cause for alarm. There, an alliance between the

[34] *The Nation*, January 11, 1994, p. 25.
[35] Welch, *The Presidencies of Grover Cleveland*, p. 132.

Populists and Republicans took control of the state legislature and carried most of the state's Congressional districts.

For the most part, voters rejected the Democrats rather than endorsed anything else. Hard times played a major role in the defeat, as did Democrats' failure to deliver tariff reform and their fierce in-fighting. Cleveland, a major asset to his party in 1892, was not so two years later, but the outcome was more than a verdict on him. Richard Bland, silver's chief congressional champion, lost his seat in Congress, and Bryan failed in his bid for a senate seat from Nebraska. Interestingly, the Populists no more than held their own among farmers and miners, and the Populist governors of Kansas and Colorado failed to win reelection. In effect, voters cast their ballots for "other," and within the American political system, that meant the Republicans.

Banking Reform: A Path Not Taken

The Panic of 1893 made it impossible for Americans to ignore the weaknesses of their financial system. The currency was inelastic—banks had trouble dealing with the surge in demand for money and credit during the harvest, much less a financial crisis. The country had eight different kinds of money in circulation—greenbacks, Treasury notes, national banknotes, gold dollars, silver dollars, gold certifications, silver certificates, and fractional silver currency. The Treasury held the country's monetary reserve, but it mixed that money with funds that it used to pay the day-to-day expenses of the federal government, so that the size of the reserve depended on Washington's cash flow. No mechanism existed to increase the supply of money and credit as the economy grew. Thoughtful defenders of "sound finance" hoped that financial reform might address these problems as well as satisfy some of the grievances of Populists and Silverites without compromising the gold standard.

The 1892 Democrat platform took a tentative step in this direction by calling for the repeal of the prohibitive 10 percent tax on notes issued by state banks. A memo from Cleveland's Secretary of Agriculture, Julius Morton, suggested that allowing state banks to issue notes was "the one means sure to prevent a revival of the silver agitation." "The repeal of this tax," he insisted, "will be the most telling blow that can be struck at the Populists."[36] State banks could, many believed, provide more currency

[36] "Memorandum on the Repeal of the Ten Percent Tax Against State Bank Currency," November 27, 1893, Cleveland Papers, reel 81.

even while maintaining its value against gold. After repeal of the Silver Purchase Act, however, the Cleveland administration gave tariff reform priority. In the summer of 1894, Democrats did introduce a bill in the House of Representatives to repeal the tax on state bank notes, but the chamber voted it down by a large margin. Only southern Democrats displayed any enthusiasm for the measure—their northern brethren joined with Republicans in opposition.[37]

State banknotes had an unhappy history. Before the Civil War, these notes had constituted most of the country's currency, but their quality had varied wildly. Some states effectively regulated the issue of notes—New York, South Carolina, Louisiana, and the New England states. Bills from banks there were generally sound. Those from elsewhere did not always merit such confidence. Many were worth less than their face value, and some were worthless. Merchants had to know the true value of the varieties of paper to avoid losses, and publishers offered volumes cataloguing the hundreds of notes in circulation and estimating their real value. By the 1890s, some believed that improvements in communications and transportation would force state banks to be more careful about issuing banknotes than they had been before the Civil War, but most were skeptical.

The "Baltimore Plan," floated in the fall of 1894, represented the first comprehensive scheme of reform to receive national attention. Members of the Baltimore Clearing House drafted and presented it to the American Bankers' Association (ABA), which was meeting in Baltimore. After a vigorous debate, the ABA endorsed the program. It called for replacing all the various notes in circulation with new bills that national banks would issue in direct proportion to their paid-in capital and retained surplus (net earnings not paid out to shareholders as dividends). Banks could issue notes equal to 50 percent of this sum, subject to a one-half percent tax that the federal government would hold to redeem the bills of any bank that went bankrupt. In an emergency, banks could issue notes equal to another 25 percent of their capital, but they would pay a stiff tax on these, encouraging rapid retirement. The Federal Treasury would print the bills, distributing them to banks. Like existing national banknotes, this money would not be legal tender, but banks would be obliged to convert it into gold, greenbacks, silver dollars, or Treasury notes on demand. Implicit in this proposal, Washington would gradually retire greenbacks and Treasury

[37] *Rock Island* (Illinois) *Argus,* June 3, 1894, p. 1.

notes. In time, the country's monetary reserve would migrate from the Treasury to private banks. Canada had a roughly similar system, and it had managed to avoid money panics as well as recurring credit crunches around the harvest. Skeptics pointed out that Canada had only about two dozen banks whereas the United States had literally thousands, but supporters contended that if the principal was sound, scale should not matter.

State banks posed a challenge. The federal government audited national banks, and most believed that it performed this function effectively. If federal auditors concluded that a national bank had $1 million in capital, then it had about $1 million in capital. Not all state banking authorities inspired such confidence. Moreover, national banks had double liability. Each share of bank stock had an official or "par" value, usually $50 or $100 a share, and if a bank failed, stockholders lost not only whatever they had paid for their shares but were also liable to the bank's creditors up to the shares' par value. In practice, collecting money from the stockholders of a defunct bank was difficult, but the very possibility encouraged caution. At the same time, the country had many state banks, some quite large and prestigious. Excluding them from the issue of notes was problematic. The Baltimore plan and many of its imitators allowed state banks to issue currency on the same terms as national ones if they submitted to the same rules, although exactly how this system would work varied.[38] This issue proved particularly divisive. One Democratic representative wrote President Cleveland, "I trust you will leave no room for a doubt as to your opposition to state banks of issue," and banker August Belmont believed that allowing state banks to issue currency was "a fundamental error."[39] State banks, however, had considerable influence. Allowing them to issue currency would secure powerful support for reform, while excluding them risked their active opposition.

The Baltimore plan represented a double-edged sword. Gretchen Ritter notes in her book *Goldbugs and Greenbacks* that it and similar proposals for reform "would have improved circulation with minimum government regulation," but that the issue of more banknotes would have reduced the role of government-issued greenbacks and Treasury notes, shifting the

[38] American Bankers' Association, *Twentieth Annual Convention, Held at Baltimore, MD, October 10th and 11th, 1894*, pp. 70–71.

[39] Thomas Springer to Grover Cleveland, November 11, 1893, Cleveland Papers, reel 80; August Belmont to N.M. Rothschilds & Sons, December 31, 1894, Belmont Papers, box 23, letter books.

balance of power in the financial sector toward private banks.[40] Such was exactly what proponents of reform desired. As one U.S. representative wrote President Cleveland, reform should "most thoroughly divorce the government from the paternal control of the currency" and "the present paternal system give way to a natural system of bank note currency, in which the government should take only the most limited and legitimate part."[41] This attitude reflected a strong ideological commitment to minimal government and a deep-seated faith in the efficacy of free markets, as well as a belief that bankers rather than politicians should make decisions about finance. One of the authors or the Baltimore Plan asserted, "Our currency must be supplied by banks—*not by the government*. The banks are the arteries of commerce, feeling instantly the change of commercial activity."[42] As a memo written for the President put it, "Banks, and not the government, should issue all notes that are to pass as currency. ... The bank directors ... are experts and are controlled by a higher power and by laws carefully drawn, and they necessarily try to issue only so many notes as the public will really want and is willing to pay interest on. But when the currency is issued direct to the people by the government, the amount of issue depends on the will of Congressmen, who are not experts, who are not controlled by any higher power or established laws, and who do not try to make the issue correspond to well-proven needs of the community, and in fact do not have in mind any test by which these needs can be gauged."[43]

Cleveland's advisor was half-right. Because they are constantly taking deposits, making loans, and trading various obligations, bankers have a knowledge of financial conditions that no legislator can match. This constant stream of transactions also makes it relatively easy for bankers to intervene in markets by expanding or contracting their credits. Bankers, however, have no special incentive to provide the ideal volume of money for the community. They turn a profit when they issue banknotes and will distribute as many as they can. Before the Civil War, some banks dispatched their notes to the far corners of the country, assuming that the paper would never find its way back to them. The notes of a Michigan

[40] Gretchen Ritter, *Goldbugs and Greenback* (New York: Cambridge University Press, 1997), p. 175.

[41] John Warner to Grover Cleveland, November 23, 1893, Cleveland Papers, reel 81.

[42] "Baltimore Plan of Currency Reform," *The Review of Reviews,* 11 (January 1895): 71. Emphasis in original.

[43] Memo for Grover Cleveland, [1894], Cleveland Papers, reel 84.

bank might circulate widely in Florida at a significant discount—a problem for the people of Florida, but not for the bank in Michigan. The First and Second Banks of the United States (BUS) had, between 1791 and 1811 and again between 1816 and 1836, imposed order by accepting all the notes of all banks at close to their face value—98 or 99 percent—and promptly cashing them. A bank that issued more notes than its customers could use soon received a visit from an officer of the BUS armed with a satchel full of its paper to clean out its vault. This prospect encouraged caution, keeping the issue of notes without bounds. The Baltimore Plan had no such provision, though it was possible that improvements in communications since the 1850s would hasten the return of banknotes to their issuers.

In his 1894 end-of-year report to Congress, Treasury Secretary John Carlisle proposed comprehensive reform based on the Baltimore Plan. He wanted to dispense with the requirement that national banks hold bonds against the currency they issued and instead authorize them to issue notes up to 75 percent of their capital and surplus, subject to depositing with the Treasury legal tenders equal to 30 percent of the notes issued. State banks willing to abide by the same requirements as national ones—including double liability for their notes—could do the same, although state authorities rather than the Comptroller of the Currency would audit these organizations.[44] The reliance on state bank regulators, whose ability varied greatly, constituted a significant weakness, as did the absence of a national system to redeem notes promptly. Both flaws, however, admitted solution within the broader framework Carlisle's proposed.

The Treasury Secretary's plan contained one radical element largely overlooked at the time and since. He wanted to do away with the requirement that national banks hold a reserve of 15–25 percent against deposits. Carlisle recognized that holding a reserve was prudent but observed that the legal requirement to do so effectively immobilized this money. Reserves exist in large part so that, if a bank comes under pressure, it has resources with which to respond. Unfortunately, a national bank that tapped these funds to pay depositors during a crisis, drawing them down below the mandated level, would put itself in violation of the law's reserve requirement—a classic Catch-22. As Carlisle put it, "When a bank stands

[44] *Annual Report of the Secretary of the Treasury, 1894* (Washington: Government Printing Office, 1894), LXVI-LXXVII; see also "A Bill to Provide for a Safe and Elastic Bank Note Currency," [1894], Curtis Papers, box 9.

most in need of all its resources it cannot use them without violating the law."[45] During the 1893 panic, banks had mobilized their reserves only by creating legally dubious clearing house certificates to substitute for cash held in reserve, freeing money to pay depositors. Carlisle argued that it was better to rely on the good sense of bankers, however imperfect, than to require them to hold a reserve that they could not use in an emergency.[46] As he put it, "Every prudently managed bank … will undoubtedly keep on hand a reasonable reserve to meet not only the ordinary demands upon it but to provide for … emergencies."[47] Though he did not say so, Carlisle also knew—as did everyone familiar with the banking system—that the reserve requirement tended to centralize finance, particularly in New York City. Banks could hold part of their reserves on deposit with other banks in "reserve cities," and banks in the latter could hold reserves with St. Louis, Chicago, or New York banks. Because deposits paid interest while cash did not, banks kept as much of their reserve on deposit as possible. Money tended to accumulate at the center, except during the harvest, when regional banks drew down their balances. By eliminating reserve requirements, reform would limit this phenomenon. Money would still move between the center and periphery, but only in response to financial conditions. Carlisle imagined a system in which bankers played a larger role but also one in which communities had more autonomy, with local bankers providing currency for transactions within the areas they served.

Inevitably, financial reform involved the politics of gold and silver. In theory, Carlisle's program would have worked as well with a silver standard as with a gold one. The Treasury Secretary and the President, however, saw reform as a way to strengthen the country's commitment to gold. As it was, the law required the Treasury to reissue all the greenbacks it received, creating what President Cleveland described as "an endless chain," depleting the government's reserve. The federal deficit

[45] *Annual Report of the Secretary of the Treasury, 1894*, LXXIX.

[46] The British banking system had a roughly comparable rigidity because the law strictly limited the Bank of England's ability to issue notes, and during a crisis, a severe shortage of currency could easily develop. In such circumstances, the British government would issue a letter temporarily suspending the limit on the issue of banknotes. The very possibility of such action reassured investors, and the government had to resort to this device only a handful of times between 1844 and 1913. American law could have provided the President or the Treasury Secretary with authority to suspend reserve requirements during a financial panic, but no one seems to have explored the possibility.

[47] *Annual Report of the Secretary of the Treasury, 1894*, LXXX.

exacerbated this problem, creating a permanent drain on the Treasury. A rush to cash greenbacks could exhaust the government's gold reserve, forcing a devaluation of the currency. A similar run on a private bank might force it into default, but such an event would not upend the gold standard. By the end of 1894, most Silverites actively sought government default. As the London *Spectator* noted, "The men who believe in silver … hope against hope that if the currency trouble grows acute, silver will be declared full money, with which they may pay their debts."[48] Any reform that reduced pressure on the Treasury was, therefore, unwelcome.

In an article he wrote in early 1895, William Jennings Bryan laid out Silverites' objections to banking reform. "The President's plan," he insisted, "gives a special privilege to a favored class; surrenders the control of the volume of paper money to private corporations; builds up an influential class which will be interested in preventing all legislation hostile to its business; substitutes non-legal tender paper for legal tender paper, and lessens the security of bank depositors." These arguments were not particularly strong. National banks already issued currency that was not legal tender, and all banks create credit—the equivalent of money—when they take deposits and make loans. Nor was it clear why changing the rules under which banks issued notes would alter the political balance of power or reduce depositors' security. Bryan stated his real objection in the last paragraph of this essay, insisting, "We suffer from a disease which is worldwide in its extent, namely, the appreciation of gold. There is but one remedy, the restoration of silver, and the longer we delay, the greater will be the difficult in applying it." Silver money would have "legal tender qualities and [be] sufficient in volume to supply the needs of commerce."[49] Silverites and supporters of greenbacks both imagined that, by substantially expanding the value of currency, their programs would reduce—ideally eliminate—the need for banks. Banking reform would make the currency far more flexible but also strengthen the position of such institutions. It was a trade-off that Silverites and Populists were unwilling to make.

In Congress, defenders of the gold standard and Silverites were evenly balanced. President Cleveland had secured an end to silver purchases in

[48] *The Spectator*, December 7, 1895, p. 810.

[49] William Jennings Bryan, "The Currency Question: A Prophetic Utterance," *The Arena* 16 (September 1896): 537. This essay was a reprint of another in February 1895.

1893 only because the financial panic created strong pressure for action and because he had used patronage aggressively. Over the following year, the stalemate reasserted itself. Had the administration introduced banking reform at the end of 1893 rather than at the end of 1894, the chances of success would have been higher, but even then, optimism would not have been in order. In 1894, the Democrats' drive for tariff reform fell short even though the party was pledged to action and, ostensibly, united. Not even the pretense of agreement existed on banking. The House Committee on Banking and Currency held extensive hearings on reform in late 1894, and some members expressed support for Carlisle's plan. Banker August Belmont reported, "There is a strong feeling among the members of Congress that for political reasons it is important that they should not adjourn without having accomplished something toward a reform of the currency," but he added "that it will result in the enactment of a law, I do not at this juncture, believe." "Owing to the great divergence of opinion on all these questions," he wrote, efforts at reform will "result in failure."[50] The House took up Carlisle's recommendations but voted them down in early 1895. A majority of Democrats supported them, but Republicans and Populists opposed them to a man, and enough Democrats defected to bring defeat.[51]

Foiled in his more ambitious plan, Carlisle subsequently fell back on relatively modest proposals. In late 1895, he recommended that national banks receive the power to organize branches that would "make the capital and resources of the parent institution available where needed." The existing ban on branches left "people in the smaller classes of towns and cities ... deprived of the advantages of the citizens of the larger places."[52] In late 1896, Carlisle suggested lowering the maximum capital necessary to organize a national bank in small towns from $50,000 to $25,000 so that citizens of these communities could create such institutions.[53] This change would not make the currency more elastic, but it might provide

[50] August Belmont to N.M Rothschild & Sons, December 31, 1894, Belmont Papers, box 23, letter books.

[51] *Topeka* (KA) *Advocate*, January 16, 1895, p. 8.

[52] *Annual Report of the Secretary of the Treasury, 1895* (Washington: Government Printing Office, 1895), LXXXIV.

[53] *Annual Report of the Secretary of the Treasury, 1896* (Washington: Government Printing Office, 1896), LXXX.

more money and credit in small towns and farming districts. Carlisle also kept up a steady drumbeat for the authority to issue gold bonds and to cancel greenbacks and Treasury notes paid into the Treasury. Congress ignored all these recommendations. Populists and Silverites had no use for national banks and their notes, and Republicans did not want to give the Cleveland administration a major victory. Instead, members of the GOP insisted that raising tariffs offered the surest path to financial stability because it would, they claimed, increase government revenue and improve the country's balance of payments by discouraging imports.

Though it yielded little, the debate over financial reform provides a valuable perspective on the financial politics of the 1890s. Without abandoning the gold standard, the country could have made more credit available to farmers and decentralized the banking system. The champions of "sound finance" were open to—in many cases enthusiastic about—such reforms, but the project suffered from its complexity and partisan infighting. Silverite opposition doomed it, however. They sought not a better place for themselves within the existing financial system but to dispense with it. As it was, local bankers and merchants controlled access to credit, and the Liverpool market determined the price of cotton and wheat. Silverites hoped by flooding the country with silver dollars to free farmers from both.

Working on the Railroads

During the 1890s, railroads defaulted on hundreds of millions of dollars in debt, dealing the economy a body blow. Bankrupt companies accounted for about a quarter of the country's rail net, and in almost every case, these roads had expanded too fast. Most suffered from undisciplined management, and often, leaders had depleted their assets through insider dealing. The problem was most acute in the West, where distances were longer and traffic lighter, but every section of the country had troubled roads. The implications were dire. Without an efficient rail net, commerce and industry would wither. Railroads also accounted for a huge part of economic activity. They were the country's largest consumers of steel and machinery and the sponsors of huge construction projects. Carnegie Steel, Illinois Steel, Baldwin Locomotive, and the Pullman Company all depended on orders from the railroads. During the depression that began in 1893, orders from railroads collapsed. The number of cars per 100 miles of track declined in the United States between 1894 and 1898 as railroad failed to replace those that wore out, and orders for steel rails fell 75 percent between 1892 and 1894.[54] Overall, capital spending by railroads fell from $300 million in 1891 to $100 million in 1896.[55]

Bankrupt railroads could not invest on the scale that their customers and the country as a whole required. Halting interest payments did provide some relief, allowing these organizations to put more of their earnings back into maintenance. The Union Pacific and Baltimore & Ohio were probably in better physical shape when they exited bankruptcy than when they first defaulted because managers spent money that had been going to creditors to catch up on deferred maintenance. In the long run, however, retained earnings were insufficient. Upgrading a bridge to accommodate heavier locomotives and trains is not only expensive but also useless without similar upgrades on all the other bridges along the line. By foregoing interest payments, a road might be able to improve maintenance, but it could not finance the sort of across-the-board improvements that would improve productivity and accommodate more traffic. To do that, railroads had to invest in more powerful locomotives, sturdier cars, heavier steel rails, more ballast, and steel trestles. Carefully managed, such improvements could pay for themselves and more besides. After 1897, E.H. Harriman rebuilt first the Union Pacific and then the Southern Pacific in this fashion.[56] Traffic increased, costs per unit of traffic fell, and earnings ballooned. To pay for improvements, however, the railroads needed credit, and that required putting them on a sound financial footing.

More broadly, reviving the railroads promised to revive the economy as a whole. They accounted for a large portion of investment in the United States. In the 1930s, economist John Maynard Keynes suggested that capital spending had a "multiplier" as those employed in it spent their earnings, and those to whom they paid this money in turn spent this cash, and so on. It worked in reverse too. When steel mills and machine shops laid off employees as the railroads cut orders, workers cut their spending, hurting the shopkeepers and merchants who catered to them. No one in the 1890s thought in Keynes' terms, but they understood the importance of the railroads to the economy.

[54] Charles Hoffmann, "The Depression of the Nineties," *Journal of Economic History* 16 (1956): 141–2.

[55] Rendig Fels, *American Business Cycles, 1865–1897* (Chapel Hill: University of North Carolina Press, 1959), p. 216.

[56] Maury Klein, *The Life and Legend of E.H. Harriman* (Chapel Hill: University of North Carolina Press, 2000).

In theory, reorganizing a railroad's finances was straightforward. A railroad in default would enter a court-approved receivership under a committee that included bankers, managers, and lawyers. This group would devise a plan to write down the company's debts by reducing interest rates on bonds and converting some of them into preferred stock, which paid a dividend only if the company earned a profit.[57] Owners of common stock usually had to pay an "assessment" if they wanted to retain their shares. The object was to reduce "fixed charges," chiefly interest payments, so that even in the worst possible circumstances—of which the mid-1890s offered a good approximation—railroads could cover them. After reorganization, most railroads usually had more capital, on paper, than before, but reductions in interest rates and the issue of stock to replace bonds reduced the costs of supporting this capital.[58] In almost all cases, the authors of these plans provided for new securities to finance what they called "betterments." Finally, most reorganization plans placed the railroad's common stock in a trust controlled by the plan's authors. These trusts typically ran five years or until the road had paid dividends on its preferred shares, whichever came second. Bankers feared that reckless leaders at railroads could undo their hard work, as had occurred after J.P. Morgan & Co.'s reorganization of the Reading Railroad in the 1880s. These trusts allowed them to enforce prudence.

In practice, these operations were fiendishly complex. The railroads involved often had tens of thousands of employees operating thousands of miles of track. Determining costs and revenue required an extensive knowledge of railroad operations, as did gauging the likely costs and benefits of capital spending. Most roads had a variety of subsidiaries with their own assets and debts, and all railways had many classes of securities with different claims—common stock, preferred stock, second preferred stock,

[57] A company must pay dividends on preferred stock before paying out anything to holders of common stock—hence the term "preferred." The dividends on preferred stock are capped, however, whereas those on common stock are not.

[58] An investor with a $1000 bond paying 6 percent from a railroad in default might receive a new $1000 bond paying 4 percent along with $400 in preferred stock paying 5 percent. Thus $1000 in capital became $1400. At the same time, fixed charges—those the railroad had a legal obligation to pay under any circumstances—declined from $60 to $40, by one-third. Should the road's income increase, it would also pay $20 on its preferred stock, giving the investor the $60 he or she would have received under the initial bond—but no more. Supporting $1400 in capital would, therefore, never cost more under the new arrangement than supporting $1000 under the old one.

car trusts, mortgage bonds, income bonds, general revenue bonds, and more.[59] Marketing the securities of railroads exiting receivership required an intimate knowledge of financial markets and investors. Only a handful of organizations had the range of expertise required. J.P. Morgan was the leader, but others such as Kuhn Loeb played important roles too. Successful reorganizations were immensely profitable for such firms. J.P. Morgan & Co. earned roughly $850,000 for sorting out the affairs of the Richmond Terminal—though most of this was in the form of common stock, whose value depended on the success of the reorganization.[60] The work was necessary and those qualified to do it few, so firms like Morgan's could set their own terms.

Most reorganizations had an international dimension—sometimes a decisive one. In many cases, foreign investors held a large portion of the securities of roads in default. Britain had committees representing the interests of creditors of the Reading, Erie, and other bankrupt roads, and similar organizations existed elsewhere in Europe. Often, reorganization entailed floating new issues in London, Paris, and Berlin. Sometimes, Europeans took a more direct hand. Baring Brothers led the reorganization of the Atchison, Topeka, and Santa Fe, while the Deutsche Bank partnered with J.P. Morgan & Co. in restructuring the troubled Northern Pacific.

The cases of the Richmond Terminal and the Union Pacific (UP) give some idea of the challenges reorganizations posed. The Richmond Terminal had long been a plaything of speculators. It was a holding company that controlled three major and two dozen minor railroads in the Southeast, dominating traffic in Virginia, the Carolinas, Georgia, and east Tennessee and stretching into Alabama and Kentucky. The system was massive, embracing over 8000 miles of track in one way or another, but management had focused on enriching itself through insider dealing

[59] The various types of stocks and bonds often had different security. The holders of mortgage bonds, for instance, had a claim on the railroad's physical property—track, stations—if the railroad defaulted. Those who held car trusts had a claim on rolling stock. Income and general revenue bonds, in contrast, were secured only by the income of the railroad. This variety of securities spoke to the inventiveness of financiers in raising money, but if a railroad collapsed, sorting out the various claims was a challenge, to put it mildly.

[60] Vincent Carosso, *The Morgans: Private International Bankers, 1854–1913* (Cambridge, MA: Harvard University Press. 1987), p. 372. $750,000 of Morgan's fee consisted of 50,000 shares of common stock in the Southern Railroad, which Morgan's valued at $15 a share, the market price at the time.

rather than coordinating and improving its extensive properties. In the early 1890s, J.P. Morgan & Co. commissioned a report that concluded, "Nearly all the rail in both systems is too light, many of the trestles need renewing, and a large number of the bridges ... are not sufficiently strong to warrant the use of heavy engines. ... The engines and cars are generally small and weak and unsuitable for main-line service. ... Other appointments, such as shops, yards, etc., are, with but few exceptions, crude and uneconomical." Large parts of the track—even sections of the main line—consisted of iron rails, which had become obsolete in the 1870s.[61] The Terminal also had a towering debt that consumed all available resources and a byzantine structure that made any sort of coordination difficult.

The Richmond Terminal's problems did not come as a shock to the financial world. The economy of the South had never fully recovered from the 1890 Baring's crisis—the region depended heavily on the export of cotton to Europe, and the Continent had slipped into recession after 1890. Weak harvests in the early 1890s compounded the problem, and the Terminal's revenue fell with the income of its customers. It first explored reorganization in 1891, and in June 1892 it defaulted on its obligations. These events inspired months of discussion and planning, but no action. The size and complexity of the Terminal's debts and the yawning gap between its costs and revenue defeated all efforts. In desperation, those who controlled the road turned to J.P. Morgan. He had a justifiably low opinion of these men and refused to undertake the task unless they gave him absolute authority over reorganization. For several months, they sought better terms, but Morgan refused to compromise, and the road's finances continued to deteriorate. On February 2, 1893, the railroad's leaders gave in and formally asked Morgan "to take up the reorganization of the Richmond Terminal and its allied properties, each pledging you our personal support and aid in full confidence that the security holders will support us in this respect."[62]

Thus J.P. Morgan & Co. began the reorganization not only of the Richmond Terminal's finances but of its entire operation. Morgan and his associates began by creating the Southern Railroad, which was authorized to issue up to $160 million in common stock, $75 million in 5 percent

[61] Quotes in Daggett, *Railroad Reorganization*, pp. 167–8.

[62] Quoted in Daggett, *Railroad Reorganization*, p. 178.

preferred stock, and $140 in bonds paying 5 percent.[63] One of Morgan's partners, Charles Coster, devised formulas for exchanging the over fifty different classes of securities that the Terminal and its subsidiaries had issued for those of the new company, forcing holders of the common and even preferred stock to pay assessments to retain their shares and reducing interest on the road's bonds. As the economy contracted during 1893 and 1894, further depressing revenue, Coster had to increase his demands. Ultimately, he reduced the system's fixed charges by $4 million a year. The assessments on common and preferred stock retired most of the road's substantial short-term debt, and Morgan somehow managed to sell $12 million of the Southern's bonds and preferred stock to investors to finance badly needed improvements.[64] Morgan also set aside $35 million in bonds to finance "betterments," with the provision that the road could sell no more than $2.5 million in any one a year. Meanwhile, Morgan's railroad expert, Samuel Spencer, investigated the various subsidiaries to see which were worth keeping. After the reorganization was complete, he would take charge of the new Southern Railroad. Morgan's lawyer, Francis Stetson, did the legal work, which over a few months in 1894 entailed two trustees' sales, one receiver's sale, ten foreclosure sales, and six conveyances without foreclosures. In all, thirty companies disappeared into the Southern Railroad.[65] The result was a company that not only paid its bills but, under Spencer's leadership, improved service substantially—albeit from a low base. In this case, J.P. Morgan & Co. had earned its hefty fee.

Though not quite as complex as the reorganization of the Richmond Terminal, the rehabilitation of the Union Pacific under the direction of Kuhn Loeb's Jacob Schiff posed special challenges. The Union Pacific, the eastern two-thirds of the nation's first transcontinental line, had a colorful

[63] In the late nineteenth century, even common stock had a "par value," usually $50 or $100 a share, that supposedly reflected the price at which the company issued it. In fact, promotors often sold stock well below par, a practice known as "watering" a stock. More important, the market price of stock depended on anticipated earnings and dividends and so often diverged considerably from the par value even when there was no "water." Financiers understood this reality perfected well. Morgan and his associates assumed that the market price of a $100 share of the Southern Railway's common stock would be about $15, which proved accurate. Unfortunately, the existence of par value often deceived unsophisticated investors and has continued to confuse later generations.

[64] Maury Klein, *The Great Richmond Terminal: A Study in Businessmen and Business Strategy* (Charlottesville; University Press of Virginia, 1970), p. 272. These securities ultimately proved a good investment, but in the mid-1890s, they seemed risky.

[65] Daggett, *Railroad Reorganization*, p. 187.

history, to put it kindly. Its promoters had created a separate company, the notorious Credit Mobilier, to build the railroad. Through it, they both overcharged the Union Pacific for construction and paid Congressmen and Senators to look the other way. From the start, the UP shouldered more debt than it could easily manage. Jay Gould rescued the road in the 1870s, bringing energetic leadership that, among other things, aggressively developed the company's extensive mineral holdings. In 1880, however, Gould had the UP purchase (at an inflated price) the Kansas Pacific, which he also controlled, plunging the road back into the sort of financial problems from which he had just rescued it. Gould, however, soon sold his stock in the company and moved on. His successor, Charles Francis Adams—the grandson and great-grandson of presidents—sought to resolve the UP's problems by acquiring feeder lines and connections—"system building." Some of these, like the link to Portland, Oregon, were valuable, but too many failed to pay their way. The UP's position was unstable even in good times, and revenue fell sharply with the financial panic. In the first half of 1893, its income dropped by $2.5 million, and the worst was yet to come.[66] By the end of that year, preparations for reorganization were under way.

The federal government's interest in the Union Pacific substantially complicated this process. In the 1860s, Washington had directly subsidized construction of the UP by transferring federal bonds to the company. The railroad was supposed to repay this money at some point, and the company and the government had been negotiating the matter since the 1870s. In some years, the company had contributed to a sinking fund set up to retire this debt, but in other years financial pressures precluded such contributions. The UP's managers never gave up the hope that they could somehow persuade Congress to write off at least part of this obligation. This outcome was unlikely. Large grants to major companies, even when they are teetering on the edge of bankruptcy, are never popular. In the case of the Union Pacific, its shady history—the Credit Mobilier scandal and Jay Gould's machinations—made concessions particularly unappetizing to politicians. By the early 1890s, the UP owed Washington well over $50 million—the sum of the original debt plus interest minus the cost of services rendered such as hauling mail. The receivers could not force the government to write down this obligation as they could with other creditors, and it defeated every attempt at reorganization for two years.

[66] Daggett, *Railroad Reorganization*, pp. 240–41.

In 1895, Jacob Schiff, the leader of Kuhn Loeb, took charge of the rescue. Before doing so, he approached Morgan, who had done a good deal of business for the UP in the past and was a member of the receivers' committee. Investment bankers of the day studiously avoided poaching clients from each other, and Schiff was cautious about intruding on what he and many others considered Morgan's turf. Morgan, however, told Schiff to proceed. Though he never explained his decision, Morgan and his associates were already busy with the reorganization of the Richmond Terminal, Erie, Reading, and Northern Pacific railroads, as well as large operations for the government. In any case, Schiff found himself in charge of a major transaction that, if successful, would yield considerable profit and prestige.

In many respects, the reorganization of the Union Pacific was typical. The receivers imposed assessments on the holders of the common stock, replaced bonds with preferred stock, and required bondholders to accept lower rates of interest. The receivers also abandoned unprofitable feeder lines to their creditors. By early 1896, such arrangements had cut fixed charges from $7 million a year to $4 million, a sum that most agreed the road could earn even in bad times. As an augur of the UP's prospects, the receivers had little trouble getting holders of common stock to pay the stiff $15 assessment per share to keep their securities.[67] The government's debt remained the chief problem. In early 1897, the receivers agreed to repay Washington all it had lent the road, plus 3.5 percent annual interest, minus funds already deposited in the sinking fund. The total obligation was $28 million. Subsequently, the government extracted another $4 million from the company by threatening to hold up proceedings on a technicality.[68] In the long run, the managers of and investors in the UP could not complain—the company did very well over the next decade as traffic grew and the railroad invested in improvements that reduced costs. In the short run, however, Kuhn Loeb and its allies had to sell millions of dollars' worth of bonds not only in New York but also in London and Berlin to satisfy the government.

In reorganizing the railroads, bankers like Morgan and Schiff probably did more for economic recovery than anyone in Washington. With their obligations reduced and secured, these railroads could not only pay their bills but finance investments that improved service and reduced costs. The

[67] Daggett, *Railroad Reorganizations*, pp. 252–4.
[68] Daggett, *Railroad Reorganizations*, p. 255.

UP spent $52 million on capital improvements between 1900 and 1907. The Northern Pacific invested $68 million in its operations between 1897 and 1907. The Southern paid $23 million for new equipment alone between 1896 and 1907. Other roads made comparable outlays. In most cases, this money went not to lay new lines but to upgrade existing ones to handle greater traffic at lower cost. In aggregate, railroads' spending on track and equipment went from an average of $250 million a year between 1890 and 1899 to $494 million a year between 1900 and 1909. The result offered a powerful stimulus to the economy while improving the country's transportation system.[69] The success of reorganization, however, depended on maintaining the gold standard. Reorganized railways sold large quantities of securities in Europe, whose investors expected to be repaid in gold. In many cases, these obligations carried a "gold clause," requiring repayment in gold even if the United States devalued the dollar. In that case, railroads' obligations would increase in proportion to any decline in the dollar's value, so abandoning the gold standard would quite likely throw them back into bankruptcy.

Unfortunately, historians of the 1890s have largely ignored these operations, leaving them to specialists in the history of business and finance. Richard White, who earned his reputation with a study of western railroads, does not mention them in his massive study of the United States in the late nineteenth century, *The Republic for Which It Stands*, nor does Scott Nelson touch on them in his history of financial crises, *A Nation of Deadbeats*.

Bonds and More Bonds

In early 1894, President Cleveland and his advisors hoped that they had stabilized the dollar by halting silver purchases and replenishing the government's gold reserve by selling bonds. Such was not the case. Both the balance of payments and the federal budget were in deficit, and these shortfalls drained the Treasury and the nation as a whole of gold. In May 1894, the Treasury's top official in New York City wrote his superiors in Washington, "As you see the work of depleting the Treasury goes 'gladly on.'"[70] The problem fed on itself. As banker James Stillman wrote,

[69] Daggett, *Railroad Reorganizations*, pp. 189, 260, 309; O'Sullivan, *Dividends of Development*, p. 63.

[70] C.N. Jordan to William Curtis, May 23, 1894, Curtis Papers, box 3.

"Foreign capitalists are alarmed at the condition of affairs here and instead of reinvesting a part of their income, as heretofore, in American investments, they are withdrawing their capital from the country."[71] Perceptions were vital. As one broker wrote, "I have a number of good securities yielding from 4 to 5 percent which I could place in Europe this moment if they were gold obligations; not being so, however satisfactory the underlying security, the far-seeing European will not buy."[72] If the American government could somehow convince European investors that the gold standard was secure, Europeans would increase their investments, thereby providing the resources necessary to preserve the standard and—perhaps—revive the economy. The situation was a classic example of the role of "confidence" in finance.

The demise of the gold standard could well have touched off another disastrous financial panic. It would have entailed a substantial devaluation of the dollar against currencies based on gold—though how much, no one could say. The many companies that had issued sterling or gold bonds would see their obligations increase in direct proportion to the devaluation, as would individuals who had debts with a "gold clause." Foreign investors might well liquidate their holdings to avoid or limit losses, intensifying the crisis. At the very least, devaluation would lead investors to postpone decisions until the value of the dollar settled, leaving the reorganization of the railroads and many other transactions in limbo. It is impossible to know exactly what would have happened had the gold standard collapsed. The results would depend heavily on the scale of devaluation. A 5 percent drop in the dollar might not have done too much damage, whereas a fall of 25 percent probably would have been disastrous. By 1894, silver was trading at half its official price of $1.29, suggesting that a shift from gold to silver could lead to a devaluation of as much as 50 percent. Free coinage would undoubtedly increase the demand for silver and raise its price relative to gold, but this increase would also elicit higher production from small silver mines in the West that had shut down because, at $0.60 an ounce, the price did not cover their costs. Even if the relative value of silver jumped 50 percent against gold, the shift to silver would still translate into a 25 percent devaluation, so alarmists had reason for concern. Further complicating matters, free coinage would not automatically follow should the government run out of gold. Washington

[71] James Tillman to William Curtis, July 31, 1894, Cleveland Papers, reel 86.
[72] H.C. Hoskier to Van Sinderen, October 8, 1894, Cleveland Papers, reel 87.

might let the dollar "float," in which case it would fluctuate between its official value in gold and that in silver. The result would be a smaller devaluation but greater uncertainty.[73]

Poor relations between Secretary Carlisle and New York's banking community did not help. Throughout 1894, these banks maintained relatively large gold reserves, which irked Carlisle, who was scrambling for gold. As the editors of *The Economist* put it, "Doubts have come to be entertained as to the ability of the Treasury to maintain the convertibility of the paper currency. The banks, therefore prefer to hold these funds in specie rather than in paper."[74] Banker James Stillman insisted, "The time will come when the reserves of the New York banks will be the only bulwark to prevent disaster to the financial interests of the country."[75] Carlisle, who was responsible for these interests, viewed their hoarding differently. He was particularly annoyed that many of those who had purchased bonds in early 1894 had secured gold to do so by converting greenbacks or Treasury notes into gold. For their part the banks, which had lost money marketing these bonds, believed that they had done the government a favor by taking them and resented Carlisle's sniping. Stillman wrote, "I was surprised to ascertain the extent of the ill feeling against Secretary Carlisle [among bankers], and the almost universal distrust of his ability to administer safely and successfully the government's finances."[76]

By November 1894, the Treasury's gold reserve had fallen to a little more than $60 million, the same level as when the year had started. Soon after the election, the Treasury announced another sale of bonds, $50 million in ten-year securities paying 5 percent, on which it hoped to realize about $58 million in gold. Secretary Carlisle was understandably concerned that buyers would again draw gold from the Treasury to pay for purchases, and even more concerned that those bidding for bonds would withdraw gold in advance of the sale so as to have enough gold on hand to pay the first installment on any purchases. Since the government was selling bonds to maintain the convertibility of its paper into gold,

[73] Both Austria-Hungary and Italy pursued such a policy in the 1880s, with Italian money fluctuating between its silver and gold value and Austrian currency trading above its value in silver.

[74] *The Economist*, December 22, 1894, p. 1571.

[75] James Stillman to David Lamont, June 23, 1894, Cleveland Papers, reel 85.

[76] Stillman to Lamont, June 23, 1894.

however, it could not very well restrict such conversions.[77] When the Treasury Secretary opened bids on November 23, he received a surprise. A syndicate organized by J.P. Morgan & Co. and the United States Trust Company offered $58.5 million for the entire issue on an "all or nothing" basis.[78] After calculating that this bid exceeded the others combined by $49,000, and no doubt anticipating that this powerful alliance of financiers could dispose of the bonds without drawing on the Treasury for gold, Carlisle accepted.[79]

The sale provided only a brief respite. Gold that the syndicate delivered did push the reserve above $100 million in early December, and less of the gold used to purchase bonds came from the Treasury itself than had been the case with the previous sale. These securities did not sell well, however, and the members of the syndicate seem to have taken a loss on the transaction. Morgan's London house, which took $1 million of these bonds, booked a loss of £673 on them.[80] More important, withdrawals of gold from the Treasury accelerated. The government lost over $31 million in gold in December 1894, and another $45 million in January 1895. By February 1, the reserve stood at only a little above $40 million.[81]

For most of the 1890s, concern about the dollar did lead to panic. As economist Rendig Fels has noted, "If the threat to the gold standard had really been considered dangerous, the outflow of gold would have assumed proportions great enough to have forced its abandonment."[82] Investors limited their exposure, accumulating gold and selling some securities, but they did not abandon hope and liquidate their holdings. In early 1895, however, the country *was* on the verge of a panic that could have forced it to abandon the gold standard. Most notably, for the first time domestic hoarding accounted for a large share of the demand for gold. Some hoarders were speculators, positioning themselves to profit if the government abandoned the gold standard. Others owed money under a "gold clause," which required repayment in gold or its equivalent, and were protecting themselves against devaluation. In any case, the government was

[77] C.N. Jordan to William Curtis, November 17, 1894, Curtis Papers, box 4; C.N. Jordan to Curtis, November 19, 1894, Curtis Papers, box 4.

[78] A syndicate is a temporary alliance among banks to market a particularly large issue of securities.

[79] Carosso, *The Morgans,* p. 317.

[80] Carosso, *The Morgans,* p. 318.

[81] [John Carlisle] to Isham Harris, June 1, 1896, Curtis Papers, box 7.

[82] Fells, *American Business Cycles*, p. 195.

experiencing a run, with creditors rushing to secure gold before Washington ran out. The uncertainty was crippling. As one Treasury official stated, "The business community is at a standstill—they dare not make time contracts" because no one knew on what basis the currency would stand in two or three months.[83]

Explaining the timing of financial crises is difficult because they have a significant psychological dimension. In late 1894, however, several factors suggested that the situation was deteriorating. Usually, the United States imported gold in the fall as it exported the harvest of cotton and wheat, and this influx helped cover the deficit for the rest of the year. In late 1894, however, the inflow of gold was negligible both because European demand was weak—the continent was still in recession—and because foreigners were selling American securities.[84] In December, Congress voted down Secretary Carlisle's plan for banking and currency reform, including the provisions to issue gold bonds at 3 percent. The program was controversial, even among advocates of "sound" finance, but Silverites saw the outcome as a victory for their cause, as did many defenders of the gold standard.[85] Finally, the President showed signs of exhaustion. In December 1894, Cleveland stated to a friend, "I am so depressed during these days."[86] In a meeting a month later with banker August Belmont and J.P. Morgan's lawyer (and Cleveland's friend and former law partner) Francis Stetson, Cleveland reportedly said "that he had discharged his duty as chief executive of the republic, and that if the legislative body, chosen by the mass of the American people, were determined to abandon the gold standard, he would not go much further in resisting their decree."[87] Events would show that Cleveland still had plenty of fight left, but late 1894 was a low point for him—and as the foremost defender of the gold standard, his mood mattered to financial markets.

As the situation deteriorated, the administration turned to August Belmont. He was both one of the few enthusiastic Democrats among the country's leading bankers and the New York agent of the powerful Rothschild's banks. On January 25, Belmont wrote Baron Edmund

[83] C.W. Jordan to William Curtis, January 25, 1896, Curtis Papers, box 4.

[84] H.C. Hoskier to Van Sinderen, October 8, 1894, Cleveland Papers, reel 87.

[85] *Topeka* (KA) *Advocate*, January 16, 1895, p. 8.

[86] Cleveland to Richard Watson Gilder, December 16, 1894, *Letters of Grover Cleveland*, p. 374.

[87] "Saving the National Credit," April 13, 1914, p. 17, Satterlee Papers, 7:7, Morgan Library.

Rothschild of the family's Paris branch, "I am going to Washington to see the President."[88] The object was a new issue of bonds that would draw gold from Europe rather than from domestic sources. Belmont cabled the London Rothschild's, "Europe's large interest in our securities should induce serious consideration of relieving the critical situation[.] Otherwise fear suspension [of the] gold standard," which would almost certainly impose heavy losses on foreign investors.[89] The London Rothschild's were not enthusiastic. "Impossible to place loan in form proposed," they cabled back on January 29, adding two days later, "We could only issue an absolute gold bond," not securities payable "in coin." At this time, all U.S. government bonds were payable "in coin," a term that included silver dollars.[90] Another cable added, "A 5 percent short term bond issued at a premium [like the previous two issues] is never really popular with the investing public on this side of the Atlantic."[91] Europeans preferred securities running twenty or thirty years and selling closer to par. Lord Rothschild, the head of the London house, was a cautious man, and he knew that the U.S. government's two previous bonds issues had not turned a profit for bankers.

Rothschild's did not rule out a deal, but they wanted support. Belmont had suggested to the U.S. Government that it should "offer to deal exclusively with you [Rothschild's]," but Rothschild's told Belmont that they had "consulted with [Walter] Burns [J.P. Morgan's brother-in-law and the manager of Morgan's substantial London operations] with whom we should act in Europe if any business resulted."[92] They added, "You had better see J.P. Morgan."[93] Undoubtedly, Rothschild's wanted to share any risk, and the leading American investment bank was the logical partner. Probably, they wanted the cooperation of Morgan himself. Belmont was a

[88] August Belmont to Edmund Rothschild, January 25, 1895, Belmont Papers, letter books, box 23.

[89] AB to NMR, January 28/9, 1895, Precis of Correspondence between Messrs. August Belmont & Co. and N.M. Rothschild & Sons, Belmont Papers, series 2, box 7, 1895

[90] NMR to AB, January 28/9, 1895; NRM to AB, February 1, 1895, both Precis of Correspondence, Belmont Papers, 1895.

[91] Cable from Rothschild's to Belmont, January 29, 1895, Rothschild's Archives, Letters, 24 January 1895 to 31 July 1895.

[92] Telegram from Belmont to Rothschild's, January 24/25, 1895, Rothschild's Archives; telegram from Rothschild's to Belmont, February 1, 1895, Rothschild's Archives, Letters, 24 January 1895 to 31 July 1895.

[93] Telegram from Rothschild's to Belmont, February 1, 1895, Rothschild's Archives, Letters, 24 January 1895 to 31 July 1895.

capable financier, but Morgan's talents and connections were unmatched, and through the syndicate with U.S. Trust, he was already familiar with the government's finances. Belmont, always sensitive to the desires of the Rothschilds, cabled back that he "fully appreciate[ed the] importance and indispensability [of the] advice and experience J.P. Morgan and intend [to] continue deferential cooperation."[94] William Curtis, Carlisle's chief lieutenant at the Treasury, probably wanted to bring Morgan into the talks as well. A New York lawyer, Curtis had business and social ties with Morgan.

In any case, Morgan soon joined the discussions. Like Lord Rothschild, he would have preferred bonds that explicitly guaranteed payment in gold, but as he cabled Burns, "The situation, however, is critical and we are disposed to do everything [in] our power [to] avert calamity and assist [the] Government under the power it actually possesses." Moreover, Morgan expected the deal "to pay good profits."[95] Whereas Lord Rothschild focused on the risks, Morgan was a more daring character and focused on the potential gains—and in finance, risk and reward go together. At a series of meetings in New York, he and Belmont negotiated an agreement with Curtis to sell $100 million in bonds for gold. These would pay 4 percent and run thirty years, thereby addressing one of the Rothschild's objections. Most observers believed that the United States could place gold bonds at 3 percent, but uncertainty about the dollar required that it pay more for securities payable "in coin" (gold or silver), and the bonds were priced to yield 3.75 percent. Should confidence in the dollar improve, so would the price of "in coin" bonds, but should the United States abandon the gold standard, their price would fall sharply. The contract would deliver either hefty profits or heavy losses.

The government announced the deal on February 1, and the news created immense relief. Withdrawals of gold from the Treasury, which had averaged close to $2 million a day in the second half of January, declined to less than $100,000 a day. As Curtis later wrote, "On February 1, 1895, the withdrawals [of gold from the Treasury] in the *morning* were $1,307,500[,] but the newspapers having announced that negotiations were in progress, deposits were made in the *afternoon* of $1,800,000."[96]

[94] Telegram from Belmont to Rothschild's, February 1, 1895, Rothschild's Archives, Letters, 24 January 1895 to 31 July 1895.

[95] Quoted in Frederick Lewis Allen, *The Great Pierpont Morgan*, (New York: Harper & Row, 1948), p. 107–108.

[96] Memo from William Curtis, December 4, 1895, Curtis Papers, box 6. Emphasis in original.

On February 4, Secretary Carlisle informed Morgan and Belmont that the deal was off. His motives are unclear. Belmont wrote, "We are completely at [a] loss to understand."[97] Carlisle and the President both realized that any private contract would generate intense criticism, and not just from Silverites. Joseph Pulitzer, publisher of the influential *New York World*, had attacked the prospect of a private deal and insisted on a public auction, stating "if the banks won't take it [the bonds], the people will."[98] Carlisle may have thought that, with the drain of gold abating, the government had more room to maneuver and could launch a public auction—a dangerous assumption since it was the prospect of a contract with Morgan, Belmont, and Rothschild's that had halted withdrawals. Some have suggested that the administration wanted a better deal. Correspondence among the bankers, however, indicates that they were willing to take the bonds at the slightly lower rate 3.625 percent, saving Washington $2 million over the life of the bonds. Since the final contract stipulated a rate of 3.75 percent, the government cannot have pushed very hard for better terms.[99] Finally, Carlisle never entirely got over his distrust of bankers and the suspicion that they were trying to exploit the government's problems for their own benefit. Belmont's and Morgan's enthusiasm for the deal raised had his suspicions.

Morgan and Belmont were horrified. They believed, probably correctly, that when news of the contract's cancellation became public, the drain of gold would resume and intensify. With no more than $40 million in gold, the government would not be able to hold out for long. Both men immediately boarded trains for Washington. Morgan brought with him Francis Stetson, his lawyer, and Robert Bacon, his youngest partner. Between his terms as president, Cleveland had been a partner in Stetson's law firm, and the two men had become good friends. Bacon was a Bostonian who had family ties to Attorney General Olney, another Bostonian. The President

[97] Belmont to Rothschild's, February 4, 1895, Rothschild's Archives, Letters, 24 January 1895 to 31 July 1895.

[98] "Gold for the Government," Belmont Papers, series II, box 7, 1895.

[99] Copies of telegrams received from and sent to Messrs. August Belmont & Co. New York, 1/5 February 1895, Sent and Received, Rothschild Archives, Letters, 24 January 1895 to 31 January July 1895. The Rothschild's strongly preferred a 3.75 percent bond, but Belmont and Morgan were open to a 3.625 percent bond. According to Belmont, the government initially wanted the bonds priced at 3.5 percent, and the bankers countered with an offer of 3.75 percent. Belmont had assumed that the two sides would settle on the midpoint between these two prices, but Curtis accepted the bankers' price.

was reluctant to see them, but Morgan persisted, and Olney arranged a meeting. The next day, Cleveland met with Morgan, Belmont, Stetson, and Bacon as well as Secretary Carlisle and Attorney General Olney, though Cleveland and Morgan did most of the talking.

In a tense meeting that lasted two hours, Morgan changed Cleveland's mind. He insisted that the government simply did not have the time to float another loan through an auction. The New York Subtreasury, where most withdrawals occurred, had only about $9 million in gold on hand, and Morgan insisted that he knew of investors who held $10 million in gold certificates that they could cash at any moment.[100] Morgan promised that the syndicate he and Belmont would lead would bring half the gold it delivered from abroad. Cleveland asked if this gold would stay in the country—a good question in light of the heavy exports of gold. Morgan replied, "Yes sir. I will guarantee it during the life of the syndicate."[101] Carlisle subsequently wrote a clause to this effect into their agreement. In this case, the Treasury Secretary's delay did allow the government to secure better terms. Morgan had, in effect, promised to control the foreign exchange market for several months—an immense undertaking that, if successful, would greatly benefit the government. Olney questioned whether the 1875 Resumption Act, under which the government would issue the bonds, authorized the sort of transaction Morgan imagined. The banker replied that an 1862 statute would allow Washington to purchase gold with bonds. After looking up the relevant legislation, Olney approved this approach. (Curtis may have first suggested this device to Morgan—sources disagree over who initially floated the idea.) Finally, President Cleveland agreed. When the talks ended and Morgan prepared to go, he realized that a brown powder covered his shoes and the cuffs of his trousers. It was tobacco. Morgan had gone into the meeting with an unlit cigar in his hand, and over the course of discussions he had, without realizing it, gradually ground the cigar to powder.[102] Subsequently, an exhausted Morgan cabled his brother-in-law Burns, in London, stating, "Impossible

[100] Technically, the gold that backed gold certificates was segregated from the general reserve. That is, in its accounts, the Treasury had $10 million in gold set aside for the certificates Morgan mentioned. Unfortunately, the New York Subtreasury had only $9 million on hand. The $10 million set aside was somewhere else in the government's coffers, and those who held gold certificates could redeem them at any Subtreasury office in the country.

[101] Quoted in Allen, *Morgan*, p. 115.

[102] Carosso, *The Morgans*, p. 327.

[to] convey any just idea of what I have been through today but we have carried our point and are more than satisfied."[103] Historian Richard White has insisted that in their talks Morgan had Cleveland "over a barrel," but that is clearly not how Morgan felt.[104]

The contract between the government and what became known as the Morgan-Belmont syndicate provided that the Treasury would buy $65 million in gold with $62.3 million in bonds that paid 4 percent and ran for thirty years. The arrangement translated into a price of $104 for bonds with a face value of $100 and an interest rate of 3.75 percent. The syndicate would sell half the bonds abroad and half at home. Belmont and Morgan would divide the domestic sales evenly, and the London Rothschild's and Morgan's London house would do the same with foreign sales. The syndicate would deliver gold at the rate of 300,000 ounces a month until the contract was complete, and until then, it would have first refusal of any further bonds the government might sell. Finally, the syndicate promised, "as far as lies in their power ... [to] exert all financial influence and ... make all legitimate efforts to protect the Treasury of the United States against withdrawals of gold." Cleveland insisted on one caveat. Congress would have ten days to authorize gold bonds paying 3 percent, in which case the syndicate would take $65 million of them rather than the 4 percent coin bonds. Most doubted that Congress would act, but the President wanted to keep the option open, not the least because such bonds would cost the government millions less over the life of the securities.[105] Morgan and Belmont agreed. The 3 percent bonds would offer less profit but entail less risk. They would also commit the United States more strongly to the gold standard, which the bankers wanted. That consideration explains why Silverites opposed such bonds, and they were numerous enough in Congress to block action.

Enlightened self-interest dictated Morgan's actions. As he told a Congressional Committee later in 1895, "I had but one aim in the whole matter—to secure the gold that the government needed and to save the panic and widespread disaster that was sure to follow if the gold was not got."[106] He was, in his own way, fiercely patriotic, and he considered the

[103] Telegram from J.P. Morgan to J.S. Morgan & Co., February 6, 1895, Rothschild's Archives, Letters, 24 January 1895 to 31 July 1895.

[104] White, *The Republic for Which It Stands*, p. 832.

[105] 1895 Bond Agreement, Belmont Papers, letter books, box 23.

[106] Quoted in "Chapter Seven, Gold for the Government," Belmont Papers, series II, box 7, 1895.

country's financial honor bound up with the gold standard. More broadly, as he cabled his brother-in-law Burns, "We all have a large interest dependent upon maintenance [of a] sound currency [in the] United States."[107] Morgan's wealth and power—like that of Belmont and many others—depended heavily on his contacts with and reputation among European investors. If the United States left the gold standard, his business would suffer immensely. In particular, the reorganization of bankrupt railroads would grind to a halt. He needed the transaction as much as Cleveland—perhaps more. That is why, in the end, Morgan went to Washington to persuade the President to approve the transaction, why he agreed to control the foreign exchange market as part of the contract, and why he was willing to offer a better price for the bonds had Cleveland pushed the point (the President did not). The banker was certainly happy to make money on the deal, but Morgan probably would have acted even if the transaction offered no profit. Similar motives drove Belmont, and besides that, handling such an important deal would enhance his reputation. Rothschild's motives are harder to discern. Probably they agreed with Belmont that "European[s] interested in our properties could serve themselves in no better way than purchasing our U.S. bonds."[108] Rothschild's had a smaller stake in the United States than either Morgan or Belmont, however. They would not embrace a risky deal simply to rescue the American government. Probably, as they canvassed prospective investors in Europe, they discovered that demand for a thirty-year 4 percent bond would be strong and concluded that the transaction would likely yield a substantial profit. In any case, they stood with Morgan and Belmont.

The bonds sold very well. The securities paid a relatively high rate of interest because investors had doubts about the American commitment to the gold standard. By replenishing the Treasury reserve, however, their sale strengthened the outlook for the dollar and made the securities themselves more attractive. On February 10, Lord Rothschild cabled Belmont, "Press here with one or two exceptions [is] very favorably disposed toward issue of bonds. Our *Times* in leader says [there is] no doubt U.S. will always pay in gold, and therefore coin bonds [are a] much cheaper

[107] Quoted in "Chapter Seven, Gold for the Government," Belmont Papers, series II, box 7, 1895.

[108] Belmont to Rothschild's, January 24/25, 1895, Rothschild's Archives, Letters, 24 January 1895 to 31 July 1895.

investment than gold bonds."[109] Two days later Belmont could report, "The sentiment here is growing more and more favorable." "There has," he continued, "been very great pressure to enter the syndicate, the probability of profit being so good."[110] The Morgan-Belmont syndicate soon embraced most of New York's banks and many in London. Ultimately, it resold the bonds at 112 ½, at which price they were "overwhelmingly subscribed,"[111] and in subsequent trading their price increased to almost 120. This escalation actually became a problem for the syndicate because many of their buyers decided to take their profits rather than hold the bonds for the long term. As Lord Rothschild wrote August Belmont, "We think ourselves that the stock [bonds] would have gone into better hands if the premium had not been driven up so much."[112] On the whole, members of the syndicate earned $4 million before taking expenses into account, and the appreciation of the bonds after the sale earned investors another $4 million. Historian Vincent Carosso, who had access to J.P. Morgan & Co.'s books, calculated its profits at $295,000 in New York and £18,500 in London.[113]

Silverites were furious. In January 1895, the country had seemed on the verge of running out of gold and adopting silver by default. At the last moment, an international syndicate of bankers had provided desperately needed gold—and earned a hefty profit in the process. The episode fit neatly into Populists' and Silverites' conspiracy theories. The Rothschilds had always been a bête noire of Silverites, and their role in the bond syndicate brought to the surface the antisemitism pervasive in American society at the time. On the floor of Congress, William Jennings Bryan ordered the clerk to read Shylock's bond from Shakespeare's *The Merchant of Venice* into the record and then demanded "that the Treasury shall be administered on behalf of the American people and not on behalf of the Rothschilds and other foreign bankers." Kansas Populist Mary Lease denounced President Cleveland as "the agent of Jewish bankers and

[109] NMR to AB, February 10, 1895, Precis of Correspondence between Belmont and Rothschild's, Belmont papers.

[110] AB to NMR, February 12, 1895, Precis of Correspondence between Belmont and Rothschild's, Belmont papers.

[111] AB to NMR, February 18, 1895, Precis of Correspondence between Belmont and Rothschild's, Belmont papers.

[112] Lord Rothschild to August Belmont, March 22, 1895, Rothschild's Archives, Letters, 24 January 1895 to 31 July 1895.

[113] Carosso, *The Morgans*, p. 339.

British gold."[114] The *Midland Journal* (Maryland) sported the headline, "Cleveland Sells the American People to the Jews."[115] Morgan received plenty of abuse too, and unlike the Rothschilds, he had no ocean to insulate himself from it. It did not help that Morgan refused to say how much his firm made on the deal. His profits were certainly ample, but his silence encouraged some to imagine that they were even larger. Perhaps the most painful criticism came from Joseph Pulitzer's *New York World*. On February 19, it complained, "In secretly selling sixty odd millions of government four percents to a syndicate for $16,000,000 more [sic: less] than they were worth, Mr. Cleveland was dealing with a former client [Morgan] through his own former partner [Stetson]." Two days later the *World* added, "Into the jobbers pockets will go $8,418,757. That is what people pay for star chamber verdancy."[116] Some historians have echoed these claims—Scott Nelson insists that Morgan netted "tens of millions of dollars" from the deal.[117]

Critics missed the point. If the government wanted to preserve the gold standard, it had little choice but to work with the Morgan-Belmont syndicate. The gold reserve had fallen so far so fast that no one else could replenish it in time. The situation also made large profits likely. The issues would either secure the gold standard, in which case the price of the securities involved would appreciate rapidly, or fail, in which case their price would drop sharply. Only by issuing bonds explicitly payable in gold could Washington have kept the profits within narrow bounds, and Silverites had foreclosed that option. The real problem was not the rapacity of bankers but the financial and institutional weakness of the American government. During this crisis, the government had to give management of its finances over to a group of private bankers, some of whom were not even U.S. citizens. In Britain, France, or Germany, the central bank would have handled a transaction like this one. Emblematic of the situation, William Curtis, the second-in-command of the American Treasury, spent several weeks in the summer of 1895 in Rothschild's London offices, filling out paperwork for the bonds.[118] As economist Frank Taussig wrote, "Even persons who

[114] Both quoted in Jean Strouse, *Morgan: American Financier* (New York: Random House, 1999), p. 349.

[115] *Midland Journal* (Maryland), February 2, 1895.

[116] Memo from Newspaper files, [1914], *New York World*, Saterlee Papers, 6:C13, Morgan Library.

[117] Nelson, *A Nation of Deadbeats*, p. 191.

[118] William Curtis to Mother, June 18, 1895, Curtis Papers, box 5.

have no sympathy with the general position of the silver men shake their heads over the gold loans, and wish that the policy which they support were not encumbered with these unfortunate and unpopular transactions." The whole thing was "humiliating to the government of a rich and prosperous people."[119]

Whatever the drawbacks, the Morgan-Belmont syndicate stabilized the currency. In financial markets, perception counts heavily, and the sale of bonds to a group comprising some of the world's most powerful banks was a tonic. On February 23, little more than two weeks after the deal closed, Cleveland's friend Arthur Farquhar wrote him, "A great change has come over the country since we met a week ago … an improvement all along the line."[120] Businessmen assumed that the worst had passed and that they could plan for the future with some confidence. An editorial published in May 1895 in *The Forum* noted, "Gradually, more money from the banks is borrowed to resume operation or to increase the hours to full time; slowly factories which have been idle are beginning to work; from time to time the newspapers print items wherein wages, cut down a year or so ago, are wholly or in part restored. … Traveling salesmen have for some time reported stocks in the hands of country dealers as low," encouraging purchases for inventory. It continued, "We must not conclude from this brief review that full prosperity is all but upon us. It is fair to say that the worst is over and that hereafter things may be expected to improve." The author added, "To this [Morgan-Belmont] syndicate we owe at this time the possibility of a better feeling, which must always precede better actual business."[121]

Most notable from a financial perspective, foreign demand for American securities revived. In April, August Belmont praised "the splendid work Mr. Morgan has done in placing American securities abroad to so large an extent."[122] The next month, Belmont noted that Rothschild's "have done most extraordinary work in London and galvanized the Londoners into life," and had sold "enormous amounts of securities."[123] In August, *The*

[119] Frank Taussig, "Bonds Sales and the Gold Standard," *The Forum*, November 1896, p. 339. The American government had sold bonds abroad before, usually through Rothschild's or Baring's, but Washington had tightly overseen the process.

[120] Arthur Farquhar to Cleveland, February 23, 1895, Cleveland Papers, reel 89.

[121] "Indications of Business Improvement," *The Forum*, May, 1895, pp. 380–82.

[122] Belmont to Lord Rothschild, April 26, 1895, Belmont Papers, Box 23, Letter Books.

[123] Belmont to Lord Rothschild, May 26, 1895, Belmont Papers, Box 23, Letter Books.

Economist listed almost $70 million in U.S. securities sold in Europe by members of the syndicate above and beyond the Treasury bonds, a total including not only issues by rock-solid companies such as the Pennsylvania and New York Central railroads but those associated with reorganizations, like the bonds of the Southern Railroad.[124] Historian Scott Nelson's assertion that the bond sale "did little to bring investors back" to the United States is simply wrong.[125] These sales relieved the balance-of-payments deficit that had plagued American finance since the 1890 Baring's crisis. This process fed on itself. If the gold standard was secure, then many American securities offered foreign investors attractive returns. At the same time, foreign purchase of American securities further reinforced the gold standard, and the influx of foreign capital helped revive the economy.

With the bonds sold and gold flowing into the Treasury, Morgan and Belmont focused on the second part of the contract.[126] Except during the incipient panic of January 1895, when domestic hoarding became common, most withdrawals of gold from the Treasury went to satisfy foreign demand. Morgan had promised to control this flow of money until September, when the syndicate would deliver its last installment of gold. That meant controlling the market for foreign exchange. Rothschild's stated, "We do not believe in any artificial manipulation of exchange," insisting "We cannot accept ... that [the] spirt [of the] contract binds us to do anything which we regard here as unbusinesslike and prejudicial."[127] Walter Burns was uncertain too, cabling his brother-in-law, "It is useless [to] attempt [to] control legitimate gold shipments for balance [of] trade."[128] J.P. Morgan, rarely plagued by self-doubt, nevertheless plunged ahead. He telegraphed Rothschild's, "We dislike your suggestion [that you] considered [our plans] unbusinesslike or prejudicial," affecting a tone that must have shocked Rothschild's, who were used to deference

[124] *The Economist*, August 10, 1895, p. 1045.

[125] Nelson, *Nation of Deadbeats*, p. 192. For foreign demand for American securities in 1895, see also Taus, *Central Banking Functions of the Untied States Treasury*, pp. 94–5.

[126] See Noyes, "The Treasury Reserve and the Bond Syndicate," pp. 573–602 and Matthew Simon, "The Morgan-Belmont Syndicate of 1895 and Intervention in the Foreign Exchange Market," *Business History Review* 42 (1968): 385–417.

[127] August Belmont to Lord Rothschild, February 12, 1895, Belmont Papers, letterpress books, box 23; Rothschild's to August Belmont, March 6 & 8, 1895, Rothschild's Archives, Letters, 24 January 1895 to 31 July 1895; Rothschild's to August Belmont, June 17, 1895, Rothschild's Archives, Letters, 24 January 1895 to 31 July 1895.

[128] Telegram from J.S. Morgan & Co. to J.P. Morgan & Co., February 28, 1895, Rothschild's Archives, Letters, 24 January 1895 to 31 July 1895.

from other bankers.[129] Morgan insisted, "Excitement [in] U.S. Congress [is] very great[,] also whole press throughout the country[;] in fact everyone discussing every phase [of] this business[.] In fact immense amount of criticism[. It is] important [to] guard every little point."[130] Belmont adopted a more conciliatory tone with Rothschild's than Morgan, but he backed his fellow New Yorker. Whereas Rothschild's (and Burns) saw the bond sale as simply another piece of business, Morgan and Belmont thought of it as part of a broader program to shore up the finances of the United States, which required managing the exchange rate until September. As residents of New York City, they also no doubt felt public criticism more acutely than did bankers living in London, and they were determined to live up to the letter of the contract.

The process began in February when, as Belmont put it, "We have endeavored to place the bonds where they would do the most good."[131] Every bank wanted part of what was shaping up to be a very lucrative transaction, and Morgan and Belmont gave every major American dealer in foreign exchange a share of it. In all, forty-eight American banks participated in the offering.[132] In turn, the syndicate expected—and received—their cooperation in managing the exchange market. The syndicate focused on the British pound, the currency of international trade. Conventional wisdom held that, when the pound sterling rose to $4.89, it became profitable to convert dollars into gold, ship the gold to Britain, and there convent it into sterling. This was known as the "gold point." Members of the syndicate, however, abstained from such operations. Between February and September 1895, whenever the exchange rate hit the gold point, they instead sold sterling at $4.90. These sales satisfied legitimate requirements for foreign exchange but put speculators in a bind. As long as the United States remained on the gold standard, there was no way that a speculator could convert pounds bought at $4.90 back into dollars at a better

129 Telegram from J.P. Morgan to Rothschild's, March 7, 1895, Rothschild's Archives, Letters, 24 January 1895 to 31 July 1895.

130 Telegram from J.P. Morgan to Rothschild's, February 19, 1895, Rothschild's Archives, Letters, 24 January 1895 to 31 July 1895.

131 August Belmont to Lord Rothschild, February 27, 1895, Belmont Papers, letterpress books, box 23.

132 List of Associates U.S. Government Bond Issue, Rothschild's Archives, 101/601F/4. The only institution involved that was not a bank was Standard Oil, which was always on the lookout for places to invest its huge profits.

price—a loss was guaranteed. Meanwhile, Morgan and Belmont sold large quantities of "sterling bills," IOUs payable in sixty days in London in pounds, to satisfy the demand for foreign exchange.[133] Other members of the syndicate assisted, albeit on a smaller scale. Morgan covered these obligations by drawing on the proceeds from the sale of American securities in Europe, while Belmont drew heavily on the reluctant Rothschild's. Their communications with Belmont during this period are full of complaints about the demands he made on them, but for the most part they went along.[134]

Inevitably, the operation unraveled. Anyone who could get around the syndicate could earn a good profit by shipping gold to Europe, and sooner or later, someone would figure out how. A large importer of coffee headquartered in New York City was the first to break through. Though not a bank, it had substantial capital and foreign contacts, and in the late summer it sent a large shipment of gold to Europe, earning a solid profit with almost no risk. By that point, however, the bond syndicate had largely run its course. No one had expected it to control the foreign exchange market indefinitely. The syndicate had undertaken to do so for about six months, until September, and it succeeded. At that point, revenue from the export of the cotton and wheat harvest would start flowing in, giving the country a payments surplus until at least the end of the year.[135]

One issue remained. By September, the syndicate had delivered $65 million in gold to the Treasury, but only about one quarter of this metal came from abroad instead of half, as the contract stipulated. Morgan and Belmont asked Carlisle to waive this portion of the contract. Though somewhat reluctant, the Treasury Secretary complied. Morgan and Belmont pointed out that the extra gold came from the vaults of banks, not the Treasury itself, as had been the case with the previous bond sales.[136] They also warned, as did some others, that the country could not import much more gold from Europe without provoking a reaction. Up to this point, the Banks of England and France had accommodated American

[133] *The Economist*, July 6, 1895, p. 876; August Belmont to Rothschild's, April 23, 1895, Rothschild's Archives, Letters, 24 January 1895 to 31 July 1895.

[134] See for instance, Rothschild's to August Belmont, February 26/28, 1895; March 6/8, 1895; March 12, 1895; March 12, 1895; March 22, 1895; June 27, 1895, all Rothschild's Archives, Letters, 24 January 1895 to 31 July 1895.

[135] August Belmont to J.P. Morgan, May 28, 1895, Belmont Papers, letterpress books, box 23.

[136] Memo, [December 17, 1895], Curtis Papers, box 9.

requirements for gold, but they were becoming leery of further exports. If they increased interest rates to halt the outflow, they could well attract more gold back from the United States. In an earlier communication, Morgan had suggested that he was in contact with the Bank of England about the bond transaction, and perhaps the Bank of France and the Reichsbank as well, presumably to make sure that they would not oppose the shipment of gold to the United States.[137] Apparently, in August he received intimations from the same channels that further exports were unwelcome. Finally—and perhaps most importantly—the syndicate had sold millions in sterling to keep gold in the United States.[138] The bond issue sought to reverse the drain of gold abroad, and to that end, foreign exchange worked as well as gold.

Venezuela and the Forth Bond Issue

In December 1895, events in Latin American once again threatened the finances of the United States. Unlike the Argentine crisis five years earlier, however, Washington created this problem itself. The occasion was a boundary dispute of fifty years standing between British Guiana and Venezuela. The British had avoided compromise because Venezuela was chronically unstable and they assumed that sooner or later circumstances would let them secure everything they wanted. After taking office in 1893, the Cleveland administration had offered to mediate, but London had ignored it. In the spring of 1895, Cleveland decided to force the issue. Unfortunately, Secretary of State Walter Gresham died in May, and the President replaced him with Richard Olney, who brought his aggressive single-mindedness to the State Department. In July, Olney communicated with Lord Salisbury, the British Prime Minister and Foreign Minister, whose Conservative Party had recently returned to power. He insisted that the border dispute "is one in which both its [the United States'] honor and interests are involved, and the continuance of which it cannot regard with indifference." To emphasize his point, Olney declared, "Today the United States is practically sovereign on this Continent," a condition that

[137] Allen, *Morgan*, p. 108. In a cable sent from New York to London early in 1895, Morgan had stated, "£5,000,000 in Banks of England, France, and Germany available [for] shipment here if necessary." How Morgan would have had better intelligence on the Bank of England than his partners in London is unclear, but Morgan's contacts on both sides of the Atlantic were legion.

[138] June 26, 1895, Diary of Charles Hamlin, Hamlin Papers, Library of Congress, reel 1.

made "any permanent political union between a European and American state unnatural and inexpedient"—claims that surprised not only most Britons but many Canadians as well.[139]

The British showed little inclination to budge. Miscalculating how serious the Cleveland administration was, Lord Salisbury did not reply until December. His answer, when it did arrive, rebutted Olney's more extravagant assertions and agreed to submit only a small part of Britain's claims to arbitration. Cleveland replied in less than two weeks, not with a diplomatic note but with a message to Congress. Olney wrote the first draft, but the President revised the message extensively, and its hawkish tone reflected his opinion. Cleveland announced that he would appoint a commission to adjudicate the boundary. "When such a report is made and accepted," his message continued, "it will, in my opinion, be the duty of the United States to resist by every means in its power, as a willful aggression upon its rights and interests, the appropriation by Great Britain of any lands in the exercise of governmental jurisdiction over any territory which after investigation we have determined of right belongs to Venezuela."[140] Many Americans viewed Britain as a rival and its Empire as a threat to the United States, and nothing else that Grover Cleveland did in his second term of office generated as much popular enthusiasm as this exercise in saber rattling. Congress promptly appropriated money for the boundary commission, and *The Economist* reported a "rush of commercial and other organizations at cities throughout the country to endorse the President's message." Senator William Stewart of Nevada, a Silver Republican who had savagely abused Cleveland for years, embraced the President's message because it promised a war that "would rid us of English bank rule."[141]

Financial markets offered a counterpoint to this enthusiasm. The prospect of war with Britain led foreign investors to withdraw money and domestic ones to hoard cash. On December 20, the head of the New York Subtreasury wrote to Washington, "The Philistines are upon us—in other words, private hoarding has begun & we must stand both foreign and internal drawings. We lost practically 4,000,000 [dollars in gold] today."[142] The next day, *The Economist*'s American correspondent wrote, "The first

[139] Quoted in Nevins, *Grover Cleveland*, p. 635.

[140] Message Regarding the Venezuelan-British Dispute, December 17, 1895, Presidential Speeches, the Miller Center, online source.

[141] Quoted in Nevins, *Grover Cleveland*, p. 641.

[142] C.N. Jordan to William Curtis, December 20, 1895, box 20, Curtis Papers.

result of the alleged war prospect was a depreciation in the price of cotton as well as of wheat," of which the British were the largest foreign buyers. He continued, "London sold Americans [securities] yesterday to the extent of at least 100,000 shares. ... There was a further depressing influence in the cancellation of foreign orders to buy bonds here, and the generally panicky feeling which followed the excited selling and rapid shrinkage of quotations was stimulated by announcements that $3,000,000 in gold would go out on today's steamer, making a total of $6,680,000 withdrawn during the week."[143] Problems quickly spread. Banker James Stillman reported on January 7, "For almost two weeks past the banks have been contracting their loans. Their deposits have been falling. The contraction has been prompted by self-preservation primarily and further by a desire to be in a position to assist the Government if the necessity therefore should arise. The result of this has been that commercial credit has been greatly curtailed and those legitimate business operations connected with manufacturing and general trade which ordinarily expect large accommodations at this season of year have been to every extent possible deferred."[144]

In the end, cooler heads prevailed. No one in Britain showed any enthusiasm for conflict with the United States, and Lord Salisbury's government immediately adopted a conciliatory line. Cleveland's and Olney's claims rankled, but the boundary of British Guiana was not worth a collision with the United States. Americans also became less bellicose as they reflected on the situation. A long-running border dispute in a lightly inhabited part of South America hardly seemed reason to threaten a great power with war. Lord Salisbury soon agreed to an arbitration panel appointed by British and American authorities—Venezuela was excluded—and this body eventually gave the British most of what they claimed. All in all, the war scare lasted less than a month. Cleveland himself apparently anticipated such an outcome, telling a friend soon after sending his message to Congress, "I now hold the whole situation in my own hands. England will be obliged to accept arbitration. Congress will not interfere."[145]

Diplomatic success carried a high price. During 1895, the American economy had showed signs of recovery. The Venezuelan crisis halted this progress. It disrupted financial markets for only a few weeks, and normally

[143] *The Economist*, January 4, 1896, pp. 14–5.
[144] James Stillman to Grover Cleveland, January 7, 1896, Cleveland Papers, reel 92.
[145] Arthur Farquhar to William McKinley, November 10, 1899, McKinley Papers, reel 8.

the country would have bounced back quickly. The recovery was still fragile, however, and the crisis was sufficient to derail it. Output shrank in 1896, and the prices of cotton and corn fell. Secretary Carlisle had opposed the President's message precisely because he feared this outcome.[146] But for the Venezuelan crisis, the administration might have entered 1896—an election year—with an improving economy. It could have plausibly claimed that its financial policies were finally bearing fruit. As it was, the situation was very different—Americans would have to wait almost two more years for full recovery. It was a high price for settling a dispute in which the United States had no direct interest.

The administration's fourth and largest sale of bonds followed hard on the Venezuelan crisis. The gradual decline of the gold reserve in the fall of 1895 forced the Treasury to consider further sales, and the drain in December, during the war scare, made action imperative. The government had over $60 million in gold, but it needed to act while it still had room to maneuver. J.P. Morgan wanted to take the lead. Five days after the President's message on Venezuela, he attended a meeting at the Treasury in which bankers and officials discussed the possibility of a new issue, and he soon began to organize a syndicate that would provide $200 million in gold. As Morgan noted, "The London market was unfortunately closed to us" because of the Venezuelan dispute, but he had little trouble lining up partners both at home and abroad, of which the Deutsche Bank was the most important.[147] The large profits earned on the previous issue made financiers eager to participate.

In early January, however, the administration decided instead to pursue a public auction, offering $100 million in thirty-year bonds paying 4 percent. The public abuse it had suffered because of the agreement with the Morgan-Belmont syndicate still rankled, and the *New York World*, at least, had promised to support an auction enthusiastically.[148] The Treasury also calculated that the situation had improved enough for the government to proceed without the backing of a syndicate. To emphasize the point, the call for bids explicitly banned "all-or-nothing" offers. As it turned out, the issue was a great success. Bidding was heavy, and though some of the gold

[146] Charles Hamlin diary, December 17, 1895, Hamlin Papers, Library of Congress, reel 3.

[147] *The Commercial & Financial Chronicle*, January 18, 1896, p. 117, Satterlee Papers, 6: C13, Morgan Library.

[148] *World* to Creelman, January 3, 1896, Cleveland Papers, reel 92.

did come from the Treasury through the cashing of greenbacks and Treasury notes, most of it came from bank vaults or private hoards. On February 8 alone, the New York Subtreasury took in over $10 million in gold for bonds—"a very good hour's work," as the Subtreasury's chief put it.[149] James Stillman wrote to the President of "the vindication in your judgment in the results attained by soliciting the people throughout the country to subscribe and by facilitating them in so doing."[150]

Still, many found the fourth loan particularly discouraging. Over less than two years, the Treasury had issued $263 million in bonds for gold, but even after the last sale, it had less than $130 million of gold in its vaults. Senator Roger Mills (D-TX) complained, "The President's bond issues were futile. It was like pouring water through a sieve. The hundred million issue a few days hence would be followed by another hundred million in a few months."[151] Though understandable, this sentiment was mistaken. The first three issues had each, in its own way, demonstrated weakness. The first sold poorly, withdrawals exhausted the second after little more than two months, and the third succeeded only because it had the backing of a powerful syndicate of bankers, not all of whom were American citizens. The fourth bond issue, by contrast, secured a large amount of gold on short notice on the government's terms. It demonstrated financial strength. Simply by weathering a series of crises, the American government had convinced the world that it would continue to pay its bills in gold. Now the question was not so much whether the United States *could* remain on the gold standard as whether it *would*.

By 1895, well informed advocates of the gold standard had another reason for optimism. For a generation, the relatively slow increase in the gold supply had limited the expansion of money and credit, fostering deflation. In the late 1880s, however, chemists working in Britain had developed the cyanide process for extracting gold from low-grade ores, and in the early 1890s, American engineers had substantially improved on it. As a petition addressed to President Cleveland in 1895 put it, "within the last two or three years … chemical processes have for the first time in fifty years affected the whole commercial world by enormously increasing

[149] C.N. Jordan to William Curtis, February 8, 1896, Curtis Papers, box 7.
[150] James Stillman to Grover Cleveland, February 8, 1896, Cleveland Papers, reel 92.
[151] "Mills Goes Back on Cleveland," clipping, [January 1896], Cleveland Papers, reel 96.

the production of the precious metal."[152] This new technology revived mines in the United States and Australia and made the exploitation of southern Africa's huge gold reserves possible. Throughout the 1880s, the world's production of gold totaled only about 130 tons a year, compared to 181 tons a year in the 1850s. With the help of the cyanide process, world output jumped to 254 tons a year in the 1890s, and in the decade after 1900 it averaged 513 tons a year.[153] In the United States alone, output jumped from $32.7 million in 1890 to $46.5 million in 1895 to $79 million in 1900. The too-small blanket of gold had become far more capacious.

[152] Petition to Grover Cleveland, [December 1895], Cleveland Papers, reel 88.

[153] Eichengreen and McLean, "The Supply of Gold under the Pre-1914 Gold Standard," p. 294.

CHAPTER 6

The Battle of the Standards

The choice between the gold standard and the free coinage of silver dominated the 1896 presidential election between Democrat William Jennings Bryan and Republican William McKinley. At the time, Americans dubbed it "The Battle of the Standards," and in retrospect, the contest seems inevitable. The grinding depression, President Cleveland's dogged defense of the gold standard, and the chorus of dissent from Silverites all pushed the money question to the front. This Battle of the Standards did not seem preordained when the year began, however. Many Republicans, including McKinley, wanted to base their campaign on tariffs, not the currency. The choice between gold and silver deeply divided Democrats, and no one knew where the party would come down, or even if the two sides might somehow reconcile. The inevitable actually had elements of contingency.

The War of Words

Hard times provided the backdrop for the Battle of the Standards. The nascent recovery of 1895 faded in 1896, with unemployment up and farm prices down. Bankruptcies rose, another large transportation system, the Baltimore & Ohio, defaulted, and capital spending by railroads fell below $100 million, the lowest level of the decade. As the American correspondent of *The Economist* wrote, "It is … very unusual to have to report so large a number of business failures with relatively such large liabilities in

W. Wells, *Financial Politics in the United States in the 1890s*,
https://doi.org/10.1007/978-3-031-86765-1_6

the third year after a panic, at a time when, judged by experience, a revival in trade is in order."[1] Conditions were not quite as bad as in 1894, but in some ways the situation was even more discouraging because 1895 had promised better.

Depression reinforced Silverites' determination. They moved aggressively, circumventing the formal structures of the major parties and taking their case directly to the people. In March 1895, a group connected with the National Bimetallic League, including A.J. Warner and Senator Stewart, declared, "There is no hope whatever that the Republican party … will change its policy [and] give up the gold standard." It continued, "No less persistent and effective is the control of the money power over the organization of the Democratic party." The situation demanded the formation of a Silver Party.[2] Mining interests dominated the new organization, often in cooperation with Silver Republicans. Despite assertions to the contrary, the creators of the new Silver Party seem to have viewed the organization chiefly as a device to put pressure on the existing parties rather than an effort to replace them.

Many Democrats were ready to embrace silver. Some like, William Jennings Bryan and Richard Bland, had long supported free coinage, but others were more opportunistic. Threatened in the South by the Populists and battered elsewhere by the Republicans, Democrats needed an issue to attract voters. As one of Cleveland's correspondents put it, some Democratic Silverites were "men who lost their seats in Congress in the last election and hope in this way [embracing free coinage] to get back."[3] Governor Altgeld of Illinois struck the first blow. He deeply resented President Cleveland's intervention in the Pullman Strike and recognized that many Democrats were desperate after their crushing defeat in 1894. He and his political allies called a special convention of the Illinois Democratic Party in April 1895 that endorsed silver coinage and denounced Cleveland.[4] In the summer of 1895, another Silver Convention met in Memphis, consisting mainly of Democrats but including Silver Republicans and Populists. It offered little new—after years of agitation,

[1] *The Economist*, October 17, 1896, p. 1350.

[2] *The Nation*, March 14, 1895, p. 195.

[3] Lambert Tree to Grover Cleveland, May 11, 1895, Cleveland Papers, reel 90.

[4] Karl Rove, *The Triumph of William McKinley: Why the Election if 1896 Still Matters* (New York: Simon & Schuster, 2015), pp. 146–9.

novelty was impossible—but it energized participants. Almost immediately thereafter, Democratic Silverites organized a Bimetallic National Democratic Committee to cultivate support for free silver among their ranks.[5] Its founders recognized that silver could attract voters from outside their party and, conceivably, allow it to recover from its devastating losses in 1894. They announced, "The success of the Democratic Party in the campaign of 1896 largely, if not wholly, depends upon the earnest and active advocacy of the free and unlimited coinage of silver."[6]

The Silverite campaign operated on several levels. Speakers like Bryan, Bland, and Ben Tillman crossed the country, spreading the gospel of free coinage. They focused on the South and West, where significant support already existed for silver, and they frequently ventured into the Midwest, where farmers were open to free coinage. In 1895 and early 1896, the National Bimetallic League hosted a series of conferences for sympathetic politicians, chiefly Democrats but also many Republicans and Populists, at which they discussed common interests and strategies.

At the time, many defenders of the gold standard attributed the enthusiasm for free silver to a conspiracy among the owners of silver mines. The National Bimetallic League certainly played a large role in mobilizing support for free coinage—Bryan wrote that its leader, A.J. Warner, "deserves to be mentioned as one of the most able and earnest advocates of bimetallism. … No one has surpassed him in unselfish devotion to the cause."[7] The League drew most of its funds from the owners of silver mines, who would profit immensely if its program had become law. At the same time, its activities were hardly secret, and support for free coinage extended far beyond those interested in silver mining. In a democracy, many organizations promote various causes, and the National Bimetallic League was simply a particularly successful example of the type.

Silverites also circulated literature, of which the most influential by far was William Harvey's *Coin's Financial School.* Published in late 1894, it consisted of a series of imaginary dialogues in which a "youth" named Coin made the case for free coinage, demolishing arguments for the gold standard. A wealth of cartoons reinforced its message, and some critics considered these illustrations the volume's most appealing aspect. This

[5] Williams, *Realigning America*, p. 68.

[6] *New York Times*, June 26, 1895, p. 2.

[7] William Jennings Bryan, *The First Battle: A Story of the Campaign of 1896* (Chicago: W.B. Conkey Co., 1897), p. 154.

short book sold between half-a-million and one million copies, and many of these moved through several hands. In April 1895, a correspondent of Secretary of War David Lamont wrote him, "A little free silver book called *Coin's Financial School* is being sold on every railroad train by the newsboys and at every cigar store," adding, "it is being read by almost everybody."[8] As the editor of one small-town paper remarked, "The advent of the book edited by Mr. Harvey has served to renew a general discussion of the uses of gold and silver money."[9] Bryan wrote, "No book in recent times had produced so great an effect in the treatment of an economic question," and he cited it in at least one important speech in New York City.[10] In this case, Silverite propaganda paid for itself—Harvey and his publishers earned a substantial profit on *Coin's School.*

Coin's School is a strange book. Coin debates not the intellectual archetypes or historical figures who usually populate such dialogues but contemporaries like economist James Laughlin and banker Lyman Gage, both of Chicago, into whose mouths Harvey puts things that they never said. Since Harvey wrote the dialogue, Coin won all the arguments. Many readers apparently believed that the events Harvey described had occurred. Gage complained, "I have had many letters from all parts of the country inquiring whether or not I was correctly reported in the alleged discussion, all of which I have answered in the negative."[11] Harvey's arguments were uneven, at best. The book devoted considerable space to whether the federal government, when it first authorized money in the 1790s, valued gold in terms of silver or silver in terms of gold. It discussed at great length the physical volume of gold and silver available for monetary purposes. None of these questions mattered in practice or theory. Harvey exhibited a fierce hatred of Britain, which he considered the chief champion of the gold standard, stating at one point, "A war with England would be the most popular on the face of the Earth. … [I]t would be the most just war ever waged by man."[12] Except for such tirades, however, *Coin's School* ignored the questions of foreign exchange and international finance. Nor

[8] Quoted in James Barnes, "The Gold-Standard Democrats and the Party Conflict," *Mississippi Valley Historical Review* 17 (1930): 431.

[9] *Worthington* (Minnesota) *Advance*, August 1, 1895, p. 1.

[10] Bryan, *First Battle*, pp. 153–4, 330.

[11] Lyman Gage to the Editor of the *Evening Post*, April 8, 1895, printed in Horace White, *Coin's Financial Fool* (New York: J.S. Ogilvie Publishing Co., 1895), pp. 62–3.

[12] William Harvey, *Coin's Financial School* (Chicago: Coin Publishing, 1894), p. 132.

did Harvey seem to recognize that, under a bimetallic regime, gold and silver did not circulate simultaneously but that the cheaper metal predominates. Other parts of the book were stronger. Willard Fisher, an economist who taught at Wesleyan University, wrote that Harvey offered "a very brief but perfected intelligible argument that falling silver tends to depreciate American wheat and cotton; and there is an incomplete but at bottom correct assessment as to how falling prices depressed industrial activity."[13] Taken as a whole, though, Fisher found "the opinions are dogmatically asserted, and are quite unsupported by evidence, even where evidence is easily to be had."[14] In response to his many critics, Harvey produced another dialogue, published in the *North American Review* in 1895, in which the chief speaker asserted, "The fair, truthful, honest arguments in *Coin's School* are met, not by counter argument, but by abuse of the book and its author."[15] He then goes on to liken Harvey to Jesus, whose crucifixion he attributes to Jesus' radical monetary doctrines.

The strength of *Coin's Financial School* lay not in the quality of its arguments but in how it affected readers. In a typical passage, Harvey charges, "Our people are losing each year hundreds of millions of dollars; incalculable suffering exists throughout the land; we have begun the work of cutting each others' throats. ... Oppression now seeks to enslave this fair land."[16] The Panic of 1893 and the subsequent depression had created terrible hardship and much frustration, and the Cleveland administration had done little about the situation except to halt silver purchases and to sell bonds to raise gold. Harvey offered an explanation for the disaster, identifying villains and proposing a straightforward solution. Fisher ascribed the popularity of *Coin's Financial School* to "skillful sophistry[,]... [a] dangerous art [in which] Mr. Harvey has great proficiency."[17]

Defenders of the gold standard were not idle. In May 1895, southern advocates of the gold standard organized a "sound money" convention in Memphis to rally support. The chief speaker was Secretary Carlisle, who had emerged as perhaps the country's most articulate defender of the gold

[13] Willard Fisher, "'Coin' and His Critics," *The Quarterly Journal of Economics* 10 (1896): 192–3.

[14] Fisher, "'Coin' and His Critics," pp. 189–90.

[15] William Harvey, "*Coin's Financial School* and its Censors," *North American Review* 161 (July 1895), p. 75.

[16] Harvey, *Coin's Financial School*, p. 145.

[17] Fisher, "'Coin' and His Critics," p. 192.

standard, and about 3000 attended. This gathering declared itself in favor of "the maintenance of all our money, whether gold, silver, or paper, on a parity" and "opposed to the free, unlimited and independent coinage of silver," and it commended President Cleveland's leadership.[18]

Advocates of the gold standard also penned many replies to William Harvey's *Coin's School*, but none approached the popularity of the original. Willard Fisher counted eight book-length responses written in 1895 alone and found most of them every bit as weak as *Coin*, writing of one, "In everything that is bad, they [the authors] surpass *Coin* immeasurably."[19] The exception was *Coin's Financial Fool* by Horace White, an experienced financial journalist who would go on to become editor of *The Nation*. White dismissed Harvey's work as "unmeaning drivel" and identified many errors in it such as confusion about the role of silver currency in the early Republic, when and why European countries abandoned silver in the early 1870s, and the public record on the "Crime of '73."[20] Fisher found much to praise in White's book, and defenders of the gold standard distributed it widely, but its audience was only a fraction of Harvey's.

These productions accounted for only a part of the literature that friends of the gold standard circulated. The New York Chamber of Commerce created a "Special Committee on Sound Financial Legislation" in early 1895, and by July it had raised $2145, mainly from bankers, to distribute literature favoring the gold standard.[21] At about the same time, the Reform Club of New York launched a larger effort along similar lines through its "Committee on Sound Currency." This group included many admirers of Grover Cleveland and sought to hold the Democratic Party in line for gold. By the spring of 1896, its program had assumed substantial dimensions, supplying regular copy to 1300 newspapers, primarily in the West and South. It also supplied the public with the text of speeches defending the gold standard by luminaries like Secretary Carlisle. The Committee's expenses were, by that point, running at about $1000 a week. It drew funds from both New York City and Boston, and it had a presence in Chicago as well.[22]

[18] *Baxter Springs* (Kansas) *News*, June 1, 1895, p. 3.

[19] Fisher, "'Coin' and His Critics," p. 194.

[20] White, *Coin's Financial Fool*, p. 110.

[21] August Belmont to Jacob Schiff, July 16, 1895, Belmont Papers, box 22, letterbooks.

[22] Calvin Tomkins to Grover Cleveland, March 13, April 7, April 17, and May 21, 1896, Cleveland Papers, reels 93–4; F.B. Sears to Charles Hamlin, August 17, 1895, Cleveland Papers, reel 91.

Nevertheless, in the South and West defenders of "sound finance" operated at a disadvantage in the struggle for control of the Democratic Party.[23] In most cases, Silverites dominated the party's organization. In the West, business interests were aligned with the Republicans and so reluctant to help. Whereas Silverites could count on financial support from the owners of silver mines, Gold Democrats could not draw on banks and merchants to the same degree. More money probably would not have mattered, however. The arguments of Silverites aligned with the understanding of most people in the South and West. As producers of commodities, they suffered particularly from deflation, and debt weighed heavily upon them. Free coinage offered a solution to these problems. President Cleveland's friend Arthur Farquhar wrote in 1895, "[I] have been pretty well over the country … traveling through twenty-four states, more than ten thousand miles, South and West. The people in that section are simply crazy upon the currency question; they cannot discuss it rationally."[24] A reporter for the *Chicago Tribune*, after visiting from a small town in Missouri, wrote, "The 'Crime of '73' is discussed in front of every grocery. … Any number of men can be found who can explain all the machinations of the Wall Street 'money sharks.'"[25]

As the debate progressed, the tone became increasingly harsh. Each side saw the other as the chief obstacle to economic progress. Supporters of the gold standard believed that the Morgan-Belmont syndicate had revived Europeans' appetite for American securities and that only Silverite agitation was keeping money from flowing into the country and restoring prosperity. Silverites contended that the Cleveland administration had done little but commit the United States to a monetary standard that promised only further deflation and hardship. One of Bryan's correspondents wrote in early 1896, "The contest upon which we must enter in this country … is reduced to its last analysis a conflict between good and bad men; the honest, the sympathetic, the human, the true men of the country will stand by the people, come weal, come woe. … The knaves or moral idiots, the depraved and impenetrable scamps, the scoundrels who make up the vast league of confederated scoundrelism in this country, will stand

[23] James Barnes, "The Gold-Standard Democrats and the Party Conflict," pp. 431–2.

[24] Arthur Farquhar to Henry Thurber, May 2, 1895, Cleveland Papers, reel 90.

[25] Quoted in Richard Franklin Bensel, *Passion and Preferences: William Jennings Bryan and the 1896 Democratic National Convention* (New York: Cambridge University Press, 2008), pp. 24–5.

for the combines, corporations, the trusts, the consolidated enemies of mankind."[26] At about the same time, the American correspondent for *The Economist* wrote, "In this fight for sound money its opponents have consisted of all that was irrational, radical, and uneconomic, of members of almost every kind of 'ism,' as well as the cranks—those who have had the preposterous or impracticable ideas about society in general, and the possibilities of our arriving at the millennium within a month or two. … it was a fight of intelligence, patriotism, and American manhood, irrespective of party."[27] A relatively disinterested observer lamented, "This is a question of enormous complexity about which men of the highest capacity, who have made a special study of the subject, are still at variance. But to read the gold papers in the country one would conclude that no man who was not a born idiot could see any merit on the silver side. And to read the silver papers one would suppose that no man not a fit subject for the penitentiary could advocate the single gold standard."[28]

The Inevitable Major McKinley

Like many talented individuals, William McKinley made his work—in his case, politics—seem easy. He was acutely sensitive to the hopes and fears of others and possessed an extraordinary sense of timing. He was also flexible, adjusting as circumstances changed. For him, conciliation and compromise were the chief principles—without these, government would falter. McKinley had focused on tariffs for so long, in part, because he thought that they offered a way to reconcile the country's many economic interests. Critics of protection like President Cleveland insisted that it heightened tensions by favoring some groups at the expense of others, but even they never denied McKinley's sincerity. He brought a similar attitude to the currency issue, an approach that differed sharply from the absolute claims of many advocates of gold and silver.

By 1890, McKinley had formed a close alliance with Mark Hanna. Hanna was an extraordinarily successful Cleveland businessman who, in the late 1880s, segued into politics, eventually attaching himself to McKinley. To McKinley's charisma and understanding of public opinion Hanna added administrative and financial expertise. McKinley's foes often

[26] David Mulvane to William Jennings Bryan, February 29, 1896, Bryan Paper, box 3.

[27] *The Economist*, February 21, 1896, p. 1534.

[28] William Dillon, "Suggestions for a Compromise," *The Nineteenth Century*, August 1896, p. 207.

described him as Hanna's puppet, but the two men were in fact a team and complemented each other in a variety of ways.

McKinley may have harbored presidential aspirations from the moment he began his political career, but others began to think of him as a prospect in 1888. At the Republican convention that year, many delegates suggested him as a "dark horse" candidate, but he refused to abandon Senator John Sherman, to whom he had pledged support. By foregoing a chance at the presidential nomination, McKinley increased his stature as a man of principle. Losing his seat in Congress in the Democratic sweep of 1890, he recouped the next year by winning the governorship of Ohio, and two years later he secured reelection by a large margin. McKinley suffered a narrow escape in the Panic of 1893 when a friend whose notes he had endorsed declared bankruptcy. At the time he had guaranteed his friend's debts, McKinley believed himself liable for up to $17,000, but the obligation was actually $130,000. McKinley had foolishly signed blank notes that his friend subsequently filled in with sums higher than those to which McKinley had agreed. This sum was far more than the Major (as McKinley liked to be called) could hope to pay. Fortunately, wealthy personal and political friends led by Hanna provided him with the money he needed, interest-free, by creating a trust to take over McKinley's debts. McKinley made regular payments into the trust for the rest of his life, but after his death, his creditors apparently wrote off these obligations. Such a financial misstep would have dented the popularity of most politicians, but it enhanced McKinley's. When news of his plight became public, over 5000 people sent him small donations, $1 or so, to assist him pay the debt—a real-life equivalent of the last scene in *It's a Wonderful Life*, when the townsfolk rescue George Bailey from bankruptcy with their contributions. McKinley returned all such donations, but they were a testimony to his extraordinary magnetism. The public saw him not as a victim of poor judgment but, rather, of the hard times that had battered them all. Notably, no prominent Democrat mentioned this episode in the 1896 presidential campaign.

Even before McKinley left Ohio's governor's mansion in early 1896, he and Hanna had launched a bid for the presidency. The Governor had campaigned heavily for Republican candidates in 1894, showing himself to party members throughout the country and putting many in his debt. Almost all observers, at the time and since, concluded that he was the first choice of the party's rank-and-file for the 1896 presidential nomination. Hanna and McKinley built on this support whenever they could. In May 1895, a confidant of the powerful Pennsylvania Senator Matthew Quay who was also well acquainted with Hanna wrote the Senator, "I find that their 'missionary work' has extended over a larger area of the country than I had supposed, and while Hanna is not boastful and has only told me the facts as he believes them, ... yet he is confident that the Governor has more strength than I had really supposed."[29]

McKinley and Hanna wanted to emphasize tariffs in the coming campaign. As Hanna wrote to a Philadelphia paper, "The tariff is by popular esteem the chief issue between the parties, and Major McKinley, sound, able, and convincing on all public questions, is its chief and most distinguished exponent. His name is a synonym for patriotism and protection."[30] Senator Quay's correspondent noted that Hanna "thinks we have got to get back on old lines, and talk more protection; pay more attention to our own industries, letting the silver question alone until it has had its run," though he noted elsewhere, "I hardly think he [McKinley] can be successful" in ignoring the currency issue.[31] Many Republicans joined with McKinley in developing a narrative that placed tariffs at the center. An essay written during the presidential campaign by one of McKinley's supporters insisted, "The business of the country had been excellent during the administration of... President Harrison," adding, "the McKinley [tariff] act had greatly aided in producing prosperity in all branches of industry and commerce." In contrast, reductions in levies under the Cleveland administration had "turned the tide of progress into a flood of adversity." "Money has by this policy been sent out of the country, to say nothing of the losses in other directions chargeable to its distress account."[32] Because of his support of tariffs, McKinley's supporters dubbed to him the "advance agent of prosperity."

From an economic and historical perspective, this argument was nonsense. The country's financial situation had begun to deteriorate before Harrison left the White House, and the McKinley Tariff and the Silver Purchase Act contributed significantly to the problem. The Democrats' tariff reductions did not go into effect until after the country had been in depression for over a year-and-a-half, and with a handful of exceptions—ceramics, wool—they were not large enough to affect producers significantly. Republicans frequently insisted that the *anticipation* of large

[29] R.A. Alger to Matthew Quay, May 8, 1895, Quay papers, box 3.

[30] Mark Hanna to The Press, Philadelphia, PA, [May 1896?], McKinley Papers, reel 1.

[31] Alger to Quay, May 8, 1895; Alger to Quay, April 1, 1895, Quay Papers, box 3.

[32] S.M. Cullom, "Blunders of a Democratic Administration: The Remedy," *The Forum*, August 1896, pp. 715, 719.

reductions in protection had retarded business investment, but were that the case, the implementation of only modest changes should have encouraged a rebound. The GOP stood on stronger ground contending that a higher tariff could help close both the government's fiscal and the country's payment deficits, which between them were draining the Treasury of gold. Under the tariff the Democrats enacted in late 1894, however, the budget deficit fell substantially, to $14 million for fiscal 1896 (which started July 1, 1895) and $19 million for fiscal 1897. Had the Supreme Court not struck down the income tax, the budget probably would have balanced in both years. By comparison, in fiscal 1894, the last full year under the McKinley tariff, the deficit had totaled $62 million. Politically, however, the tariff issue offered Republicans a variety of benefits. It focused attention on an issue on which they agreed, appealed to urban workers who produced goods in competition with imports, and promised to reinforce the gold standard without further issue of bonds or controversial legislation—and McKinley was a politician, not an economist or banker.

McKinley's desire to avoid the currency issue irritated many partisans of the gold standard. In the 1870s, as a new member of Congress, he had voted for a bill providing for the free coinage of silver. Since then, he had not strayed too far from the precepts of "sound finance," but he had favored limited silver coinage, including the much-maligned Silver Purchase Act of 1890. *The Nation* sneered that McKinley "has no more idea of the laws of currency than one of his negro delegates at [the] St. Louis [convention] will have of higher mathematics." (Racism was not solely the province of southern Whites.) It continued, "The particular question in the arena today is far too important to allow any delay or subterfuge about it."[33] Privately, J.P. Morgan complained that McKinley was a "straddler" with a "backbone of jelly." Learning of Morgan's opinion, an Ohio banker who was acquainted with both him and Hanna arranged a meeting between the two—oddly, the paths of these two powerful businessmen had never crossed, even though both had large interests in the iron and steel industry. At this meeting, Hanna demonstrated his own powers of persuasion, convincing Morgan that the Major was "sound" on the money question and that McKinley's cautious approach was appropriate. He agreed to consult Morgan about the currency plank of the GOP's platform and secured from the banker large donations for McKinley's presidential campaign.[34]

[33] *The Nation*, May 21, 1896, p. 890.

[34] Carosso, *The Morgans*, pp. 292–3; Whitelaw Reid to William McKinley, June 13, 1896, McKinley Papers, reel 1.

McKinley and Hanna had to translate the Major's considerable popularity into delegates at the Republican convention at St. Louis in June. Success was not assured. During the 1880s, John Sherman and James G. Blaine were the most prominent figures in the GOP, but Sherman never received the nomination, and when Blaine got the nod in 1884, dissident Republicans had helped elect Cleveland. In other years, "dark horse" candidates like Harrison and James Garfield carried the convention. Unlike Sherman and Blaine, who had plenty of enemies as well as supporters, McKinley did not stir powerful animosity, but complacency was not in order. Starting in 1895, McKinley and Hanna worked to line up support from GOP leaders throughout the country. They had a good case—McKinley was probably the strongest candidate the party could field. Hanna also reminded Republicans that, if victorious, McKinley would control patronage with which he would reward supporters, though Hanna refused to move beyond such generalities. He insisted, "The Governor [McKinley] should stand without a single fetter, before the people, if he receives the nomination."[35]

This approach ran into trouble in the important states of New York and Pennsylvania. Senators Matthew Quay and Thomas Platt dominated the GOP in these states, and their support would probably have guaranteed McKinley the nomination. Both had unhappy memories of 1888, when they had supported Harrison only to fall out with him once he had assumed office. They gave Hanna a list of demands that included control of all federal appointments in their states and Platt's appointment as Treasury Secretary in a McKinley administration, and they insisted that the Governor concede their demands in writing. At least one of Quay's confidants who also knew McKinley and Hanna warned Quay and Platt that they were overplaying their hand, writing, "If we were to make a demand, they would use it in playing the role of extreme virtue, and ask for support, because they had done so."[36] The man was a good prophet. McKinley rejected Quay and Platt's demands and, after brief hesitation, resumed his drive for the nomination under the slogan, "The People Versus the Bosses."

The campaign broke precedent. Hanna assigned his own men to each state to rally support for McKinley, if necessary bypassing the local Republican leadership. The Major did not always triumph, but his

[35] Alger to Quay, May 8, 1895, Quay Papers, box 3.

[36] Alger to Quay, June 8, 1895, Quay Papers, box 3.

supporters won more often than they lost. Hanna opened another front in the South, spending the winter of 1895–1896 in Georgia. McKinley spent three weeks visiting with Hanna there, canvassing southern Republicans. The region's GOP was not yet the empty shell that it would eventually become, but in most states it was weak and depended heavily on federal patronage. Its leaders wanted a candidate who could win and direct federal largess their way, and after meeting McKinley, most concluded that he represented their best hope for victory.

When the Republican convention met in June 1896, McKinley had a clear majority of the delegates. Hanna deserved much of the credit, but he had a good product to sell—McKinley was a stronger candidate than his chief opponents, Senator William Allison of Iowa and Speaker of the House Thomas Reed. The platform that emerged from the convention bore McKinley's stamp. It soundly condemned the Cleveland administration, and the largest section by far dealt with tariffs. "The policy of protection," it asserted, was "the bulwark of American industrial independence, and the foundation of American development and prosperity." The tariff bill enacted under the Cleveland administration was "injurious to the public credit and destructive of business enterprise." Though considerably briefer, the section on the currency was forthright as well. McKinley had wanted a cautious plank that condemned devaluation but avoided the word "gold" or explicit condemnation of silver coinage. A clear majority of the delegates wanted something stronger, however, and McKinley acceded to their wishes. The platform stated, "The Republican Party is unreservedly for sound money. … We are unalterably opposed to every measure calculated to debase our currency." The document went on to declare that the party was "opposed to the free coinage of silver, except by international agreement with the leading commercial nations of the Earth."[37] As a practical matter, champions of the gold standard could not have asked for more.

The currency plank delivered the convention's only real drama. For months, Silver Republicans had discussed what do to if the convention embraced the gold standard. Many had participated in a meeting in February convened by the National Bimetallic League that had called for a convention in August to launch a new Silver Party, but others were reluctant to abandon the GOP. On all issues except the currency, they were

[37] 1896 Republican Platform, Presidency Project, UCSB; Rove, *The Triumph of William McKinley*, pp. 223–7.

Republicans—for instance, all wanted tariffs to defend western products like wool, lead, and hides against foreign competition. Nevertheless, western voters increasingly demanded the free coinage of silver, and despite its nod toward international bimetallism, the GOP platform held out little hope for silver's partisans. Senators Teller and Wolcott of Colorado embodied the two options. Though an enthusiastic supporter of free coinage, Wolcott insisted that he would not leave the GOP. He wrote, "I desire to be counted as a Republican, proud of the traditions of my party, glorying in its achievements."[38] Teller, on the other hand, warned, "Whenever the political organization to which I belong ceases to represent my sentiments and my judgment on great and fundamental principles I shall cease to act with it."[39] Teller proved as good as his word. On the floor of the convention, he sought to amend the platform in favor of free coinage, and when defeated, he walked out. Only twenty-two delegates followed him, however. Free silver had little support in the GOP outside the Mountain West, and even most that region's Republicans stayed with the party. They were reluctant to cut their ties to the GOP, particularly since most expected McKinley to win in November. Voters in the Mountain States were more enthusiastic—Teller received a hero's welcome on his return to Denver after the convention. Later, Wolcott wrote of McKinley's support in Colorado, "Our vote was small, pitifully small."[40] Teller was undoubtedly in tune with his constituents and the Republican rank-and-file in the Mountain West.

The Road to Chicago

The contest for the Democratic nomination revolved around issues rather than personalities. Almost every major figure in the party was identified with one side of the currency issue or the other, and deciding on a nominee was impossible until the party decided where it stood on this key question. The party's rules reinforced this inclination. The nomination required a two-thirds majority. Silverites were almost certain to have a majority, but supporters of gold might well have enough delegates to deadlock the convention. Senator David Hill of New York and former Governor William

[38] *New York Times*, April 29, 1896, p. 5.

[39] Topeka, Kansas, *The Advocate*, May 8, 1896, p. 1.

[40] Oliver Wolcott to Mark Hanna, Nov. 9, 1896, Hanna Family Paper, Western Reserve Historical Society, Volume I, bound letters.

Russell of Massachusetts were personally popular despite their support for gold, and one of them might emerge as a compromise candidate. By contrast, a simple majority could decide the party platform. If Silverites could commit the party to free silver *before* selecting a candidate, defenders of the gold standard would have little choice but to leave the nomination to one of their opponents. Until then, discussing personalities could only divide the supporters of silver. As William Jennings Bryan told one correspondent, "I don't think it wise to encourage a contest for the nomination until [the] platform is adopted."[41] Bryan had his own reasons for delay, but he read the situation correctly.

Silverites had the advantage in this contest. Starting in 1895, they had begun to organize, particularly in the South and West. They hoped to take control of state conventions so that they could send delegations committed to free silver to the national convention in Chicago, which was scheduled for July 1896. Speakers like Bryan, Richard Bland, and Ben Tillman toured the country touting the virtues of free coinage, both catering to and reinforcing the growing enthusiasm for silver. Local activists put pressure on Democratic leaders. More calculating politicians also began to see the virtues of silver. The drubbing they had received in 1894 and the growing strength of Populism in the South alarmed them. The failure of tariff reform in 1894, which was largely the Democrats' own fault, made it unlikely that they could capitalize on that question. Silver offered Democratic politicians an issue with which to revitalize their party.

More than any other individual, William Jennings Bryan coordinated this movement. He not only delivered many speeches lauding free coinage but kept in contact with its supporters throughout the country, suggesting various strategies, most notably language for resolutions endorsing silver.[42] He had neither the organization nor the money that Mark Hanna commanded, but his impact was nevertheless profound. An Alabama correspondent expressed a common sentiment when he commended Bryan for "the splendid service you rendered in this state in the cause of silver, which in my judgment largely contributed to the great victory we won recently here" in the state Democratic convention.[43]

[41] William Jennings Bryan to Mr. Miller, April 23, 1896, William Jennings Bryan Papers, Library of Congress, box 1.

[42] See, for example, Josephus Daniels to Bryan, May 8, 1896, Bryan Papers, box 4.

[43] Jonathan Tomlinson to Bryan, May 18, 1896, Bryan Papers, box 4.

The Gold Democrats had no such moving spirit. The New York Reform Club ran an extensive campaign in the press, and Secretary Carlisle delivered effective speeches throughout the country, but the Silverites had more newspapers and speakers. President Cleveland was not running for reelection, but he refused to take himself out of the race explicitly, which made it difficult for his followers to rally around someone else. The leading candidate from the East, Senator David Hill, was on poor terms with the President. In mid-March, Secretary Carlisle—a logical heir to Cleveland—announced his candidacy, but support failed to materialize, and he abandoned the race just three weeks later.[44] The Republicans were gradually closing ranks around "sound money," but that did Gold Democrats little good. Cleveland still controlled government patronage, and his appointees usually weighed in for the gold standard, but most Democrats considered the President a spent force. In the South and West, much of the party's rank-and-file was actively hostile to him. Often, state conventions voted down anodyne resolutions commending Cleveland's faithful service to the country, an honor routinely extended to those leaving office.

Cleveland did intervene in Michigan in March 1896, mobilizing Don Dickinson, a capable political manager from the state who had served in his first administration as Postmaster General. The President wrote him, "If our prospects look dark, that should stimulate action instead of tempting inaction. Who can tell what change may be brought about in three months? Besides, I do not believe the real condition of silver prospects are by any means up to the volume of bluster and brag we hear."[45] Cleveland hoped that a victory for gold in a midwestern state like Michigan would derail the campaign for silver or, at least, deny Silverites a two-thirds majority at the convention. Dickinson was not enthusiastic. He wrote back, "The sound-money men are all demoralized and out of service, while free silver is in full control of all the organizations, all the offices." He added, "It seems to me that if a bad defeat was to come anyway, it had better be *with* a crank platform. … A bad defeat with a good platform would encourage our worst element and depress our best, whereas the same defeat when the silver men had their way would enable us to rally under the banner of sound principle and reorganize the party." Nevertheless, Dickinson agreed to "buckle to and do our duty from now on, as *you* see fit."[46]

[44] Robert Merry, *President McKinley* (New York: Simon & Schuster, 2017), p. 131.

[45] Cleveland to Don Dickinson, March 19, 1896, *Letters of Grover Cleveland*, p. 432.

[46] Dickinson to Cleveland, March 31, 1896, *Letters of Grover Cleveland*, p. 435. Emphasis in original.

Dickinson delivered one of the few victories for "sound finance." In May, Michigan's Democratic state convention produced both a platform and a delegation for the national convention committed to the gold standard. This success stood in isolation, however. Less than two weeks after receiving news of this success, Cleveland wrote Dickinson, "People whom I see here who believe with us appear to be thoroughly impressed with the idea that nothing can be done to stem the tide of silverism at Chicago. … It is hard to call on friends to maintain a struggle which seems so hopeless."[47] In June, Cleveland made one last plea to the public, stating, "I refuse to believe that … there will be engrafted upon our Democratic creed a demand for free, unlimited, and independent coinage of silver. … Such a course will inflict a very great injury upon every interest of our country … and will result in lasting disaster to our party."[48] Cleveland wrote in vain. In early June, over a month before the Democrats formally convened, an operative for Richard Bland, who was both a prominent champion of silver coinage and a leading candidate for the nomination, insisted, "The battle for 'Free Silver at 16 to 1' has been fought and *won* as far as controlling the Chicago convention is concerned."[49] One of Cleveland's allies wrote to the President just two weeks later, "Our friends have no hope of controlling [the] convention," and then announced that he intended to go on vacation.[50] Silver was the question of the moment, and Democrats from the South and West fervently embraced it. To them, the gold standard signified all that was wrong in the United States—not only low prices and depression but also the power of banks, railroads, and industrial trusts. Governor John Peter Altgeld of Illinois insisted at his state's convention, "It is the people against the plutocracy. The common people against the unfeeling avarice of organized wealth … against the gold fetters with which the eastern bondholders would enslave us."[51]

At the Democratic convention, the platform came first. Silverites were determined that it endorse free silver, and they made sure that the convention would vote on the matter before selecting a candidate, thereby dictating the nature of the campaign regardless of the nominee. To solidify its position, the Silverite majority replaced some of Michigan's delegates who

[47] Cleveland to Dickinson, June 10, 1896, *Letters of Grover Cleveland*, p. 438.
[48] Cleveland to Democratic Voters, June 16, 1896, *Letters of Grover Cleveland*, pp. 440–1.
[49] George Allen to Bryan, June 5, 1896, Bryan Papers, box 4. Emphasis in original.
[50] M. Doran to Cleveland, June 22, 1896, Cleveland Papers, reel 90.
[51] Quoted in Bensel, *Passion and Preference*, p. 31.

favored the gold standard with men who supported silver coinage, giving Silverites a majority among the delegation and rendering Dickinson's labors vain. Since the party in that state followed the "unit rule," with the majority determining the vote of the entire delegation, the result was a shift large enough to give Silverites a two-thirds majority in the convention as a whole. Under Hill's leadership northeastern Democrats put up a good fight, but they lacked the votes. Forensic honors went to the thirty-six-year-old William Jennings Bryan who electrified the convention when he declared, "You shall not press down upon the brow of labor this crown of thorns, you shall not crucify mankind upon a cross of gold!"[52]

The platform that emerged embraced not only free coinage of silver but a variety of other reforms. After stating "the money question is paramount to all others at this time" and "demand[ing] the free and unlimited coinage of both silver and gold at the present legal ratio of 16 to 1 without waiting for the aid or consent of any other nation," the platform called for the abolition of national bank currency, a ban on "gold contracts" and the issue of "gold bonds" in private transactions, tighter regulation of the railways, a large reduction in tariffs, and an income tax. It also implicitly called for restrictions on the power of the federal judiciary, deprecating the decision that had invalidated the income tax as well as court injunctions against organized labor such as that used against the American Railway Union during the Pullman strike.[53]

With the adoption of free coinage, the Democrats had only to decide on a candidate. Supporters of the gold standard abstained from the contest, but even had they tried to block the nomination of a Silverite, they would have failed. With Michigan's delegation now in favor of silver, supporters of free coinage had a two-thirds majority. The well-informed Hanna expected Richard Bland, the party's stalwart champion of silver, to carry the prize.[54] Silver Republicans and Populists both encouraged delegates to select Henry Teller, a distinguished figure behind whom Silverites of all stripes could unite. Yet Bland lacked gravitas, and Teller was not a Democrat. After several ballots, the choice fell on Bryan. At the time and since, many attributed Bryan's triumph to his extraordinary "Cross of

[52] Bryan, *The First Battle*, p. 206

[53] 1896 Democratic Platform, The Presidency Project, UCSB. Gold bonds were bonds payable in gold or its equivalent, and gold contracts required payment in the same. They protected lenders against the sort of devaluation the free coinage of silver might create.

[54] Merry, *President McKinley*, p. 130.

Gold" speech. His oratory was decisive, but Bryan's papers reveal that more was at work. As early as August 1895, a Silverite who had attended a conference on the currency reported, "Nearly everyone I talked with was in favor of nominating you for president."[55] One politically active Texan wrote Bryan before the convention, "The nation ought to give you a vote of thanks by making you its president for the valiant services you have rendered in the cause of silver."[56] An Alabama newspaper editor wrote in May, "I think if the convention would nominate you, it would create great enthusiasm with the young Democracy of the nation."[57] Josephus Daniels, the editor of the influential Raleigh (NC) *News and Observer*, had promised Bryan his support, as had Ben Tillman.[58] Despite his relative youth, Bryan had probably done more to win his party over to free coinage than anyone else, and he was arguably the greatest orator of the age. Democratic Silverites had made a point of emphasizing the platform rather than a specific candidate, and so the contest for the nomination had remained amorphous until the last minute, with even those publicly committed to a particular candidate remaining open to persuasion. All knew of Bryan's efforts on behalf of silver, and most thought of him as a contender, though perhaps not a leading one. His great speech turned these musings into a conviction that he was the strongest candidate that the party could offer—which he almost certainly was.

The Democratic Party's embrace of the free coinage of silver appalled eastern Democrats. Most of the delegates who defended the gold standard at the Chicago convention abstained during the contest for the nomination because, they contended, they could not support any candidate who ran on the party's platform. Though President Cleveland had anticipated the triumph of silver, he nevertheless wrote during the convention that he was "so dazed on the political situation that I am in no condition for speech or thought about it."[59] William Curtis reported that, soon after Bryan's nomination, "'The Great Chief' is sulking in his tent and won't say or do anything."[60] Senator David Hill, when asked about the situation,

[55] Jonathan Tomlinson to Bryan, August 26, 1895, Bryan Papers, box 3.

[56] George Carden to Bryan, June 8, 1896, Bryan Papers, box 4.

[57] Jonathan Tomlinson to Bryan, May 10, 1896, Bryan Papers, box 4.

[58] Jonathan Daniels to Bryan, April 30, 1896, Bryan Papers, box 3; Charles Rosser to Bryan, May 6, 1896, Bryan Papers, box 4.

[59] Cleveland to Richard Olney, July 13, 1896, *Letters of Grover Cleveland*, p. 446.

[60] Curtis to Mother, July 20, 1896, Curtis Papers, box 7.

replied, “I still am a Democrat—very still.”[61] Whereas the Silver Republicans had bolted from their party, Gold Democrats felt that their party had ejected them. Some, including Hill, would make their peace with Bryan, who graciously welcomed their support—Bryan was not a vindictive man. Even easterners like Hill who accepted Bryan, however, merely resigned themselves to the situation rather than embraced it, and many remained bitter.

Coalitions Coalesce

As 1896 began, the Populists faced a difficult decision. They had won more elections and survived as a force longer than any third party in American history, and they had probably won more votes in 1894 than they had in 1892. Nevertheless, evidence suggested that their support was cresting. In 1894, they had lost control of every state government in the West that they had won in 1890 and 1892. The party did better in the South, but with the important exception of North Carolina, they controlled no state governments, and the Democrats had made it clear that they would spare no effort to retain power, resorting to fraud and violence if necessary. As an insurgent movement that promised followers radical transformation, the Populists had to deliver victories or risk disillusion among their supporters and the evaporation of their strength.

Populism’s appeal had clear limits. The party had a large mass of supporters in the Wheat and Cotton Belts, but even in these regions it was probably short of a majority. Elsewhere their numbers were far smaller. Historians Charles Postel and Scott Nelson have written of the links between Populists and urban radicals like the Knights of Labor and Eugene Debs’ unions, but however interesting, these ties did not translate into many votes.[62] San Francisco, which elected a Populist as mayor in 1894, represents the proverbial exception that proved the rule. The candidate was Adolph Sutro, who had made a huge fortune mining silver—hence his attraction to Populism—and had spent much of it on philanthropy in San Francisco. As a historian of the city’s politics put it, “Sutro would have won on any ticket. … His victory represented a non-partisan tribute to a very highly esteemed old man.” Other Populist candidates carried barely

[61] Quoted in Nevins, *Grover Cleveland*, p. 706.

[62] Postel, *Populist* Vision, pp. 205–42; Nelson, *Nation of Deadbeats*, pp. 198–200.

more than 10 percent of San Francisco's voters.[63] The Populist had strong support in states in which silver mining was an important industry, but in most cases, these voters were really Silverites, and they would bolt if either of the major parties embraced free coinage. The party's support was negligible in the Northeast—rural districts as well as urban ones—and not much stronger in the Industrial Midwest. Populism was largely a regional phenomenon, and the regions in which it was competitive were nowhere near a majority in the nation as a whole.

Fusion had delivered the most impressive Populist victories. Success in Kansas and Nebraska in 1890 and 1892 had depended on cooperation with Democrats, and the triumph in North Carolina in 1894 owed to an alliance with Republicans. In the Mountain West, Populists were often a minority in their own party—Silver Republicans had absolute control of the Populist Party in Nevada and played a leading role in other states. After 1894, many of the party's leaders saw fusion at the national level as the party's best hope and free silver as the means to accomplish it. At the time, the Populists alone among the nation's major parties supported free coinage. James Weaver, the party's presidential candidate in 1892, wrote early in 1896, "I shall favor going before the people in 1896 with the money question alone, unencumbered with any other contention whatsoever."[64] He feared that including the Subtreasury plan and nationalization of the Railroads in the Populist platform would make it impossible to win over Silverites from the two major parties.

Others were doubtful. Many Populists had long considered free coinage of silver a second-best policy, preferable to the gold standard but far inferior to a system of fiat money—greenbacks. Populists from the Grain Belt considered control of the railroads as important as reform of the currency. Many in the party were reluctant to abandon these positions. The editor of one leading Populist newspaper actually hoped that "the party not grow too quickly," lest it lose its radical edge.[65] Those united behind Populism's full demands described themselves as adhering to the "middle of the road," and they feared that the sort of alliances with Democratic and Republican Silverites that Weaver imagined would submerge the

[63] Alexander Saxton, "San Francisco Labor and the Populist and Progressive Insurgencies," *Pacific Historical Review* 34 (1965), p. 426.

[64] Quoted in Hicks, *The Populist Revolt*, p. 344.

[65] Quoted in Goodwyn, *The Populist Moment*, p. 243.

People's Party within those organizations, not only destroying its character but weakening the cause of reform in the country as a whole. Fusion would put the party at the "tail end of the procession when it ought to have been in the lead."[66]

Divisions within the party reflected self-interest and experience as much as ideology. Those who had won public office saw fusion as their best chance of holding onto their positions. Populist lecturers and editors, on the other hand, feared that fusion would render them superfluous. Populists in the Grain Belt had enjoyed fruitful cooperation with Democrats, but those in the South had suffered fraud, intimidation, and even violence at the hands of southern Democrats.

Historian Lawrence Goodwyn depicts Silverites as political cuckoos who displaced real Populists and took over their party. If anything, the reverse was the case. Populists like Weaver sought to harness Silverites to the Populist wagon. Free coinage was the issue of the day. There was no groundswell for the Subtreasury or anything else that the People's Party was advocating. Free coinage of silver not only offered Populists an opportunity but threatened them with irrelevance if they ignored it.

The conflict among Populists soon assumed a bitter edge. Weaver complained in a letter to William Jennings Bryan early in 1896, "We have had quite enough middle of the road nonsense."[67] Another leading fusionist, Herman Taubeneck, grumbled that his opponents within the party had "gone over to the Socialists."[68] Those who adhered to the middle of the road professed, "We are getting very tired of these vexatious self-seekers, these mouthing men at Washington and elsewhere who have no visible means of support except scheming in questionable politics."[69] One publication insisted that the movement for fusion, "like a Kentucky militia regiment[,]... consists of all colonels and no privates."[70] Tom Watson wrote that the focus on free silver "is a trap, a pitfall, a snare, a menace, a fraud, a crime against common sense and common honesty."[71]

Fusionists controlled the national party machinery and used it to secure their ends. In February 1896, they scheduled the party's national

[66] Quoted in Hicks, *The Populist Revolt*, p. 345.
[67] Quoted in Goodwyn, *The Populist Moment*, p. 247.
[68] Quoted in Goodwyn, *The Populist Moment*, p. 243.
[69] Quoted in Goodwyn, *The Populist Moment*, p. 237.
[70] Quoted in Hicks, *The Populist Revolt*, p. 345.
[71] Quoted in Woodward, *Tom Watson*, p. 337

convention so that it not only convened two weeks after the Democrats' but met at the same time and in the same city as that of the new Silver Party. It was clear that the Republicans would not embrace free coinage of silver. Though the Democrats were still debating the matter, Weaver and his fusionist allies believed that President Cleveland and the party's strong Northeastern wing would hold Democrats in line behind the gold standard. At the very least, the requirement for a two-thirds majority for the presidential nomination would result in some sort of compromise on the matter. Should that occur, the Populists would emerge as the sole champion of the free coinage of silver, putting them in a position to absorb dissidents from both parties. To this end, Weaver forged ties with the National Bimetallic League and maintained correspondence with Democratic and Republican Silverites like Bryan and Teller. If their parties endorsed the gold standard, he argued, they should walk out of their conventions and ally with the Populists. This strategy was risky, but if successful it could catapult the People's Party to control of the federal government or, at least, allow the Populists to replace the deeply divided Democrats as the country's second major party.

The growing strength of Silverites within the Democratic Party wrecked this plan. If the Democrats embraced free coinage, the Populists would have little choice but to accept whomever they nominated. To do otherwise risked splitting the vote for silver and guaranteeing McKinley's victory. By May, Weaver realized that he had lost control of the situation. He urged Bryan that the Democrats' "nomination be advisory simply and not final. This will afford opportunity to confer with our [Populist and Silver] conventions at St. Louis and open the way for union."[72] Bryan and the Democratic convention ignored this plea. It lacked precedent, and the Democrats had no intention of giving the Populists a veto over their nominee. Several leading Populist fusionists attended the Democrats' convention as honored guests, and they urged the nomination of Senator Teller because it would be easier for them to negotiate cooperation with the Democrats and maintain their identity if a Republican headed the ticket. Ultimately, of course, Bryan won the nomination. He was the Democrat most acceptable to the Populists, but even his choice was a mixed blessing. With Bryan at the top of the ticket, Populist voters would be more inclined to desert to the Democrats.

[72] James Weaver to Bryan, May 29, 1896, Bryan Papers, box 4.

When the Populist convention met in St. Louis in August, fusionists were discouraged and the "middle of the road" faction furious. Southern Populists recoiled at an alliance with the Democrats, who had so long abused them. Those who hewed to the middle of the road complained that, by nominating Bryan, the Party would be acceding to "a surrender of the People's Party movement and the destruction of their present magnificent organization."[73] The Populists had little choice, however. Bryan and the Democratic platform embraced not only the free coinage of silver but several other reforms supported by the People's Party. If the Populists nominated their own candidate, they would either divide the vote for silver, guaranteeing McKinley's victory, or see their supporters desert en masse to the Democrats, destroying their credibility. The party accepted the inevitable and nominated Bryan but asserted its independence with its vice-presidential nomination. Bryan might be inevitable and even appealing in many ways, but not so his vice-presidential candidate, Arthur Sewall, a Maine businessman who deviated from orthodoxy only in his support for free silver. Though Weaver and many other fusionists urged Sewall's nomination, the convention opted for Tom Watson of Georgia and made Bryan's nomination conditional on his accepting Watson. They reasoned that if they accepted the Democrats' candidate for the presidency, the Democrats should accept their man for the second slot. Many—including Watson—believed that the Democrats had agreed to drop Sewall for the Populist candidate, but in this they probably deceived themselves.[74] Certainly, the Democrats refused to abandon Sewall. Some Populists no doubt hoped that Watson, long a thorn in the side of Georgia's Democrats, would prove unacceptable to Bryan, opening the way for the Populists to put forward their own nominee for president.

Bryan resolved this dilemma by ignoring it. He followed the advice of Governor James Hogg of Texas, who wrote him, "Take time. Do not let anyone rush you."[75] It turned out that, in 1892, the Populists had not formally notified James Weaver of his nomination, and he had never formally accepted the honor. Weaver made sure the Democrats knew of this

[73] Quoted in Hicks, *The Populist Revolt*, p. 358.

[74] In *The Climax of Populism: The Election of 1896* (Lexington: University of Kentucky Press, 1965), pp. 37–41, historian Robert Durden analyzes this question in detail and concludes that the Populists who thought the Democrats would drop Sewall were engaged in wishful thinking. He seriously doubts that the leaders of the Democratic Party ever made any such promises, even implicitly.

[75] James Hogg to Bryan, July 28, 1896, Bryan Papers, box 4.

precedent, and Bryan simply observed that he had received the nomination of the People's Party without even mentioning Watson. In many states, the Populists and Democrats arranged a joint slate of electors, all committed to Bryan but divided between Sewall and Watson. For his part, Watson conducted a campaign in which he spent almost as much time denouncing Sewall as praising Bryan. These events consumed a lot of time and occasioned much heartburn, but they do not seem to have hurt the appeal of the man at the top of the ticket.[76]

As the Populists decided their political future, the other loose pieces on the political board fell into place. Senator Teller had always insisted that the silver issue was paramount. He acted promptly, writing Bryan after the Democratic convention, "Your nomination was more than satisfactory to me. I think we shall be able to consolidate all the forces of free coinage in your support, and if we do this, I believe you will be elected."[77] The new Silver Party, in which western Republicans loomed large, embraced Bryan and Sewall at its convention.[78] Its members had never sought an independent existence but rather hoped to convert one of the two major parties to its cause. With Bryan's triumph at Chicago, they had succeeded. Republicans Silverites nevertheless maintained their autonomy, organizing a Silver Republican Party, which had a substantial presence in the Mountain States. They agreed with the Democrats on little besides free coinage and wanted to maintain their freedom of maneuver. Being stronger than the Democrats or Populists in this region, they could insist on their own organization. In that party of the country, the contest often pitted Silver Republicans against McKinley Republicans, even though Bryan led the Silverite ticket.

Gold Democrats, stunned and bitter, took longer to coalesce. Many embraced McKinley. In Minnesota, "National Democrats" (as they styled themselves) insisted, "The election of Mr. Bryan would surely be followed by disaster and dishonor to the country. No one can believe that such consequence would follow the election of Mr. McKinley." Despite their strong disagreement with the GOP over tariffs, they concluded that gold Democrats could "best serve our country by voting for the Republican

[76] Durden, *The Climax of Populism*, pp. 91–110.

[77] Teller to Bryan, July 15, 1896, *The Watchman and Southron* (Sumter, SC), July 22, 1896, p. 6.

[78] *Iron County* (MO) *Register*, July 30, 1896, p. 2.

candidate."[79] Others were not so sure, fearing that some Democrats opposed to free silver might nevertheless refuse to support a Republican and opt for Bryan, particularly in the South. Moreover, they wanted to stake a claim to the future of the Democratic Party after November, when they assumed the party would suffer a crushing defeat. In early September, a convention of Gold Democrats met in Indianapolis and nominated its own ticket, which Senator John Palmer led (D-IL). Not surprisingly, the platform called for the maintenance of the gold standard and the reduction of tariffs, and the delegates "heartily endorse[d] the financial policy and the administration of Grover Cleveland." The party demonstrated its relative narrow base by advocating direct election of U.S. Senators, not by the population as a whole, but by those who made "payment of at least one hundred dollars yearly taxes upon real property."[80] For the most part, they fixed their gaze on the period after the election. As a group of Chicago's Gold Democrats put it, "Democrats should defeat Bryan in order to preserve for future usefulness the Democratic Party." They continued, "Although there is no possibility of their [the Gold Democrats candidates'] election. ... Every vote so cast will be a vote for the perpetuity and the honor of the Democratic Party—a party whose principles are eternal."[81]

The Cleveland administration had to perform a delicate balancing act. Privately, the President was "delighted with the outcome of the [Gold Democrats'] Indianapolis Convention ... and as a Democrat I feel very grateful to those who have refreshed the bad political atmosphere with such a delicious infusion of fresh air." At the same time, he knew that Palmer had no hope of carrying even a single state, and he firmly believed that Bryan's victory would be a catastrophe. Accordingly, Cleveland did his best to ensure McKinley's election. Publicly, he remained silent. He doubted that anything he might say would help the situation, and besides, "For years, officially and unofficially, I have, in season and out of season, declared my opinions on the subject of sound money."[82]

Cleveland suffered one more painful political blow in the summer of 1896 when his Secretary of the Interior, Hoke Smith, announced that he

[79] *To the National Democracy of Minnesota*, Bryan Papers, box 5.

[80] "Synopsis of Platform," September 2, 1896, Cleveland Papers, reel 95.

[81] T.A. Moran et al., Cook County Democratic Central Committee, October 28, 1896, Bryan Papers, box 4.

[82] Cleveland to William Vilas, September 5, 1896, *Letters of Grover Cleveland*, pp. 456–7.

would support Bryan—though he did refuse to endorse the party's platform. Smith, the Cabinet's only southerner, wrote to Cleveland, "The local situation is such in my own state [Georgia] that I consider the protection of person and property involved in the local democrat success which can only continue through democratic organization."[83] Cleveland had a remarkable bond with his cabinet, which had remained united through many difficulties, and Smith's defection hurt. The President wrote Smith that he considered Smith's distinction between the platform and the candidate "like straining at a gnat and swallowing a camel," and retorted sharply, "I suppose much was said about the 'local situation' in 1860."[84] In fact, Smith's defection was predictable. He had little interest in or convictions about the currency—William Curtis had to tutor him on the subject so that he could defend the administration's policy coherently[85]—and he was ambitious. The future of the Democratic Party lay with Bryan, and Smith knew it.

President Cleveland misunderstood the Democratic Party of the South. He firmly believed in minimal government and free markets and accepted at face value the assurances of southern Democrats that they did the same. The real principle of southern Democrats was white supremacy, however. Against that, the currency was insignificant. As Josephus Daniels of North Carolina wrote Bryan, "We are fighting not only for 'sound money' as we understand 'sound money' [free coinage of silver], but for the preservation of our home government in the hands of intelligence."[86] An African-American living in North Carolina was blunter, stating, "It is a question of free silver or free nigger."[87] Southern Democrats would support any issue that united white voters under their banner. Cleveland, like many Democrats outside the South, ignored this ugly reality. He would never have won election to the White House without carrying the South, nor could he have governed without the support of southern Democrats in the House and Senate. Though not free of the prejudices common among white Americans of his generation, Cleveland did not embrace white supremacy and segregation with the same enthusiasm as Bryan. For instance, during his first term as president, Cleveland had hosted Frederick

[83] Hoke Smith to Cleveland, July 20, 1896, Cleveland Papers, reel 95.
[84] Cleveland to Hoke Smith, August 4, 1896, Cleveland Papers, reel 95.
[85] William Curtis to Mother, August 3, 1893, Curtis Papers, box 3.
[86] Josephus Daniel to Bryan, April 30, 1896, Bryan Papers, box 3.
[87] Quoted in Durden, *The Climax of Populism*, pp. 110–12.

Douglass and his wife (who was white) at receptions in the Executive Mansion.[88] Instead, Cleveland deceived himself about the motives of his southern allies. Smith's defection injected an uncomfortable dose of reality into this illusion.

The Bankers' Syndicate

By embracing the free coinage of silver and nominating Bryan, the Democrats created the possibility of a financial panic. If either foreign investors or Americans holding currency believed that Bryan would win, they would probably sell securities and cash in greenbacks and Treasury notes for gold, which would quickly drain the country's reserve of gold. Even the possibility of a Democratic victory could encourage hoarding. At the very least, businesses would avoid long-term commitments until the future of the currency was clear. For instance, banker Jacob Schiff could not complete the reorganization of the Union Pacific because this operation involved selling a large quantity of bonds in Europe, and investors there would not make any commitment until they knew whether the country would be on gold or silver. As a result, the economic slowdown evident in the spring continued over the summer and into the fall. In late October, *The Economist*'s American correspondent reported, "Investments are not being made. Banks, bankers, and stock brokers have discouraged bull speculation. … London has evidently decided on an extreme conservative course with respect to our market, doubts as to the success of the sound money cause now being surprisingly in evidence there."[89]

The prospect of a financial panic during the election campaign alarmed the Cleveland administration and all other defenders of "sound finance." It might well force the country onto a silver basis even before the people voted, rendering the campaign moot. Even if gold standard held, a panic could well strengthen Bryan's prospects, suggesting that prosperity and the gold standard were mutually exclusive. Right after the Democratic convention adjourned, Treasury Secretary Carlisle dispatched William Curtis to New York "to impress upon them [New York's bankers] the great importance of preventing a condition that should necessitate a bond issue." He continued, "I think this is of the greatest importance in view of

[88] Richard Welch provides an intelligent discussion of Cleveland's views on race in *The Presidencies of Grover Cleveland*, pp. 65–9.

[89] *The Economist*, November 14, 1896, p. 1498–9.

the political situation—and our friends ought to help us, if necessary, to the full extent of their means. What the syndicate did to prevent withdrawals in the summer of 1895, can certainly be done by the associated banks of New York at this time."[90] Thus encouraged, J.P. Morgan sprang into action. A strong personality, he did not hesitate to take charge during a crisis, and such was his prestige and force of character that others usually fell in line. As a result, Curtis wrote in the summer, "We see the curious spectacle of the U.S. finances being controlled by a committee of which J.P. Morgan is the chairman, & the majority of whom are Hebrews, while the Secretary of the Treasury sits, practically powerless, in his office."[91] (Silverites had no monopoly on antisemitism in American society.)

Fortunately for these bankers, the country's underlying financial situation was stronger than a year earlier. The federal deficit had fallen substantially, to $14 million for fiscal 1896 (which ended July 1, 1896), and $19 million for fiscal 1897. In the last two bond issues, the government had raised close to $175 million in gold. Critics pointed out that about half of this gold had flowed out of the Treasury by the summer of 1896, but these operations had another effect. Those who drew gold out of the Treasury bought it with greenbacks and Treasury notes, and as economist Frank Taussig wrote, "For a period of about a year—from November 1895 to October 1896—the Treasury locked up in its vaults continuously the huge sum of 100 millions [*sic*] of legal tenders."[92] Earlier, the federal deficit would have forced the Treasury to disgorge these notes, but with the shortfall much smaller, most of this paper stayed put. With less currency in circulation, interest rates increased, attracting foreign capital and encouraging those who held gold to deposit it in banks, where it would earn a return.[93] In late 1893, supporters of issuing bonds had imagined that, by doing so, the federal government would limit the supply of money and raise interest rates, attracting capital from abroad and mobilizing gold held in private hoards. The process took four issues of bonds over three years, but by 1896 it had finally borne fruit.

Meanwhile, the country's international position had improved. In the first eight months of 1895, the country had imported $46 million more in

[90] John Carlisle to Cleveland, July 16, 1896, Cleveland Papers, reel 94.

[91] William Curtis to Mother, July 23, 1896, Curtis Papers, box 7.

[92] Frank Taussig, "The United States Treasury, 1894–1896," *Quarterly Journal of Economics* 13 (1899): 206.

[93] William Curtis to Charles Dabney, October 14, 1896, Curtis Papers, box 8.

goods than it exported, but during the same period in 1896, it exported $96 million more than it bought abroad—a shift in favor of the United States of $142 million.[94] This improvement reflected a large surge in exports, particularly of manufactured goods. The brutal decline of prices in the United States had made its products more competitive in world markets, while economic recovery in Europe, which had begun in earnest in 1895, increased demand.

Morgan's combine operated in favorable circumstances, but success was not guaranteed. Political considerations often overwhelm economic ones. The group intervened twice. In July, Bryan's triumph at the Democratic convention badly rattled foreign investors, who began to sell securities and withdraw gold from the United States. In response, as Custis wrote, "The bankers of New York … agree[d] to furnish bills of exchange at rates under the gold shipping point." This action "inspired so much confidence that normal conditions prevailed and the situation cured itself."[95] By August, however, uncertainty about the outcome of the presidential campaign had encouraged a new wave of withdrawals, draining $2.5 million in gold from the Treasury in one week and prompting the head of the New York Subtreasury to urge another bond issue.[96] Instead, the combine put $20 million in gold into the Treasury, taking greenbacks and Treasury notes in exchange.[97] By September, conditions were improving rapidly. Relatively high interest rates and European payments for grain and cotton brought money into the country, giving it a payments surplus. *The Economist*'s American correspondent reported that on September 12 alone, $12 million in gold arrived in New York City from abroad.[98] At the same time, McKinley's growing strength discouraged speculation against the dollar.[99]

In contrast with the syndicate of the previous year, this combine did not advertise its activities. It was not a secret. One journalist wrote in August "that a strong combination of foreign and domestic bankers were in a praiseworthy or patriotic endeavor to maintain the Treasury gold reserve."[100] Nevertheless, few mentioned the combine during the campaign, and most forgot about it afterward. Silverites did not want to

[94] Curtis to Dabney, October 14, 1896.
[95] Curtis to Dabney, October 14, 1896.
[96] C.N. Jordan to William Curtis, August 7, 1896, Curtis Papers, Box 7.
[97] *The Economist*, August 15, 1896, pp. 1068–9.
[98] *The Economist*, September 26, 1896, p. 1254
[99] *The Economist*, September 19, 1896, 1221–2.
[100] *The Economist*, September 5, 1896, p. 1157.

advertise that the very prospect of Bryan's victory had created the possibility of a financial panic, and McKinley's supporters did not want to trumpet his alignment with New York's most powerful financiers. Many otherwise solid accounts of the 1896 election, such as those of Paul Glad, Hal Williams, and Karl Rove, overlook the episode entirely.[101]

The incident said much about the country's financial institutions. Most European governments could manage the sort of operations Morgan's group conducted through their central banks, which were privately owned but cooperated very closely with finance ministries. The United States had no such institution and had to rely on and ad hoc association of private bankers.

The Decision

The 1896 presidential campaign constituted perhaps the greatest political spectacle in American history. For months, political speakers attracted overflowing crowds, political parades commanded the streets, and political literature flooded the mails. In their very different ways, Bryan and McKinley reached far more voters than had any previous candidates for the presidency. The question of the currency crowded out all others, and on it, both Bryan and McKinley sought to win over undecided voters and sway those in opposition. Republicans denounced Bryan as a dangerous radical, and Democrats insisted that McKinley was a tool of special interests, but the candidates and their literature rarely if ever descended into personal vituperation. Mark Hanna described McKinley's campaign as "educational," and Bryan could have said the same of his effort.

The stakes justified the effort. Advocates of free silver sought to reorient the country's financial system by devaluing the dollar. This would both raise prices (in dollars) for commodities like cotton and wheat sold on international markets and increase the volume of the currency substantially. At the same time, free silver would alienate foreign investors who had provided vast resources for economic development, quite likely sparking a financial panic as those holding dollars scrambled to convert them into gold while they still could. Bryan insisted that free coinage would not lead to devaluation, but as economist Frank Taussig wrote, "Those who

[101] Paul Glad, *McKinley, Bryan, & the People* (Chicago: Ivan Dee, 1964); Williams, *Realigning America*; Rove, *The Triumph of William McKinley*.

make the suggestion cannot have real faith in it."[102] Free coinage would have to double the market value of silver against gold, reversing a trend of twenty-five years that even the massive purchases under the Silver Purchase Act had failed to slow. In fact, most Silverites actively courted devaluation because it would raise the price, in dollars, of commodities like cotton and wheat that farmers exported. From a purely economic point of view, free coinage was a risky proposition. The issue went beyond simple calculations of profit and loss, however. As Governor Altgeld of Illinois stated, "If all the talk about gold going to a premium were true, it would not meet the question. The question is, shall republican institutions be maintained in this country?"[103] Most Silverites opposed the direction of economic development in the United States in the late nineteenth century. The centralization of economic power in railroads, large industrial companies, and the New York money market appalled them. They hoped that free silver would decentralize the system, giving the population—particularly farmers—greater control over their economic destiny. As Bryan said, "Thomas Jefferson, in his immortal inaugural, after summing up the true principles of government, said, 'Should we wander from them in moments of error or alarm, let us hasten to retrace our steps and regain the road which alone leads to peace, liberty and safety.' The supremacy of the bondholders in our government shows that we have neither peace, liberty, nor safety before us. We have reached Jefferson's sign-board of danger. It is time to turn back."[104] In contrast, McKinley was comfortable with the transformation of American society then underway. His natural constituents were the commercial farmers, businessmen, and workers of the Midwest. He spoke not of turning back but of strengthening the emerging system, advocating policies "protective to all our interests," particularly tariffs.[105]

Bryan's campaign depended on the candidate. Though for a generation the country's businessmen had leaned toward the Republican Party, there had always been plenty of exceptions who provided the Democrats with funds. In the last three presidential contests, the Republicans had outspent the Democrats, but Cleveland's efforts had not suffered from a lack of

[102] Frank Taussig, *The Silver Situation in the U.S.* (New York: Putnam's, 1896), p. 156.

[103] John Peter Altgeld, *Live Questions: Comprising his Papers, Speeches, and Interviews* (Chicago: George Bowen & Sons, 1899), p. 602.

[104] Address of William Jennings Bryan to Bland Club of Chicago, reproduced in Charles Stevens, *Free Silver and the People* (New York: F.T. Neely, 1896), pp. 14–5.

[105] *Indianapolis Sunday Journal*, October 19, 1896, p. 1.

money. With the Democrats' embrace of free silver and alliance with the Populists, however, this support dried up. Only those engaged in mining silver remained, and their resources were a fraction of those available to McKinley from railroads, banks, and manufacturers. Bryan was always short of money, and it is unlikely that his campaign spent more than a tenth of the huge sums Hanna mobilized for McKinley.

The problem for the Democrats went deeper than the lack of cash, however. During the first half of the campaign, Bryan had to book his own railroad tickets and hotel rooms and even carry his own luggage. He already had an exhausting schedule, and such niggling tasks were a heavy and unnecessary burden. Only in early October did the Democratic National Committee finally provide the candidate with his own train car.[106] The failure to make such arrangements earlier is shocking evidence of poor organization. The Democrats were short of money, but not that short.

The shift in the Democrats' geographic focus exacerbated these problems. Since the Civil War, the party had been strong in the Northeast—stronger than in the Midwest and far stronger than on the Great Plains or in the Mountain West. Free coinage, however, was anathema in the Northeast, which had an efficient banking system and numerous commercial and financial ties with Europe. Bryan had no chance of carrying these states, and he realized it. The leader of the Democrats' campaign in New Jersey lamented in late October, "We have had no [national] Democratic speaker here this campaign as yet. But Republican speakers have been very thick." He insisted, "The balance … will be in our favor if you [Bryan] should come."[107] The candidate knew better. Bryan focused on states where free coinage had support but where, too often, the Democratic organization was weak. In states like Iowa and Minnesota, silver had appeal, but the Democrats lacked the dense network of local operatives to mobilize voters that the party possessed in large parts of the Northeast.

Bryan's oratory constituted his chief asset. His extraordinary "Cross of Gold" speech had swung a majority of uncommitted delegates to his side at the Democratic convention, and many Democrats believed that his words would do the same among the population at large, if only the people heard him. Accordingly, Bryan embarked on an unprecedented speaking campaign that ultimately covered thousands of miles and reached

[106] Rove, *Triumph of William McKinley*, pp. 339–40.
[107] W.E. Pailing to Bryan, October 22, 1896, Bryan Papers, box 4.

hundreds of thousands of voters. Traditionally, candidates for the presidency did not actively campaign, relying on surrogates—"the office seeks the man," as the saying went. Bryan himself was the strongest weapon in his own arsenal, however. If he wanted to win, he had little choice but to break with precedent. Though he appeared at least once in almost every state, Bryan concentrated on the Midwest and the Great Plains. McKinley seemed certain to carry the Northeast, while almost all conceded the South and the far West to Bryan. Victory would go to the candidate who won the middle section of the country. Throughout the campaign, Bryan demonstrated almost superhuman endurance and retained his basic good nature and optimism despite immense strain. On one day in October, he spoke twenty-three times, and over three days in Chicago, he delivered thirty speeches.[108] In total, he spoke to over a million people—probably well over a million. No previous presidential candidate had reached half as many.

Bryan insisted that the currency was "the paramount issue. ... When we have restored the money of the Constitution [silver,] all other necessary reforms will be possible; but until that is done there is no other reform that can be accomplished." The gold standard, he warned, sacrificed American interest to those of foreign creditors, "surrender[ing] the right of self-government and place[ing] the legislative control of our affairs in the hands of foreign potentates and powers." "It is the issue of 1776 over again."[109] Bryan emphasized the problem of deflation while insisting that free coinage of silver would not lead to devaluation. "An absolutely honest dollar," he contended, "would not vary in its general purchasing power. ... A dollar which increases in purchasing power is just as dishonest as a dollar which decreases in purchasing power." "During the last twenty-three years legislation has been creating an additional demand for gold, and this law-created demand has resulted in increasing the purchasing power of each ounce of gold. We contend that free and unlimited coinage by the United States alone will raise the bullion value of silver to its coinage value, and thus make silver bullion worth $1.29 per ounce in gold throughout the world." The point was important. The likelihood that the free coinage of silver would lead to a large devaluation of the dollar and create a financial crisis was the strongest argument against it, as Bryan well understood. "It

[108] Merry, *President McKinley*, p. 138.
[109] Bryan, *The First Battle*, pp. 204, 206.

certainly is asserted," he said, "that the gold standard will enable us to borrow more money from abroad. I reply that the restoration of bimetallism will restore the parity between money and property, and thus permit ... the American people to become loaners of money instead of perpetual borrowers."[110]

Bryan did not hesitate to appeal to regional prejudice. "We say not one word against those who live upon the Atlantic coast," he claimed, "but the hearty pioneers who have braved all the dangers of the wilderness, who have made the desert blossom as the rose—pioneers away out there [pointing to the west], who rear their children near to nature's heart. ... It is for these that we speak." "The great cities," he continued, "rest upon our broad and fertile prairies. Burn down your cities and leave our farms, and your cities will spring up again as if by magic, but destroy our farms and the grass will grow in the streets of every city in the country."[111] Such rhetoric fired the southern and western farmers who were Bryan's chief constituents, but it repelled easterners and urbanites.

Bryan's tours sparked immense enthusiasm. In August in Albany, New York—hardly a center of support for free coinage—newspapers reported, "The crowd began to gather in the city hall square two hours before the meeting and when Mr. Bryan faced them the people were packed in solid masses over several acres of pavement and sod, with adventurous men perched like bouquets in the branches of trees and climbing telephone and lamp posts. His appearance ... kindled a fierce shout, which swelled into three cheers, with hundreds of hats and handkerchiefs in the air."[112] Another paper described his visit to Decatur, Illinois, on October 23: "Excursionists by the hundreds were in town and the streets were crowded long before the candidate's train rolled in. So dense was the mass of humanity that a passageway could not be cleared from the [train] carriage to the platform, and Mr. Bryan was obliged to make his address from the vehicle." Later that day, in Mattoon, Bryan arrived to find that "every white horse in the vicinity ... had been pressed into service to assist several sets of silver-clad young men to carry out the symbolization of 16 to 1." Accompanying them were "several golden queens, each with sixteen marks of honor." Soon thereafter Bryan arrived in Peoria, where he delivered

[110] Bryan, *The First Battle*, pp. 321, 325, 330.
[111] Bryan, *The First Battle*, pp. 200, 205.
[112] *Kansas City Daily Journal*, August 28, 1896, p. 1.

three speeches, one after the other, in three packed venues, talking until close to midnight.[113]

William McKinley's campaign followed very different lines. He had a much stronger organization than Bryan—or for that matter, than any previous candidate for the presidency. Mark Hanna, who led it, operated out of New York, where he focused on raising money and keeping the Northeastern states in line. Though no definitive accounting exists, he raised at least $3.5 million, including $250,000 each from J.P. Morgan & Co. and Standard Oil, which Hanna's longtime friend John D. Rockefeller dominated. Overall, McKinley had twice as much money as Harrison's campaigns had enjoyed in 1888 or 1892.[114] McKinley's organization had a second headquarters in Chicago in recognition of the central importance of the states of the Midwest and Great Plains. The candidate's protégé Charles Dawes managed the Chicago office, and by August 1, he had assembled a disciplined organization in which "no contract is made … without my approval, and no contract is let without being subject to competitive bids." Dawes noted that the personnel came "from business associates and not from politicians," and he concluded, "The Traveling Men's Bureau, the Speakers' Bureau and the Literary Bureau are all in good shape."[115] In this fashion, McKinley and Hanna largely bypassed the state GOP organizations that traditionally ran campaigns, giving the candidate and his agents more control over the contest as well as reducing the claims of state leaders upon him should he win.

Organization did not constitute strategy, however. Bryan left the Chicago convention with considerable momentum. His triumph there had not only energized committed Silverites but also made an impact on many of the undecided. As one anonymous correspondent later wrote Hanna, "Had the election taken place immediately after the Chicago convention the results would have been quite different."[116] This statement may exaggerate Bryan's initial strength, but McKinley and Hanna soon realized that a contest that they had hitherto considered one-sided would be hard-fought. As the *New York Times* observed, "It will not be enough to declare from the East that the Silverites are crazy. … [T]he fallacies of the fiat-money men must be exposed by men who know how to talk

[113] *Birmingham State Herald*, October 24, 1896, p. 1.

[114] Merry, *President McKinley*, p. 137.

[115] Charles Dawes to McKinley, August 1, 1896, McKinley Papers, reel 1.

[116] Anonymous letter to Mark Hanna, November 17, 1896, Hanna Papers, Volume 1.

sound-money clearly and forcibly, with illustration and with humor."[117] Right up until Bryan's nomination, McKinley and Hanna had planned to focus their campaign on tariffs. Now they recognized that they had no choice but to pivot toward the currency.

First, Republicans had to decide the candidate's role. Hanna warned McKinley, "You've got to stump or [you] will be defeated." McKinley refused, insisting, "I cannot take the stump against that man [Bryan]." "I might just as well put up a trapeze on my front lawn and compete with some professional athlete as go out speaking against Bryan."[118] Probably no other American of the day could match Bryan's oratory, and McKinley understood that to try would simply emphasize his opponent's greatest strength. Instead, McKinley waged a "front porch" campaign, as had James Garfield in 1880 and Harrison in 1888. A steady stream of delegations from all over the country visited McKinley's home in Canton, Ohio, and he met with and delivered speeches to them, which the press reprinted and the campaign circulated. In this milieu, McKinley excelled. He had an extraordinary ability to connect with others one-on-one even in brief encounters, and the front porch strategy allowed him to exploit this strength to the utmost. The family of President Richard Nixon told a story of how Nixon's father, Frank, when a young man living in Ohio, had a horse of which he was immensely proud. At one point, McKinley visited Frank's hometown, and Nixon rode this horse in the parade that greeted McKinley. During the festivities, McKinley stopped, sized up Frank, and praised Frank's mount. Frank, heretofore a Democrat, converted to the Republican Party on the spot.[119]

Though McKinley's campaign had precedent, it operated on a scale far larger than any of its predecessors. With generous funding as well as enthusiastic cooperation from the railroads, McKinley's organization brought thousands of people to Canton every day from as far afield as Vermont and Nebraska. A band greeted each group of visitors at the railroad station and led it to McKinley's house, where the leader of the delegation gave a brief address and the candidate responded with a speech of his own and shook hands with his guests. McKinley made a point of vetting his visitors' remarks in advance to make sure that they contained

[117] *New York Times*, July 22, 1896, p. 2.

[118] Quoted in Merry, *President McKinley*, pp. 138–9.

[119] Stephen Ambrose, *Nixon: Education of a Politician, 1913–1962* (New York: Simon and Schuster, 1987), p. 15.

nothing that might embarrass the campaign, and he tailored his remarks to his audience—McKinley had different speeches for Army veterans, coal miners, and traveling salesmen. One newspaper reported that this process went on from 9:00 in the morning until 11:00 at night and stated that the crowds "filled the yard, took possession of the porches, and peered in at the windows [of McKinley's house]. When one set of visitors left another immediately supplied their places."[120] Overall, roughly 750,000 passed by McKinley's front porch during the campaign, putting him in contact with more voters than any other candidate for the presidency thus far in American history—except Bryan. Considering that the pilgrims who traveled to Canton undoubtedly told their friends and neighbors all about their adventures, the effect probably matched that of Bryan's tours, at least in the critical midwestern states.

These visitors responded to McKinley's low-keyed but formidable charisma. One from Nebraska wrote, "I heard him make an address to 1000 ex-confederate soldiers that came to see him from the Shenandoah Valley, Virginia. … Some of these old ex-confederates were lacking a leg and many of them were short one arm"—an impressive demonstration of McKinley's appeal, considering that he had served with distinction in the Union Army during the Civil War. This observer continued to describe his own experience, "It was about the best time taking everything into consideration that we could have gone there. I tell you McKinley is a grand man and he can make a grand speech. … Tell the McKinley club that I represented them and the county at McKinley's house and that he gave me a second shake of the hand to carry back to the boys of Nebraska."[121]

Though McKinley tailored his speeches to the audience, sound money and protection were the recurrent themes. The Democrats, he said, "are urging us to attempt by legislation to make fifty cents' worth of silver pass current as a legal tender one hundred cents dollar, good for all public and private obligations. The mere statement of the proposition ought to lead to its instant rejection. We cannot by law make every man honest, but we will certainly never make a law encouraging them to be dishonest."[122] To a delegation from the coal fields he stated, "When the miners … have dug their coal by their honest toil they want to be paid in dollars that are equal to the best dollars in the world … and will be as good on one day in one

[120] *The San Francisco Call*, September 19, 1896, p. 3.
[121] George Huntsberger to W.R. Clements, October 12, 1896, McKinley Papers, reel 2.
[122] *Orleans County Monitor* (VT), September 21, 1896 p. 2.

country as in another."[123] To another group he insisted, "No nation has even benefitted by poor money or injured by good money. … Good honest dollars hurt no one. If we have not as much good money as we ought to have let us get more, and we will get more whenever the country requires it. But we will not get it as long as we are proposing to adopt the financial policy of China or Mexico," which based their money on silver.[124] To a delegation of railroad employees the candidate contended, "You cannot improve the market by destroying the credit of the country, for the credit of the country lies at the foundation of capital and prosperity. The moment you have destroyed the credit of the country you have taken away from the manufacturer the ability to get money with which to conduct his business. … The farmer can no more increase the value of his wheat by diminishing the value of the American dollar than he can increase the quantity of his hay by diminishing the hay wagon on which he hauls it."[125] Indeed, McKinley insisted, "It is the proposition to debase our currency standard that has created consternation in every business center of the country, has made times hard, has driven money from active industry and put it behind barred doors, where it will be kept until confidence is again restored."[126] Such arguments resonated. One periodical cited a man who worked as a printer saying, "When things are in a more settled state, we are assured that large sums of money will be put into productive enterprises in this country by small investors in Europe if they can be sure of getting three and one half or four percent."[127]

McKinley insisted that protection offered the real solution to the country's economic problems. Supposedly problems began with the election of 1892, which put those determined to reduce tariffs into power. "Its effect was immediately felt," he asserted. "While months were to elapse before the new administration went into power, its acts were in part, at least, foreseen and anticipated. … Orders for machinery were cancelled, contracts were annulled, buying and selling curtailed, plans which had been formed for the extension of business were abandoned, works already built were not equipped with machinery, doubt and uncertainty hung over the country."[128] The Democrats went on to confirm these doubts by reducing

[123] *Topeka State Journal*, September 25, 1896, p. 8.
[124] *The Indianapolis Journal*, October 18, 1896, p. 1.
[125] *The Indianapolis Journal*, September 30, 1896, p. 1.
[126] *The Indianapolis Journal*, October 11, 1896, p. 1.
[127] *Overland Monthly*, 28 (October 1896): 481.
[128] *The Indianapolis Journal*, October 11, 1896, p. 1.

protection, a policy McKinley promised to reverse. He offered workers "American wages, the wages that he had for thirty years from 1860 to 1890, under the glorious policy of a protective tariff."[129]

Protection promised to win over many who were uncertain about the gold standard but found Bryan too radical. It appealed not only to those engaged in manufacturing, who would benefit directly from restrictions on imports, but to dairy and truck farmers as well as those raising cattle and hogs for the meatpackers because protection promised to expand the urban market on which they depended. Those who raised sheep naturally looked to the protection of wool from foreign competition. The man in charge of the campaign in and around Toledo, Ohio, reported to Hanna, "Anti-free-silver literature was largely used in the city, while we reached the farmers largely with protective literature."[130] One of the GOP's travelling orators wrote, "In West Virginia and Maryland [which McKinley would win] I found the tariff the potent factor which I endeavored to inculcate."[131]

After the contest was over, a political operative from the Golden State asserted, "California was carried on the tariff and not on the money question. This is a strong silver state."[132] Bryan has no such second string in his bow. The Democratic Platform advanced other reforms, but in his oratory, the candidate spent more time discussing free silver than all other matters combined—usually far more. Finally, whereas Bryan played to regional and class resentments, McKinley insisted, "The man who would array the poor against the rich, labor against capital, class against class or section against section is not the friend of the country but an enemy of the very best interest of every citizen."[133]

Dawes' Chicago office churned out huge volumes of literature with which it blanketed the country, drawing heavily on McKinley's speeches but tapping into many other sources too. The program had parallels in the campaign of New York's Reform Club in 1895 and early 1896, but its scale dwarfed that effort. Every day the Chicago headquarters dispatched boxcars full of material to every corner of the country, and it followed up to ensure distribution. Over a dozen weeks, it distributed 200 million

[129] *The Indianapolis Journal*, October 18, 1896, p. 1.
[130] M. Loenshal to Hanna, November 10, 1896, Hanna Papers, Volume I.
[131] L.C. Schilling to Hanna, November 10, 1896, Hanna Papers, Volume I.
[132] L.A. Sheldon, November 10, 1896, Hanna Papers, Volume I.
[133] Bryan, *The First Battle*, p. 200; *The Indianapolis Journal*, October 18, 1896, p. 1.

pamphlets, fliers, and broadsides, or more than twelve for each voter. These ran the gamut from general surveys of the currency to productions aimed at specific groups—veterans, coal miners, farmers, immigrants, and more—and came in several languages.[134] The man in charge of the campaign in Toledo claimed, "The city of Toledo was covered twelve times, the thirteen townships outside of Toledo, eight times," and he added that a substantial volume of the literature was in French, German, Polish, Italian, and Yiddish. His office alone mailed 252,000 pieces of campaign literature to voters.[135] At the same time, McKinley's campaign directed a swarm of speakers who blanketed the country, particularly the all-important states of the Midwest—1400 at the height of the effort. By the last weeks of the contest, it had speakers running both ahead of and behind Bryan to refute his arguments.[136]

Two groups received special attention—Midwestern farmers and urban workers. The former were decisive. Whichever candidate carried the Midwest and the Great Plains would win the election, and there farmers were a majority. The latter offered the GOP a margin of error. Though farmers still predominated in most of the United States, large victories in the cities could compensate for narrow defeats in the countryside. McKinley and Hanna thought of their campaign as "educational." They would fight on the issues, defending the gold standard and touting protection as the answer to the country's economic problems.

Farmers posed the greater challenge. By devaluating the dollar, free coinage of silver would almost certainly raise the price of wheat and cotton sold abroad. Bryan was a product of rural Illinois and Nebraska, and his rhetoric resonated with Midwestern farmers. Republicans responded in a variety of ways. They insisted that the fall in the price of wheat in the United States reflected "the enormous increase in the amount of wheat annually produced." Since the 1870s, the US output of wheat had doubled, while the country's population had increased only about 60 percent, and competition from farmers in Russia, India, and Argentina for foreign markets had intensified. As a result, as one campaign publication put it, "Wheat has fallen in price of necessity, in obedience to the law of supply

[134] Williams, *Realigning America*, pp. 138–9.

[135] Loenshal to Hanna, November 10, 1896. Loenshal described some of the literature as being in "Hebrew," but presumably he meant Yiddish.

[136] Rove, *The Triumph of William McKinley*, p. 355.

and demand, and altogether independent of the money standard."[137] McKinley contended, "We cannot cut down the competition which they [farmers] have in India and Russia and the Argentine Republic or increase consumption at home of their product by cutting down the value of the currency of the United States. The only way farmers can be benefitted is through a larger consuming class."[138] This protection could do by increasing the country's manufacturing base. Such arguments particularly resounded with truck and dairy farmers, who sold most of their output within the United States, and those who raised livestock for the rapidly growing meatpackers.

The Republicans enjoyed one great piece of good luck during the campaign. News of poor harvests in Europe and India drove the price of wheat up in the fall of 1896. The advance was temporary—harvests abroad were indeed poor, but it would be months before the shortfall translated into larger purchases of American wheat—but the jump occurred right before the election. It naturally heartened wheat growers, and it contradicted the assertions of Silverites that prices could not advance under the gold standard. One of Hanna's correspondents from Oregon thanked him "for your magnificent effort in raising and maintaining the prices of wheat so markedly during the past few weeks. It is worth millions to us [Oregon's farmers]."[139] Hanna was a capable man, but raising the price of wheat in world markets was beyond even his powers. McKinley was simply fortunate.

Winning over workers proved easier. Populists and Silverites thought of themselves as the champions of the worker, and some radicals like John Altgeld and Eugene Debs supported Bryan. Debs wrote Bryan, "Under your administration the rule of the money power will be broken."[140] Frank Parsons, a respected engineer and educator, declared, "It is a question not of the remonetization of silver, but of the remanitization of government—a question of entrusting the federal power to men in hearty sympathy with the great common people, or to men in sympathy with Wall Street and the whole army of parasites and monopolies."[141] For men like Altgeld, Debs, and Parsons, free silver was the thin edge of a wedge of reform that would

[137] "Wage-Earners and the 200-Cent Dollar," [1896], McKinley Papers, reel 1.
[138] *The Indianapolis Journal*, September 30, 1896, p. 1.
[139] H. Yongue to Hanna, November 9, 1896, Hanna Papers, Volume I.
[140] Eugene Debs to Bryan, July 27, 1896, Bryan Papers, box 4.
[141] Frank Parsons, "The Issue of 1896," *The Arena*, 16 (November 1896): 881.

break the political power of banks, railroads, and industrial trusts, opening the way for a radical transformation of American society.

Free coinage itself deterred workers, however. Bryan insisted, "Wage-earners know that while a gold standard raises the purchasing power of the dollar, it also makes it more difficult to obtain possession of the dollar; they know that employment is less permanent, loss of work more probable, and reemployment less certain."[142] Parsons argued, "When prices go up [because of free coinage] wages will also rise, and employment will become more continuous and secure. The first effect will be that a *day's* wage will buy somewhat less than at present—prices will be lifted first—then the resulting stimulation of business will call for more labor, mills and factories will run full time instead of half or a third of the time, men at work will have work for a larger part of the year, and many not at work at all will be able to get work; the result will be that a *year's* wages will buy a good deal more than at present."[143] Republicans, however, hammered away at the impact of devaluation and rising prices on the purchasing power of wages. One GOP publication insisted, "Wages are always the last factor to feel the advance. An increase in the price paid for labor comes very slowly and the increase, in this case, could not come at all until the business of the country has been readjusted to confirm to the silver basis."[144] Another piece of campaign literature asserted, "Older men recollect that in the years following the [Civil] war, wages were not near as high in proportion as other things were."[145] Speaking to a group of railway workers, McKinley said, "Nearly $500,000,000 are paid annually to the railroad employees alone. Does the railroad employee propose to aid any party to enact legislation which will cut his pay from 25 to 50 percent?"[146] Instead of inflation, Republicans insisted that workers should look to protection against foreign competition, which would let them claim higher wages. This argument resonated. Workers did not need to accept platitudes about the common interests of management and labor to realize that both could profit from protection.

Few workers showed much enthusiasm for free coinage. Deb's American Railway Union, as one irritated Republican put it, "urge[d] railway

[142] Bryan, *The First Battle*, p. 322.
[143] Parsons, "The Issue of 1896," p. 884. Emphasis in original.
[144] "Wage-Earners and the 200-Cent Dollar."
[145] "A Farmer's Letter on the Silver Question."
[146] *The Indianapolis Journal*, September 30, 1896, p. 1.

employees to ignore the money question, to regard their employees as their enemies, and to regard the opposition of the railroad officers to Mr. Bryan and his principles as a sure indication that he is their friend."[147] Workers, however, were not inclined to ignore what Bryan himself insisted was the chief issue of the campaign. During the grinding depression of the 1890s, prices fell faster than wages—though of course, total employment had declined as well.[148] Still, lower prices had offered workers some consolation amid hard times. During the inflation that had accompanied the Civil War—the only case of persistent inflation in living memory—wage increases had indeed lagged well behind advancing prices. Even the reform-minded editors of journals like the *New England Magazine* and *The Forum* concluded that the gold standard served workers' interests better than free coinage of silver. The mercurial Terence Powderly, the former leader of the Knights of Labor who had cooperated with the Populists in the past, gave a speech in New York City during the campaign denouncing free coinage, warning that it would erode workers' purchasing power.[149] Republicans circulated a letter by leaders of three unions representing railway workers "denouncing the attempt at free coinage of silver at sixteen to one, believing it to be directly against the interests of labor."[150]

A cultural gap further separated Bryan from workers. He was a product of rural America and spoke in the idiom of the revivalist preacher. Most workers were immigrants or the children of immigrants and had little in common with Bryan. Though McKinley did not spring from the working class, he was a type with which most of its members were familiar—if they were fortunate, they worked for men like McKinley (or Hanna).[151] McKinley's record contained much that appealed to immigrants and workers. When serving as governor of Ohio, McKinley publicly rebuffed demands by the American Protective Association (APA) that he fire

[147] An Address to Railroad Employees, [September 1896], McKinley Papers, reel 1.

[148] Charles Hoffmann, "The Depression of the 1890s," *The Journal of Economic History* 2 (1956); 150–1.

[149] Rove, *The Triumph of William McKinley*, pp. 323–4.

[150] *New York Times*, October 28, 1896, p. 2.

[151] Hanna's political enemies created stories of violent strikes and abuse of workers at his businesses, but in fact, labor relations at Hanna's enterprises were, by the standards of the day, quite good. No one would mistake him for a champion of organized labor, but he listened to and often acted on workers' complaints. Supposedly, Hanna said of George Pullman during the Pullman Strike, "A man who won't meet his men half-way is a God-damned fool." The quotation may be apocryphal, but those who knew Hanna considered it in character.

Catholic guards at the state prison.[152] The APA was a secretive, nativist organization hostile to both immigrants and the Catholic Church. In the spring of 1896, it lodged a series of complaints against McKinley. It alleged that he had refused to meet with its leaders, that he was a member of the secretive Ancient Order of Hibernians (a group of Irish Catholics), that Marc Hanna was a Catholic, and more. It concluded that it could not support McKinley's nomination. McKinley authorized Hanna to make a mocking riposte, noting that all the specific allegations of the APA were false. The APA's leaders had never asked for a meeting with the Major, Hanna was an Episcopalian, and while McKinley belonged to six fraternal associations, the Hibernians were not among them—nor was the APA.[153] Ordinarily, McKinley's campaign followed a softer line. He recognized that in politics, neither friendship nor enmity was permanent, and sought to avoid alienating anyone. As a firm believer in compromise and conciliation, however, he had little time for an organization like the APA that had no interest in either. McKinley also had a balanced record toward organized labor, acting forcefully to prevent violence by workers during the 1894 coal strike in Ohio, but also supporting relief efforts for the families of striking miners as well as legislation to punish employers who fired workers for joining a union. In labor relations as in most other areas of national life, McKinley favored compromise.

Silverites often treated workers as members of the Southern Alliance treated black farmers, assuming an identity of interests without delving deeply into their concerns. The Democratic Platform condemned the use of court injunctions in labor disputes, such as President Cleveland had secured during the Pullman strike, but Bryan rarely devoted more than a sentence to the subject in his speeches. In contrast, the GOP circulated literature to immigrants and their children in their own languages and organized clubs that appealed to various ethnic groups. In Indiana, for instance, the Republican National Committee had an operative who apparently did nothing but organize clubs among Poles in support of McKinley.[154] The Democrats had nothing vaguely comparable.

After the election, Bryan complained "Many employees were either directly or indirectly compelled to support the Republican ticket."

[152] Rove, *The Triumph of William McKinley*, pp. 228–9.

[153] *The American* (Omaha), April 24, 1896, p. 5; Rove, *The Triumph of William McKinley*, pp. 175–8.

[154] L.M. Kucharski to Hanna, November 10, 1896, Hanna Papers, Volume I.

Historian John D. Hicks seconded this charge in his generally excellent history of Populism, as did Robert Durden at considerably greater length in his *Climax of Populism*.[155] Certainly, few employers concealed their preferences. In an open letter to workers, the chief manager of the Chicago, Peoria, & St Louis Railroad wrote, "I know that our prosperity as employees of this railroad largely depends on the prosperity of the road, and I do not want any false political theories to be adopted in the country which will depress or ruin the business out of which we make our living." "The company's bonds," he continued, "are payable in gold, and it is admitted on all sides that if free coinage wins, gold will be hard to get, and the effect upon the company will doubtless be bankruptcy." Meanwhile, free coinage would increase the cost of supplies, further squeezing the road. As a result, "The cost of your living would very largely increase, and there would be absolutely no earthy probability of your securing an advance in your rates of pay." He concluded, "Some misguided people may think their business would be benefitted by free silver. If they think so, let them vote for it; but do not let us be fooled into voting for something that would benefit the other fellow and be a positive detriment to us."[156] The economy was weak during the summer and fall of 1896, and some factories and mines closed. In many cases, managers followed the line of the man in charge of a St Louis ironworks who blamed layoffs on "the Free Silver agitation, and … the [Democrats'] Chicago platform."[157] Such statements not only reflected managers' understanding of the situation but had the added advantage of deflecting workers' resentment away from management. In fact, uncertainty about the currency had led many businesses to postpone major decisions until the situation was clearer. Even those with doubts about the gold standard wanted to know the financial ground on which they stood before making any large commitments. They would wait until after the election.

Gauging the impact of employers' statements is difficult. Managers like the one at the Chicago, Peoria, & St Louis Railroad certainly pulled no punches, but neither did they threaten retaliation against dissenters,

[155] Bryan, "Has the Election Settled the Money Question?" p. 710; Hicks, *The Populist Revolt*, p. 375; Durden, *The Climax of Populism*, pp. 131–4.

[156] To the Employees of the Chicago, Peoria & St Louis Railroad, September 19, 1896, McKinley Papers, reel 1.

[157] Quoted in Durden, *The Climax of Populism*, p. 139.

warning only of general financial calamity if Bryan won. Robert Durden cited an incident that seems to be the proverbial exception that proves the rule. When a St Louis department store dismissed a dozen workers because its manager believed that they supported Bryan and free coinage, the public backlash was such that he had to rehire them almost immediately.[158] By 1896, most of the heavily industrialized states had adopted the "Australian" or secret ballot, so an employer could not be sure how a worker voted. One of Bryan's correspondents, writing from Cleveland, stated that employers there had given workers a day off with pay on the understanding that they would march in a parade for McKinley, but he continued, "I know a great many of the working men. Many of them are wearing McKinley badges, but if they know you quite well, they will show you a Bryan badge on the inside of their vest and tell you that is the way they will vote."[159]

After the election, Grover Cleveland's friend Arthur Farquhar wrote him, "The silent vote among the working people went to sound money after all as you told me it would."[160] In fact, some workers did vote for Bryan—one GOP operative attributed the party's defeat in Kansas to Bryan's support among miners and railway workers, and another lamented that the party did not do as well in Chicago's working-class districts as he would have liked.[161] On the whole, however, McKinley received the large majority of workers' votes. They had perfectly good reasons to prefer the gold standard and protection to the free coinage of silver, and it is best to attribute their support for the GOP to such calculations.

Bryan's complaint about intimidation was more than a little hypocritical. The Democratic Party in the South owed its power, in large part, to fraud and intimidation, which it practiced on a scale unmatched in American history to deny the franchise to African-Americans, who overwhelmingly supported the GOP. One of Hanna's correspondents from Alabama complained, "We have been counted out everywhere," and another from Virginia asserted, "I doubt if there was a fair count given at any place; I know there was not at the precinct where I voted." As another

[158] Durden, *Climax of Populism*, p. 140.

[159] Braxton Davenport to Bryan, October 22, 1896, Bryan Papers, box 4.

[160] Arthur Farquhar to Cleveland, November 12, 1896, Cleveland Papers, reel 93.

[161] Albert Horton to Hanna, November 5, 1896, Hanna Papers, Volume I; Murray to Hanna, November 4, 1896, Hanna Papers, Volume I.

Virginian described the canvass in his town, "Our voters were intimidated very much and there were 150 votes thrown out and a good many were waiting in line at sundown but they were denied," and he concluded by noting that Bryan carried the town by only 191 votes.[162] Bryan was immensely popular among southern Whites, Populists, and Democrats, but in South Carolina and Mississippi, where African-Americans were the majority, he probably would have lost if they had enjoyed equal access to the ballot box.[163] In Virginia and Tennessee, McKinley's popularity in the cities and persistent Republican strength in the mountains might well have allowed the GOP to carry both states with a fair count. In a completely honest canvass, Bryan almost certainly would have done worse—perhaps much worse.

As the election neared, McKinley seemed to gain traction. In late October, August Belmont wrote one of the Rothschilds, "I am satisfied that the coming election will result in the most overwhelming defeat … which any party has received since the war. … The campaign of education has been a very thorough one and has been conducted with great skill and on high principles from the Republican headquarters."[164] On the eve of balloting, William Curtis could report, "There is no run on the Treasury for gold. … If there was any deep-seated fear of Bryan's election this would not be so."[165]

As returns came in during the night of November 3, it became clear that McKinley had won a great victory. He carried not only the Northeast but also the Industrial Midwest by large margins, as well as border states like Maryland, West Virginia, and Kentucky. He divided the Farm Belt with Bryan, winning Iowa, Minnesota, and North Dakota by solid margins while the Democrat carried Kansas, Nebraska, and South Dakota. Bryan won the South and most of the far West by substantial majorities, although McKinley carried California and Oregon. Though his support was strongest in the cities and among farmers who produced livestock,

[162] W. Carris to Hanna, November 17; Wm. Vaughn to Hanna, November 10, 1896; and J. Nichols to Hanna, November 6, 1896, all Hanna Papers, Volume I.

[163] By 1896, both Mississippi and South Carolina has revised their state constitutions to deny African-Americans the vote, replacing ad hoc and extra-legal devices with legal and systematic ones.

[164] August Belmont to Alfonse Rothschild, October 22, 1896, Belmont Papers, letter books, box 23.

[165] William Curtis to Mother, October 31, 1896, Curtis Papers, box 8.

dairy products, or fruits and vegetables for the cities, McKinley also turned in a respectable performance among those who raised grain for export. The electoral vote was 271 to 176 in McKinley's favor. The popular vote was closer, 7.1 million to 6.5 million, but McKinley's margin was still larger than that of any other presidential candidate for over twenty years. The Republicans lost some ground in the House of Representatives, but they retained a very large majority there, and their numbers in the Senate increased. Throughout the country, defenders of the gold standard heaved a collective sigh of relief.

CHAPTER 7

The Triumph of Gold

According to most histories, William McKinley's victory in the 1896 election secured the gold standard. At the time, the future did not seem so clear. The economy remained weak—conditions at the end of 1896 were probably worse than a year earlier. By some estimates, the economy did not bottom out until the summer of 1897. The legal status of the currency remained unsettled—the government relied on a variety of ad hoc measures to keep the various types of money in circulation at par with the gold dollar. William Jennings Bryan believed that, by pushing the currency to the forefront, the 1896 campaign had resulted in "temporary defeat, but permanent gain for the cause of bimetallism." The fortunes of the parties had shifted dramatically in 1890 and again in 1894, and they might well do so again. "The contest for financial independence will go on," he insisted.[1] Bryan had risen to prominence as the champion of the free coinage of silver and was loath to concede defeat, but he had a point. The 1896 election did not so much settle the question of the currency as give William McKinley the opportunity to settle it.

[1] Bryan, "Has the Election Settled the Money Question?" pp. 704, 710.

W. Wells, *Financial Politics in the United States in the 1890s*,
https://doi.org/10.1007/978-3-031-86765-1_7

The New Administration

As he took office, President McKinley showed remarkably little interest in the currency. Aside from the usual platitudes about sound currency, his inaugural address contained only two statements on the subject. "The question of international bimetallism will have early and earnest attention," he promised. "It will be my constant endeavor to secure it by cooperation with the other great commercial powers of the world."[2] He also urged Congress to authorize a commission to study the currency. (It refused.) The new president showed far more interest in tariffs. "We should have more revenue, and that without delay," he insisted. "Nothing has ever been made plainer at a general election than that the controlling principle in the raising of revenue from duties on imports is zealous care for American interests and American labor."[3] This statement was jarring. The choice between gold and silver had dominated the 1896 campaign. Nevertheless, during the contest McKinley had clearly endorsed a higher tariff, and the President called a special session of Congress to convene on March 15 to consider new tariff legislation.

McKinley's party supported his approach. Senator Thomas Platt of New York, who had clashed with McKinley in the past, stated in early 1897, "No legislation is now necessary for the maintenance of the gold standard. When we have replenished the Treasury, restored public credit, and set the country's industries again on their feet, there will be time enough … to revise our, no doubt, disordered currency system."[4] Later in the year, Senator James Allison, one of the most influential men in the upper house, said, "We will be able to get along if we do not get any currency legislation."[5]

This attitude irritated more doctrinaire advocates of the gold standard. The editors of *The Economist* insisted, "There cannot be a permanent improvement in the condition of affairs in the United States … until the questions affecting the currency are effectively dealt with, and there is no early prospect of such a consummation."[6] Economist Laurence Laughlin

[2] McKinley Inaugural, March 4, 1896, Presidency Project, UCSB.
[3] McKinley Inaugural.
[4] *The Economist*, January 30, 1897, p. 156.
[5] Newspaper clipping, [November 1897], McKinley Papers, reel 2.
[6] *The Economist*, August 7, 1897, p. 1138.

complained, "Why should the President have allowed himself to open the special session of Congress [on March 15] with a message in which there was not one word in regard to monetary legislation—the main question of the [1896] campaign?"[7]

The economic outlook was indeed unclear. Many observers had hoped that McKinley's victory, by removing uncertainty about the gold standard, would restore prosperity. Yet as Laughlin wrote, "The feeling of confidence immediately after the election caused a great rise in the price of securities—only to be followed, within a month or two, by a steady and disheartening decline. Since then industry has moved with leaden feet." During the year after the election, good news alternated with bad. In December 1896, a minor panic rattled banks in Illinois, Wisconsin, and Minnesota.[8] At the same time, poor harvests in Europe and a good one in the United States translated into higher prices for and larger exports of wheat over 1897. As a result, gold flowed into the country, pushing the Treasury's reserve over $150 million for the first time in years. *The Economist* reported "improved and growing demand … for farm implements, wagons, and for pianos and organs" from rural districts, but the same article noted, "The … great manufacturing industries, iron and steel, … cotton and woolen goods, remain … relatively unfavorable." Notably, weak demand had led some textile mills to close for several weeks.[9] Railroads laid more track in 1897 than they had for several years, but the total remained well below the boom years of the 1880s. Two of the major rail systems that had defaulted, the Union Pacific and the Baltimore & Ohio, remained in receivership. The situation in 1897 resembled that of 1895, promising but well short of prosperous.

Political conditions made significant financial reform unlikely. The Republicans were in firm control of the House of Representatives, but their grip on the Senate was weak. There they were the largest party by far, with forty-four members, but that was short of a majority in the ninety-member chamber. There were thirty-four Democrats, five Populists, and seven who identified themselves as members of the Silver Party or as Silver

[7] J. Laurence Laughlin, "The McKinley Administration and Prosperity," *The Forum*, July 1897, p. 562.

[8] Andrew Jalil, "A New History of Banking Panics in the United States, 1825–1929: Construction and Implications," *American Economic Journal: Macroeconomics*, 7 (2015), p. 305.

[9] *The Economist*, August 7, 1897, pp. 1144–5.

Republicans. Moreover, several Republican Senators from the West were sympathetic to silver. An effort to confirm the gold standard would almost certainly fail in the Senate, increasing rather than reducing uncertainty. With the Treasury flush with gold, the administration had every reason to avoid such a collision. Besides, the situation was likely to improve. State legislatures elected Senators, and gains by the GOP in these bodies since 1894 made it almost certain that, in many states, Republican senators would soon replace Democratic ones.[10]

In 1897, Republicans focused on tariffs, an issue on which they agreed and that allowed cooperation with Silver Republicans. The House of Representatives had conducted extensive hearings in the winter session of the outgoing Congress. When the new Congress met in a special session starting March 15, it had ready a bill that Speaker Thomas Reed managed to push through by the end of the month. As usual, the Senate moved at a more leisurely pace, spending most of April on hearings and May and June on debate and amendments. In most respects, however, its final bill resembled the House measure, and the two chambers quickly resolved their differences in conference. The new tariff, known as the Dingley tariff, largely restored the levies imposed under the 1890 McKinley Tariff and even, in some cases, increased them. By most measures, it was the steepest tariff thus far in American history.

The bill held out benefits to farmers and, particularly, inhabitants of the West. It restored the duty on raw wool, imposing proportional levies on wool cloth to compensate textile producers. Because American farmers sold a large portion of what they raised on world markets, in most cases tariffs did them little good. Wool was the great exception. The United States imported large volumes of it, so this levy benefitted those raising sheep, particularly western ranchers. The new tariff also imposed levies on imported hides and lead, which heretofore had entered the country duty-free. Westerners were, again, the primary domestic producers of both. From an economic perspective, these changes were dubious. They raised the prices of key raw materials for important industries—woolen textiles, shoemaking, and paint—that employed more people than sheep ranching, leather curing, and lead mining. Laurence Laughlin condemned the bill as "a tariff of exaggerations, a tariff of scandals, and tariff of barbarians, a

[10] Warner Sutton to McKinley, June 22, 1898, McKinley Papers, reel 3.

tariff which antagonized both Republicans and Democrats."[11] Politically, however, it served its purpose, demonstrating to Silver Republicans that the GOP could benefit their constituents.

The Wolcott Mission

Instead of seeking to reinforce the gold standard, President McKinley launched talks for an international agreement to remonetize silver. The Republican platform had promised to explore this option, as had McKinley himself during the campaign. The President was no purist in monetary affairs—if the country could coin silver without devaluation, he saw no reason not to do so. Success seemed possible. In 1895 and 1896, the British House of Commons, the French Chamber of Deputies, and the German Reichstag had all passed non-binding resolutions urging their governments to explore the possibility of an agreement remonetizing silver.[12] From a political perspective, the President had little to lose. An honest effort would demonstrate goodwill toward Silverites, and success would cut the legs out from under Bryan and his supporters. Even failure would serve a purpose, convincing many uncertain about the financial future that the gold standard represented the country's only realistic option.

Supporters of the gold standard displayed mixed reactions. Laurence Laughlin declared the initiative "a shock to confidence not easily borne in silence."[13] *The Economist* declared, "One international conference after another has been held, and all have proven abortive. To convene another would be equally futile."[14] On the other hand, August Belmont wrote, "It is … necessary to fulfill the promises made in the 1896 campaign," though he added, "No one believes Europe is prepared to discuss such a question."[15] Even the editors of the thoroughly orthodox *London Times* remarked, "In a well-regulated state it ought not to excite astonishment that he [McKinley] is now endeavoring to redeem these promises [made during the campaign] to pursue an agreement."[16] For the most part,

[11] Laughlin, "The McKinley Administration and Prosperity," p. 561.

[12] Russell, *International Monetary Conferences*, p. 433–8.

[13] Laughlin, "The McKinley Administration and Prosperity," p. 559.

[14] *The Economist*, March 6, 1897, p. 341.

[15] Belmont to Leopold Rothschild, January 12, 1897, Belmont Papers, box 23, letter books.

[16] *London Times*, April 13, 1897, McKinley Papers, reel 2.

Silverites reserved judgment. Their papers reported on the progress of talks without comment. The success of negotiations would accomplish their goal but severely damage their political credibility, whereas failure would strengthen advocates of the gold standard. Among politicians, only Silver Republicans showed real enthusiasm. An international agreement would allow them to reconcile with the GOP without compromising their support for silver.

President McKinley oversaw the talks himself. He had appointed Senator John Sherman Secretary of State, but though eminent, Sherman was failing (he probably suffered from Alzheimer's). McKinley knew of Sherman's weakness but gave him the post anyway because he wanted to make Sherman's Senate seat available for Mark Hanna. (Hanna indeed secured election to the Senate from Ohio in Sherman's place.) The result created a vacuum at the top of a key department for the first year of McKinley's administration—Sherman resigned in April 1898. For monetary talks, McKinley himself filled the gap. He believed, probably correctly, that another international conference on silver would yield little unless the key participants had agreed on a program in advance. Accordingly, he dispatched a three-man commission to Europe to conduct bilateral talks. Senator Edward Wolcott, a Silverite who had stayed loyal to the GOP in 1896, led the group. It also included Adlai Stevenson, a Democrat who had both served as Cleveland's Vice President and supported Bryan in 1896, and Charles Paine, a politically active Boston financier with more orthodox views on finance. Wolcott, a strong personality, dominated the group, which became known as the Wolcott Mission. As Wolcott told the British Prime Minister, Lord Salisbury, he intended "to ascertain, as definitively as possible, in advance of an International Bimetallic Conference, if one should be called, the views of the governments that might participate therein."[17] During the course of talks, Wolcott and the US ambassadors in London and Paris all communicated directly with McKinley as well as with Secretary Sherman, and the President apparently drafted their instructions himself. Most observers believed that the German government had no interest in an agreement on silver, so the mission would go first to Paris and, if it made progress there, proceed to

[17] Memorandum of a Meeting held at the Foreign Office, July 12, 1893, "Correspondence Respecting on the Proposals on Currency Made by the Special Envoys from the United States," October 1897, NA, T 173/953. 1897.

London.[18] If successful in these capitals, Wolcott would be in a strong position to initiate talks in Berlin.

As Wolcott and his associates prepared to depart, the American embassies in Paris and London canvassed opinion there. The new ambassador to Britain, the urbane John Hay, wrote the President, "In my first interview with Lord Salisbury I told him I should soon ask his attention to the matter of a bimetallic conference."[19] In another letter, Hay reported that he was "gratified to find that British opinion is by no means so unanimously hostile to us [on silver] as has been pretended."[20] Horace Porter, the ambassador in Paris, wrote, "The officers of the government [here] have expressed at all times in my conversations with them, an earnest disposition to cooperate heartily with the United States in this matter, and a determination to act in entire good faith."[21]

The French government received the Wolcott Mission warmly. France had abandoned silver in the 1870s under pressure, and support for bimetallism remained strong there. The financier and economist Henri Cernuschi, the most articulate champion of international bimetallism, had lived in Paris and had made his fortune in its money market. Wolcott and his associates spent several weeks there, meeting with the French President and members of the government and engaging in direct talks with officials in the Foreign and Finance ministries.

By early July, Wolcott had worked out with the French government not only a tentative agreement but a joint approach to the British, whose cooperation all considered vital to success. France and the United States would resume free coinage of silver at the French ratio of fifteen and a half to one. This rule would entail inconvenience for the United States, which would have to alter its legal ratio of sixteen to one and recoin its silver dollars, but it was necessary. If the two countries maintained their different ratios, the entire burden of maintaining the value of silver would fall on France, which assigned silver a higher price than the United States. Only after France had exhausted its gold reserves would silver flow to American mints. The French naturally refused to consider such a one-sided arrangement. The point of an international agreement was to mobilize the resources of several nations to stabilize the relative price of silver and gold.

[18] John Hay to John Sherman, May 20, 1897, McKinley Papers, reel 2.
[19] John Hay to William McKinley, May 9, 1897, McKinley Papers, reel 2.
[20] John Hay to John Sherman, July 17, 1897, McKinley Papers, reel 2.
[21] Horace Porter to John Sherman, June 29, 1897, McKinley Papers, reel 2.

The joint approach to Britain demonstrated similar realism. The British had based their money on gold for seventy-five years, far longer than any other major power. For them, bimetallism represented not a return to old practices but a new departure. Moreover, the country was prosperous, which weighed heavily against monetary innovation. The Americans and French would lead with a request that Britain open its mints to the free coinage of silver, but they were ready with an alternative when London refused. They would ask the British to reopen India's mints to free coinage, reversing a policy adopted only four years earlier. Before then, the Subcontinent had absorbed large quantities of silver, and presumably it could do so again. In addition, the Americans and the French would ask the British to mint more silver coins of small denominations and to increase the size of transactions for which they were legal tender—a change that would increase demand for silver somewhat but not dramatically alter the overall situation.

Armed with these agreements, Wolcott and his associates decamped to London. There as in Paris they received a warm reception, meeting extensively with the Prime Minister, Lord Salisbury, and other members of the government as well as officials of the Foreign Ministry, the Treasury, and the India Office. Queen Victoria formally received them at Windsor Castle. The French ambassador participated in many of these meetings, demonstrating that, as Ambassador Hay put it, "France is heartily with us, which they [the British] seemed to doubt."[22] Hay reported that, in all discussions, Salisbury "said, with great frankness, that the government were not entirely of one mind in relation to this matter. … He added that it was by no means certain that the opinion of the Indian government, and the leading people there, was so strongly in favor of bimetallism as it formerly was." Arthur Balfour, the leader in the House of Commons, was "thoroughly in favor of bimetallism through international agreement," but the Chancellor of the Exchequer (Finance Minister) strongly opposed any change.[23] Diplomatic considerations figured in as well. Balfour told the Cabinet that it was "of the first importance that if the negotiations started at Washington are to fail, the blame for their failure should not rest at our door. Such a result would probably injure our international relations with the United States," which had improved significantly since the Venezuelan crisis. Balfour added that "some well-informed persons"

[22] John Hay to William McKinley, July 16, 1897, McKinley Papers, reel 2.
[23] Hay to Sherman, May 20, 1897, McKinley Papers, reel 2.

believed that the American initiative was not sincere. The McKinley administration simply wanted to appease Silverites at home and would, as Balfour put it, "hail with unbounded satisfaction the chances of throwing all the odium of ill-success upon England." Such considerations, he insisted, made it all the more important to be conciliatory.[24] On August 7, Salisbury announced that his government needed to conduct extensive study and discussion before replying to the American and French proposals.[25]

On October 11, after two months of government conferences, inter-ministry discussion, and lobbying, Lord Salisbury announced, "It would be most unwise to reopen the mints [of India] as part of the proposed arrangements," effectively killing prospects for an international agreement.[26] McKinley's biographer H. Wayne Morgan believed that London never had any intention of agreeing to anything and that all of this activity was simply for show, to say "no" in as polite a way as possible.[27] On the other hand, Lewis Gould, in his history of the McKinley administration, suggested that the British were eager for an agreement until officials from the India Office elbowed their way into the discussion and nixed the accord.[28] Documents from British archives paint a more nuanced picture. They make it clear that London seriously considered the American and French proposal but had no intention of acting without carefully considering the situation in India. Ultimately, the situation in the Subcontinent was decisive, not larger questions of the virtues and defects of the gold standard. When the British closed India's mints to silver in 1893, they had created, in John Hay's words, "most serious consequences to the prosperity of the people in India."[29] A currency that had been expanding rapidly suddenly became static, creating a shock that led to a severe recession. As a report by officials in India put it, "India has since 1893 passed through a period of serious tension and embarrassment alike to trade and to the

[24] Arthur Balfour to the Cabinet, October 12, 1897, NA, CAB 37/45.

[25] John Hay to John Sherman, August 7, 1897, McKinley Papers, reel 2.

[26] John Hay to John Sherman, [October 23, 1897], McKinley Papers, reel 2; clippings from *London Times*, October 23, 1897, McKinley Papers, reel 2.

[27] H. Wayne Morgan, *William McKinley and His America* (Syracuse, NY: Syracuse University Press, 1963), pp. 282–5.

[28] Lewis Gould, *The Presidency of William McKinley* (Lawrence: The Regents Press of Kansas, 1980), pp. 44–7.

[29] Hay to Sherman, August 7, 1897.

Government."[30] By 1897, however, the India Office believed "that our difficulties are now nearly over, and that we shall, in the near future, succeed in establishing a stable exchange." London had "pegged" the Indian currency to sterling, buying and selling rupees to keep the rate stable, a system that allowed the gradual expansion of money and credit.[31] The rupee remained a silver coin, but the link to sterling gave it a value in gold higher than the market price of the silver it contained, not unlike silver dollars in the United States. This peg valued the silver in the rupee relative to gold at twenty-three to one, well above the market prices but far below the fifteen-and-a-half-to-one ratio sought by the United States and France.[32] Should an international agreement secure the latter ratio, the value of the rupee would appreciate by almost half against currencies backed by gold. Officials in the India Office feared that such a large rise in the rupee's value "would shatter, for the time at least, the export trade of India, would gravely affect the balance between the State as landlord and the cultivating classes, would diminish the receipts from the State railways, and would give a shock to commercial and social relations."[33] The government of India added that all of this would entail "acute individual suffering."[34] Even Balfour, who strongly supported an agreement on silver, conceded, "The suddenness of the jump from the old to the new value of the rupee" might cause serious problems.[35] If, on the other hand, the attempt to remonetize silver failed to raise its price to the official ratio—and British officials believed "the probability is that they [the Americans and the French] will fail to secure that result"—then India would be back where it had been in 1893, with a depreciating silver currency.[36] Balfour thought it possible to frame an agreement that would avoid these pitfalls, but his memo on the subject offered few specifics. In

[30] Government of India to India Office, September 16, 1897, "Correspondence Respecting Proposals on Currency."

[31] The great economist John Maynard Keynes wrote his first book, *Indian Currency and Finance* (1913), about India's currency regime, describing its complexities in great detail.

[32] The rupee was worth more than the silver it contained because the government limited the supply of coins, which were legal tender in India, giving the silver rupee a position similar to that of silver dollars in the United States.

[33] Clippings from *London Times*, October 23, 1897, McKinley Papers, reel 2.

[34] Government of India to India Office, September 16, 1897, "Correspondence Respecting Proposals on Currency."

[35] Arthur Balfour to the Cabinet, October 12, 1897, NA, CAB 37/45, 1897.

[36] Government of India to India Office, September 16, 1897, "Correspondence Respecting Proposals on Currency."

fact, it is hard to imagine how India could have implemented such a huge revaluation without substantial economic disruption. British officials had good reason to stand pat.

Reviewing the course of talks, John Hay wrote the President, "I do not see what more could have been done. Wolcott has been untiring in energy, tactful and persuasive in argument, has made a most favorable impression on friend and foe. … But circumstances have worked against us more powerfully than any argument."[37] Prosperity in Europe robbed the issue of its impact, and every informed official knew that gold production was increasing rapidly, raising doubts about the need for silver money. With respect to India, the passage of time had made the restoration of the free coinage of silver difficult and perhaps even dangerous. Its experience represents a classic example of what economists call "path dependency." In 1893, the closure of India's mints to silver had badly dislocated the subcontinent's economy. Had the United States and France asked Britain to reopen India's mints to silver soon thereafter as part of a larger effort to remonetize silver, London might well have acquiesced. Four years later, after the British had stabilized the rupee on their own, the answer was different—the cost to India of retracing its steps was simply too high.

President McKinley's hopes for these negotiations are unclear. He rarely revealed his thoughts to anyone—not even Mark Hanna. Had the Wolcott Mission succeeded, he certainly would have implemented the results. Given the political situation and his own pledges, he could hardly have done otherwise. With the mission's failure, he could plausibly argue that the gold standard constituted the country's only viable option. McKinley was first and foremost a politician, and he undoubtedly realized both that the political situation demanded a serious effort to negotiate and that, even if talks failed, they would yield political benefits. He quite possibly thought no further.

Reform and War

While the McKinley Administration secured a new tariff and dispatched the Wolcott Mission to Europe, advocates of the gold standard pursued their own agenda. On November 18, 1896, barely two weeks after the election, the Indianapolis Chamber of Commerce issued an invitation to other such organizations throughout the country for a conference on

[37] John Hay to William McKinley, October 11, 1897, McKinley Papers, reel 2.

financial reform. The Monetary Conference convened in Indianapolis in January 1897 with over 300 delegates representing 100 cities. After a vigorous discussion that defined the larger issues, the Convention appointed a Commission to study financial reform and offer recommendations. The Convention expressed hope that Congress would adopt and expand on this Commission, action President McKinley endorsed in his inaugural address. Congress refused to act, presumably because Silverites realized that such a commission would almost certainly endorse the gold standard. In any case, the Commission proceeded on its own, holding a series of hearings and issuing a voluminous *Report of the Monetary Commission* in January 1898.[38]

Laurence Laughlin, a thoroughly orthodox advocate of the gold standard, had more influence on the *Report* than anyone else. It recommended that Congress pass legislation that would: (1) explicitly promise to redeem all currency in gold coin, including silver dollars, rendering the de facto gold standard in place since 1879 official, (2) create a new bureau in the Treasury Department devoted solely to redeeming currency in gold, (3) equip the new bureau with its own gold reserve, insulating the monetary standard from fluctuations of the federal budget, (4) authorize gradual retirement of all greenbacks and Treasury notes, and (5) allow national banks to issue notes based, not on bonds deposited with the Treasury, but on their paid-in capital and surplus, with the proviso that notes in excess of 60 percent of their capital would pay a tax of 2 percent, and those in excess of 80 percent a tax of 6 percent. This arrangement would allow banks to expand their circulation in an emergency but give them a strong incentive to reduce it when the crisis had passed. The *Report* also suggested technical reforms to strengthen the audits of national banks, make it easier for investors to purchase government bonds, and facilitate the organization of national banks in small towns.[39]

The publication of the *Report* gave the champions of financial orthodoxy a substantial advantage. Already, the defeat of Bryan in 1896 and the failure of the Wolcott Mission had effectively foreclosed the free coinage of silver in the foreseeable future. Silverites were increasingly on the defensive, able to block change but not to initiate it. The *Report* crystalized the tenets of financial orthodoxy and backed them with several hundred pages

[38] *Report of the Monetary Commission of the Indianapolis Convention* (Chicago: University of Chicago Press, 1898, pp. 3–18.

[39] *Report of the Monetary Commission*, pp. 60–74.

of analysis and statistics. No other program of monetary reform could boast such intellectual backing or such broad support within the business community. As historian Charles Postel has noted, Populists spent a good deal of time studying the monetary system, but they never had the resources to produce anything so comprehensive, and their allergy to banking always left a huge gap in their analysis. Beyond the broad question of gold versus silver, most Americans—including President McKinley—cared little about the details of the financial system but simply wanted an arrangement that offered stability and prosperity. This the *Report* seemed to offer.

Already McKinley's Secretary of the Treasury, Lyman Gage, had recommended a similar package of reforms. Gage, who had worked his way from modest beginnings to the leadership of Chicago's largest bank, was a noted defender of the gold standard. He was among those bested in absentia by Coin in William Harvey's *Coin's School*. Gage was a political independent who leaned Republican but had supported Grover Cleveland for President in 1884. McKinley wanted a Treasury Secretary from the Midwest who would command the respect of New York's financiers. After exploring several options, he settled on Gage, despite the objections of some Republicans.[40] In his annual report to Congress at the end of 1897, the Treasury Secretary observed that the country's financial condition was strong because, with exports increasing, gold was flowing into the United States and the Treasury. "Unfortunately," he wrote, "the continuation of these good conditions cannot be assured to us." To strengthen the country's financial position, he recommended creating a separate fund at the Treasury with $125 million in gold devoted solely to redeeming notes, reissuing notes redeemed for gold only in exchange for the metal (notes used to pay taxes would be used again), allowing the Treasury to issue bonds that guaranteed payment in gold, and basing the issue of national banknotes on banks' total capital rather than on bonds deposited with the government. Finally, he wanted to authorize national banks with capital of as little as $25,000 to provide banking facilities in small towns.[41]

Not surprisingly, Silverites had little use for Gage's proposals. The *Lincoln County Leader* (Oregon) christened them a "monstrosity of goldbugism" that would "unite all opponents of the single gold

[40] David Baillie to McKinley, [January 28, 1897], McKinley Papers, reel 1.

[41] *Annual Report of the Secretary of the Treasury, 1897* (Washington: Government Printing Office, 1897), LXXIII–LXXVII.

standard."[42] The Topeka *Advocate and News* warned, "The bankers want to get the note-issuing business into their own hands so that they and not the government may control the volume of circulation."[43] Silverites had enough votes in the Senate to kill any reform measure, and they did just that, shelving a bill based on the Monetary Commission's *Report* that had passed the House. Senator Teller, however, decided to stake out a stronger position. He introduced a resolution stating that the United States could, if it so desired, pay the interest on its debts with silver dollars. The measure was not binding but allowed Silverites to raise doubts about any bonds issued to replenish the gold reserve or to retire greenbacks. Moreover, the resolution was undoubtedly correct about the law, which required the payment of bonds "in coin," a term that included silver dollars. Because the resolution entailed no action, supporting it represented an easy way for Senators from the West and South to demonstrate their continuing loyalty to silver. In early February, the Senate passed Teller's resolution by a vote of forty-seven to thirty-two, with the support of western Republicans like Wolcott as well as of Democrats, Populists, and Silver Republicans.[44]

In retrospect, Teller and other Silverites in Senate overplayed their hand. Teller based his resolution on one adopted in 1878, when the currency still consisted of greenbacks unsupported by gold. Bond owners of that day had bought their securities with paper money and had no moral claim to repayment in gold—or in silver, for that matter. Since 1879, however, anyone who had purchased government bonds had used gold or its equivalent, and they *did* have a moral claim to repayment in the same. With his resolution, Senator Teller unwittingly confirmed the charge that free coinage would defraud creditors, and President McKinley pounced on the opportunity. For a year, he had avoided specific statements on the currency, letting the Wolcott Mission proceed. In his annual message at the end of 1897, the President had endorsed Gage's proposals but insisted that their object was "keeping all of them [various types of money] at par with gold," holding open the possibility of a role for silver.[45] In late January 1898, however, at a meeting of the National Association of Manufacturers in New York City, he declared, "The money of the United

[42] *Lincoln County Leader* (Oregon), January 28, 1898, p. 1.
[43] Topeka, KA, *Advocate and News*, March 30, 1898, p. 11.
[44] Ellis, *Henry Moore Teller*, pp. 297–9.
[45] William McKinley, State of the Union Address, 1897, Presidency Project, UCSB.

States is and must forever be unquestioned and unassailable. If doubts remain, they must be removed." He continued, "Nothing should tempt us—nothing ever will tempt us—to scale down the sacred debt of the nation through a legal technicality. Whatever may be the language of the contract, the United States will discharge all its obligations in the currency recognized as the best throughout all the civilized world." McKinley then went further than the rhetoric he had used in the 1896 campaign, insisting, "It will not suffice for citizens nowadays to say simply that they are in favor of sound money. ... The people's purpose must be given the vitality of public law."[46]

In 1898, the growing crisis in Cuba and the resulting war with Spain dominated public life, pushing financial issues aside for the moment. Behind the scenes, however, the question remained potent. As always, the prospect of war created financial uncertainty. Secretary Gage later wrote, "The simpler-minded depositors in savings banks made withdrawals of their funds; the commercial banks in the larger cities sympathetically suffered through loss of cash to savings institutions. The rate of interest rose; the price of securities declined."[47] As August Belmont noted, however, "The country's position, financially, is so favorable that I do not look to any serious complications in that respect resulting from hostilities."[48] New York's banks were flush with gold, the Treasury's reserve of the gold stood above $175 million, growing exports were drawing more gold into the country, and American miners were bringing more gold to the surface. Unease did not give way to panic, and over the summer calm returned as the United States won a series of engagements against the Spanish. Belmont, who was skeptical of the conflict, wrote that Democrats "committed the stupendous folly of advocating this war, in the belief it was going to help the silver cause, and that the necessity of such large expenditures would require some radical treatment of our monetary system, and that silver would then be recognized as the cure. I said at the time ... a war would strengthen the gold standard as well as be a great card for the

[46] William McKinley, *The Speeches and Addresses of William McKinley* (New York: Doubleday, 1900), pp. 63–4.

[47] *Annual Report of the Secretary of the Treasury, 1898* (Washington: Government Printing Office, 1898), XCIII–XCIV.

[48] August Belmont to F.M. Rothschild & Sons, April 8, 1898, Belmont Papers, series I, letterpress books, box 23.

Republican Party, both of which have turned out to be the case."[49] Belmont was probably too cynical—Americans of all stripes, Silverites included, were furious with Spain's brutal campaign against Cuban rebels and supported the island's independence. Silverites did hope, however, that the demands of war would demonstrate the inadequacy of the gold standard, and events proved their calculations flawed.

The war strengthened the forces of financial orthodoxy. Congress quickly authorized an issue of $200 million in bonds paying 3 percent to finance the conflict, half of which would go to the public at par. There was no repetition of the bitter debates during the Cleveland administration over bond issues. Having declared war, Congress had to fund it, and legislators naturally sought money on the best terms. This bond issue had important monetary implications. Casual observers doubted that Washington could sell these securities except at a significant discount, but Secretary Gage calculated otherwise. National banks, he believed, would happily take up the entire issue. These institutions could issue notes equal to 90 percent of the face, or par, value of bonds they owned. Most federal securities bore interest rates of 4–6 percent, and with the decline of interest rates since the late 1870s, these securities commanded a significant premium in the market. As a result, banks had to tie up as much as $120 in capital to issue $90 in notes. The new 3 percent bonds, which would trade close to par, offered a better deal, requiring banks to tie up only $100 to issue $90 in notes. Gage estimated that, used in this fashion, 3 percent bonds would earn banks 1.4 percentage points more on their investment than those carrying higher rates. He added, "This was quickly perceived in the money market."[50] Still, Gage took no chances and arranged for a syndicate of New York Bankers, including National City Bank and J.P. Morgan & Co., to take whatever the public did not. In the event, the issue was heavily oversubscribed, and Washington disposed of it at a slight premium without having to call on the syndicate.[51]

This issue financed the war and changed the monetary landscape. Because of the premium on federal bonds, the volume of national banknotes in circulation had fallen from $350 million in 1882 to $160 million in 1892. By 1897, the amount of these notes had increased to

[49] August Belmont to A.M. Weller, July 12, 1898, Belmont Papers, letterpress books, box 22.

[50] *Report of the Secretary of the Treasury, 1898*, XCIII–XCIV.

[51] *Esther Rogoff Taus, Central Banking Functions of the United States Treasury, 1789–1941* (New York: Columbia University Press, 1943), pp. 96–7.

$220 million, presumably because many of the bonds issued by the Cleveland administration ended up with national banks. Between 1898 and 1900, however, the volume of these notes grew to $300 million—a jump of $80 million in just two years—and this increase almost certainly reflected the issue of federal bonds to finance the Spanish War. At least one Populist, Tom Watson, had anticipated this outcome, writing, "The new bonds will give them [bankers] the basis for new banks, and their power is prolonged."[52] This increase in currency reduced pressures for silver dollars or greenbacks, but it also reduced pressure to allow national banks to issue currency backed by their overall capital rather than bonds.

Silverites did manage to include in the legislation financing the war a provision which required the Treasury to coin $1.5 million in silver dollars each month, tapping its surplus of silver—"coining the seigniorage." This operation proceeded smoothly—the economy was growing and people could use the money. The impact, however, was much smaller than that of the new bonds.

Denouement

The 1898 elections allowed the administration to enact financial reform. The GOP went into the contest in a strong position. The United States had just decisively defeated Spain despite a good deal of administrative confusion at the start of mobilization. Perhaps more important, the tentative recovery of 1897 had turned into a genuine boom, and prosperity always helps the party in power. August Belmont wrote in the summer of 1898 that the economy "is now better than at any time since I have been in business."[53] In 1898, the output of steel and coal reached historical highs, and the mileage of new railroad track laid began to approach that of the early 1890s. The last of the major railroads that had gone bankrupt completed their reorganizations. The prices of cotton and wheat had stabilized—if farmers were not flush, neither were they desperate. Perhaps most striking, exports surged—particularly shipments of manufactured goods. Sales of cotton textiles abroad had increased 70 percent since 1890, exports of machinery had more than doubled in the same period, and shipments of iron and steel had jumped six-fold. This activity not only employed American workers and factories but brought more gold into the

[52] Quoted in Woodward, *Tom Watson*, p. 397.
[53] Belmont to A.M. Weller, July 12, 1898.

country, even as higher production from domestic mines further increased the supply of gold from that direction. New technology—the cyanamide process—had revived gold mining and, with it, expanded the currency. In the late 1890s, the value of gold mined in Colorado, the home of Senators Teller and Wolcott, surpassed that of silver.[54] Gold was more plentiful than at any time since the 1850s.

The 1898 campaign lacked focus. The question of imperialism—particularly the annexation of the Philippines—which would loom large in the 1900 contest, had little impact because the administration had yet to sign a peace treaty with Spain or to formulate a policy toward the Philippines. Republicans naturally emphasized prosperity and talked up the victory over Spain. To the degree that they looked to the future, they echoed the issues of 1896, championing sound finance and protection. Mark Hanna, who managed the campaign, insisted, "The St. Louis platform [from 1896] should be the issue,"[55] both to build on the success of 1896 and to reinforce party unity. Many Democrats echoed the themes that Bryan had emphasized in 1896, but others focused on local concerns, which seemed to offer more promise for victory. In New York, Democrats recovered some of the ground they had lost in 1894 and 1896, not because the voters of the Empire State had revised their opinion of silver coinage but because the electorate turned its attention to state matters. Bryan did not campaign much. He had volunteered for military service during the war and spent most of the fall on garrison duty in Cuba. In his few appearances, he concentrated his fire on the confusion that had accompanied mobilization for the war. McKinley did make a tour, but for the most part he confined his remarks to praise for the country's soldiers and sailors.

The 1898 election witnessed the steep decline of the Populists. In 1896, it had sent four senators and twenty-two representatives to Washington, its best showing by far.[56] This performance reflected, in large part, alliances between Democrats and Populists in the Farm Belt and Mountain States. In Kansas, the Populists had received the Democrats' endorsement for all their candidates for the US House and for most state offices in exchange for supporting Bryan and Sewall in the presidential

[54] Eric Stene, "The Historical Statistics of the Colorado Mining Industry," *Mining History Journal* 3 (1996): 124.

[55] Mark Hanna to McKinley, November 10, 1898, McKinley Papers, reel 5.

[56] Senator Richard Pettigrew of South Dakota won election as a Republican in 1888 and again in 1894, but he joined the Populists in the summer of 1896, giving them five members in the upper house.

contest. In 1898, two factors cost the Populists heavily in the West. First, the Republicans recouped some of the ground lost in the Grain Belt in 1896. Better prices for wheat had restored prosperity, and as the party in power, the GOP received credit. Mark Hanna campaigned in the Farm Belt himself—a bold move, since Populists and Democrats had repeatedly cast him as the incarnation of plutocracy. He apparently made a good impression. Voters expecting a monster found instead a plain-spoken man who possessed blunt charm. In the Dakotas, Nebraska, and Kansas, Republicans captured seven House seats from the Populists. Second, in the Mountain States many Silver Republicans who had flirted with Populism began to edge back toward the GOP. The combination of prosperity and rising gold output had convinced many that free coinage had little future as an issue, and this question had been their chief link to Populism. Reunion would require several years, and there were exceptions—Senator Teller became a Democrat. Nevertheless, the process had begun.

Populism was in retreat in the South as well. In the 1898 campaign, Democrats emphasized white supremacy even more than usual and utilized fraud and intimidation to win elections. The contest in North Carolina was particularly vicious. There, an alliance between Republicans and Populists had controlled the government since 1894, and the Democrats used every device, fair and foul, to regain control in 1898. In Wilmington, they violently overthrew the duly elected Republican government of the city, killing several people in the process. Overall, the number of Populist representatives from the region declined from six to one, and the party's organization was a shambles. The party was not yet dead, but it was dying.

The Alliance and Populism had rested on two pillars—hard times and the indifference of political leaders. By 1898, both were crumbling. Farm prices were increasing and would continue to advance through World War I. Agrarian radicals had been right to attribute the deflation of the last quarter of the nineteenth century to a shortage of money, but their solutions—the Subtreasury and the free coinage of silver—promised to create new problems. Instead, a fortuitous expansion of gold production throughout the world raised prices without upending the financial system. Populism was always as much a political protest as an economic one, based on the too-often correct assumption that government officials were more interested in the well-being of banks and railroads than that of the average citizen, particularly those who cultivated the land. Bryan's nomination had put a champion of farmers at the head of one of the major parties. The political upheaval of the 1890s badly rattled many western Republicans and southern Democrats, leading them to embrace the cause of reform. "Middle of the Road" Populists discounted the efforts of Bryan and other reformers in the major parties as half-measures, and indeed these fell well short of the most radical Populist demands—the Subtreasury and government ownership of the railroads. At the same time, political leaders were paying more attention to farmers' concerns and, more important, acting on them. Populists had promised a radical transformation of American society, and this prospect had energized the activists and voters who were the movement's strength. Defeat had rendered this promise remote, discouraging adherents and weakening the organization. Like success, failure fed on itself. In this context, the moderate but nevertheless significant reforms offered by the major parties, like the regulation of railway rates, had considerable appeal for Populist voters.

The 1898 election substantially strengthened the administration. Republicans lost ground in the House of Representatives but nevertheless retained a solid majority. In the Senate, the GOP picked up ten seats, expanding its total to fifty-four out of ninety. Many of these gains represented the delayed fruits of victories in 1894 and 1896, as state legislatures with Republican majorities got the opportunity to select Senators, but the advance was impressive nevertheless. In the last two off-year elections, 1890 and 1894, the party in power had suffered devastating losses, so when the Republicans emerged from the 1898 elections in a strong position, their success was even more striking. Summing up, Hanna told McKinley, "It was a splendid victory for an off-year and a splendid tribute to you."[57]

President McKinley, ever patient, waited until the new Congress convened in late 1899 before pressing financial reform. In the meantime, the rising tide of prosperity and the higher output of gold strengthened advocates of the gold standard. The former reinforced McKinley's and the Republicans' popularity, while the latter robbed Silverites of their strongest argument. As Secretary Gage wrote to labor leader Samuel Gompers, "We may reasonably expect that the world's greatly increased output of gold in the present decade will in the immediate future destroy whatever pertinence … present criticism of the gold standard may possess."[58] Even

[57] Mark Hanna to McKinley, November 15, 1898, McKinley Papers, reel 5.

[58] Lyman Gage to Samuel Gompers, January 10, 1898, McKinley Papers, reel 3.

Senator Teller conceded as much, though he was less optimistic that the supply of gold would continue to increase over the long term.[59] Of course, the change wrought by the expansion of the gold supply also indicated that Silverites had been right to attribute the deflation of recent decades to a shortage of gold. Financial reform, however, addressed the future, not what had gone before.

Republicans, eager to settle the matter before the 1900 election, began framing a measure in the spring of 1899.[60] A consensus existed within the party on many key points. Almost all wanted to make gold the official basis of the currency, formally guaranteeing the redemption of greenbacks, Treasury notes, and even silver dollars and certificates in gold. Republicans also agreed on creating a separate bureau in the Treasury to redeem currency in gold and providing it with its own reserve to do so—ultimately $150 million in gold. Heretofore, the government had redeemed notes out of Treasury balances, which also financed its day-to-day expenses, thereby tying the monetary standard to Washington's short-term financial fortunes. In 1894 and 1895, Silverites had consistently blocked legislation authorizing bonds needed to cover the government's deficit because the money raised would also reinforce the gold standard. Creating a separate bureau with its own reserve to manage redemptions would avoid or at least reduce such problems in the future, insulating the gold standard from questions of taxing and spending. Should the new office's gold decline below $100 million, it would have the authority to issue bonds paying 3 percent in gold to replenish its stock of the metal. Had these arrangements been in place during the Cleveland administration, the gold standard would never have been in doubt.

The future of greenbacks and Treasury notes occasioned the sharpest disagreement. Purists wanted to eliminate them completely and replace them with notes issued by banks. At the same time, many staunch supporters of the gold standard feared withdrawing so much currency from circulation. Greenbacks had served the country well enough for thirty-five years, and it was unlikely that national banknotes could, under the existing law, completely replace them. Such notes needed the backing of federal bonds, and the supply of these securities was limited, even with the substantial issue that accompanied the Spanish War. Basing banknotes on institutions' total capital rather than bonds might offer a solution, but

[59] Ellis, *Henry Moore Teller*, p. 320–1.
[60] *The Economist*, May 27, 1899, pp. 754–5.

many legislators were wary. As it was, the population accepted national banknotes without question because bonds backed every note, dollar for dollar. No one knew if people would do the same with notes that depended on the resources of individual banks. Nor did anyone know if the federal government could effectively regulate notes issued by literally thousands of national banks. Even the administration lacked consensus on the matter—Secretary Gage favored a currency based on banks' capital, but Charles Dawes, his Comptroller of the Currency, preferred the existing system.[61] Creating an asset-based currency entailed risks that many Republicans refused to run. The final proposal represented a compromise. It continued to base national banknotes on federal bonds but allowed institutions to issue notes up to 100 percent of the face value of bonds rather than 90 percent. At the same time, the Treasury's new redemption office would not reissue greenbacks redeemed for gold except in exchange for gold. (Notes used to pay taxes would go into the Treasury's general fund rather than to the new redemption bureau, and the Treasury would reissue them to pay the government's expenses.)

The bill made one modest concession to Silverites. It provided that, as Treasury notes came into the government to pay taxes, Washington would replace them with silver dollars or silver certificates. This process would simplify the currency somewhat by gradually eliminating one of the several types of money, and few would lament the passing of the Treasury note. The government had issued these notes to buy silver at prices well below the official one of $1.29 an ounce. As a result, replacing Treasury notes with silver dollars struck at the rate of $1.29 would leave the government with a good deal of extra silver—about $55 million at the official price. Washington had already been coining 1.5 million silver dollars a month to pay for the Spanish War, and the financial reform bill guaranteed that this process would continue until the government had exhausted its surplus silver. The bill's authors assumed, correctly, that with the economy and the demand for money both growing, "coining the seigniorage" would impose no new pressures on the country's gold reserve. At the same time, the volume of silver money would increase, and the Treasury would dispose of its huge stock of idle silver, the "overhang," which tended to depress its market price.

One little-noted aspect of financial reform had great impact. The measure authorized the organization of national banks with capital of as little

[61] Gould, *The Presidency of William McKinley*, pp. 169–70.

as $25,000 in small towns. Hitherto, the law had required such organizations to have at least $50,000 in capital, and many small towns lacked the resources to create such a bank. Throughout the 1890s, farmers had complained about the difficulty in obtaining credit, but with the exception of the Alliance's utopian Subtreasury Plan, reformers had not addressed this demand. Advocates of free coinage believed that flooding the country with silver money would reduce the need for credit. Their suspicion of financial institutions in general and of national banks in particular inclined them against any expansion of such organizations. Advocates of the gold standard had no such qualms. Under the new rule, rural entrepreneurs would organize hundreds of small national banks. In the ten months after the law first authorized them, investors organized 266 of these new banks, thirty in Iowa alone, and this growth continued into the new century.[62] In the Dakotas, the number of national banks increased from 52 to 256 in just a few years.[63] Nationwide, the number of national banks expanded from 3700 in 1900 to 5600 in 1905, with much of the growth in small towns.[64] Meanwhile, the volume of notes issued by national banks increased to $471 million by 1905, an advance of 57 percent over 1900.[65] This outcome vindicated those advocates of the gold standard who had insisted that banking reform could address at least some of the grievances of farmers without altering the monetary standard.[66]

Reform did not deal with the problem of "elasticity." As the editors of *The Economist* put it, "There is no machinery by means of which the volume of the currency can be made to expand and contract in accordance with the varying requirements of the country," such as during the harvest

[62] William McKinley, State of the Union Address, 1900, Presidency Project, UCSB.

[63] Ostler, *Prairie Populism*, p. 19.

[64] US Bureau of the Census, *Historical Statistics of the United States, Colonial Times to 1970, Bicentennial Edition, Part 2* (Washington, DC, 1975), p. 1025.

[65] Milton Friedman and Anna Schwartz, *A Monetary History of the United States, 1867–1960* (Princeton: Princeton University Press, 1963), p. 179.

[66] Solutions frequently create their own problems. The rising tide of rural prosperity in the first two decades of the twentieth century raised up these small national banks. After World War I, however, prices for crops fell sharply, and hundreds of these institutions failed. Their fortunes depended on one community, and their relatively small resources meant that they could not diversify their risks much. In retrospect, the country might have done better to permit existing national banks to set up branches in smaller towns, but in the 1890s, increasing the reach of national banks was controversial, to put it mildly. It was easier to secure approval for new national banks than to allow those that already existed to open branches.

or a financial crisis.[67] In Europe, central banks performed this function, and the proposal to allow banks to issue notes based on their capital rather than bond holdings might have done the same, had it worked as advertised. As it was, the American financial system remained inflexible.

Congress took up financial reform over the winter of 1899–1900. After a decade of bitter debate on the subject, the result was anticlimactic. The administration had the votes—President McKinley had been at work among lawmakers for quite a while, using his formidable powers of persuasion to line up support. Senator Teller did the best he could, warning that the increase in gold output "will cease—because in the history of the world it has always ceased … [and then] there will be discovered in the business world a sliding scale toward lower prices."[68] The public, however, was far more interested in the question of imperialism and, in particular, annexation of the Philippines, while Republicans wanted to go before the country in 1900 having resolved the currency issue. Reform passed relatively easily.

In the three years since he had taken office, President McKinley had not set a foot wrong on the money issue. In 1897, knowing that he lacked a majority in the Senate and that many in the country remained undecided, he had let the matter simmer. The Wolcott Mission explored international bimetallism while the commission appointed by the Indianapolis Monetary Conference had laid out a program of financial reform designed to stabilize the gold standard. With the failure of the Wolcott Mission, McKinley had come down for the gold standard, using the pretext offered by Teller's amendment to announce his decision. He then displayed further patience, waiting until the GOP had a working majority in the Senate. Finally, in 1900 he secured reform that embraced all the important recommendations of the Monetary Commission, with the important exception of a currency based on bank assets. Perhaps most remarkably, McKinley made it all seem easy. He was lucky, particularly with the increase in gold production after 1895, but he had made the most of his good fortune.

[67] *The Economist*, December 2, 1899, p. 1694.
[68] Quoted in Ellis, *Henry Moore Teller*, p. 321.

CHAPTER 8

Conclusion

The Battle of the Standards turned on finance—specifically, international finance. The gold standard connoted not merely rules for coinage but a complex financial system that governed trade and investment throughout much of the world. In the late nineteenth century, Americans availed themselves of this system to secure capital for their country's rapid economic development. When champions of gold identified it with "progress" and "civilization," they referred to this process. Rapid economic change is always disruptive, however, not the least because benefits accrue unevenly and, for some, not at all. Hitherto, communities and individuals in the United States had enjoyed considerable economic autonomy. In the last quarter of the nineteenth century, economic development created powerful, centralized institutions such as railway systems, industrial trusts, and the New York money market, whose activities affected the well-being of millions. The railroads and the New York money market depended heavily on foreign capital, and large industrial corporations depended heavily on the railroads and the New York money market. Many Americans found this process deeply unsettling, even if they profited from it. To those who lost ground, it was positively obscene.

Between 1870 and 1895, the world's supply of gold did not grow as fast as the volume of transactions that it had to support, fostering deflation. Falling prices hit Americans who grew wheat and cotton particularly hard because most of them carried substantial debts. Their plight was

W. Wells, *Financial Politics in the United States in the 1890s*,
https://doi.org/10.1007/978-3-031-86765-1_8

especially poignant because, by selling their crops abroad, they earned the foreign exchange to pay interest and dividends to foreign investors. Those opposed to the gold standard rallied around the free coinage of silver. It would, by devaluing the currency, increase the price of wheat and cotton, in dollars, and it would sever the ties between the United States and the international financial system, restricting railroads' and the New York money market's access to foreign capital. The result would shift the economic balance of power in the United States from the cities to the countryside and from the center to the periphery. When champions of silver identified it with "tradition" and "patriotism," they referred to this prospect. These were the questions that William McKinley and William Jennings Bryan debated in the 1896 presidential election.

In the Battle of the Standards, the defenders of gold had a substantial advantage. The transformation of the American economy and society—the growth of railroads, manufacturing, and cities—had already proceeded quite far. The country depended on capital from abroad to finance investment, its international trade, and even some of its domestic commerce. Any measure like the free coinage of silver that could alienate foreign investors risked disaster. The 1893 Panic and the subsequent depression occurred, in large part, because foreigners stopped making new investments in the United States. Free coinage might well lead them to liquidate existing holdings, creating chaos. John Carlisle, President of Cleveland's Treasury Secretary, disapproved of many of the economic changes underway in the United States, and he hoped that the reform of tariffs and banking would slow or even halt them. At the same time he insisted, "We cannot preserve our trade relations with the best customers for our surplus unless we maintain a monetary system substantially in accord with them."[1] Free coinage of silver, he feared, would create a financial panic that would overwhelm everyone, even farmers of wheat and cotton who hoped to profit from the devaluation of the dollar. Some urban radicals like Eugene Debs and John Altgeld supported free coinage because they believed that it would cripple the power of bankers and industrialists, opening the way for other reforms. These men had significant support among workers, but in this instance, most of their followers refused their lead. Inflation held no appeal for those who depended on cash wages, and the possibility of financial panic frightened them. No one can know what would have happened had the United States embraced free coinage, but it was a risky

[1] *New York Times*, May 21, 1895, pp. 1, 9.

proposition, as a majority of voters in 1896 understood. Bryan's cause was not hopeless—he appealed to values that most Americans cherished—but against an opponent as capable as McKinley, victory was unlikely.

In this contest, the Populists played a supporting rather than leading role. They represented the latest incarnation of the anti-monopoly sentiment that had animated the Grange, the Greenback Party, the Knights of Labor, and others concerned by the centralization of economic life in the United States during the last quarter of the nineteenth century. Populism was a regional phenomenon concentrated among farmers of cotton and wheat. It had a negligible following in the Northeast and Industrial Midwest, the wealthiest and most densely populated parts of the Union. It was a protest movement that attracted those who believed, often with good reason, that the leaders of the established parties had no interest in their concerns. In states where the established parties seriously addressed at least some of these issues, such as Iowa and South Carolina, Populism made little impression. The centerpiece of the Populist program, the Subtreasury, was not only impractical and potentially dangerous but had little appeal outside of Populism's core constituency. The party's chances of securing national power on its own were nil.

The free coinage of silver was always the key issue. Enthusiasm for it predated the Alliance and Populism and developed independent of them. Silver Republicans secured passage of the ill-considered Silver Purchase Act in 1890, and when President Cleveland secured the repeal of this act in 1893, he pushed silver to the top of the national agenda. The Populists had embraced silver almost as an afterthought, but it accounted for much of their success. The issue delivered three of the four states the Populists carried in the 1892 election (Colorado, Idaho, and Nevada) and may have made the difference in the fourth (Kansas). Senators Peffer and Allen, the Populist leaders in the Senate, came to national attention in 1893 by leading the filibuster against repeal of the Silver Purchase Act. In 1896, Populists like James Weaver hoped to ride silver into the White House, perhaps under the leadership of a Silverite such as Senator Henry Teller. Silverites were happy to ally themselves with the People's Party but maintained their separate identity and remained open to better offers. When the Democrats made such an offer in 1896, Silverites took it, and the Populists had little choice but to follow.

The Battle of the Standards, and particularly the role of Populists within it, has long served as a sort of Rorschach test for historians. John D. Hicks saw the Alliance and the People's Party as forerunners of Progressive reform whose efforts ultimately guaranteed that "the people now rule."[2] Charles Postel offered a subtler version of this analysis, seeing the Populists as more egalitarian precursors of Progressivism. Richard Hofstadter believed that anxiety among farmers about status and position drove the Alliance and the People's Party, while Lawrence Goodwyn imagined that these organizations could have radically reshaped American society had Silverites not commandeered the movement. Richard White described the Battle of the Standards as a contest between a laissez-faire view of society and a more flexible concept that held out the possibility of state action against social ills. Lawrence O'Malley saw the contest as a debate over "the nature and authenticity of the self."[3] Many of these analyses are useful. Hicks's and Postel's work had much to teach about Populism, Hofstadter identified Populism's penchant for xenophobia and conspiracy theories, and Goodwyn recognized the radical potential of Populism. Yet all skate around the central issue.

The Battle of the Standards constituted a referendum on social and economic change. Would railroads, factories, and cities continue to grow, or would the country move back toward its rural, agricultural roots? Of course, a single question cannot, in and of itself, encompass such a huge social change, but the currency came as close to doing so as anything before the American people in the 1890s. Bryan represented those opposed to change, offering paeans to farmers and warning that it was time to "turn back." McKinley defended change, touting "progress" and offering tariffs as a device that could balance the country's various interests—a primitive example of what political scientists call the "broker state." Despite trepidation, Americans endorsed McKinley and the new order. Afterward, they would sometimes gaze back longingly at their country's agrarian past, but few seriously considered returning to it.

[2] Hicks, *The Populist Revolt*, p. 422.
[3] O'Malley, *Face Value*, p. 161.

Appendix A

Timeline

1862	February	Legal Tender Act authorizes first issue of greenbacks; United States effectively leaves the gold standard
1863	February	Congress passes first National Banking Act creating national banks and a national currency
1864	June	Congress passes second National Banking Act, imposing a prohibitive tax on the notes of state banks
1873	April	Congress ends coinage of silver dollars, effectively demonetizing silver, an action later christened "The Crime of '73"
1874		First appearance of organizations that will coalesce into the Southern Farmers' Alliance
1875	January	Congress authorizes return to the gold standard in January 1879 and the sale of bonds to raise gold to this end
1877	March	Northern Farmers' Alliance organized
1878	February	Congress passes Bland-Allison Act, authorizing limited coinage of silver dollars
1879	January	United States returns to the gold standard
1880	October	First national meeting of what would become the Farmers' Alliance in Chicago
1886	December	Colored Farmers' Alliance organized
1887	January	Texas Farmers' Alliance launches the Texas Exchange
	December	President Grover Cleveland announces support for major reductions in the tariff
1888	May	Texas Exchange faces financial crisis that will force it to close in 1889

(*continued*)

W. Wells, *Financial Politics in the United States in the 1890s*,
https://doi.org/10.1007/978-3-031-86765-1

(continued)

	November	Benjamin Harrison elected President with Republican majorities in both houses of Congress
1889	January	Farmers' Alliance proposes the Subtreasury Plan
	November	First Silver Convention
1890	July	Congress passes the Silver Purchase Act, buying large quantities of silver with Treasury Notes
	October	Congress passes the McKinley Tariff, sharply raising duties on most imports
	November	Democrats triumph in off-year elections, gaining control of House of Representatives and many state governments
	November	Financial crisis in London; the Bank of England rescues Baring Brothers
	December	Southern Farmers' Alliance issues "Ocala Demands," which will be the basis for the Populist platform
1892	February	Democrats and Silver Republicans defeat the "Force Bill," which sought to protect the voting rights of African-Americans in the South
	February	First national convention of Peoples' Party (Populists)
	May	Second National Silver Convention; Bimetallic League launched
	August	Austria-Hungary adopts the gold standard
	November	Grover Cleveland elected President, with Democratic majorities in both houses of Congress
	December	Brussels Conference fails to secure agreement on silver coinage
	December	Gold begins to flow out of the United States, progressively tightening credit
1893	February	Reading Railroad declares bankruptcy
	May	National Cordage declares bankruptcy; financial stringency turns into financial panic
	June	British government closes India's mints to silver
	June	Doctors remove cancerous growth from President Cleveland's mouth
	August	Special session of Congress meets to repeal the Silver Purchase Act
	August	New York Clearing House issues "clearing house certificates;" the financial panic abates
	October	Congress repeals the Silver Purchase Act
1894		William Harvey publishes *Coin's Financial School*
	January	Treasury Secretary John Carlisle announces sale of government bonds to raise gold
	March	President Cleveland vetoes bill "coining the seigniorage"
	July	President Cleveland sends the Army into Chicago to crush the Pullman Strike
	August	Wilson-Gorman Tariff becomes law without President Cleveland's signature
	October	American Bankers' Association proposes the "Baltimore Plan"

(*continued*)

(continued)

	November	Democrats suffer crippling losses in off-year elections
	November	Second sale of federal bonds to raise gold
1895	February	Third sale of federal bonds to raise gold (Morgan-Belmont Syndicate)
	March-September	Morgan-Belmont Syndicate manipulates the foreign exchange market to prevent export of gold from the U.S.
	December	Venezuelan Crisis
1896	January	Fourth sale of federal bonds to raise gold
	March	Bimetallic League announces formation of the Silver Party
	June	Republicans nominate William McKinley for the presidency on a platform of protection and the gold standard
	July	Democrats nominate William Jennings Bryan for the presidency on a platform of free coinage of silver
	July	Populists nominate William Jennings Bryan for the presidency but choose Tom Watson as their vice presidential candidate
	July	Silver Party nominates William Jennings Bryan for the presidency
	July	J.P. Morgan, with encouragement from Treasury Secretary Carlisle, organizes a syndicate to support the gold standard during the election
	September	Gold Democrats nominate John Palmer for the presidency
	November	McKinley wins the presidency by a large margin; Republicans control Congress
1897	March	President McKinley dispatches Wolcott Mission to Europe to negotiate agreement on silver coinage
	July	Congress enacts a tariff sharply raising duties on most imports
	October	British government refuses to negotiate on silver coinage
1898	January	*Report of the [Indianapolis] Monetary Commission* released
	January	President McKinley endorses formalizing the gold standard
	April	Spanish-American War begins
	August	Spanish-American War ends
	November	Republicans win off-year elections, solidifying their control of the Senate
1900	March	Gold Standard Act becomes law

Appendix B

Elections

Presidential Election, 1888

State	*Republican (Harrison)*	*Electors*	*Democrat (Cleveland)*	*Electors*
Alabama	57,177 (32.7%)		117,314 (67.0%)	10
Arkansas	59,752 (38.0%)		86,062 (54.8%)	7
California	124,816 (49.7%)	8	117,729 (46.8%)	
Colorado	50,772 (55.2%)	3	37,549 (40.8%)	
Connecticut	74,584 (48.4%)		74,920 (48.7%)	6
Delaware	12,950 (43.5%)		16,414 (55.1%)	3
Florida	26,529 (39.9%)		39,557 (59.5%)	4
Georgia	40,499 (28.3%)		100,493 (70.3%)	12
Illinois	370,475 (49.9%)	22	348,351 (46.6%)	
Indiana	263,366 (49.0%)	15	260,990 (48.6%)	
Iowa	211,607 (52.3%)	13	179,876 (44.4%)	
Kansas	182,845 (55.2%)	9	102,739 (31.0%)	
Kentucky	155,138 (45.0%)		183,830 (55.3%)	13
Louisiana	30,660 (26.5%)		85,032 (73.4%)	8
Maine	73,730 (57.5%)	6	50,472 (39.4%)	
Maryland	99,986 (47.4%)		106,188 (50.3%)	8
Massachusetts	183,892 (53.4%)	14	151,590 (44.0%)	

(*continued*)

W. Wells, *Financial Politics in the United States in the 1890s*, https://doi.org/10.1007/978-3-031-86765-1

(continued)

State	*Republican (Harrison)*	*Electors*	*Democrat (Cleveland)*	*Electors*
Michigan	236,387 (49.7%)	13	213,469 (44.9%)	
Minnesota	142,492 (54.1%)	7	104,372 (39.7%)	
Mississippi	30,095 (26.0%)		85,451 (73.8%)	9
Missouri	236,252 (45.3%)		261,943 (50.2%)	16
Nebraska	108,417 (53.5%)	5	80,522 (39.8%)	
Nevada	7229 (57.5%)	3	5303 (42.2%)	
New Hampshire	45,734 (50.4%)	4	43,382 (47.8%)	
New Jersey	144,360 (47.5%)		151,508 (49.9%)	9
New York	650,338 (49.2%)	36	635,965 (48.1%)	
North Carolina	134,784 (47.1%)		148,336 (51.9%)	11
Ohio	416,054 (49.6%)	23	395,456 (47.1%)	
Oregon	33,291 (53.8%)	3	26,518 (42.8%)	
Pennsylvania	526,091 (52.7%)	30	446,633 (44.8%)	
Rhode Island	21,969 (53.9%)	4	17,530 (43.0%)	
South Carolina	13,737 (17.2%)		65,824 (82.3%)	9
Tennessee	139,511 (45.8%)		158,779 (52.2%)	12
Texas	93,991 (25.9%)		236,290 (65.0%)	13
Vermont	45,193 (71.2%)	4	16,788 (26.4%)	
Virginia	150,399 (49.5%)		152,004 (50.0%)	12
West Virginia	78,171 (49.0%)		78,677 (49.3%)	6
Wisconsin	176,553 (49.8%)	11	155,232 (43.8%)	
Total	5,449,825 (47.8%)	233	5,539,118 (48.6%)	168

Source: The American Presidency Project, University of California, Santa Barbara

Presidential Election, 1892

State	*Republican (Harrison)*	*Elect.*	*Democrat (Cleveland)*	*Elect.*	*Populist (Weaver)*	*Elect.*
Alabama	9184 (3.9%)		138,135 (67.0%)	11	84,984 (36.5%)	
Arkansas	47,072 (31.8%)		87,834 (59.3%)	8	11,831 (8.0%)	
California	118,072 (43.8%)	1	118,151 (43.8%)	8	25,331 (9.4%)	
Colorado	38,620 (41.1%)		0 (0%)		53,584 (57.1%)	4
Connecticut	77,030 (46.8%)		82,395 (50.1%)	6	809 (0.5%)	
Delaware	18,077 (48.5%)		18,581 (49.9%)	3	0 (0%)	
Florida	0 (0%)		30,154 (84.8%)	4	4843 (13.6%)	
Georgia	48,305 (21.6%)		129,386 (57.8%)	13	42,937 (19.2%)	
Idaho	8599 (44.3%)		0 (0%)		10,520 (54.2%)	3
Illinois	399,308 (45.7%)		426,281 (48.8%)	24	22,207 (2.5%)	

(*continued*)

(continued)

State	*Republican (Harrison)*	*Elect.*	*Democrat (Cleveland)*	*Elect.*	*Populist (Weaver)*	*Elect.*
Indiana	255,615 (46.2%)		262,740 (47.5%)	15	22,208 (4.0%)	
Iowa	219,795 (49.6%)	13	196,367 (44.3%)		20,595 (4.6%)	
Kansas	156,134 (48.3%)		0 (0%)		162,888 (50.3%)	10
Kentucky	135,462 (39.7%)		175,461 (51.5%)	13	23,500 (6.9%)	
Louisiana	27,903 (23.6%)		87,922 (74.3%)	8	2462 (2.1%)	
Maine	62,878 (54.2%)	6	48,024 (41.4%)		2045 (1.8%)	
Maryland	92,736 (43.5%)		113,866 (53.4%)	8	796 (0.4%)	
Massachusetts	202,814 (51.9%)	15	176,813 (45.2%)		3210 (0.8%)	
Michigan	222,708 (47.7%)	9	202,396 (43.3%)	5	20,031 (4.3%)	
Minnesota	122,836 (45.9%)	9	101,055 (37.8%)		29,336 (11.0%)	
Mississippi	1398 (2.7%)		40,030 (76.2%)	9	10,118 (19.3%)	
Missouri	227,646 (42.0%)		268,400 (49.6%)	17	41,204 (7.6%)	
Montana	18,871 (42.4%)	3	17,960 (39.8%)		7338 (16.5%)	
Nebraska	87,213 (43.6%)	8	24,956 (12.5%)		83,134 (41.5%)	
Nevada	703 (6.5%)		2811 (26.0%)		7226 (66.7%)	3
New Hampshire	45,658 (51.1%)	4	42,081 (47.1%)		292 (0.3%)	
New Jersey	156,059 (46.2%)		170,987 (50.7%)	10	969 (0.3%)	
New York	609,350 (45.6%)		654,868 (40.0%)	36	16,429 (1.2%)	
North Carolina	100,346 (35.8%)		132,951 (47.4%)	11	44,336 (15.8%)	
North Dakota	17,519 (48.5%)	1	0 (0%)	1	17,770 (49.0%)	1
Ohio	405,187 (47.7%)	22	404,115 (47.5%)		14,850 (1.7%)	
Oregon	35,002 (44.7%)	3	14,243 (18.2%)		26,875 (34.3%)	
Pennsylvania	516,001 (51.4%)	32	452,264 (47.5%)		8714 (0.9%)	
Rhode Island	26,975 (50.7%)	4	24,336 (44.7%)		228 (0.4%)	
South Carolina	13,325 (18.9%)		54,680 (77.6%)	9	2407 (3.4%)	
South Dakota	34,888 (49.5%)	4	9081 (12.9%)		26,544 (37.6%)	
Tennessee	100,537 (37.8%)		136,368 (51.4%)	12	23,918 (9.0%)	
Texas	77,478 (18.3%)		239,148 (56.6%)	15	99,688 (23.6%)	
Vermont	37,992 (68.1%)	4	16,325 (29.3%)		42 (0.1%)	
Virginia	113,098 (38.7%)		164,136 (56.2%)	12	12,275 (4.2%)	
Washington21.	36,459 (41.4%)	4	29,802 (33.9%)		19,165 (21.8%)	
West Virginia	80,292 (46.9%)		84,487 (49.4%)	6	4167 (2.4%)	
Wisconsin	171,101 (46.1%)		177,325 (47.7%)	12	9919 (2.7%)	
Wyoming	8454 (50.6%)	3	0 (0%)		7722 (46.2%)	
Total	5,186,793 (44.0%)	145	5,554,617 (46.0%)	277	1,029,357 (8.5%)	22

Source: The American Presidency Project, University of California, Santa Barbara

Presidential Election Results 1896

State	*Republican (McKinley)*	*Electoral*	*Democrat (Bryan)*	*Electoral*
Alabama	55,673 (28.6%)		130,298 (67.0%)	11
Arkansas	37,512 (25.1%)		110.103 (73.7%)	8
California	146,688 (49.1%)	8	123,143 (41.2%)	1
Colorado	26,271 (13.9%)		161,005 (84.9%)	4
Connecticut	110,285 (63.2%)	6	56,740 (32.5%)	
Delaware	16,883 (53.5%)	3	13,425 (42.6%)	
Florida	11,298 (24.3%)		30,683 (66.0%)	4
Georgia	60,107 (36.8%)		94,733 (58.0%)	13
Idaho	6324 (21.3%)		23,135 (78.1%)	3
Illinois	607,130 (55.7%)	24	465,593 (42.7%)	
Indiana	323,754 (50,8%)	15	305,538 (48.0%)	
Iowa	289,293 (55.5%)	13	223,744 (42.9%)	
Kansas	158,484 (47.5%)		173,049 (51.5%)	10
Kentucky	218,171 (48.9%)	12	217,894 (48.9%)	1
Louisiana	22,037 (21.8%)		77,175 (76.4%)	8
Maine	80,403 (67.9%)	6	34,587 (29.2%)	
Maryland	136,959 (54.7%)	8	104,150 (41.6%)	
Massachusetts	278,976 (69.5%)	15	104,150 (41.6%)	
Michigan	293,336 (53.8%)	14	237,164 (43.5%)	
Minnesota	193,503 (56.6%)	9	139,735 (40.9%)	
Mississippi	4819 (6.9%)		63,355 (91.0%)	9
Missouri	304,940 (45.2%)		363,667 (54.0%)	17
Montana	10,509 (19.7%)		42,628 (79.9%)	3
Nebraska	103,064 (46.2%)		115,007 (51.5%)	8
Nevada	1938 (18.8%)		7802 (75.6%)	3
New Hampshire	57,444 (68.7%)	4	21,271 (25.4%)	
New Jersey	221,367 (59.7%)	10	133,675 (36.0%)	
New York	819,838 (57.6%)	36	551,369 (38.7%)	
North Carolina	155,122 (46.8%)		174,408 (52.6%)	11
North Dakota	26,335 (55.6%)	3	20,686 (43.6%)	
Ohio	525,992 (51.9%)	23	474,882 (46.8%)	
Oregon	48,700 (50.0%)	3	46,739 (48.0%)	
Pennsylvania	728,300 (61.0%)	32	427,125 (35.8%)	
Rhode Island	37,437 (63.8%)	4	14,429 (26.4%)	
South Carolina	9313 (13.5%)		58,801 (85.3%)	9
South Dakota	41,040 (49.5%)		41,225 (49.7%)	4
Tennessee	148,683 (46.3%)		167,168 (52.1%)	12
Texas	163,413 (31.7%)		267,803 (51.9%)	15
Utah	13,491 (17.3%)		64,607 (82.7%)	3

(*continued*)

State	Republican (McKinley)	Electoral	Democrat (Bryan)	Electoral
Vermont	51,127 (80.1%)	4	10,179 (15.9%)	
Virginia	135,379 (45.9%)		154,708 (52.5%)	12
Washington	39,153 (41.8%)		51,646 (55.2%)	4
West Virginia	105,379 (52.2%)	6	94,480 (46.8%)	
Wisconsin	268,135 (59.9%)	12	165,523 (37.0%)	
Wyoming	10,072 (47.8%)		10,376 (49.3%)	3
Total	7,105,076 (51.1%)	271	6,370,897 (45.8%)	176

Source: The American Presidency Project, University of California, Santa Barbara

Congressional Election 1888

House of Representatives

State	Republican	Democrat	Other
Alabama	1	7	
Arkansas	1	3	1 (Labor)
California	4	2	
Colorado	1	0	
Connecticut	3	1	
Delaware	0	1	
Florida	0	2	
Georgia	0	10	
Idaho[a]	1	0	
Illinois	13	7	
Indiana	3	10	
Iowa	10	1	
Kansas	7	0	
Kentucky	2	9	
Louisiana	1	5	
Maine	4	0	
Maryland	3	3	
Massachusetts	10	2	
Michigan	9	2	
Minnesota	5	0	
Mississippi	0	7	
Missouri	4	10	
Montana[b]	1	0	
Nebraska	3	0	

(*continued*)

(continued)

State	*Republican*	*Democrat*	*Other*
Nevada	1	0	
New Hampshire	2	0	
New Jersey	4	3	
New York	19	15	
North Carolina	3	6	
North Dakota[c]	1	0	
Ohio	16	5	
Oregon	1	0	
Pennsylvania	21	7	
Rhode Island	2	0	
South Carolina	1	6	
South Dakota[d]	2	0	
Tennessee	3	7	
Texas	0	11	
Vermont	2	0	
Virginia	4	6	
Washington[e]	1	0	
West Virginia	2	2	
Wisconsin	7	2	
Wyoming[f]	1	0	
Total	179	152	1 (Labor)

[a] Admitted during the course of Congress
[b] Admitted during the course of Congress
[c] Admitted during the course of Congress
[d] Admitted during the course of Congress
[e] Admitted during the course of Congress
[f] Admitted during the course of Congress

Senate

State	*Republican*	*Democrat*	*Other*
Alabama	0	2	
Arkansas	0	2	
California	1	1	
Colorado	2	0	
Connecticut	2	0	
Delaware	1	1	
Florida	0	2	
Georgia	0	2	
Idaho[a]	2	0	

(*continued*)

(continued)

State	*Republican*	*Democrat*	*Other*
Illinois	2	0	
Indiana	0	2	
Iowa	2	0	
Kansas	2	0	
Kentucky	0	2	
Louisiana	0	2	
Maine	2	0	
Maryland	0	2	
Massachusetts	2	0	
Michigan	2	0	
Minnesota	2	0	
Mississippi	0	2	
Missouri	0	2	
Montana[b]	2	0	
Nebraska	2	0	
Nevada	2	0	
New Hampshire	2	0	
New Jersey	0	2	
New York	2	0	
North Carolina	0	2	
North Dakota[c]	2	0	
Ohio	1	1	
Oregon	2	0	
Pennsylvania	2	0	
Rhode Island	2	0	
South Carolina	0	2	
South Dakota[d]	2	0	
Tennessee	0	2	
Texas	0	2	
Vermont	2	0	
Virginia	0	2	
Washington[e]	2	0	
West Virginia	0	2	
Wisconsin	2	0	
Wyoming[f]	2	0	
Total	51	37	

Source: Wikipedia, 51st United States Congress

[a] Admitted during the course of Congress

[b] Admitted during the course of Congress

[c] Admitted during the course of Congress

[d] Admitted during the course of Congress

[e] Admitted during the course of Congress

[f] Admitted during the course of Congress

Congressional Election 1890

House of Representatives

State	*Republican*	*Democrat*	*Other*
Alabama	0	8	
Arkansas	0	5	
California	4	2	
Colorado	1	0	
Connecticut	1	3	
Delaware	0	1	
Florida	0	2	
Georgia	0	9	1 (Populist)
Idaho	1	0	
Illinois	6	14	
Indiana	2	11	
Iowa	5	6	
Kansas	2	0	5 (Populist)
Kentucky	1	10	
Louisiana	0	6	
Maine	4	0	
Maryland	0	6	
Massachusetts	5	7	
Michigan	3	8	
Minnesota	1	3	1 (Populist)
Mississippi	0	7	
Missouri	0	14	
Montana	0	1	
Nebraska	0	1	2 (Populist)
Nevada	1	0	
New Hampshire	0	2	
New Jersey	2	5	
New York	11	23	
North Carolina	1	8	
North Dakota	1	0	
Ohio	7	14	
Oregon	1	0	
Pennsylvania	18	10	
Rhode Island	0	2	
South Carolina	0	7	
South Dakota	2	0	
Tennessee	2	8	
Texas	0	11	
Vermont	2	0	

(*continued*)

(continued)

State	*Republican*	*Democrat*	*Other*
Virginia	0	10	
Washington	1	0	
West Virginia	0	4	
Wisconsin	1	8	
Wyoming	1	0	
Total	87	236	9 (Populist)

Senate

State	*Republican*	*Democrat*	*Other*
Alabama	0	2	
Arkansas	0	2	
California	2	0	
Colorado	2	0	
Connecticut	2	0	
Delaware	1	1	
Florida	0	2	
Georgia	0	2	
Idaho	2	0	
Illinois	1	1	
Indiana	0	2	
Iowa	2	0	
Kansas	1	0	1 (Populist)
Kentucky	0	2	
Louisiana	0	2	
Maine	2	0	
Maryland	0	2	
Massachusetts	2	0	
Michigan	2	0	
Minnesota	2	0	
Mississippi	0	2	
Missouri	0	2	
Montana	2	0	
Nebraska	2	0	
Nevada	2	0	
New Hampshire	2	0	
New Jersey	0	2	
New York	1	1	
North Carolina	0	2	
North Dakota	2	0	

(*continued*)

(continued)

State	*Republican*	*Democrat*	*Other*
Ohio	1	1	
Oregon	2	0	
Pennsylvania	2	0	
Rhode Island	2	0	
South Carolina	0	2	
South Dakota	1	0	1 (Independent)
Tennessee	0	2	
Texas	0	2	
Vermont	2	0	
Virginia	0	2	
Washington	2	0	
West Virginia	0	2	
Wisconsin	1	1	
Wyoming	2	0	
Total	47	39	1 (Populist) 1 (Independent)

Source: Wikipedia, 52nd United States Congress

Congressional Election 1892

House of Representatives

State	*Republican*	*Democrat*	*Other*
Alabama	0	9	
Arkansas	0	6	
California	2	4	1 (Populist)
Colorado	0	0	2 (Populist)
Connecticut	1	3	
Delaware	0	1	
Florida	0	2	
Georgia	0	11	
Idaho	1	0	
Illinois	11	11	
Indiana	2	11	
Iowa	10	1	
Kansas	2	1	5 (Populist)
Kentucky	1	10	
Louisiana	0	6	
Maine	4	0	
Maryland	0	6	

(*continued*)

(continued)

State	Republican	Democrat	Other
Massachusetts	9	4	1 (Independent Democrat)
Michigan	7	5	
Minnesota	4	2	1 (Populist)
Mississippi	0	7	
Missouri	1	14	
Montana	1	0	
Nebraska	3	1	2 (Populist)
Nevada	0	0	1 (Silver Party)
New Hampshire	2	0	
New Jersey	2	6	
New York	14	20	
North Carolina	1	8	
North Dakota	1	0	
Ohio	10	11	
Oregon	2	0	
Pennsylvania	20	10	
Rhode Island	0	2	
South Carolina	1	6	
South Dakota	2	0	
Tennessee	2	8	
Texas	0	13	
Vermont	2	0	
Virginia	0	10	
Washington	2	0	
West Virginia	0	4	
Wisconsin	4	6	
Wyoming	0	1	
Total	124	220	11 (Populist) 1 (Silver Party) 1 (Independent Democrat)

Senate

State	Republican	Democrat	Other
Alabama	0	2	
Arkansas	0	2	
California	1	1	
Colorado	2	0	
Connecticut	2	0	
Delaware	1	1	
Florida	0	2	

(*continued*)

(continued)

State	*Republican*	*Democrat*	*Other*
Georgia	0	2	
Idaho	2	0	
Illinois	1	1	
Indiana	0	2	
Iowa	2	0	
Kansas	0	1	1 (Populist)
Kentucky	0	2	
Louisiana	0	2	
Maine	2	0	
Maryland	0	2	
Massachusetts	2	0	
Michigan	2	0	
Minnesota	2	0	
Mississippi	0	2	
Missouri	0	2	
Montana	2	0	
Nebraska	1	0	1 (Populist)
Nevada	1	0	1 (Silver Party)
New Hampshire	2	0	
New Jersey	0	2	
New York	0	2	
North Carolina	0	2	
North Dakota	1	1	
Ohio	1	1	
Oregon	2	0	
Pennsylvania	2	0	
Rhode Island	2	0	
South Carolina	0	2	
South Dakota	1	0	1 (Populist)
Tennessee	0	2	
Texas	0	2	
Vermont	2	0	
Virginia	0	2	
Washington	2	0	
West Virginia	0	2	
Wisconsin	0	2	
Wyoming	2	0	
Total	40	44	3 (Populist) 1 (Silver Party)

Source: Wikipedia, 53rd United States Congress

Congressional Election 1894

House of Representatives

State	*Republican*	*Democrat*	*Other*
Alabama	2	5	2 (Populist)
Arkansas	0	6	
California	6	1	
Colorado	1	0	1 (Populist)
Connecticut	4	0	
Delaware	1	0	
Florida	0	2	
Georgia	0	11	
Idaho	1	0	
Illinois	22	0	
Indiana	13	0	
Iowa	11	0	
Kansas	7	0	
Kentucky	6	5	
Louisiana	0	6	
Maine	4	0	
Maryland	3	3	
Massachusetts	12	1	
Michigan	12	0	
Minnesota	7	0	
Mississippi	0	7	
Missouri	11	4	
Montana	1	0	
Nebraska	5	0	1 (Populist)
Nevada	0	0	1 (Silver Party)
New Hampshire	2	0	
New Jersey	8	0	
New York	29	5	
North Carolina	3	2	3 (Populist)
North Dakota	1	0	
Ohio	19	2	
Oregon	2	0	
Pennsylvania	28	2	
Rhode Island	2	0	
South Carolina	1	6	
South Dakota	2	0	
Tennessee	4	6	
Texas	1	12	
Utah[a]	1	0	
Vermont	2	0	
Virginia	2	8	

(*continued*)

(continued)

State	Republican	Democrat	Other
Washington	2	0	
West Virginia	4	0	
Wisconsin	10	0	
Wyoming	1	0	
Total	253	94	7 (Populist) 1 (Silver Party)

[a] Admitted during the course of Congress

Senate

State	Republican	Democrat	Other
Alabama	0	2	
Arkansas	0	2	
California	1	1	
Colorado	2	0	
Connecticut	2	0	
Delaware	0	2	
Florida	0	2	
Georgia	0	2	
Idaho	2	0	
Illinois	1	1	
Indiana	0	2	
Iowa	2	0	
Kansas	1	0	1 (Populist)
Kentucky	0	2	
Louisiana	0	2	
Maine	2	0	
Maryland	0	2	
Massachusetts	2	0	
Michigan	2	0	
Minnesota	2	0	
Mississippi	0	2	
Missouri	0	2	
Montana	2	0	
Nebraska	1	0	1 (Populist)
Nevada	0	0	2 (Silver Party
New Hampshire	2	0	
New Jersey	1	1	
New York	0	2	
North Carolina	1	0	1 (Populist)
North Dakota	1	1	
Ohio	1	1	

(*continued*)

(continued)

State	*Republican*	*Democrat*	*Other*
Oregon	2	0	
Pennsylvania	2	0	
Rhode Island	2	0	
South Carolina	0	2	
South Dakota	1	0	1 (Populist)
Tennessee	0	2	
Texas	0	2	
Utah[a]	2	0	
Vermont	2	0	
Virginia	0	2	
Washington	2	0	
West Virginia	1	1	
Wisconsin	0	2	
Wyoming	2	0	
Total	44	40	4 (Populists) 2 (Silver Party)

Source: Wikipedia, 54th United States Congress

[a] Admitted during the course of Congress

Congressional Election 1896

House of Representatives

State	*Republican*	*Democrat*	*Other*
Alabama	1	7	1 (Populist)
Arkansas	0	6	
California	3	2	2 (Populist)
Colorado	0	0	1 (Populist) 1 (Silver Republican)
Connecticut	4	0	
Delaware	0	1	
Florida	0	2	
Georgia	0	11	
Idaho	0	0	1 (Populist)
Illinois	17	5	
Indiana	9	4	
Iowa	11	0	
Kansas	2	0	6 (Populist)
Kentucky	4	7	

(*continued*)

(continued)

State	*Republican*	*Democrat*	*Other*
Louisiana	0	6	
Maine	4	0	
Maryland	6	0	
Massachusetts	12	1	
Michigan	10	2	
Minnesota	7	0	
Mississippi	0	7	
Missouri	2	12	
Montana	0	0	1 (Silver Republican)
Nebraska	2	0	4 (Populist)
Nevada	0	0	1 (Silver Party)
New Hampshire	2	0	
New Jersey	8	0	
New York	29	5	
North Carolina	3	1	5 (Populist)
North Dakota	1	0	
Ohio	15	6	
Oregon	2	0	
Pennsylvania	26	3	1 (Independent Republican)
Rhode Island	2	0	
South Carolina	0	7	
South Dakota	0	0	2 (Populist)
Tennessee	2	8	
Texas	1	12	
Utah	0	1	
Vermont	2	0	
Virginia	4	6	
Washington	0	1	1 (Silver Republican)
West Virginia	4	0	
Wisconsin	10	0	
Wyoming	0	1	
Total	206	124	22 (Populist), 3 (Silver Republican), 1 (Silver Party), 1 (Independent Republican)

Senate

State	*Republican*	*Democrat*	*Other*
Alabama	0	2	
Arkansas	0	2	
California	1	1	
Colorado	1	0	1 (Silver Republican)
Connecticut	2	0	
Delaware	0	2	
Florida	0	2	
Georgia	0	2	
Idaho	1	0	1 (Populist)
Illinois	2	0	
Indiana	1	1	
Iowa	2	0	
Kansas	1	0	1 (Populist)
Kentucky	1	1	
Louisiana	0	2	
Maine	2	0	
Maryland	1	1	
Massachusetts	2	0	
Michigan	2	0	
Minnesota	2	0	
Mississippi	0	2	
Missouri	0	2	
Montana	1	0	1 (Silver Republican)
Nebraska	1	0	1 (Populist)
Nevada	0	0	2 (Silver Party)
New Hampshire	2	0	
New Jersey	1	1	
New York	1	1	
North Carolina	1	0	1 (Populist)
North Dakota	1	1	
Ohio	2	0	
Oregon	2	0	
Pennsylvania	2	0	
Rhode Island	2	0	
South Carolina	0	2	
South Dakota	0	0	1 (Silver Republican) 1 (Populist)
Tennessee	0	2	
Texas	0	2	
Utah	0	1	
Vermont	2	0	

(*continued*)

(continued)

State	Republican	Democrat	Other
Virginia	0	2	
Washington	1	0	1 (Silver Republican)
West Virginia	1	1	
Wisconsin	1	1	
Wyoming	2	0	
Total	44	34	5 (Populist) 2 (Silver Party) 5 (Silver Republican)

Source: Wikipedia, 55th United States Congress

Congressional Election 1898

House of Representatives

State	Republican	Democrat	Other
Alabama	1	8	
Arkansas	0	6	
California	6	1	
Colorado	0	0	1 (Populist) 1 (Silver Republican)
Connecticut	4	0	
Delaware	1	0	
Florida	0	2	
Georgia	0	11	
Idaho	0	0	1 (Silver Republican)
Illinois	14	8	
Indiana	9	4	
Iowa	11	0	
Kansas	7	0	1 (Populist)
Kentucky	2	9	
Louisiana	0	6	
Maine	4	0	
Maryland	4	2	
Massachusetts	10	3	
Michigan	12	0	
Minnesota	7	0	
Mississippi	0	7	
Missouri	3	12	
Montana	0	1	
Nebraska	2	1	3 (Populist)
Nevada	0	0	1 (Silver Party)
New Hampshire	2	0	

(continued)

(continued)

State	Republican	Democrat	Other
New Jersey	6	2	
New York	16	18	
North Carolina	3	5	1 (Populist)
North Dakota	1	0	
Ohio	15	6	
Oregon	2	0	
Pennsylvania	29	10	
Rhode Island	2	0	
South Carolina	0	7	
South Dakota	2	0	
Tennessee	2	8	
Texas	1	12	
Utah	0	1	
Vermont	2	0	
Virginia	1	9	
Washington	2	0	
West Virginia	3	1	
Wisconsin	10	0	
Wyoming	1	0	
Total	188	160	6 (Populist) 2 (Silver Republican) 1 (Silver Party)

Senate

State	Republican	Democrat	Other
Alabama	0	2	
Arkansas	0	2	
California	2	0	
Colorado	1	0	1 (Silver Republican)
Connecticut	2	0	
Delaware[a]	0	1	
Florida	0	2	
Georgia	0	2	
Idaho	1	0	1 (Populist)
Illinois	2	0	
Indiana	2	0	
Iowa	2	0	
Kansas	1	0	1 (Populist)
Kentucky	1	1	
Louisiana	0	2	

(*continued*)

(continued)

State	*Republican*	*Democrat*	*Other*
Maine	2	0	
Maryland	2	0	
Massachusetts	2	0	
Michigan	2	0	
Minnesota	2	0	
Mississippi	0	2	
Missouri	0	2	
Montana	1	1	
Nebraska	2	0	
Nevada	0	0	2 (Silver Party)
New Hampshire	2	0	
New Jersey	2	0	
New York	2	0	
North Carolina	1	0	1 (Populist)
North Dakota	2	0	
Ohio	2	0	
Oregon	2	0	
Pennsylvania	2	0	
Rhode Island	2	0	
South Carolina	0	2	
South Dakota	0	0	1(Populist) 1 (Silver Republican)
Tennessee	0	2	
Texas	0	2	
Utah	1	1	
Vermont	2	0	
Virginia	0	2	
Washington	1	0	1 (Silver Republican)
West Virginia	2	0	
Wisconsin	2	0	
Wyoming	2	0	
Total	54	26	4 (Populists) 2 (Silver Party) 3 (Silver Republicans)

Source: Wikipedia, 56th United States Congress

[a] Extended vacancy

Appendix C

Economic Statistics

Output and Prices

Year	*Total Output (current prices)*[a]	*Total Output (1929 prices)*[b]	*Change in Output*	*Change in Prices*[c]
1880	$10,619	$17,939		
1881	$10,495	$18,115	1.2%	(2.3%)
1882	$11,543	$19,401	6.9%	2.0%
1883	$11,353	$19,469	0.4%	(2.0%)
1884	$11,132	$20,167	3.6%	(5.5%)
1885	$10,544	$20,393	1.1%	(6.8%)
1886	$11,022	$21,602	5.9%	(1.4%)
1887	$11,470	$22,282	3.1%	1.0%
1888	$11,415	$21,875	(1.9%)	1.4%
1889	$11,944	$22,750	4.0%	(3.2%)
1890	$12,560	$24,514	7.8%	(2.6%)
1891	$12,918	$25,632	4.6%	(1.8%)
1892	$13,649	$28,194	10.0%	(4.3%)
1893	$13,172	$26,701	(4.2%)	0.1%
1894	$11,904	$25,758	(3.5%)	(6.1%)
1895	$12,202	$29,091	12.9%	(9.5%)
1896	$12,509	$28,416	(2.3%)	4.8%

(*continued*)

W. Wells, *Financial Politics in the United States in the 1890s*,
https://doi.org/10.1007/978-3-031-86765-1

(continued)

Year	*Total Output (current prices)*[a]	*Total Output (1929 prices)*[b]	*Change in Output*	*Change in Prices*[c]
1897	$13,804	$31,125	9.5%	0.8%
1898	$14,418	$31,488	1.2%	3.2%
1899	$16,318	$34,578	9.8%	3.8%
1900	$17,705	$35,678	3.2%	4.9%

Source: Susan B. Carter et al., editors, *Historical Statistics of the United States: Earliest Times to the Present, Millennial Edition* (New York: Cambridge University Press, 2006), vol. 3, 3–59, 3–60

[a] Gross National Product in millions of dollars
[b] Gross National Product in millions of dollars
[c] The Gross National Product deflator, not the change in consumer prices

Production of Selected Products

Year	*Steel*[a]	*Bituminous Coal*[b]	*Railroad Track Laid*[c]
1880	1.397	50,757	6706
1881	1.779	51,945	9846
1882	1.945	58,917	11,569
1883	1.874	64,860	6745
1884	1.737	71,737	3923
1885	1.917	71,773	2975
1886	2.870	74,645	8018
1887	3.733	88,562	12,876
1888	3.238	102,040	6900
1889	3.784	95,685	5162
1890	4.779	111,302	5427
1891	4.349	117,901	4806
1892	5.492	126,857	3161
1893	4.471	128,385	3024
1894	4.889	118,820	1760
1895	6.785	135,118	1420
1896	5.849	137,640	1692
1897	7.940	147,618	2109
1898	9.888	166,594	3265
1899	11.739	193.323	4569
1900	11.227	212,316	5368

Source: US Bureau of the Census, *Historical Statistics of the United States, Colonial Times to 1970, Bicentennial Edition, Part 2* (Washington, DC, 1975), pp. 590, 693–4; Susan B. Carter et al., editors, *Historical Statistics of the United States: Earliest Times to the Present, Millennial Edition* (New York: Cambridge University Press 2006), vol. 4, 4–917

[a] Millions of tons
[b] Millions of tons
[c] Miles

Capital Spending by Railroads

Year	*Current Dollars (millions)*	*Constant (1929) Dollars (millions)*
1880	$272	$616
1881	$306	$683
1882	$320	$711
1883	$294	$652
1884	$247	$551
1885	$223	$507
1886	$216	$498
1887	$222	$514
1888	$238	$552
1889	$244	$570
1890	$271	$642
1891	$307	$738
1892	$200	$729
1893	$267	$657
1894	$229	$568
1895	$158	$395
1896	$87	$223
1897	$84	$207
1898	$112	$262
1899	$139	$321

Source: Melville J. Ulmer, *Trends and Cycles in Capital Formation by United States Railroads, 1870–1950*, National Bureau of Economic Research working Paper, 1954

Balance of Payments: Current Account[a]

Year	*Exports*	*Imports*	*Services (net)*[b]	*Payments on Foreign Investments (net)*	*Unilateral Transfers*[c]	*Balance*
1880	$929	($694)	($41)	($79)	($4)	$111
1881	$936	($672)	($39)	($88)	($5)	$132
1882	$824	($747)	($48)	($84)	($13)	($68)
1883	$875	($748)	($50)	($89)	($22)	($34)
1884	$822	($730)	($61)	($90)	($24)	($83)
1885	$792	($635)	($59)	($86)	($27)	($15)
1886	$781	($698)	($67)	($93)	($28)	($105)
1887	$774	($759)	($74)	($98)	($28)	($185)
1888	$750	($791)	($78)	($107)	($30)	($256)
1889	$841	($817)	($73)	($118)	($44)	($210)
1890	$921	($866)	($80)	($125)	($45)	($195)
1891	$997	($875)	($77)	($134)	($50)	($140)
1892	$1084	($888)	($73)	($143)	($54)	($74)
1893	$974	($898)	($56)	($139)	($44)	($163)

(*continued*)

(continued)

Year	*Exports*	*Imports*	*Services (net)*[b]	*Payments on Foreign Investments (net)*	*Unilateral Transfers*[c]	*Balance*
1894	$943	($692)	($39)	($113)	($54)	$44
1895	$855	($774)	($82)	($126)	($55)	($182)
1896	$1048	($816)	($76)	($122)	($49)	($15)
1897	$1136	($803)	($74)	($127)	($41)	$91
1898	$1304	($653)	($75)	($133)	($44)	$400
1899	$1363	($735)	($77)	($124)	($68)	$359

Source: Susan B. Carter et al., *Historical Statistics of the United States: Earliest Times to the Present* (New York: Cambridge University Press, 2006), vol. 5, 5–454, 5–455

[a] Millions of dollars

[b] Chiefly shipping

[c] Such as remittances by immigrants and spending by tourists

Selected Exports[a]

Year	*Raw Cotton*	*Leaf Tobacco*	*Wheat & Flour*	*Meat*	*Cotton Textiles*	*Iron & Steel*	*Machinery*
1880	$212	$16	$226	$114	$10	n.a.	n.a.
1881	$248	$19	$213	$134	$14	n.a.	n.a.
1882	$200	$19	$149	$69	$13	$1	$14
1883	$247	$19	$175	$61	$13	$1	$17
1884	$197	$18	$126	$64	$12	$2	$16
1885	$202	$22	$125	$63	$12	$1	$11
1886	$205	$27	$89	$54	$14	$1	$10
1887	$206	$26	$143	$53	$15	$1	$11
1888	$223	$22	$111	$52	$13	$2	$12
1889	$238	$19	$87	$59	$10	$2	$16
1890	$251	$21	$102	$78	$10	$3	$20
1891	$291	$21	$106	$81	$14	$3	$21
1892	$258	$20	$237	$83	$13	$3	$21
1893	$189	$22	$169	$79	$12	$3	$22
1894	$211	$23	$129	$80	$14	$3	$22
1895	$205	n.a.	$95	$81	$14	$3	$24
1896	$190	n.a.	$92	$81	$17	$5	$29
1897	$231	n.a.	$116	$88	$21	$11	$38
1898	$230	$22	$215	$104	$17	$19	$44
1899	$210	$25	$177	$109	$24	$29	$61

Source: Susan B. Carter et al., *Historical Statistics of the United States: Earliest Times to the Present* (New York: Cambridge University Press, 2006), vol. 5, 5–547 to 5–551

[a] In millions of dollars

Farm Prices

Year	*Corn ($/bu.)*	*Wheat ($/bu.)*	*Cotton ($/lb.)*	*Hogs ($/head)*	*Cattle ($/head*
1880	$0.39	$0.95	$0.098	$4.80	$17.80
1881	$0.63	$1.20	$0.107	$6.00	$18.67
1882	$0.48	$0.89	$0.091	$6.74	$20.93
1883	$0.35	$0.91	$0.091	$5.64	$23.87
1884	$0.32	$0.65	$0.092	$5.06	$25.26
1885	$0.36	$0.77	$0.084	$4.30	$24.40
1886	$0.43	$0.69	$0.081	$4.60	$22.20
1887	$0.33	$0.68	$0.086	$5.12	$21.18
1888	$0.42	$0.93	$0.085	$5.80	$19.39
1889	$0.28	$0.70	$0.086	$4.80	$18.77
1890	$0.50	$0.84	$0.086	$4.24	$16.95
1891	$0.40	$0.83	$0.072	$4.65	$16.49
1892	$0.39	$0.62	$0.083	$6.37	$16.81
1893	$0.36	$0.53	$0.070	$6.06	$17.00
1894	$0.45	$0.49	$0.046	$5.09	$16.84
1895	$0.25	$0.51	$0.076	$4.50	$16.56
1896	$0.21	$0.72	$0.067	$4.36	$17.86
1897	$0.26	$0.81	$0.067	$4.70	$18.62
1898	$0.29	$0.58	$0.056	$4.67	$22.79
1899	$0.30	$0.59	$0.070	$5.36	$24.53
1900	$0.35	$0.62	$0.092	$6.08	$26.50

Source: Susan B. Carter et al., *Historical Statistics of the United States: Earliest Times to the Present* (New York: Cambridge University Press, 2006), vol. 4, 4–97, 4–102, 4–111, 4–165

Gold Flows[a]

Year	*Gold Mined*	*Imports (Exports) of Gold*	*Balance of Payments*	*Net Foreign Investment*
1886	$34.820	($22)	($105)	$137
1887	$33.086	$33	($185)	$231
1888	$33.107	$26	($256)	$287
1889	$32.921	($50)	($210)	$202
1890	$32.797	($4)	($195)	$194
1891	$33.127	($68)	($140)	$136
1892	$32.962	$0	($74)	$41
1893	$35.893	($88)	($163)	$146
1894	$39.443	($5)	$44	($68)
1895	$46.543	($30)	($182)	$137
1896	$53.004	($78)	($15)	$40
1897	$57.276	$45	$91	($23)
1898	$64.536	$105	$400	($279)
1899	$70.940	$51	$359	($229)

Source: US Bureau of the Census, *Historical Statistics of the United States, Colonial Times to 1970*, Washington, D.C, 1975, pp. 606, 867, 885; Susan B. Carter et al. *Historical Statistics of the United States: Earliest Times to the Present* (New York: Cambridge University Press, 2006), vol. 5, 454–5

[a] In millions of dollars

Government Finances[a]

Year[b]	*Total Income*	*Customs*	*Internal Revenue*	*Other*[c]	*Outlays*	*Surplus (Deficit)*
1885	$323	$181	$112	$35	$260	$63
1886	$336	$192	$117	$27	$242	$94
1887	$271	$217	$119	$35	$268	$103
1888	$279	$219	$124	$36	$268	$111
1889	$387	$224	$131	$32	$299	$88
1890	$403	$230	$143	$31	$318	$85
1891	$392	$220	$146	$27	$366	$26
1892	$354	$177	$154	$24	$345	$9
1893	$385	$203	$161	$21	$383	$2
1894	$306	$131	$147	$27	$368	($62)
1895	$324	$152	$143	$29	$356	($32)
1896	$338	$160	$147	$31	$352	($14)
1897	$347	$177	$147	$24	$366	($19)
1898	$405	$150	$171	$85	$443	($38)
1899	$515	$206	$273	$36	$605	($90)
1900	$567	$233	$295	$39	$521	$46

Source: US Bureau of the Census, *Historical Statistics of the United States from Colonial Times to 1970*, Washington, DC, 1975, p. 1104, 1106

[a] In millions of dollars

[b] The fiscal year ran from July 1 of the previous year to June 30 of the year in question. Fiscal 1890, therefore, ran from July 1, 1889, to June 30, 1890

[c] Includes net revenue from the Post Office and the sale of land

Currency Supply[a]

Year	*Gold*	*Silver Dollars*	*Subsidiary Coins*	*Greenbacks*	*Gold Certificates*	*Silver Certificates*	*National Banknotes*	*Treasury Notes*
1879	$110	$8	$61	$301	$15	$0	$321	
1880	$225	$20	$48	$327	$7	$5	$337	
1881	$315	$29	$46	$328	$5	$39	$349	
1882	$358	$32	$46	$325	$5	$54	$352	
1883	$344	$35	$46	$323	$59	$72	$347	
1884	$340	$40	$45	$318	$71	$96	$330	
1885	$341	$39	$43	$331	$126	$101	$308	
1886	$358	$52	$46	$323	$76	$88	$307	
1887	$376	$55	$48	$326	$91	$142	$276	
1888	$391	$55	$50	$308	$121	$200	$245	
1889	$376	$54	$51	$316	$117	$257	$207	
1890	$374	$56	$54	$334	$130	$297	$181	
1891	$407	$58	$58	$343	$120	$307	$162	$40

(*continued*)

(continued)

Year	*Gold*	*Silver Dollars*	*Subsidiary Coins*	*Greenbacks*	*Gold Certificates*	*Silver Certificates*	*National Banknotes*	*Treasury Notes*
1892	$408	$56	$63	$339	$141	$326	$167	$98
1893	$409	$56	$65	$330	$92	$326	$174	$140
1894	$495	$52	$58	$325	$66	$326	$200	$143
1895	$476	$51	$60	$319	$48	$319	$206	$115
1896	$454	$52	$60	$256	$42	$330	$215	$95
1897	$517	$51	$59	$306	$37	$357	$226	$83
1898	$657	$58	$64	$310	$35	$390	$222	$98
1899	$679	$61	$69	$328	$32	$402	$237	$92
1900	$610	$65	$76	$317	$200	$408	$300	$75

Source: Susan B. Carter et al. *Historical Statistics of the United States: Earliest Times to the Present* (New York: Cambridge University Press, 2006), vol. 3, 3–609

[a] In millions of dollars

Volume of Bank Deposit

Year	*Bank deposits*[a]
1880	$1.36
1881	$1.66
1882	$1.79
1883	$1.93
1884	$1.96
1885	$2.07
1886	$2.32
1887	$2.48
1888	$2.55
1889	$2.73
1890	$2.99
1891	$3.12
1892	$3.47
1893	$3.26
1894	$3.35
1895	$3.52
1896	$3.46
1897	$3.72
1898	$4.26
1899	$4.99
1900	$5.39

Source: US Bureau of the Census, *Historical Statistics of the United States, Colonial Times to 1970, Bicentennial Edition, Part 2* (Washington, DC, 1975), pp. 992–3

[a] In billions of dollars

Gold and Silver Production in the United States[a]

Year	*Gold*	*Silver*
1860	2225	116
1861	2080	1547
1862	1896	3480
1863	1935	6574
1864	2230	8508
1865	2575	8701
1866	2588	7734
1867	2502	10,441
1868	2322	9281
1869	2395	9281
1870	2419	12,375
1871	2104	17,789
1872	1742	22,236
1873	1742	27,650
1874	1620	28,868
1875	1619	24,530
1876	1932	29,996
1877	2269	30,778
1878	2477	35,022
1879	1882	31,566
1880	1742	30,319
1881	1679	33,258
1882	1572	36,197
1883	1451	35,733
1884	1490	37,744
1885	1538	39,909
1886	1687	39,694
1887	1603	41,722
1888	1604	45,793
1889	1595	50,094
1890	1589	54,516
1891	1605	58,330
1892	1597	65,500
1893	1739	60,000
1894	1911	49,500
1895	2255	57,727
1896	2568	58,835
1897	2775	53,860
1898	3118	54,438
1899	3437	54,764
1900	3830	57,647

Source: US Bureau of the Census, *Historical Statistics of the United States, Colonial Times to 1970, Bicentennial Edition, Part 2*, Washington, DC, 1975, p. 606

[a] Thousands of fine troy ounces

Silver Prices

Year	*Price ($/oz.)*
1870	$1.33
1871	$1.33
1872	$1.32
1873	$1.30
1874	$1.28
1875	$1.24
1876	$1.16
1877	$1.20
1878	$1.15
1879	$1.12
1880	$1.15
1881	$1.18
1882	$1.14
1883	$1.11
1884	$1.11
1885	$1.07
1886	$1.00
1887	$0.98
1888	$0.94
1889	$0.94
1890	$1.05
1891	$0.99
1892	$0.88
1893	$0.78
1894	$0.63
1895	$0.65
1896	$0.67
1897	$0.60
1898	$0.58
1899	$0.60

Source: Bureau of the Census. *Historical Statistics of the United States, Colonial Times to 1970, Bicentennial Edition, Part I*, Washington, DC, 1975, p. 606

Selected Bibliography

Primary Sources

Archives

American Presidency Project. University of California at Santa Barbara (Internet).

Chronicling America, Historic American Newspapers. Library of Congress, Washington, DC (Internet).

Columbia University Archives, New York, NY.
Belmont Family Papers.

Library of Congress, Washington, DC
Benjamin Harrison Papers.
Charles Hamlin Papers.
Grover Cleveland Papers.
Manton Marable Papers.
Mathew Quay Papers.
William Curtis Papers.
William Jennings Bryan Papers.
William McKinley Papers.

W. Wells, *Financial Politics in the United States in the 1890s*,
https://doi.org/10.1007/978-3-031-86765-1

Morgan Library, New York, NY.
Morgan Papers
Satterlee Papers

National Archives, Kew, England.
CAB 37/34. 1893.
CAB 37/31. 1893.
CAB 37/45. 1897.
MINT 12/247. 1893.
T 173/953. 1897.

Rothschild's Archives, London, England.

Western Reserve Historical Society, Cleveland, OH.
Hanna Family Papers.

Government Documents

Annual Report of the Secretary of the Treasury, 1890. Washington: Government Printing Office.

Annual Report of the Secretary of the Treasury, 1893. Washington: Government Printing Office.

Annual Report of the Secretary of the Treasury, 1894. Washington: Government Printing Office.

Annual Report of the Secretary of the Treasury, 1895. Washington: Government Printing Office.

Annual Report of the Secretary of the Treasury, 1896. Washington: Government Printing Office.

Annual Report of the Secretary of the Treasury, 1897. Washington: Government Printing Office.

Annual Report of the Secretary of the Treasury, 1898, Washington: Government Printing Office.

US House of Representatives. 52nd Congress, 1st session, Committee on Coinage, Weights, and Measures. *Free Coinage of Gold and Silver.* 1893.

US House of Representatives. 52nd Congress, 2nd session. *National Money System: Views of the Minority*, 1893.

US House of Representatives. 52nd Cong. 2nd sess. *Repeal of the Sherman Act.* February 7, 1893.

US House of Representatives. 53rd Cong. 1st Sess. Message of the President of the United States. August 8, 1893.

US Senate, 53rd Congress, 1st session. *Letter from Ernest Seyd to Samuel Hooper on the Subject of Coinage.* 1893.

Proceedings, Reports, & Other Documents

American Bankers' Association. *Twentieth Annual Convention, Held at Baltimore, MD, October 10th and 11th, 1894.*

Proceedings of the First National Silver Convention at St. Louis November 26, 27, and 28, *1889.* St. Louis: Buxton & Skinner Stationery Co. 1889.

Proceedings of the Second National Silver Convention held at Washington,May 26th, 27th, and 28th 1892, Including the Organization of the American Bimetallic League. Washington, DC: Geo. R. Gray. 1892.

Report of the Monetary Commission of the Indianapolis Convention. Chicago: University of Chicago Press. 1898.

Warner, A.J. *Opening Address of A.J. Warner Delivered Before the Silver Convention (1893).* Washington, DC: Geo. R. Gray. 1893.

Articles

Bryan, William Jennings. "Has the Election Settled the Money Question?" *North American Review* 163 (December 1896): 703–710.

Carnegie, Andrew. "Mr. Bryan, the Conjurer." *North American Review* 164 (1897): 106–118.

Fisher, Willard. "'Coin' and His Critics." *The Quarterly Journal of Economics* 10 (1896): 187–208.

Harvey, William. "*Coin's Financial School* and its Censors." *North American Review* 161 (July 1895): 71–79.

Hoxie, Robert F. "The Silver Debate of 1890." *Journal of Political Economy* 1 (September 1893): 535–587.

Noyes, Alexander. "The Treasury Reserve and the Bond Syndicate." *Political Science Quarterly* 10 (1895): 573–602.

Taussig, Frank. "Bonds Sales and the Gold Standard." *The Forum* 16 (November 1896): 325–45.

Books

Altgeld, John Peter. *Live Questions: Comprising his Papers, Speeches, and Interviews.* Chicago: George Bowen & Sons. 1899.

Bryan, William J. *The First Battle: A Story of the Campaign of 1896.* Chicago: W.B. Conkey Co. 1897.

Carpenter, Kenneth, ed. *Gold and Silver in the Presidential Campaign of 1896.* New York: Arno Press. 1974.

Cleveland, Grover. *The Letters of Grover Cleveland.* Allan Nevins, ed. New York: Houghton Mifflin Company. 1933.

Donnelly, Ignatius. *The American People's Money.* Chicago: Laird & Lee, 1896.

Emery, Sarah. *Seven Financial Conspiracies which have Enslaved the American People, 3rdEdition*. Lansing, MI, 1896.

Harvey, William Hope. *Coin's Financial School*. Chicago: Coin Publishing Company. 1894.

McKinley, William. *The Speeches and Addresses of William McKinley*. New York: Doubleday. 1900.

Sherman, John. *Recollections of Forty Years and the House, Senate, and Cabinet: An Autobiography*. Chicago: The Werner Company. 1895.

Silver Speeches in the U.S. Senate. Google Books (Internet).

Stevens, Charles, ed. *Free Silver and the People*. New York: F.T. Neely. 1896.

Taussig, Frank. *The Silver Situation in the U.S*. New York: Putnam's. 1896.

White, Horace. *Coin's Financial Fool*. New York: J.S. Ogilvie Publishing Co. 1895.

Secondary Sources

Books

Adler, Dorothy, *British Investment in American Railways, 1834–1898*. Charlottesville: University of Virginia Press. 1970.

Allen, Frederick Lewis. *The Great Pierpont Morgan*. New York: Harper & Row, 1948.

Barners, James A. *John G. Carlisle: Financial Statesman*. Gloucester, MA: Peter Smith. 1967.

Bensel, Richard Franklin. *Passion and Preferences: William Jennings Bryan and the 1896 Democratic National Convention*. New York: Cambridge University Press, 2008.

———. *The Political Economy of American Industrialization, 1877–1900*. New York: Cambridge University Press. 2000.

Calhoun, Charles. *Benjamin Harrison*. New York: Times Books. 2005.

———. *Minority Victory: Gilded Age Politics and the Front Porch Campaign of 1888*. Lawrence, KA: University of Kansas Press. 2008.

Campbell, E.G. *Reorganization of the American Railroad System, 1893–1900*. New York: Columbia University Press. 1938.

Vincent Carosso. *The Morgans: Private International Bankers, 1854–1913*. Cambridge, MA: Harvard University Press. 1987.

Daggett, Stuart. *Railroad Reorganization*. New York: August Kelly. 1967.

Durden, Robert. *The Climax of Populism: The Election of 1896*. Lexington: University of Kentucky Press, 1965.

Ellis, Elmer. *Henry Moore Teller: Defender of the West*. Caldwell, ID: Caxton Press. 1941.

Fels, Rendigs. *American Business Cycles, 1865–1897*. Chapel Hill: University of North Carolina Press. 1959.
Ferguson, Niall, *The House of Rothschild; The World's Banker, 1849–1999*. New York: Viking. 1999.
Friedman, Milton, and Anna Schwartz. *A Monetary History of the United States, 1867–1960*. Princeton: Princeton University Press. 1963.
Glad, Paul. *McKinley, Bryan, & the People*. Chicago: Ivan Dee. 1964.
Goodwyn, Lawrence. *Democratic Promise*. New York: Oxford University Press. 1976.
——— *The Populist Moment: A Short History of the Agrarian Revolt in America*. New York: Oxford University Press, 1978.
Gould, Lewis. *The Presidency of William McKinley*. Lawrence, KA: The Regents Press of Kansas. 1980.
Grodinsky, Julius. *Transcontinental Railway Strategy, 1869–1893: A Study of Businessmen*. Philadelphia: University of Pennsylvania Press, 1962.
Hicks, John D. *The Populist Revolt*. Minneapolis: University of Minnesota Press. 1931.
Hofstadter, Richard. *The Age of Reform*. New York: Vintage Books. 1955.
Kazin, Michael. *A Godly Hero: The Life of William Jennings Bryan*. New York: Alfred A. Knopf. 2006.
Klein, Maury. *The Great Richmond Terminal: A Study in Businessmen and Business Strategy*. Charlottesville; University Press of Virginia. 1970.
Koenig, Louis W. *Bryan: A Political Biography of William Jennings Bryan*. New York: Capricorn Books. 1975.
Kynaston, David. *The City of London: Volume I, A World of Its Own*. London: Pimlico. 1994.
———. *Till Time's Last Stand: A History of the Bank of England, 1694–2013*. London: Bloomsbury. 2017.
Lauck, W. Jett. *The Causes of the Panic of 1893*. Boston & New York: Houghton, Mifflin and Company. 1907.
Laughlin, J. Lawrence. *The History of Bimetallism in the United States*, 4th Edition. New York: D. Appleton & Co. 1900.
Merry, Robert. *President McKinley*. New York: Simon & Schuster. 2017.
Morgan, H. Wayne. *William McKinley and His America*. Syracuse, NY: Syracuse University Press. 1963.
Nelson, Scott Reynolds. *Nation of Deadbeats: An Uncommon History of America's Financial Disasters*. New York: Alfred A. Knopf. 2012.
Nevins, Allan. *Grover Cleveland: A Study in Courage*. New York: Dodd, Mead & Co., 1932.
Nugent, Walter T.K., *The Money Question During Reconstruction*. New York: W.W. Norton & Co., 1967.

Ostler, Jeffrey. *Prairie Populism: The Fate of Agrarian Radicalism in Kansas, Nebraska, and Iowa, 1880–1892.* Lawrence: University of Kansas Press. 1993.

O'Sullivan, Mary. *Dividends of Development: Securities Markets in the History of U.S. Capitalism.* Oxford: Oxford University Press. 2016.

Postel, Charles. *The Populist Vision.* New York: Oxford University Press. 2007.

Reitano, Joanne. *The Tariff Question in the Gilded Age: The Great Debate of 1888,* University Park, PN: Pennsylvania State University Press, 1994.

Reti, Stephen P. *Silver and Gold: The Political Economy of International Monetary Conferences, 1867–1892.* Westport, CN: Greenwood Press. 1998.

Ritter, Gretchen. *Goldbugs and Greenbacks: The Antimonopoly Tradition and the Politics of Finance in America, 1865–1896.* New York: Cambridge University Press. 1997.

Rove, Karl. *The Triumph of William McKinley: Why the Election of 1896 Still Matters.* New York: Simon & Schuster. 2015.

Russell, Henry B. *International Monetary Conferences.* New York: Harper & Brothers. 1898.

Socolofsky, Homer E. and Allan B. Spetter, *The Presidency of Benjamin Harrison.* Lawrence: University of Kansas Press. 1987.

Sharkey, Robert. *Money, Class, and Party: An Economic Study of Civil War and Reconstruction.* Baltimore: Johns Hopkins Press. 1959.

Strouse, Jean. *Morgan: American Financier.* New York: Random House. 1999.

Taus, Esther Rogoff. *Central Banking Functions of the United States Treasury, 1789–1941,* New York: Columbia University Press. 1943.

Welch, Richard E., *The Presidencies of Grover Cleveland.* Lawrence: University of Kansas Press. 1988.

White, Richard. *The Republic for Which It Stands: The United States During Reconstruction and the Gilded Age, 1865–1896.* New York: Oxford University Press. 2017.

Wilkins, Mira. *The History of Foreign Investment in the United States to 1914.* Cambridge MA: Harvard University Press. 1989.

Williams, R. Hal. *Realigning America: McKinley, Bryan, and the Remarkable Election of 1896.* Lawrence: University Press of Kansas. 2010.

Woodward, C. Vann. *Tom Watson: Agrarian Rebel.* Charlottesville: University of Virginia Press. 1955.

Ziegler, Philip. *The Sixth Great Power: A History of One of the Greatest of all Banking Families, the House of Barings, 1762–1929.* New York: Alfred Knopf. 1988.

Articles

Ali, Omar H. "Standing Guard at the Door of Liberty: Black Populism in South Carolina, 1886–1895. *The South Carolina Historical Magazine* 107 (2006): 190–203.

Barnes, James. "The Gold-Standard Democrats and the Party Conflict." *Mississippi Valley Historical Review* 17 (1930): 422–450.

Beeby, James. "Grass Roots Populism in North Carolina." *North Carolina Historical Review* 78 (2001): 156–86.

Bordo, Michael, and Hugh Rockoff. "The Gold Standard as a 'Good Housekeeping Seal of Approval.'" *Journal of Economic History* 56 (June 1996): 389–428.

Calomiris, Charles W. "Greenback Resumption and Silver Risk: The Economics and Politics of Monetary Regime Change in the United States." In Michael Bordo and Forrest Capie, eds., *Monetary Regimes in Transaction*. Cambridge: Cambridge University Press. 1993, pp. 86–132.

Cotter, Christopher and Peter Rousseau, "Correspondent Banking, Systemic Risks, and the Panic of 1893." *Munich Personal RePEc Archive*. Paper No. 113340. June 15, 2022.

DeCanio, Samuel. "Populism, Paranoia, and the Politics of Free Silver." *Studies in American Political Development* 25 (2011): 1–26.

Eichengreen, Barry, and Ian W. McLean. "The Supply of Gold under the Pre-1914 Gold Standard." *Economic History Review* 47 (1994): 288–309.

Frieden, Jeffry A. "Monetary Populism in Nineteenth-Century American: An Open Economy Interpretation." *Journal of Economic History* 57 (June 1997): 367–395.

Friedman, Milton. "The Crime of 1873." *Journal of Political Economy* 98 (1990): 1159–94.

Goetzmann, William and Andrey Ukhov. "British Investment Overseas, 1870–1914: A Modern Portfolio Theory Approach." *Review of Finance* 10 (2006): 261–300.

Gorton, Gary. "Clearinghouses and the Origins of Central Banking in the United States." *The Journal of Economic History* 45 (1985): 277–83.

Hannah, Leslie. "J.P. Morgan in London and New York before 1914." *Business History Review* 85 (Spring 2011): 113–150.

Hoffmann, Charles. "The Depression of the 1890s." *Journal of Economic History* 16 (1956): 137–164.

Jalil, Andrew. "A New History of Banking Panics in the United States, 1825–1929: Construction and Implications." *American Economic Journal: Macroeconomics* 7 (2015): 295–330.

Miller, Victoria. "Exchange Rate Crises with Domestic Bank Runs: Evidence from the 1890s. *Journal of International Money and Finance* 15 (1996): 637–56.

Nichols, Jeannette Paddock. "The Politics and Personalities of Silver Repeal in the United States Senate." *American Historical Review* 41 (October 1935): 26–53.

Ostler, Jeffrey. "The Rhetoric of Conspiracy and the Formation of Kansas Populism." *Agricultural History* 69 (1995): 1–27.

Pierce, Michael. "Farmers and the Failure of Populism in Ohio, 1890–91." *Agricultural History* 74 (2000): 58–85.

Saxton, Alexander. "San Francisco Labor and the Populist and Progressive Insurgencies." *Pacific Historical Review* 34 (1965): 421–438.

Simon, Matthew. "The Morgan-Belmont Syndicate of 1895 and Intervention in the Foreign Exchange Market." *Business History Review* 42 (1968): 385–417.

Sylla, Richard. "Federal Policy, Banking Market Structure, and Capital Mobilization in the United States, 1863–1913." *The Journal of Economic History* 29 (1969): 657–86.

Taussig, Frank. "The United States Treasury, 1894–1896." *Quarterly Journal of Economics* 13 (1899): 204–218.

Timberlake, Richard H. "Repeal of Silver Monetization in the Late Nineteenth Century." *Journal of Money, Credit, and Banking* 10 (February 1978): 27–45.

Wellborn, Fred. "The Influence of the Silver-Republican Senators, 1889–1891." *The Mississippi Valley Historical Review* 14 (March 1928): 462–480.

Wells, Wyatt. "The Rhetoric of the Standards: The Debate over Gold and Silver in the 1890s." *Journal of the Gilded Age and Progressive Era* 14 (2015): 49–68.

———. "Silver and Segregation," *Historically Speaking* 14 (November 2013): 2–5.

Index[1]

[1] Note: Page numbers followed by 'n' refer to notes.

W. Wells, *Financial Politics in the United States in the 1890s*,
https://doi.org/10.1007/978-3-031-86765-1

T

www.ingramcontent.com/pod-product-compliance
Lightning Source LLC
Chambersburg PA
CBHW072041101025
33682CB00040B/113
* 9 7 8 3 0 3 1 8 6 7 6 4 4 *